the MEANING *of life in the world religions*

THE LIBRARY OF GLOBAL ETHICS AND RELIGION

General Editors: Joseph Runzo and Nancy M. Martin

Volume I, *The Meaning of Life in the World Religions*, ISBN 1–85168–200–7
Volume II, *Love, Sex, and Gender in the World Religions*, ISBN 1–85168–223–6
Volume III, *Ethics in the World Religions*, ISBN 1–85168–247–3

RELATED TITLES PUBLISHED BY ONEWORLD:

Avatar and Incarnation, Geoffrey Parrinder, ISBN 1–85168–130–2
Believing – An Historical Perspective, Wilfred Cantwell Smith, ISBN 1–85168–166–3
Celebrate, Margo Westrheim, ISBN 1–85168–199–X
Concepts of God, Keith Ward, ISBN 1–85168–064–0
Faith and Belief: The Difference Between Them, Wilfred Cantwell Smith, ISBN 1–85168–165–5
The Fifth Dimension, John Hick, ISBN 1–85168–191–4
God and the Universe of Faiths, John Hick, ISBN 1–85168–071–3
God, Chance and Necessity, Keith Ward, ISBN 1–85168–116–7
God, Faith and the New Millennium, Keith Ward, ISBN 1–85168–155–8
In Defence of the Soul, Keith Ward, ISBN 1–85168–040–3
Jesus and the Muslim, Kenneth Cragg, ISBN 1–85168–180–9
Life After Death, Farnáz Ma'sumián, ISBN 1–85168–074–8
Muhammad and the Christian, Kenneth Cragg, ISBN 1–85168–179–5
Muslims and Christians Face to Face, Kate Zebiri, ISBN 1–85168–133–7
Patterns of Faith Around the World, Wilfred Cantwell Smith, ISBN 1–85168–164–7
The Phenomenon of Religion, Moojan Momen, ISBN 1–85168–161–2
Religious Truth for our Time, William Montgomery Watt, ISBN 1–85168–102–7
The Sense of God, John Bowker, ISBN 1–85168–093–4
Sexual Morality in the World's Religions, Geoffrey Parrinder, ISBN 1–85168–108–6
Ultimate Visions, edited by Martin Forward, ISBN 1–85168–100–0
The Universe Within, Anjam Kursheed, ISBN 1–85168–075–6
A Wider Vision, Marcus Braybrooke, ISBN 1–85168–119–1

the MEANING *of life in the world religions*

EDITED BY

Joseph Runzo and Nancy M. Martin

Volume I
in
The Library of Global Ethics and Religion
General Editors: Joseph Runzo and Nancy M. Martin

ONEWORLD
OXFORD

THE MEANING OF LIFE IN THE WORLD RELIGIONS

Oneworld Publications
(Sales and Editorial)
185 Banbury Road
Oxford OX2 7AR
England
http://www.oneworld-publications.com

Oneworld Publications
(US Marketing Office)
160 N Washington St.
4th Floor, Boston MA 02114

A CIP record for this title is available
from the British Library

ISBN 1-85168-200-7

Cover design by Design Deluxe
Typeset by LaserScript, Mitcham, UK
Printed and bound in England by Clays Ltd, St Ives plc

This volume is dedicated to

JOHN HICK AND HUSTON SMITH

Mentors and Friends

Twenty men crossing a bridge,
Into a village,
Are twenty men crossing twenty bridges,
Into twenty villages,
Or one man
crossing a single bridge into a village.

Wallace Stevens

CONTENTS

Part III MEANING AND ASIAN RELIGION

Part IV LOVE, RELATIONSHIPS, AND RELIGION

Part V GLOBAL VIEWS

ILLUSTRATIONS

Photographs: Joseph Runzo and Nancy M. Martin

CONTRIBUTORS

MASAO ABE is Professor Emeritus in Philosophy of Religion at Nara University in Japan and has been a visiting professor at distinguished universities in the United States and elsewhere. A member of the Kyoto School of Philosophy, he is an eminent spokesperson for Buddhism in Buddhist–Christian dialogue today, with particular expertise in Zen Buddhism and Buddhist, Japanese, and Western Philosophy. His publications include *Buddhism and Interfaith Dialogue*, *A Study of Dogen*, and *Zen and Western Thought.*

JOHN BERTHRONG is Director of the Institute for Dialogue Among Religious Traditions, Associate Dean for Academic and Administrative Affairs, and Assistant Professor of Comparative Religion in the School of Theology at Boston University. As a leading proponent of interreligious dialogue and a renowned scholar of Confucian studies, his research interests include not only Chinese philosophy and religion but also comparative theology and philosophy. Among his most recent books are *All Under Heaven: Transforming Paradigms in Confucian-Christian Dialogue* and *Transformation of the Confucian Way.*

KAREN McCARTHY BROWN is Professor of the Sociology and Anthropology of Religion at the Graduate and Theological Schools of Drew University. She has won numerous awards for her book *Mama Lola: A Vodou Priestess in Brooklyn* and is currently working on a study of race and gender in eighteenth-century Bermuda. She is the director of the Newark Project funded by the Ford Foundation, engaging both graduate and theological students in urban ethnography, field-based education, curriculum development, advocacy work, and community organization in Newark, New Jersey.

CHRISTOPHER KEY CHAPPLE is Professor of Theological Studies and Director of Asian and Pacific Studies at Loyola Marymount University. He has published eight books on such topics as karma, non-violence in Asian traditions, ecology, and the Jesuits, including *Nonviolence to Animals, Earth and Self in Asian Traditions*, and *Karma and Creativity*, and he is co-translator of *The Yoga Sutras of Patanjali*. His current research focuses on the Jaina Yoga texts of Haribhadra, and the application of Asian ethics to the field of environmentalism.

CHARLOTTE ELISHEVA FONROBERT is an Assistant Professor of Talmud at the University of Judaism in Los Angeles. Her research focuses on feminist interpretations of rabbinic texts and the relationship between the religious cultures of rabbinic Judaism and early Christianity, especially concerning gender issues. She has just completed a book entitled *Menstruation and the Construction of Gender in Talmudic Culture*, forthcoming with Stanford University Press.

JOHN HICK is a world-renowned authority on religious pluralism. Currently a Fellow of the Institute for Advanced Research in the Humanities at the University of Birmingham in England, he has also taught at Cambridge University and Birmingham University in England, and at Cornell, Princeton, and Claremont Graduate School in the United States. He has published twenty-six books, including *Faith and Knowledge*, *Evil and the God of Love*, *Death and Eternal Life*, *God and the Universe of Faiths*, *God Has Many Names*, and his monumental study, *An Interpretation of Religion*. His latest book is entitled *The Fifth Dimension: An Exploration of the Spiritual Realm*.

ANNE C. KLEIN is Professor and Chair of the Department of Religious Studies at Rice University where she teaches Buddhist thought and culture, women's studies, and Tibetan language. The author of four books on Tibetan Buddhism including *Knowledge and Liberation* and *Meeting the Great Bliss Queen: Buddhists, Feminists and the Art of the Self*, she is currently translating and researching a philosophical text from the Tibetan Bon tradition, *The Authenticity of Innate Awareness*, previously unknown to the West.

JULIUS LIPNER is a distinguished member of the faculty of Divinity at Cambridge University and a Fellow of Clare Hall, Cambridge. Working in the field of the comparative study of religion, he has special interests in Buddhist, Hindu, and Christian traditions. Among his books are *The Face of Truth* (on Ramanuja), *Hindu Ethics: Purity, Abortion and Euthanasia*, and *Hindus: Their Religious Beliefs and Practices.* He is currently working on a book on God and love.

SALLIE McFAGUE is Carpenter Professor of Theology and former Dean at Vanderbilt Divinity School. She is a prominent and powerful voice in contemporary feminist theology. Her books include *Speaking in Parables: A Study in Metaphor and Theology, Metaphorical Theology: Models of God in Religious Language, Models of God: Theology for an Ecological, Nuclear Age*, and *The Body of God: An Ecological Theology*, and *Super, Natural Christians: How we Should Love Nature.*

F.E. PETERS is a Professor in the Department of Near Eastern Languages at New York University with joint appointments in History and Hebrew and Judaic Studies. Recognized for his monumental work on the Western monotheisms, he is the author of fourteen books on subjects ranging from Greek philosophy to classical Judaism, Christianity, and Islam. His books include *Judaism, Christianity and Islam: The Classic Texts and their Interpretations* in three volumes, *Jerusalem, The Hajj*, and *Muhammad and the Origins of Islam.*

PHILIP L. QUINN taught at Brown University before assuming his current position as John A. O'Brien Professor of Philosophy at the University of Notre Dame. Having published over one hundred articles and reviews in various areas of philosophy, he is also the author of *Divine Commands and Moral Requirements* and the co-editor of *A Companion to Philosophy of Religion.* More recently he has developed strong interests in the analysis of pluralism and inter-religious dialogue.

NINIAN SMART is J.F. Rowny Professor Emeritus of Comparative Religions at the University of California, Santa Barbara, and was the founding professor of the first major Department of Religious Studies in England at Lancaster University. He has published thirty-two books, both technical and popular, addressing the history of religions, Indian philosophy, philosophy of religion, methodology and theory, religious dialogue, education, politics, and Christian thought. His comprehensive range of books includes *Beyond Ideology: Religion and the Future of Western Civilization, Concept and Empathy, Dimensions of the Sacred*, and *The World's Religions.*

HUSTON SMITH is Thomas J. Watson Professor of Religion and Distinguished Adjunct Professor of Philosophy Emeritus, Syracuse University, and a visiting professor at the University of California, Berkeley. He is renowned for his contribution to educating people around the globe about the world's religions through numerous books and articles, films and television series. His *The World's Religions* is one of the standard texts in the field, and he has also published *Beyond the Post-Modern Mind*, *Forgotten Truth*, and *Essays on World Religion.*

KEITH WARD, an eminent philosopher of religion and theologian, was a Fellow and Dean of Trinity Hall at Cambridge University and Professor of History and Philosophy of Religion at the University of London before being appointed to his current position as Regius Professor of Divinity at Oxford University. He is a Canon of Christ Church Cathedral. His numerous books focus on a wide variety of theological issues, and among his more recent works are *Images of Eternity; God, Chance and Necessity; In Defence of the Soul;* and his monumental comparative theology: *Religion and Revelation; Religion and Creation*; and *Religion and Human Nature.*

The Editors

NANCY M. MARTIN received her MA from the University of Chicago Divinity School and her PhD from the Graduate Theological Union, Berkeley. An Assistant Professor of Religious Studies at Chapman University, she is a historian of religion with expertise in Asian religions, gender issues, and comparative mysticism. Involved in extensive fieldwork in Rajasthan, her research focuses on devotional Hinduism, women's religious lives, and the religious traditions of low-caste groups in India. She is the recipient of a Graves Award for the Humanities and is currently completing a book on the sixteenth-century saint Mirabai, entitled *Mirabai Manifest: The Many Faces of a Woman Poet-Saint in India.*

JOSEPH RUNZO received his MA and PhD in philosophy from the University of Michigan and MTS in philosophical theology from Harvard Divinity School. He is Professor of Philosophy and Religious Studies at Chapman University and Life Fellow of Clare Hall, Cambridge University. He is the recipient of five National Endowment for the Humanities Fellowships and Awards. Working in the fields of philosophy of religion, epistemology, and ethics, he has published five books: *Reason, Relativism, and God, Religious Experience and Religious Belief, Is God Real?, Ethics, Religion and the Good Society,* and *World Views and Perceiving God.* He is currently working on a book entitled *Religion, Sex and Love: Reflections of the Divine* and also on an Introduction to the Global Philosophy of Religion.

Acknowledgments

This volume is the first in a projected series offering a pluralistic and global perspective on questions of religion and ethics: The Library of Global Ethics and Religion, to be published by Oneworld Press. The editors wish to thank Novin Doostdar and Juliet Mabey of Oneworld for their enthusiastic support of this project. The present volume has benefited from the pluralistic vision of not only the dedicatees, John Hick and Huston Smith, who were pioneers in religious pluralism, but also of Masao Abe, Julius Lipner, and Keith Ward who have inspired our work. The initial impetus for this volume was a conference held at Chapman University in 1997, which was made possible through the Huntington and Griset Lectureship Funds. We also wish to acknowledge all those who participated in the conversation there, including many of the contributors in this volume, but also James Kellenberger, Brian Smith, Cynthia Humes, Mark Juergensmeyer, Dale Wright, Zayn Kassam, Juan Campo, Katherine McCarthy, Jody Myer, James Fredericks, Glenn Yocum, and Nathan Tierney.

We are grateful to our friends Yukihiro Aizawa and Dr. and Mrs. Robert G. Albertson for their generous support in our pursuit of a cross-cultural perspective, which also made possible many of the photographs in this volume. We would also like to thank a number of our students: Joie Karnes, Jason Bricker, and especially Beverly Worden for their help with the conference that first brought many of us together; Katie DeFriese, Jessica Cioffi, and especially Jessie Stevens for their help with the manuscript; and Shanna Murray for her work on the index and so much more.

Finally, this book benefited in so many ways from the co-operative efforts of the Global Ethics and Religion Forum, a new society of scholars in Europe, Canada, India, and the United States, dedicated to promoting a wider understanding both of religious pluralism and of ethical issues among the world religions in a global context. We wish to thank our friends in the Forum, a number of whom have essays in the present volume, for their steadfast support.

INTRODUCTION

Aristotle defined humans as the "rational" animals. We might better be defined as the "religious" animals, the animals with religious worldviews. Other animals might share rationality with humans, but they do not seek meaning in a Transcendent; they do not long to confer significance on themselves and their existence through something "beyond" the transient phantasmagoria of the physical world.

Bertrand Russell, despite his eventual atheistic conclusion, speaks to the uniquely human drive behind all religions when he says:

> In the spectacle of death, in the endurance of intolerable pain, in the irrevocableness of a vanished past, there is a sacredness, an overpowering awe, a feeling of the vastness, the depth, the inexhaustible mystery of existence ... In these moments of insight, we lose all eagerness of temporary desire, all struggling and striving for petty ends, all care for the little trivial things that, to the superficial view make up the common life of day by day ... all the loneliness of humanity amid hostile forces is concentrated upon the human soul, which must struggle alone, with what of courage it can command against the whole weight of a universe that cares nothing for its hopes and fears ... From that awful encounter of the soul with the outer world, renunciation, wisdom, and charity are born; and with their birth a new life begins.[1]

This is the apotheosis, and the challenge, of being human. The world religions respond to this challenge, encapsulated in the Socratic dictum that "the unexamined life is not worth living" (*Apology* 38a), by pointing in various ways to a source of ultimate value that transcends our individual lives, our social world, and physical existence itself. Upon seeing the golden calf the Hebrews had created, Moses smashed the tablets containing the Ten Commandments in order to refocus his people upon Yahweh (see Plate 2). Jesus went to his death mourning and saying, "Father forgive them, for they know not what they do," his ministry becoming triumphant only after the crucifixion (see Plate 1). Seeing sickness, old age, and death for the first time, Siddhartha Gautama renounced the "pleasure palace" of his youth and began his search for liberation. Or, as the Islamic mystic poet Rumi said,

> Empty the glass of your desire
> so that you won't be disgraced.
> Stop looking for something out there
> and begin seeing within.[2]

This drive in the human heart to seek something beyond this world became manifest around 4500 years ago when the great world religions began to coalesce, first in the form of Hinduism on the broad well-populated river plains of the Indus and later the Ganges Rivers (see Plate 4) of India, followed closely by the rise of the Hebrew tradition in the ancient desert Mediterranean regions lying between Asia and the largely undeveloped West. These two great strands of world religiosity became marked by a hope for either salvation from sin (a more Western perspective) or liberation from ignorance and bondage to this world (a more Asian perspective).

Further salient developments in world religion as a seeking of salvation/liberation occurred during what Karl Jaspers has called the "axial age" – around 800 to 500 BCE – when in India, even as the philosophical pursuit of meaning flowered within Hinduism itself, Buddhism and Jainism arose out of Hinduism, great Prophets addressed the nation of Israel, and Taoism and Confucianism became established in China. Five centuries passed, and then Christianity developed in the Western religious crucible of the Mediterranean during the first century, the same area where, six centuries later, the great Western monotheisms were transformed once again with the rise of Islam. Still later, India once again became the source of a major development with the growth of the *bhakti* tradition of devotion to God, beginning in the sixth century, and the rise of the Sikhs in the fifteenth century, while in the West the Islamic tradition saw the advent of the Baha'i Faith in the nineteenth century.

As we now move into the twenty-first century, there are over four-and-a-half billion adherents of the world religions. Christianity, a proselytizing tradition, has spread globally until there are nearly two billion Christians today, over half of whom are Roman Catholic, while about a quarter of Christians are in various Protestant denominations and half of the remainder are in the traditions of Eastern Orthodoxy. The other actively proselytizing world religion, Islam, has a billion adherents around the globe with Indonesia being the most populous Islamic nation. Hinduism itself has nearly one billion adherents, while Buddhism has about three hundred and fifty million. Important, smaller traditions in the world today include approximately twenty million Sikhs, fourteen million Jews, six million Baha'is, and perhaps four million Jains, not to mention the indeterminate millions who are influenced today by Confucian thought. Indigenous traditions, such as those originating in Africa, make up the remainder. This remarkable panoply of living traditions, with their central place on the world stage, bring valuable and divergent perspectives and resources to the question of the meaning of life, for they carry wisdom which has been tempered by centuries and strengthened by the testament of devout lives.

The present volume brings together many of the most prominent voices for religious pluralism at the close of the twentieth century, and in their essays the authors offer authoritative expositions of Hinduism, Jainism, Confucianism, Buddhism, Judaism, Islam, Christianity, and even Haitian Vodou, as well as comprehensive overviews and philosophical perspectives on the world's religious traditions. Keith Ward and Ninian Smart begin the volume, exploring the nature of religion and the possibilities of dialogue and comparison across religions. Ward argues strongly for a distinctly religious perspective on life's meaning, as do Joseph Runzo, Huston Smith, and John Hick in subsequent chapters, although each characterizes this perspective in a somewhat different way. Specific formulations of life's meaning within particular traditions are then presented, with Philip Quinn's essay beginning this portion of the book. He first lays out clear parameters of what would constitute a meaningful life in any context, before turning specifically to the case of Christianity. F.E. Peters and Charlotte Fonrobert then offer us vivid portraits of life's meaning for those following the tenets of Islam and

Judaism. Turning to Asia, Julius Lipner creates an overarching vision encompassing the many varieties of religiosity that fall under the name of "Hinduism." Christopher Chapple then compares Hindu yogic traditions with Jainism, and Masao Abe invites us into a Buddhist experience of a radically interdependent world in which we become free to live truly through a direct confrontation with death and the fullness of Buddhist emptiness. John Berthrong concludes the section by taking us into the very different world of Confucianism, which grows side by side with Buddhism in China.

Next Joseph Runzo, Nancy M. Martin, Anne C. Klein, and Karen McCarthy Brown explore more deeply the fundamental relationality that underlies religious approaches to life's meaning. Runzo offers us a framework for exploring the meaning and nature of that love which marks the human–divine relationship, while Martin provides an in-depth example from Hindu devotional traditions of this type of all encompassing love. Klein explores Buddhist understandings of relationality through the cultivation of mindfulness and the guru or deity visualization practices of Tibetan traditions, and Brown introduces us to the spirits and healing traditions of Haitian Vodou with its deeply African roots.

In the concluding essays Huston Smith, John Hick, and Sallie McFague offer us global perspectives as they return to broad questions about the religious point of view and religious pluralism. Both Smith and Hick present comprehensive formulations of what the religious perspective can offer us in terms of life's meaning, pointing to a supreme valuing of life coupled with a cosmic optimism about the potential for solving the human condition. McFague takes up the specific case of Christianity, leaving behind exclusivist claims and proposing an inclusive and cosmic vision of Christianity's message to a world, a vision of the world as the body of God.

These essays collectively present the reader with the necessary historical understanding, comparative analysis, and philosophical insights of the world's religions and of leading contemporary thinkers, to arrive at an informed personal understanding of life's meaning. Perhaps the meaning of life is best found in the combined cumulative wisdom of the world religions. Or it may be that there is no one meaning but a plurality of meanings for life to be found among the world religions. Or perhaps a universal core to the meaning of life underlies an irreducible plurality of perspectives among the world religions. The answers to these questions are left to the reader to decide. Whatever answers the reader arrives at for him/herself, these essays present a compelling case for using the rich resources that the world's diverse religions bring to questions of life's meaning.

NOTES

1. Bertrand Russell, "A Free Man's Worship," in his *Why I am not a Christian* (New York: Simon & Schuster, 1957), pp. 113–114.
2. Jelaluddin Rumi, *Love is a Stranger*, trans. Kabir Helminski (Battleboro: Threshold Books, 1993), p. 74.

Part I

THE RELIGIOUS PERSPECTIVE

Some world religions espouse belief in God; others do not. Some world religions enjoin a life of meditation; others prescribe prayer for the faithful. Some world religions posit resurrection and an afterlife; others subscribe to reincarnation followed by a very different afterlife; and still others subscribe to reincarnation but no afterlife. There are numerous differences among the world's great religions, but what do the world religions have in common such that they are all, appropriately, understood as religions? Part of what we mean when we call something a distinct "religion" is that it offers a particular view of the meaning of life. But is there an identifiable "religious perspective" on the question of life's meaning that is, in some sense, shared by diverse religious traditions around the globe? In this opening section Keith Ward and Ninian Smart offer insight into these fundamental questions, drawing diverse examples from the religious traditions of the world and laying the foundation for the subsequent in-depth discussions of particular religious traditions.

Defining what we mean by the term "religion" is no easy task. Taking an essentially cognitive approach, Keith Ward asserts that all religions are most fundamentally belief-systems giving answers to the question of life's meaning. He suggests that beliefs about the nature and meaning of life underlie other aspects of religion and are essential to defining a given tradition. It is beliefs that impart meaning to social and individual religious actions, whether ethical or ritual in nature, and to personal experiences and narratives identified as religious (all key dimensions of religions identified and discussed by Ninian Smart). Religions cannot be reduced to beliefs, but religious beliefs are especially important to questions of the meaning of life. These belief-systems are sustained by communities drawing on particular sources of authority, including religious teachers and canonical scriptures, the whole of the tradition developing over time as new interpretations are needed to address changing circumstances and knowledge.

Going beyond, though fundamentally agreeing with Ward's view that beliefs are key and underlie other dimensions of religion, Ninian Smart expands our understanding of the phenomenon of religion by mapping out additional dimensions. Blending the non-cognitive dimension of religion with the cognitive, he points to stories of religious leaders and divinities, ethical attitudes, personal religious experiences, rituals, and material expressions such as art and architecture. He shows clearly how these aspects of religion – along with beliefs – articulate, reinforce, and embody religious understandings of life's ultimate value, purpose and meaning.

In Smart's view, mythic and narrative dimensions provide models and trajectories for the meaningful life and articulate belief in an embodied way that is fundamentally different from doctrinal formulations. Religious experiences give authority and lived reality to intellectual affirmations of belief, whether that experience is one of awe before a transcendent deity or of mystical union or the passing away of the self. The ethical dimensions of religions often draw on expressive emotive examples of extraordinary individuals, and ground ways of acting in the world toward others in a higher purpose and more encompassing understanding of reality. Rituals, in turn, serve in myriad ways to articulate, teach, and reinforce understandings of the world and human life as meaning filled and purposeful. And religious values and meaning find expression and cultivation in the aesthetic dimension: music and material arts such as the architecture of temple and shrine and cathedral and mosque and other sacred spaces. Smart suggests that all these dimensions, cognitive as well as non-cognitive, make up the phenomenon we call religion and speak to the question of life's meaning.

But this raises a more fundamental question. Can we really compare religions? On the one hand, are the belief-systems of the great world religions so different that comparison is impossible, as if two people were trying to communicate when they speak different and mutually unintelligible languages? Or, on the other hand, are religions really all basically saying the same thing? Ward offers us a middle path, steering away from both extremes and suggesting that religious belief-systems are generally comparable but usually incompatible because they view the world and human nature in distinctly different ways. The same will be true of other dimensions of religion, because of the underlying different world-views operative in each. On this view, you can compare different religions; what you cannot do is simultaneously adhere to two different religions.

Does this mean that following a religious path is the only way to live a meaningful life? No. Clearly non-religious sources of meaning can be found. Yet, arguably there is a distinctly religious perspective on life's meaning. According to Ward, religions claim to offer the greatest meaning by articulating "the highest possible value of a human life" and "the most nontrivial purpose of human life" and showing the way to attain this highest value and purpose, whether the goal be *moksha*, nirvana, or the experience of God. They posit a supreme value that they claim has a universal and objective reality and advocate the absolute fulfillment of human potentiality, with the journey toward fulfillment itself infused with purpose.

Ward then suggests that the highest values for human life articulated by religions share the idea of a final state of "wisdom, compassion and bliss" and require a movement away from self toward care for others as an essential part of the path toward that state. Of course, within this broad shared framework are varied beliefs and widely divergent practices (which other scholars will address in this book, offering vivid detail for specific traditions). But the religious perspective is marked by a shared claim of ultimate value and purpose rooted in a reality (some Buddhists would not want to use this term) beyond the constructions of the human mind and human communities. Yes, Ward says, one can live a meaningful life without religion, but if a set of religious beliefs about the ultimate meaning and purpose of human life are true, then, unless one follows them, one will actually miss out on the real meaning of life.

Finally, both Ward and Smart also speak to the problem of meaninglessness. Ward suggests that what we often mean by statements such as "Life is meaningless" is that the things that happen to and around us do not seem to fit into any kind of overall pattern and that human life has no ultimate goal. For Ward, the world religions address precisely these issues. Taking a different tack, Smart asserts that it is when our worldviews and our highest values no longer seem plausible that meaning begins to fall apart. We lose hope and a vision for the future; we lose our sense of the value of human life and of an overarching purpose to life and history. Smart concludes his chapter with a call to reexamine our views of the world in the light of our expanding scientific knowledge – "to rethink, and indeed to re-feel, the cosmos." He challenges us to transform our religions and our world-views, reinfusing them with plausibility and seeing once again how they give meaning to our lives.

1

RELIGION *and the* QUESTION OF MEANING

Keith Ward

Religions are belief-systems which articulate, with different degrees of systematization, competing theories about the meaning of human life. All the claims made by these belief-systems cannot be true, though it may seem unlikely that all the claims made by any one of them at any given time are true. It may be, however, that one can identify a core of important beliefs that are shared by many systems, which may be held to be central to any reflective religious view, and which do provide a particular religious perspective on the meaning of human life. It may then be possible to speak of a convergence of belief about life's meaning between some major religious traditions, insofar as this core can be regarded by them as of fundamental importance. I shall refer to Buddhism, one sort of Hinduism (Vaishnava), and Christianity in outlining the possibility of such a convergent view. But there will remain differences in the detailed analysis of life's meaning in diverse systems, and thus conflict as well as convergence will remain characteristic of religion for the foreseeable future. There will be differing views about the importance and extent of such conflict.

It may seem obvious that religions are belief-systems. But Wilfred Cantwell Smith has complained that to see religions as belief-systems is basically to misrepresent the phenomena of faith. The very word "religion," he claims, is so inadequate and misleading that "it should be dropped."[1] The paradox of his suggestion is that there is little doubt of the sorts of human beliefs and practices he is concerned with: they are religious beliefs and practices. However difficult it may be to provide exact definitions, and however many borderline cases there may be, we do in general know what is meant by a "world religion." We know what the central cases of world religions are.

However radical or traditional one's own beliefs may be, one would have to accept that a person who accepts the Four Noble Truths, who regards Siddhartha Gautama as an enlightened human being, who reads the Pali canon to obtain inspiration and guidance, and who practices meditation to obtain the stilling of selfish desires, is a Buddhist. There are Buddhist societies one can join, there are Buddhist symbols one can use, and above all there is the Sangha, the society of monks, which represents the ideal of a Buddhist life. All these facts are conveniently expressed by saying that Buddhism, however internally diverse it might be, is a distinct religion.

Cantwell Smith, however, dislikes the term "religion," which, he says, implies the idea of a true or false system of beliefs. In its place, he recommends a two-fold terminology of "faith" and "cumulative tradition." But, one must ask, what sort of cumulative tradition does he have in mind? It is not politics or art, language or social ethics that he has in mind. It is, of course, a religious tradition. But now it looks as though he is using precisely the concept he is trying to drop, for how can one identify a religious tradition, as opposed to a social or political or cultural tradition?

He does it by saying that "the materials of a cumulative tradition serve each generation as the ground of a transcendent faith," and that gives the game away.[2] Religious cumulative traditions are humanly constructed sets of symbols or doctrines or practices which seek to express or sustain "faith," the second component of his recommended conceptual revision. Faith, it quickly becomes clear, is a matter of inner personal experience. At one point he speaks of a "personal confrontation with the splendor and the love of God;" at another of "man's personal sense of the holy."[3] More generally, his concern is with human "relation with transcendence," and he usually describes "the transcendent" as a personal, living reality.[4] One immediately apparent problem with this definition is that it does not fit Buddhism very well. Admittedly Buddhism can be used as a counter-example to most attempted definitions of religion, but it is still unsatisfactory to have a description of faith which does not easily apply to what is generally regarded as a major world religion.

Faith, as Cantwell Smith describes it, is a living relation to the transcendent, and cumulative traditions are the constantly changing human conceptualizations of faith. The obvious problem is that if one thinks there is a transcendent with which one can have a living relationship, and if one says anything at all about its relation to the cosmos and the conditions of human existence, one is already committed to a specific belief-system, even if a very vague, fluid and ill-defined one. Wilfred Cantwell Smith's belief-system is squarely in the liberal Christian tradition of Schleiermacher and Otto, finding the most vital fact about religion to be its evocation of a relationship to a more or less personalistically conceived transcendent reality, and characterizing doctrines as provisional and revisable attempts to preserve the records of and reflections upon such inner experiences.

Cantwell Smith wants to distinguish what he calls "faith" from the "cumulative tradition," the variegated set of beliefs and practices that have accumulated in various cultures over the years. However, if one subtracts beliefs and practices, including the belief that there is a transcendent and the practice of cultivating a deeply felt relationship with it, nothing would be left. Personal experience may indeed be important to religion, but one cannot disentangle it from the very beliefs that say just what sort of experience it is. Nor are religious practices quite so contingently related to "faith" as Cantwell Smith's account seems to suggest.

Practices include the ritual, moral, and social behaviors, which are three dimensions of Ninian Smart's valuable analysis of religion, and these all ultimately depend upon some set of beliefs. Rituals with no belief element are simply dances. To be a religious ritual, something must be believed to be accomplished by the ritual, whether it is a participation in some spiritual reality or a cleansing from impurity. In the case of Buddhism, the chanting of mantras makes sense because it is considered to be a way of achieving mental states conducive to enlightenment, and to release from *dukkha* or the suffering of impermanence. In Hinduism and Christianity, the rituals of sacrifice and of the Eucharist are primarily ways of relating human lives properly to the divine, and that entails beliefs that there is such a divine reality, with which a relation symbolized by sacrifice is possible and appropriate.

The moral and social behavior of religious believers is distinguished from purely secular, interpersonal morality by being rooted in the will of some supernatural being, in the case of Christianity, or by having some relation to what is believed to be an attainable but in some sense suprahuman goal, in Buddhism and Hinduism.

Similarly, the stories and experiences that are further elements of Ninian Smart's analysis could not exist without specific beliefs. If I tell a creation myth, I must at least believe that it gives some important insight into the human condition, so it enshrines some truths. If the Genesis creation myth does not at least say that humans are created by God, and have some God-like properties, if it is pure fiction, it is impossible to see why I should regard it as more important than any other myth. Similarly, the stories of the Buddha and of Krishna, even if many of them are legendary, are told to give insight into what an ultimate state of wisdom and freedom from suffering, or a state of joyful love, is like.

As for experiences, if I have heart-throbbing experiences of "absolute dependence" or "awe before the transcendent," I must at least believe that there is something upon which I am absolutely dependent, or some greater reality of which I may appropriately stand in awe. If I experience the deep calm of nirvana, I must believe that there is a state beyond duality which is the attainable goal of ascetic practice. There is no belief-free experience.

So while being religious is not just a matter of having theoretical beliefs, it is necessarily a matter of having beliefs about some of the most important aspects of the human condition, which are grounded in appropriate experiences and give rise to appropriate feelings and actions. In other words, one can properly regard a religion as a set of beliefs, together with the rituals and stories, experiences and practices that they imply or suggest. Different religions can reasonably be viewed as different belief-systems. As they are belief-systems about the same general subject matter, they will be comparable but usually incompatible. For it is difficult to have two different belief-systems covering the same range of general facts about the universe which never conflict as to matters of fact.

In saying this, I am denying two views that are quite often expressed about religion – first, that different religions, being different "language games," are incommensurable and cannot be compared, and second, that all religions in some sense really believe the same thing. It seems obvious that different religions are both comparable, given enough patience and time, and usually incompatible, in at least some respects.

What I think is correct and helpful about Cantwell Smith's proposal is the insight, stated in slightly more general terms than he usually uses, that the beliefs proper to religious rites, moral and social codes, stories and experiences, are beliefs about some suprahuman spiritual reality or states – what he calls "the transcendent" – to which one can be appropriately related by specific practices. Such beliefs may be very vaguely defined. Cantwell Smith stresses the fact that in China there has been no discrete, authoritatively defined belief-system. People have turned to Confucian, Taoist, and Buddhist rituals at various times. Nevertheless, there is a Taoist canonical text, which expresses beliefs about the properly balanced human way of life, and which at many points conflicts with the Confucian canon and its notions of conventional social order, even if many people overlook such conflicts. The fact that people may turn to different religious practices at different times does not mean that those practices are not rooted in competing belief-systems. It just means that people are not very much concerned with consistency in religion, and that most people, when not aroused by political or racial factors, are content to leave detailed religious controversies to others – thank goodness! They tend to treat religions as pragmatically useful, and are therefore not surprised if different doctrines seem to be useful or helpful on different occasions. But such pragmatic utility is rarely acceptable to the professional apologists of a religion as a justification of their religious beliefs. They tend to seek some coherent and plausible systematization of the beliefs that are most characteristic of their religion.

Cantwell Smith might say that this is a very Western, intellectualist way of viewing the matter, and that what we tend to call religions are much more complex and diverse than just belief-systems. One of the best examples to support his argument is the religion we call "Hinduism," which consists of many conflicting belief-systems. What makes someone a Hindu, it may be said, is that they are born in India – Indian nationalist political parties do say that. And there is certainly a very strong link between ethnicity and religion, as Judaism and Sikhism both make clear. One can be born into a religion, before any conscious deliberation about beliefs takes place, so is religion not more like a culture, a form of life, than like a set of beliefs?

It must be agreed that "Hinduism" can be a very misleading term, if it is used to cover everything from the Brahmo Samaj to Vaishnavism. It is misleading precisely if it makes one think that all such Hindus share the same beliefs. In that respect, it is rather like speaking of the Abrahamic traditions of religion. That would refer to a group of religions which trace an important beginning of their beliefs back to Abraham, but which differ from each other on many issues. So the Hindu traditions may trace their beliefs back to the Veda and Upanishads, which they agree to accept as sacred texts, but interpret and supplement in many ways. At a high level of generality, one may speak of Hinduism as a set of traditions having a historical source different from that of the Abrahamic faiths. Whether it is useful to do so depends upon the level of generality one is considering, on the set of beliefs to which it is being, at least implicitly, opposed, and on the sort of social unity one is interested in achieving.

Despite the BJP (a Hindu nationalist party active in India today), it is possible to be Indian without being Hindu. One can do so most obviously by rejecting the Vedas as sacred texts, and by rejecting the associated social rites (such as the Brahminical sacrificial rites). When the BJP says that "to be Indian is to be Hindu," they are partly opposing Islam and Christianity as alien influences, and so stressing the agreement of Hindus, at a rather general level, to accept a set of common texts, social origins, and customs. At a lower level of generality, it is not unusual to find Vaishnavites (devotees of Vishnu) and Shaivites (devotees of Shiva) attacking one another, where they are not united against a common enemy. It is in fact fairly easy to specify particular Indian religions in terms of their distinctive beliefs, which are usually traced back to a particular authoritative teacher. "Hinduism" is only a good case for Cantwell Smith's argument because it is an umbrella term for a number of different religions. His argument collapses because those different religions are distinguished precisely in terms of their beliefs.

If religions are defined primarily in terms of beliefs, one might be tempted to think that any change of belief would constitute a new religion. However, that would overlook the fact that religions constitute themselves as social groups, and trace their beliefs and practices to some authoritative source. Whitehead's definition of religion as "what a man does with his solitariness" misses the aspects of community and authority completely, and so is grossly inadequate. To be Indian may not be identical with being Hindu, but one can understand, even if one views with suspicion, the attempt to create a society with a range of common beliefs and values, rooted in a common tradition.

It is part of the belief-structure of most religions that there should be a particular society which protects and sustains its basic values and beliefs, within which one may pursue the ideal human goal, as defined within the society. Since humans have to learn in each new generation, and since they usually have not the time or inclination to reflect deeply on religious matters, it is important to have a society that can preserve and teach the basic truths and practices of religion. This means that there must be a canonical source of basic beliefs, an authoritative set of texts based on the teachings of those thought to be in the best position to know the truth of such beliefs. And there must exist some social mechanism for interpreting beliefs in the light of new knowledge or new social conditions. This suggests that the "same religion" continues to exist if the same canonical texts are used, with a continuous and authoritative tradition of interpreting them and applying them in new conditions.

It is when one group feels so strongly about specific belief changes that it breaks away from an existing group, or when it ejects a new group, that one has a new religion. Thus many early Christians probably wished to remain within the Jewish faith. But the claim that the Messiah had come and had been rejected by the Jewish authorities proved, unsurprisingly, to be unacceptable to those authorities. So Christianity was born as a new religion. At the Protestant Reformation, the authority of the Church to interpret the faith was rejected, and one can say that a number of new religions were born, each with its own authoritative line of interpreters. Ecumenically minded Christians, stressing the identity of the basic canonical texts between these religions, seek ways of reuniting the interpretative traditions. What is at stake is not whether the actual beliefs all agree, but whether a new agreement can be forged about the social mechanism for reformulating beliefs in new conditions. Such a mechanism could leave many disputes about beliefs formally undecided. Just as religions can split, so they can unite, but only if they agree to identify the canonical and interpretative authorities by which the society is to be bound.

Thus there can be religions within which there are actual but unformalized divisions, as when some Baptist churches do not exchange preachers with other Baptist churches, realizing that their beliefs are in conflict. They remain in the same group of churches because they share the same canonical authority, and the same general attitude to interpretative authority – namely, the consensus of a local congregation, prayerfully seeking the guidance of the Holy Spirit.

What this means in practice is that individual churches do follow particular traditions of interpretation, which can be traced to the teachings of various notable Baptists. But these differences do not usually become formalized. Each Baptist church is in one sense a different religion, but they are bound together in loose alliances, all of which accept some fundamental beliefs, by which they are sharply differentiated from other groups (in this case, the rejection of infant baptism). Baptists, and perhaps Protestant Christians in general, are rather like Hindus, in being alliances of differing and constantly splintering interpretative traditions, bound together by acceptance of a common canonical text, and some core beliefs and practices.

A religious community, then, may be seen as a group that defines itself in terms of a set of canonical beliefs about the ultimate powers and values that bound human existence, traced back to a founding authority, with a set of practices sustaining appropriate relations to those powers and values. For such groups, the main and most important purpose of human life is to establish such a relation. Its highest value lies in the experience of that relation. The meaning of a human life lies in the way events, actions, and experiences in that life aid or impede the final goal, for oneself or for others.

Cantwell Smith's own construal of religion fits this pattern, in taking "the transcendent" to be of supreme value, and the highest purpose of life to consist in sustaining a living relation with it. So, despite Cantwell Smith's protests, one can fairly, if paradoxically, interpret his book *The Meaning and End of Religion* as offering a characterization of religion as a belief-system which claims to describe a reality of supreme value, in relation to which human life realizes its true purpose. In other words, a religion is a belief-system articulating one view of the meaning of human existence.

Religions are concerned with actual life problems, with facing factors that seem to deprive life of value and attainable purpose, factors such as suffering, death, depression, and anxiety. They are concerned with reinforcing social and personal values and sustaining worthwhile patterns of life together. They are concerned with whether there is any purpose or goal that human life has. The crucial religion questions are: How can I best cope with my life problems? What is a worthwhile life? And what may I hope for in life?

Religions, when they are functioning positively, try to teach a way of coping with life and of becoming a more integrated and fulfilled person. They encourage a search for what gives self-worth and lasting satisfaction. They encourage positive thinking about life's prospects. They often provide group affirmations to establish such positive patterns more effectively. They aim at strong, affirmative, creative attitudes, and the overcoming of negative and self-destructive tendencies. They offer forms of training which may overcome destructive impulses and lead to greater wisdom, equanimity, and happiness.

So in Buddhism, meditation is used to overcome the sense of self and of attachment to finite goods. It is meant to lead to states of joy and tranquillity, and the overcoming of greed, hatred, and delusion. Similarly, in Vaishnava Hinduism, devotion, meditation, and ritual activity are all used to awaken the mind to the consciousness of the Supreme Self, which lies within, as the core of one's illusory desiring consciousness. And in Christianity, prayer is a training in reverence, gratitude, self-examination, and compassionate love, which is meant to help in building up a cooperating and loving community, with a vocation to reconcile the world to God.

Life can have meaning even if one has no religious beliefs. One finds a meaning in life if one discovers and pursues things that are intrinsically worth doing, which are satisfying and enjoyable. To do that, one has to have a good knowledge of one's own dispositions and motives, and an acceptance of the sorts of values human life can offer. One has to have a good deal of wisdom and sensitivity, but one does not need any religious beliefs. We can find meaning in pursuing projects that use our potentialities in enjoyable and worthwhile ways, and in being content with the limited goods we can reasonably attain.

Philip Quinn very clearly analyzes what it is for a human life to have meaning in terms of the concepts of "positive intrinsic value" and "non-trivial purposes of value." Religions are concerned with the meaning of life, in both these respects. They aim to give human life a positive complete meaning by showing what the highest possible value of human life is, and by showing that the most non-trivial purpose of human life is to achieve that value in a way that the religion claims to specify.

What distinguishes religious meaning is that one sort of intrinsic value, perhaps a very complex one, is claimed to be objectively the highest and proper value attainable by humans, or by any being whatsoever. In saying that this is objectively the case, I mean that many, or even most, humans might not see it to be a value. Yet it remains a supremely overriding value, whether or not they see it. Humans might not see the value of nirvana, or of the vision of God. But if they do not do so, they are mistaken. Indeed, it is a fundamental feature of most religions that the majority of humans are said to be suffering from illusion, ignorance, or depravity, which makes them unable to see what the highest value actually is.

In saying that the value is the highest, I mean that there is no other possible state that is of greater value, and that this value overrides all others, in the case of any conflict. For Buddhists, every human experience and state is tinged with suffering or unsatisfactoriness. Only nirvana is limpid, pure, cool, and untouched with sorrow. When it is rightly perceived, this value outweighs all others, and it does so for every sentient being. For Vaishnavas, all worldly existence leads to involvement in suffering, but an experience of the loving presence of Krishna gives a foretaste and promise of a realm beyond suffering. The supreme value is that of pure bliss, which comes by the transcending of attachment to the values of the world. For Christians, the experience of God is such that no other experience compares with it. In the classical formulation of Anselm, God is "that than which nothing greater [of greater value] can be conceived," and the experience of that reality is itself the greatest value attainable by created beings.

What distinguishes a religious view of non-trivial purpose is that all positive human purposes are subordinate to the one objective purpose of attaining the supreme goal of union with, or fulfilling relation to, the supreme value, which in itself exists unchangeably and indestructibly. Having established what the supreme value is, religions typically go on to construct a view of human nature that posits that its fulfillment is to be found in relation to that supreme value. Human beings are thus seen as intrinsically teleological. They have a purpose, that purpose belongs to human existence as such, and it consists in the fullest development of what is essential to human nature. This is clearest in the Christian case, where God creates human beings for a purpose. The purpose is not invented by humans; it exists in the mind of the creator. That purpose consists in a fulfillment of the potentialities for understanding, creativity, and community that have been implanted by the creator. It is completed by a conscious, co-creative fellowship with the creator, which is, in its fullness, a dynamic personal relation to a being of supreme value.

The purpose of human life does not have to be some end-state which terminates the process of human life. It may well lie in the process itself. The process attains its purpose when it exists as it is intended by God to exist. In the case of human lives, God intends humans to live in a freely chosen conscious loving fellowship with God and with other sentient beings. When they do so, and when all that restricts or impedes such fellowship is removed, the objective (divinely intended) purpose of human life is achieved.

Such a notion of divine intention that a process of a certain sort should exist is not available to Buddhism, since the idea of a creator is usually rejected or at least ignored. Nevertheless, one can still speak of an objective purpose or aim, which is the release from suffering and desire, and the attaining of nirvana. What makes that purpose objective is that the universe is so structured that desire inevitably causes suffering, and the overcoming of desire leads to the cessation of suffering. There is no purpose in life as such. That is, there is no positive reason for the existence of human beings. But, if one exists there is an objective goal of life, which alone can bring an end to suffering, and that is the attaining of nirvana. In some versions of Mahayana Buddhism, a stronger sense of purpose has developed, in that one aims to cultivate universal compassion for all beings and work for their release from suffering. On such views, there is often a close relation to theism, since the whole universe can be seen as pervaded by the Dharmakaya, the cosmic body of the compassionate Buddha-nature, which can be incarnate in many particular enlightened humans, and in which one aims to participate. Even though there is no creator, there is a community of compassionate beings of wisdom and bliss, exemplifying the ultimate nature of reality as concerned to end suffering and lead all beings to endless bliss.

It may seem odd to speak of purpose, in Buddhism, as a fulfillment of human nature. Yet the Buddhist account of human nature is that there is no central substantial self, so that the truth of human nature is indeed realized in the realization of freedom from individual projects and desires. In Buddhism, as in Christianity, the religious account of purpose is that there is one objective goal of human activity, which is conceptually connected with the realization of "true" human nature, and release from defective or mistaken views of what human nature is.

Vaishnava shares with Buddhism the same general cosmology of a beginningless and endless universe, into which humans are born many times and in which they are trapped by desire and attachment. But it has an explicit doctrine of the creator, Vishnu, and of the avatars of finite manifestations of Vishnu, especially Krishna, with whom devotees can be related in ecstatic love. It is disputed whether Vishnu intended this universe to exist, with its endless chain of sorrows. But once it exists, Vishnu does intend all beings to obtain release from suffering and experience the divine love. Here again the idea of an objective purpose is validated by being rooted in the desires of a supreme divine being. The purpose is release from rebirth, but this is not understood negatively, as an ending of individual life. It is rather understood as an entrance into a truer form of life, where humans can be fulfilled in love. In all three of these religious views, the most important non-trivial human purpose is objectively defined by an account of human nature and its most desirable fulfillment or realization.

A religious view of the meaning of life might want to add to Philip Quinn's account the element of pattern or significance. Human life not only has a positive goal, which lies in relation to a reality of supreme value. In addition, the events that happen in a human life are meaningful, in that there is an intelligible pattern to them, giving to each one a significance which it holds because of its unique relation to the others. When people complain that life is meaningless, they often mean that they cannot see how the events that happen to them fit into any overall pattern. To see the meaning of a human life would be to see how its various elements fit into a unique, complex, and integrated pattern.

Some Christians would say that God directs every event as a punishment, a discipline, or an opportunity for salvation. A more subtle account might say that all events are caused by the complex interaction of many freely choosing agents, partly rebelling against and partly cooperating with the general persuasive action of God to bring all things to the fulfillment God wills. To see the meaning of a life fully would be to understand how good and evil actions are necessarily interwoven and productive of good and bad consequences over time, and to see how they can be used by God to further a redemptive purpose, in which no action for good will ever be in vain, and in which evil will eventually bring about its own destruction.

Hindus and Buddhists typically say that what happens to one in life is determined by one's past deeds in other lives, either as a reward or punishment. The pattern of life is built up by karma, the law of spiritual retribution and reward. There is a specific reason why everything happens as it does, and this reason is connected with the egoistic and desire-filled acts of moral agents, or with their moral or spiritual development. Rebirth arises from *avidya*, ignorance, and the events of life teach humans how to overcome illusion and realize eternal bliss.

Secular views of human nature can speak about intrinsically worthwhile states, and about efficient ways to obtain them. They can recommend mental practices such as meditation to obtain such states, and there can be authoritative teachers who encourage such practices, and authoritative texts which expound them. In fact the secularized forms of yoga and meditation often found in the West do precisely that. We do not speak of these as religions, because they exclude appeal to a supernatural being or trans-human state, a certain sort of relation to which is claimed to be the one true goal of human life, and they do not usually claim that each life has a pattern which provides an intelligible reason for the occurrence of every event, in relation to the attainment of the proper human goal.

For secular views, there is no one true goal of life, and there are no supra-human states of any interest to us. So there is no reference to God, to Brahman, or to nirvana. There is usually an alternative account of human existence, and the best one is perhaps the neo-Darwinian account of an evolution of mind out of design, design out of order, and order out of chaos. There is no objective purpose of human existence. One can regard some states as intrinsically worthwhile, though there will be a certain subjectivity about that. Different people might choose very different values to pursue. Yoga and meditation will appeal to stressed-out or passive types, whereas drag-racing and football will appeal to more active and extrovert characters. Meditational practices become optional therapies, and are largely matters of taste and one's personal psychology.

Religions typically claim that their selection of intrinsic values is appropriate for all human beings, that everyone sooner or later will have to aim at them or face immense suffering, and that these values are rooted in a supra-human reality, a right relation to which is essential to realizing them. They would have to say that they can authoritatively teach the way to release from suffering and the realization of ultimate value, for all human beings.

Can religions not aim at less than this? A tribal religion may seek to establish right relations of the tribe with spirits and the powers of the natural world, but not insist that this is a universal way for all people. Jews seek to follow Torah, but do not insist that Gentiles do. Or a very liberal person may claim that all religions offer different ways toward human fulfillment. So maybe religions do not have to make the universal, even imperialistic, claims that I have suggested.

However, insofar as tribal religions claim truth at all, they are committed to the belief that there really are spiritual powers which relate to a particular tribe in a particular way. On reflection, such a view has to be generalized to cover all human groups, so one does have a universal claim that there are many spirit powers, relating in various ways to human beings. Unless the tribe is regarded as hugely abnormal, the sort of relation it should have to the spirits must be regarded as the sort of relation people in general should have to spirits. No tribal member would say that they are bound not to kill and steal, but it may be allright for other humans to do so. Other tribes must have at least analogous relations to spirits.

So if one tribe has rituals for cleansing misdeeds and expressing penitence, they may not wish other tribes to have just the same rituals, which were handed down by a particular group of teachers. But they will, if they are rational, expect that other tribes will have some rituals that effect the same sort of thing, that express penitence and offer forgiveness. There can be a variety of customs but a similarity of basic relationship to the spirits. Any tribe that does not have some rituals for relating to the spirits in gratitude, reverence, and penitence will be missing something important.

Tribal religions do speak of a proper goal of human existence, but they limit consideration of this goal to the purpose of their own tribe, which stands in relation to a particular set of spirits. Other tribes and nations must have analogous goals, set by the spirits. Since the human race is one, all these goals must cohere in some way. This can be done by accepting a huge pantheon of gods or spirits, all of whom serve some larger purpose and goal – perhaps the goal of leading humans to an awareness of the unity of all beings in one all-inclusive spiritual reality. That is the way taken by some main Indian traditions. Or it can be done by insisting that the tribal god is in fact the one true God, and all other ways of worship will ultimately converge on it. That is the way taken by the Hebrew prophets.

So Jews would not expect Gentiles to keep Torah. They take a pride in having a distinctive law. Yet Jews must, on reflection, think that all peoples should worship the one true God in some appropriate way, that is, some way analogous to the Jewish way. Again it is a matter of having many culturally diverse ways of expressing the same set of basic relationships and attitudes. Jews think that religions that worship many spirits are in fact defective in some ways, since there is only one creator God. Gentiles do not have to keep the Sabbath: that is a special rule for only some people. But that rule is given by one creator God, and all people have to worship that one God. So universal claims about the nature of supreme value and the final human goal are inseparable from reflective religion.

It seems that there is a core of general agreement in the major reflectively systematized religions about the supreme value and final goal.

The supreme value is a reality or state of wisdom, compassion, and bliss. Most theists would agree that God is such a reality. Most Buddhists would agree that nirvana is such a state. So, while God is a personal creator and nirvana is a non-dual state of being, there are high-level agreements about some of the most important properties of the ultimately desirable being or state. If a theist accepts that the essential nature of God is incomprehensible and radically unlike any finite being – as most orthodox theology has done – and if a Buddhist accepts that nirvana is beyond literal description – as most Buddhists do – then it might be reasonable to say that there is a common human goal of wisdom, compassion, and bliss.

Any path toward it must tend to overcome egoism and encourage altruistic action and a concern for the well-being of others. By this criterion a great number of religious beliefs and practices stand condemned. Practices that encourage egoism, by seeing prayer as a means of getting what one wants, or that encourage hatred of others, by seeing them as enemies of God, or that recommend the performance of purely ritual acts or calling on the name of a god as a means of salvation, or that encourage barbaric or grossly ascetic practices, by seeing them as means of gaining merit, have been condemned by both Jesus and Gautama. By the same token, however, many religious beliefs and practices would be conducive to realization of the human goal.

Unfortunately one cannot resolve all religious disputes by alleging that there is a very general level of undisputed absolute truths, while everything else is culturally conditioned and therefore relatively unimportant. After all, even those very general beliefs are highly disputed by many human beings. On what basis can one say that there exists a reality of wisdom, compassion, and bliss? That there is just one such supreme reality, and these are its properties? Or why should one believe that there is just one proper human goal, pursuit of which may require great personal sacrifices?

The attempt to answer these questions inevitably leads to the consideration of lower-level beliefs, which might justify or explicate the higher-level beliefs. There must be some basis for saying that there is one supreme compassionate being. One important part of such a basis must be that there are plausible cases in history where such compassion, wisdom, or bliss has been experienced. In other words, there must be some persons who reliably claim knowledge of the wisdom, compassion, and bliss of the supreme.

Similarly, there must be persons who claim knowledge of the proper human goal – which may, of course, be precisely the attaining of such a knowledge of the supreme. In other words, consideration of the claims of religion leads to consideration of more particular claims about religious authorities – people in whom, it is said, self has been overcome, supreme bliss has been attained, and unlimited compassion has been realized. The way of religious faith, for most of us, is a way of discipleship, following one who is believed to be selfless, renounced, compassionate, established in bliss, knowing the Supreme Self, who conveys the divine love and presence to others. Are there any such? If there were, we could only know it by the testimony of those who knew that person well, over a reasonable period of time. In the history of religions, there are a number of testimonies to the existence of selfless, compassionate, joyful teachers. They cannot be accepted without question, but neither should they be rejected out of hand.

We have to consider claims about the life and person of the alleged authority. We also have to consider what might be independently ascertained about the truth of the teachings of that authority, for what religious leaders teach will naturally be qualified by the conceptual scheme available to them in their culture. Religions are belief-systems founded on a general interpretative context as well as authoritative experience. The personal experience and quality of life of a religious teacher may justify a claim that there is a supreme goal, that it has the nature of compassion and bliss, and that it can be attained in the way they teach. Yet they could be wrong about such things as the age of the universe, the rules of social ethics, or the future of the earth. They need not, after all, be infallible in all their beliefs, as long as they are reliable about the things that are conducive to liberation or salvation. And in fact it is simply not possible to accept all religious teachers as correct in even the major claims they make about the supreme value and final goal.

Suppose one very sensibly took both Siddhartha Gautama and Jesus to be selfless, wise, and liberated religious teachers. One could follow them as reliable guides to the way of overcoming egoism and becoming conscious of a state or being of supreme wisdom, compassion, and bliss. Yet in the case of Jesus, if he was wrong about the Kingdom of God, about the historical purpose of God, and about the love of God, he would be importantly wrong. In the case of Siddhartha, if he was wrong about the non-existence of a substantial self, about the possibility of enlightenment, and about rebirth, he would be importantly wrong. Siddhartha saw the whole world as immersed in suffering, and taught that such suffering can be wholly ended by learning non-attachment. He believed in rebirth and in the possibility of final release from rebirth. In the end, Buddhist practice is made intelligible by a certain sort of belief in rebirth and karma. Either there is rebirth, or there is not. Either there is a law of karma, or there is not. Either there is an existence beyond duality and attachment, or there is not. There are many more or less straightforwardly factual claims made by religions which affect the sorts of descriptions they give of the supreme value and final goal of human life, and consequently of the appropriate way to attain that goal. There is a common structure to the sort of meaning religions give to life, but each religion gives a different particular interpretation of that structure. Such pluralism of views can be taken as a positive virtue, since freedom of diverse interpretation is conducive to self-criticism, to the effort to expand one's horizons, and to recognition of one's own very partial and culture-bound opinions. What it cannot reasonably lead one to do is to accept every one else's interpretations as just as good as one's own.

Disputes about the meaning of life are inevitable. Religion is not necessary to give meaning to life, though it is necessary to any claim that there is one state or being of supreme intrinsic value, that there is one overridingly important human purpose, and that there is an objective, morally ordered pattern in human experience. So a religious view of life may begin to seem attractive if one begins to wonder whether there are any truly objective values, any ends of human activity that really are of great intrinsic worth, whether people think so or not. Such ends may, for example, be morally binding ends, in the realization of which authentic humanity would be found. The Semitic traditions typically stress this aspect of the moral obligations of justice and mercy, which are not simply options, but requirements. Or they might be values that could only be rightly perceived if one realized the extent to which one was misled by the egoistic self. The Indian traditions emphasize the extent to which hatred, greed, and delusion give a false view of the self and its true nature.

Again, one might wonder if the true objectivity of such values did not imply their attainability. If it is obligatory to realize a society of justice and mercy, or if a right view of human existence brings one to desire liberation from the bondage of the egoistic self, must not such a society or such a liberation be possible? Of course the answer is "no." The moral ends of life may be unattainable, because the universe is just uninterested in human moral concerns. But such a perception may lead one to find life meaningless, in the sense that its most worthwhile purposes can usually not be realized, at least for most people.

Or one might wonder if there is any pattern to one's experience, if the things that happen to one and the things one achieves or fails to achieve hold any ultimate significance. Sometimes human lives can seem without any shape or coherence. But at other times one may feel that one can speak of a human life in terms of a learning, developing, and experiencing that seems fortuitous. The hint of such a pattern in one's experience, however hidden it may often be, may lead to a sense that one is discovering the meaning of one's life, not simply inventing it.

These three points, the question of the objectivity of value, of its attainability, and of the pattern of a life that seeks value, often lead to the postulation of a religious view. The major world religions have a common or analogous structure which reflects these three elements of a religious quest for meaning. They posit a supra-mundane state or being of supreme value. They posit a human goal or purpose which lies in a certain conscious relation to that value. They posit a way to the goal that enables one to "map" one's life story in terms of a pilgrim's (or rake's) progress, in community with others, and following the path of an authoritative teacher or teachers who have attained or disclosed the goal in a definitive way.

Within that common structure, however, there are a great number of diverse particular beliefs, which seem to fill in just about all the possible alternative positions provided by the structure. The supreme value can be construed in a number of ways along a continuum from a non-dual state of inactive bliss to a personal and active subject who grieves for and rejoices with the world and interacts with it. Theravada Buddhism describes nirvana as a state beyond desire, limpid and serene, but not in any causal or active relation to the world of action and desires. Vaishnava Hinduism sees it as a Supreme Self, perfect intelligence and bliss, which is manifest in the person of Krishna, of which one is always a part, and of which one can become conscious through loving devotion and meditation. Christianity affirms the existence of a personal and self-existent God, usually thought of as complete without the universe, but giving supreme fulfillment to disciples through the beatific vision of its essential nature.

In accordance with these interpretations of the Real, the final goal varies from being conceived as a complete union with the non-dual, in which all the constituent parts of finite human personality fade away (in Theravada Buddhism), to being a continuing individual personality in a loving relationship with a personal God (in Christianity), or to being a soul liberated from the body and made part of the Supreme Cosmic Self (in Vaishnava Hinduism). The convergence here is that the final human purpose is to come to knowledge by acquaintance with a state of bliss, wisdom, and compassion. The divergence is as to whether this is a unitive or a relational goal.

Practices for attaining the goal range from rigorous forms of renunciation, in some forms of Buddhism, to devotional singing and dancing, in Vaishnava Hinduism, and to possession by the Spirit, in some forms of Christianity. They may be seen as extending over many lives or as confined to one human life. Each way requires an overcoming of egoism, a transcendence of the finite self in relation to an objective supreme value, and obedience to a way of discipleship which has been disclosed by a revered teacher.

It is therefore possible to speak of a religious view of the meaning of life, and to think of a particular religion as giving one set of interpretations of such a view. Most of these interpretations are incompatible in detail, and it may be that none of them contains a complete and unrevisable set of truths. It is also true that within any one tradition, all these diverse ideas can be found in some degree, obviously in different positions of relative importance. So it is important to learn about other systems, to extend one's view of the possibilities of interpretation open to one, and to learn which members of one's own set of beliefs may need revision. But if the core beliefs of a specific religion seem coherent and plausible, if its claim for its canonical authority seem well justified, and if its most obviously culture-relative beliefs can be revised in accordance with new knowledge (for instance, in the natural sciences) without undue strain, then that religion may be said to offer a rationally acceptable account of the meaning of life. My judgment is that many will do so, but most will not.

A human life can have meaning without an objective purpose, value, or pattern. We can construct our own values and purposes in a morally patternless world. The irony of a wholly pragmatic view of religion is that it treats religions as useful to attaining values and purposes which we construct. But the consequence is that religions will no longer be dealing with the meaning of life at all. They will be means to constructing a sense of meaning in our lives. One should not accept a religion just because it seems to make an otherwise meaningless life meaningful. But if a specific set of religious beliefs is true, those who do not accept it, however meaningful their lives may seem to be, will indeed have missed the meaning of life.

Notes

1. Wilfred Cantwell Smith, *The Meaning and End of Religion* (San Francisco: Harper & Row, 1978), p. 48.
2. Ibid., p. 144.
3. Ibid., pp. 31, 39.
4. Ibid., p. 123.

2

THE NATURE *of* RELIGION: MULTIPLE DIMENSIONS *of* MEANING

Ninian Smart

It is normal for us intellectuals to think of the meaning of life in terms of philosophical or religious doctrines. I shall indeed start there, but as a way into what may be thought of as the mythic, experiential, ethical, social, and material aspects of the notion. The fact is that just as religions, and for that matter embodied ideologies such as nationalisms, are complex, so are the qualities of the meaning of life.

First, it seems that people tend to think of the meaning of life in relation to the place they have in the scheme of things. This might be conceived of as their cosmology. For instance, what is their picture of the cosmos, their view of whether there is a creator who presides over it, of the nature of history, and of the prospects of human life? Let us pause to reflect on these matters. Regarding human prospects, there is the question of whether there is such a thing as liberation. If there is, what is it freedom from? Naturally the idea of salvation is polyvalent, depending on what you are to be saved from. Is it from sin, as in traditional Christianity? Is it from psychological causes of suffering (or dissatisfaction, *dukkha*), as in Buddhism? Is it from this impermanent world, as often in Hinduism? There are, no doubt, overlaps between religions. But the ideas of liberation are context dependent and hinge on doctrines of a wide-ranging nature. There are some faiths that involve reliance on God, as in Islam, Sikhism, Judaism, Christianity, and some important versions of the Hindu tradition. They have differing mythic narratives about that God, but they all affirm God's creative power. That in turn means that they derive human existence and values from the creator – and not just human values, but also the powers of animals, fish, insects, and stars and suns and moons. Of course, there are differences (sometimes at different times) in the conceptions of the scale of the universe. Indeed, our knowledge of the size of the universe has expanded dramatically in the last fifty years or so, since Hubble first demonstrated that the galaxies' red-shift means that they are fleeing from each other. The God we see is awe-inspiring; and the proper response to her or him is worship. In return, the holiness that in principle is God's alone may be conferred upon humanity. This is sometimes referred to as the operation of grace. So the first rather simple idea is that the meaning of life lies in worship or devotion to the Divine, from whom we get our salvation or liberation.

Sometimes, to complicate matters (as often in the Hindu world), the particular items of value we derive from the Divine are devolved, so that we turn to more immediate deities or spirits or saints to funnel particular goods to us. Sarasvati, for instance, is the goddess of learning, so success at school can come through her. But ultimately, liberation comes through the one Divine, it is thought by those who know. Another way of putting God's function is to say that he or she conserves value: the values of life are maintained by God through the conferral on us of eternal life.

On the other hand, some religions, and notably Buddhism, do not have a Creator. The god Brahma, thought by Hindus to be the Creator, actually suffers from an illusion; because he is the first being to come into existence (by karmic force) in a new world era, he thinks that those who come after him must have come into existence *because* of him. But he is wrong; they come into being through the same sort of karmic force that brought him into being. *Post me propter me* he fallaciously reasons. So in Buddhism, at least very clearly in Theravada, there is no adoration of God. It is true that in Theravadin countries you may stop off to give a coconut or some offering to a deity. But such deities are in principle no more important or permanent than the mayor or the tycoon. Similarly Jainism has no Creator. But the highest value lies in nirvana or *kevala*. This transcends rebirth and is the only escape from suffering. The enormous cosmos contains (in Buddhism) many worlds where animals and humans exist, perpetually (or almost) being reborn, whether as ghosts, animals, humans, or gods – all destined to suffering at various levels. Humans live together in society, and its projects may give some meaning to life, but ultimately it is nirvana that is the most significant achievement. The monks and nuns signify the final reality of a level beyond our world. So though it is true that there is no transcendent God in Buddhism, there is a transcendent state. In both cases ultimate meaning refers to something "outside" our world. I put the word "outside" in quotation marks here, because for one thing to be literally outside a certain space, it has to be in another part of space and hence in this cosmos.

But there is a complication here, because in Mahayana sometimes nirvana and *samsara* (the round of rebirth or the empirical world) are identified. Why is this? We can explicate this in terms of mystical or contemplative experience, in which subject–object distinction, common to external perception, is abolished. One who perceives emptiness (*shunyata*) *is* that emptiness. But emptiness is the nature of things and so is the nature of *samsara* and is the liberating perception of emptiness or nirvana. By the same token we all have the Buddha-nature within us. So in Mahayana, where this equation is affirmed, what we are liberated from is the ignorance or delusion, before we have perceived emptiness. The knowledge of emptiness is the liberation we seek.

In regard to secular philosophies, such as humanism and Marxism, there is nothing strictly speaking that is transcendent. Among humanists there is perhaps a supreme value, namely reverence for persons. Somewhat similar is philosophical Confucianism which, though it emphasizes collectivity in that the welfare of society is important, also sees the meaning of life as bound up with moral and mental self-improvement. We may note that reverence for persons is also affected by the way society is viewed; thus society includes ancestors both among Confucianists and Africans and other peoples.

So much briefly for various doctrinal patterns relating to the meaning of life. But supreme beings and states (such as nirvana) are incarnated in myths or sacred narratives or realized in the life and deeds of holy persons or groups, and these, too, give plot and shape to meaningful lives and provide embodied models. Judaism, for example, does not only have a Supreme Being but one with a history, as delineated through the books of the Hebrew Bible and in the Talmud. The meaning of life is found, for the pious Jewish woman, in her relationship to this God, and through the daily practice of the Torah. If she is Orthodox, her daily acts are suffused, for example, with the requirements of *kashrut,* the very preparation of all her and her family's food. So the meaning of life has both a doctrinal and a narrative dimension. For the Christian the mythic narrative overlaps somewhat with that of the Jew, but above all the Christian focuses on Christ, whose life, death, and resurrection constitute the essential story. The story of Genesis even varies from that of the Jewish selfsame text. Christ is Creator, too, and the story of Adam and Eve is of a profound fall. Original sin is so strong a doctrine in Christianity because it paves the way for the salvation by Christ's sacrifice on the cross. The story, of course, does not end there; for both Jews and Christians there is a tale of the future, the restoration of the land of Israel in the one case and the Second Coming in the other. But the story of God in Islam is different again, even though it also overlaps with that of the others (e.g., the story of Abraham, the teachings of Jesus, and the tale of the Last Judgment in the future). But above all the biography of God intersects with that of the Prophet Muhammad and with the subsequent great success of Islam. Also, the narratives of Muhammad's life become a narrative pattern for guiding the life of every Muslim. Similarly those about Ali and Fatima and others hold up models and ideals.

In the Hindu tradition there is a great wealth of mythic options. The stories of the various avatars or incarnations of Vishnu weave together many motifs of divine manifestation. Most notably there are the stories of Rama and Krishna, which are reenacted in dramatic performances in the cities and villages of India, and most recently on television. When I talk about "options," this is important, because to some degree the system is one of the *ishtadevata* or chosen God. You can choose which ideal to follow. You can emphasize God's justice or his love of souls or his power or her creativity. In the theologies of Ramanuja, Chaitanya, and a number of others (probably the dominant actual kind of religion on the ground in India), the emphasis is on the mutual love of God and individuals, and so on God's warm grace.

In Buddhism the narrative dimension exploits the doctrinal in drawing on fictional and fabulous descriptions of the previous lives of the Buddha to illuminate conduct. The edifying tales contained in the *Jatakas* or *Birth Stories* point to ideals of human behavior and to concepts illuminating the virtues. Also, these are supplemented by the autobiographical poems known as the *Therigathi* and the *Theragatha,* the *Verses of the Nuns and Elders.* These purportedly (and it is no doubt true in many cases) tell of real-life events happening to holy recluses, and keep people aware of the ultimate goal of nirvana. All this occurs within a framework of history, with the theory being proposed that as we get further from the time of the

Buddha so there is a decline in the possibility of self-help in salvation. Thus, in Japan we have the idea of *mappo* – the age of the end of the dharma – when we have to rely on the help of the Buddha in attaining to the Pure Land. This pattern of salvation, by the way, is much closer to the doctrines of Christianity and Hinduism than it is to those of Theravada. The agent of this salvation is Amida, a Buddha (or rather from the Pure Land point of view, especially as expressed by Shinran, *the* Buddha). But in Mahayana, a special place is reserved for the mythic figure of the Bodhisattva, one who is destined for Buddhahood but who puts off his or her liberation in order to save others. A prominent role is played for instance by the figure of Avalokitesvara, the One who looks down with Compassion, who, by the way, underwent a sex-change in China and beyond and became the supremely caring person of Kuanyin (Kannon in Japan). She is reminiscent of the Virgin Mary. The narrative of the latter fills out the work of the saving God, by injecting a womanly figure into the (so to speak) pantheon. There are even impulses in the contemporary Catholic church, some of them on high, to promote the cause of Mary as being co-saviour with Christ.

The idea of rebirth is essential to the Buddhist and Hindu accounts of liberation, and it goes with a huge cosmology. From early Buddhism such beliefs in the pulsating universe took a grip on what was later the Hindu imagination. The *kalpas* and *yugas* revolve endlessly. The Western cosmology is laughably small-scale by comparison. But rebirth or reincarnation can bring on a sense of ennui. This is important as a stimulus for a more burning desire for liberation, and also suggests that the process is most difficult to get out of or at least that great power on the part of some Other would be required to do so. The belief in rebirth puts life in such a different perspective. Ennui after all subtracts from the sense of the meaning of life. The glories of existence may seem to fade when endlessly repeated. A column of ants may cause Indra pause if he thinks that each ant is a former Indra. Suppose you were offered the chance of living for a million or a billion years? It is a very different scenario from the single-shot cosmology of the Christian and Islamic faiths. It also suggests that you can carry on making progress toward holiness. The educational theory behind rebirth is more relaxed than implicit in one-life opportunities. It also, by the way, fits with the idea of accumulated merit and karma. So we have multivalent signals contained in belief in rebirth. On the one hand, it enhances ennui and so tends to assign this-worldly activity to a lower level of value. It also may reduce the ultimate value of heaven. On the other hand, it provides a framework for making sense both of moral action and of merit.

The belief in a Creator, however, leads to a short-circuiting of karma. Karma becomes the instrument by which the Creator distributes lives, rewards actions, punishes vice, and so on. But that means that by the Creator's grace he or she can pluck you from this world, to exist in heaven close to him or her. Sometimes (as according to Madhva) the Creator simply realizes what is predestined. But generally grace comes to override merit. The same applies in the Pure Land traditions.

As for the experiential dimension of meaning, basically we can consider two basic forms here – on the one hand the numinous experience, put on the map by Rudolf Otto, and on the other hand the mystical or contemplative experience. There are other varieties, of course, but these two lie behind many of the key ideas in religion.

The numinous experience of the Other can dynamize our daily activities and fellowship in a given community. The prophets were an example, and the awe-inspiring finds its response in the worship of God. The inferior worshiper feels humble and soaked in inadequacy. The holy Creator is seen as the sole source of holiness and indeed wholeness; hence, there evolves out of the numinous experience the sense of receiving grace. So God though frightening is also the merciful giver. He or she therefore expresses above all love. That the Divine Reality is, as well as being fearful, also loving, merciful, and compassionate is found sooner or later as a sentiment in the varying major religious traditions. This reinforces the feeling that God confers salvation; it is relationship with the Divine Being that constitutes the true meaning of life. This is evident in doctrine, narrative, and experience.

In India the numinous God unites with the religion of *bhakti* or devotionalism. The effects are similar to those in the Western monotheisms, though the atmosphere is different – doubly so when we see the contrasts between Hindu and Buddhist *bhakti*. Probably the most representative of all Hindu theologians is Ramanuja, partly because he also encapsulated the regionalism of India through his expression of the values of the Tamil poets. Also, his followers diverged into differing views about grace. The question was how we are to draw out the logic of the numinous experience of the loving Other. For the so-called "cat" school we are utterly dependent on the divine grace in getting us from here to heaven (like the kitten who is picked up by the scruff of the neck); for the so-called "monkey" school the soul has to do something – to cling to the Lord, as a little monkey clings to its mother's waist. God as Other manages our karma and is creator of the Vaikuntha heaven, a beauteous region where we are in the presence of the Lord. Incidentally, the whole cosmos, including heaven, is the body of the Lord, in the intimate control of Vishnu. We must recognize that this theology is in a powerful way an expression of spiritual experience.

Honen and Shinran appealed to a similar experience – based on an Indian original Pure Land theme, this strand of divine-flavored worship displays a like logic. But perhaps Amitabha (Amida) is less fearful than the Hindu Lord. In any case, the Buddhist tradition nearly always put the contemplative path at the center of its values, at least in theory. This softened its harder edges.

Let us now turn to this second main kind of religious experience – the mystical. Contrasted to, but not at all in contradiction with, the values of the numinous is the contemplative experience. Since the imagery of light is often used to point to it, and since the word "mystical" has a number of other, unrelated uses, I shall use the word "luminous" to refer to it, with a touch of light-heartedness. The contrast between the two is as follows. The luminous experience is without subject and object, typically. The numinous reveals the Other. The one diminishes the gap; the other affirms it. Even where the side of luminous love is emphasized, there is a relationship (a love of I and Thou). Secondly, the luminous is pure consciousness; it involves the purification of consciousness and the elimination of distracting perceptions and thoughts. The numinous typically contains visionary or auditory contents. The luminous experience calms turbulence in the soul, but the numinous one often enhances it – so awe-struck and afraid is the percipient. The luminous typically is indefinable, incomprehensible, ineffable: it is the progenitor of the *via negativa.* It is true that the numinous is also ineffable, but in a slightly different manner. The overwhelming Holiness of the Other strikes us dumb, but we cannot express sufficiently the divine greatness. The luminous experience is without features. The One cannot be praised enough, and so is, as it were, performatively off the ends of the scale. This is different from indescribability. The luminous typically appears outside time and suffused in bliss, or maybe beyond bliss. The numinous is often seen, as having to do with God or the gods, as immortal. So it frequently happens that the mystic, seeking the immortal within, thinks of her luminous experience as involving some kind of union (or even identity) with the numinous. The lack of clear subject–object distinction leads the contemplative to say that he is one with the Real, but the mode of that oneness becomes crucial.

For the numinous is the Holy, and sometimes, as in Islam, Judaism and Christianity, is exclusively so. To claim to be equal to God is blasphemy, yet sometimes the mystic perceives himself or herself as being in a subject–object-less relationship with God. If, of course, you do not believe in God, that is, not seriously, then there is no question of union here. That is why the Theravadin does not affirm some kind of communion or union with ultimate reality. For him, he is in a transcendent state. The options are identity (Shankara), union (Eckhart), communion (Teresa), and non-union (nirvana). Where union occurs, inevitably the imagery of sexual union crops up, as in Tibetan tantra, and in the play on the union of Christ with his church. Sometimes literal sexual techniques are used to achieve the highest bliss. The analogy between sexual love is taken seriously, for sex takes you out of your mind. Such experiences, whether of numinous or luminous encounter, establish an unshakable ground for meaning and action for the individual and generate religious narratives.

We have already noted that the narratives of holy persons and leaders of religion suffuse the ethical dimension of a meaningful life. I can find, through devotion, loyalty and admiration directed toward the prophets, avatars, sages and heroes of the tradition, a shape to my ethical beliefs. I can be noble like Muhammad, self-humbling like Christ, insightful like the Buddha, spirited like Shembe, sagacious like Confucius, courageous like Gobind Singh, loving like Krishna, heroic like David, harmless like Mahavira, and free like Zhunangzi. The myths permeate the style of ethical conduct, in principle, of the follower. Also, ethical demands are not simply individual matters, but can flow from societies, in particular those societies within society such as the Sangha and the Church. They in turn may become universal and embrace the whole of society, as with the medieval Church and with Islam, in certain regions and at some times. Their examples can be important. But in modern times we have invented the nation, often as the most important community shaping our values. This leads to split allegiances: I may be American as a citizen, but religiously I may be Episcopalian. So often we are driven back on our individual judgment on what we believe to be right (with regard to landmines or euthanasia, for instance).

Religious meanings are often most profoundly reinforced by and expressed through their ritual dimension. Rituals help to underline, and give feeling to, all the values and ideas we have so far discussed. Thus, rituals such as devotional acts, rites of passage, pilgrimages, and so on help to express (for instance) the transcendence and majesty of God, the sacredness of human beings and the sublimity of human consciousness. Without ritual a sense of the depth of human life disappears. Without the handshake and the wave, the clasped hands and the salute, the baptism and the funeral procession, the prostration and the pilgrimage, the hymns or chants to the Lord and the immersion, the sanctity of our condition begins to fade away. The taste of personhood turns flat and the vision of meaning in life blurs.

The ritual dimension spreads too. Study in Judaism becomes a means of worship. *Laborare est orare* epitomizes an old Benedictine world. Life itself is seen as a pilgrimage, wonderfully and obliquely portrayed in Bunyan's famous work. Rituals also reenact the stories that animate our tradition, and the Jewish year portrays in ritual so many key episodes in the history that Jews tell themselves. Likewise the paintings and sculptures that adorn temples and churches are "frozen rituals" representing the key heroes and events of the liberation that our saviors and holy ones enable us to attain.

Rituals enhance the feelings that help to animate our faiths. For instance, a powerful role is played by hymn-singing in church and synagogue. They are ritual in that they are part of what constitutes the way in which we express worship. They are also stimulators of religious emotions and experience.

Both music and representational art are vital sides of our being. It is true that some religions are aniconic – Judaism, portions of Protestantism, the Lingayata, Sikhism, Islam, and so forth. Yet although they may draw the line at representing God (and humans), they have other ways of decorating their meeting places. Also, the scriptures often have within them beauties, through which our passions may be aroused. There is a kind of music in literature, which is played for us through the recitation of the scriptures and in the call to prayer.

There is, then, also a material dimension to the way meaning in life is developed and represented. The cathedrals of Europe (for instance) and the noble architecture of the Mughals in India, the complex and gracious architecture of Borobodur and Angkor, and the highly decorated temples of Hinduism and the sublime frescoes of Assisi and Sri Lanka all testify to the ways in which divine or transcendent glory is expressed materially. There are also to be considered in this connection the appearance of secular music and art. The paintings by the Impressionists do not convey a religious art *per se*; and the architecture of the Bauhaus does not overtly contain a sacred message. A modern architect may venture occasionally upon a religious building, such as Le Corbusier (Jean Jeannaret) with his chapel in the southeast of France at Ronchamp and Basil Spence with his famous new Coventry Cathedral, begun in 1954. The skyscrapers of the modern city, the stadium in the city, the monuments to war, the houses in the countryside, the dams and the laboratories and museums – all these convey a certain ethos of the secular: the proud can-do culture of the modern world. Their values are interpretable, but they do not overtly reflect nirvana or the Divine. But in modern times, too, religious architecture has burgeoned, and it signifies pluralism, for in the West lots of temples and mosques arise, as once Western churches and the occasional synagogue peppered South Asia, China, and elsewhere.

If through our doctrines, myths, experiences, ethics, communities, rituals, and material art we create those values that in summation constitute the meaning of religion, how can we delineate the way meaning fades? How can we think of the meaningless? Perhaps the most poignant aspect is the failure of hope. This is, so to speak, the failure of the future. But it can also be seen as the waning of the eternal, the lack of permanent meaning in anything. God by being there somehow guarantees that our values (endorsed by her or him) will remain when we are gone. Meaninglessness is a failure of the absolute value of what we worship, what we are devoted to, what we esteem. The worldview we once held to, which gave us confidence in the future and in the reality of value of the present, may have faded in plausibility. Perhaps God is no longer plausible, nirvana an illusion, our hopes illusory. Humans may no longer appear sacred, and history may be without any ongoing thrust, no ultimate purpose.

In brief, the meaning of life is related to the varied dimensions that worldviews, or more narrowly religions, display. It has to do with cosmology and with the narratives we tell, above all of our gods or heroes. It has to do with our experiences and sentiments. Even those who have not had a primary infusion of the numinous have a sense of it and feelings of awe; even those whose inner life has not attained a sense of the luminous can yet have intimations of it in the lives of elders and mystical saints. The meaning of life can in part be gleaned from the ethical dimension, in the evidences of love and compassion in the lives of humans. It is found, too, in the solidarities of communities, whether nations, the Sangha, families, mosques, or wherever. Finally, we may see it expressed in the stones of churches, the wood of temples, the paintings of sacred buildings and the arts of music across the world.

The meaning of life can be said to reside in the maintenance of values and their production in the various dimensions. Typically what gives meaning to life consists in a collage of values, differing between persons and cultures. And, of course, these values can be subject to criticism. Often the values need at least in part to be teleological: your purpose in life may relate to an ongoing process, such as being conducive to the welfare of your family or your nation or your profession. There are various ongoing webs of purposes, through which your life gains its meaning. But the process must itself be valuable. The purposive should conduce to the production or manifestation which is in itself valuable. And religion gives all this a deeper significance, because it concerns those values that are ultimate or profound, among others.

Let me use all this as background to comment on some of the issues arising from the chapters in this volume on the varied traditions dealt with. One item developed by Charlotte Fonrobert's treatment of the Jewish heritage has to do with study. Study of the Torah is a remarkable phenomenon as undertaken in Judaism. With the dispersal of Jews through the Roman world and with the destruction of the Temple, it was not altogether surprising that synagogue worship should spread and that rabbinic Judaism should come to dominate the tradition. Yet it is surprising that the study of (say) sacrifice or the agricultural year should become equivalent in value to the sacrificial process itself – no longer possible without the Temple, of course. Now an analog to this might be found in the Benedictine *laborare est orare*, as we have noted above. One might say *studiare est orare*. But there is a subtle difference. By hoeing turnips in a monastery field or by weaving cloth in a nunnery, we might indeed worship God with the right intention, but with study we understand something about God – the revealed shape of God's mind. The Benedictine way is to take something "secular" (that is, definable apart from religion) and sanctify it; the Jewish way here is to take something religious and interpret it through another religious meaning.

But studying can have a secular meaning as well and has greatly benefited from the habit of religious studying.

In general the case is somewhat different with Christianity (and in particular Catholic Christianity). Catholic and Orthodox Christianity, not to mention Anglican and some other forms, are sacramental in essence (and more radical forms of Protestantism would not eschew the adjective). That partly reflects Christ's incarnation. Quinn notes, however, that we should not be seduced into an arrogant anthropocentrism. His careful philosophical analysis is much to be commended, but we remain with a question of how we know that a person's purposes have positive value. They perhaps have to be seen in the eye of faith, but from an "objective" point of view they are only probably to be affirmed. Incidentally, Jainism, as Christopher Chapple has indicated clearly, is a most rigorous religion. But despite the importance of commitment to such an austere faith, it is soft epistemologically, for it also espouses *syadvada* or "maybe-ism" – and this should govern all faiths.

When we come to compare Christianity with Islam, we have overlaps, of course, but we also have vital divergences. Islamic law lays down rather different rules and values from those of Christianity. F.E. Peters depicts them magisterially. The divergence of revelations can hardly be resolved, and outside faith in a given revelation there is no decisive way of choosing between them. We have here a paradox in faiths. A religious tradition seems to demand certitude, but objective knowledge is at best uncertain. This especially becomes a problem where cultures are intermingling, as in the present global world. Even where religious experience (for instance the luminous certitude of the Sufi) brings a kind of knowledge, there are diverse ways of interpreting mystical experiences. This is an extra reason for espousing a liberal or modernist position, where toleration reigns. Because also in science knowledge is often revised, the open society is desirable. For the advancement of knowledge, some sort of democracy is desirable within the Islamic (and other) worlds. It happens, by various misfortunes, to be singularly lacking in Muslim countries, except Malaysia and one or two others. But a revival of mainstream values, such as Sufism, may be coming, once the hard-edge militancy of Islam has passed by.

Karen McCarthy Brown among other things introduces us to the world of Greater Africa. African movements and religions abound in the New World, including Haitian Vodou which she has so perspicuously illuminated. A feature of these religions is their capacity to live alongside

Catholicism. In Africa there are well over ten thousand new religious movements which also synthesize Christian and traditional or classical African values. This illustrates something important about meanings. A faith has to make sense of deeply held values arising from your own tradition. Western Christianity has made important advances in Africa, but it often failed to be true either to the biblical writings or to classical culture in that continent. For instance Western medicine, good as it is at rooting out some diseases, neglects many motifs in African healing; likewise, it does not repeat the faith healing and miracle working of Christ in the gospels. Also the stories of the Exodus and of Christ reflect the suffering and experiences of the terrible cruelty of slavery.

Incidentally, African religion is not alone in transforming itself whether in Brazil, the Caribbean, or the American mainland. Other religions, mostly relatively small-scale, have reacted by forming new movements or by consolidations. By consolidations, I refer to the way new larger blocks have been created such as Native American religion or African religion itself – these are modern concepts pioneered by thinkers such as Mbiti or sages such as Black Elk. Western scholars have also contributed with researchers in Polynesia and circumpolar regions expanding our understandings of cultural regions and religious themes. Gradually the religions under pressure from the great traditions are gathering strength, either by absorbing values and meaning from those traditions, or by consolidating themselves, or both.

Julius Lipner deals with Hinduism which also displays a great transformation in modern times. In the course of the rise of Indian nationalism, the ideology of Vivekananda was particularly appealing, since it managed to synthesize the differing strands of the tradition together with those of other religious loyalties, such as Islam, Sikhism, the Parsees, Christianity, and so on. The unity of religions could mean that Indians of all persuasions could join together to struggle for freedom. It is interesting that this major Indian theme is amplified in John Hick's theory, which he presents tellingly here, and Huston Smith's presentation echoes a not dissimilar theme. Vivekananda readapted the great Shankaracharya, but Lipner is correct in seeing a greater centrality in actual religious life in the *bhakti* theology of Ramanuja. The rise of the BJP (a powerful Hindu nationalist political party) is, however, a real danger to India. The toleration of the Republic of India hitherto has held the diverse communities together (admittedly with occasional riotous conflicts).

It must be remembered that there are about one hundred and ten million Muslims in India. If they ever became seriously disaffected, India would be in deep trouble. Perhaps the same lesson applies to the global world: those who peddle narrowness and hostility between faiths may end up seriously undermining what there is of a sense of common humanity.

Christopher Chapple has written a rich chapter on the values of Jainism, with its austere regard for living beings. He also deals with the philosophy and practice of Yoga. Together with Buddhism and one or two other movements these traditions go back to the Shramanic strand of Indian religion, and maybe to the Indus Valley culture, as he argues. If Jainism enshrines *tapas*, the heat of austerity, Yoga develops the mystical tradition (as does Buddhism in its own way). Jainism gives a vital valuation of non-violence in its reverence for life. Gandhi's innovative interpretation of this led to a relatively peaceful transition to Indian independence (except for the vast ethnic cleansing that marked partition).

The tradition of Jainism is perhaps more akin to Theravada Buddhism than it is to Mahayana, although the seeds of the Greater Vehicle are already contained in Theravada. It is the Mahayana main perspective on the meaning of life that is explicated by Masao Abe. Here there is a particular blend of both philosophical insight and experience. The realization of the identity of nirvana and *samsara* is a special sort of knowledge. It involves penetrating to Emptiness (which yet involves a kind of Fullness). Further, it is because the human being has self-consciousness that he or she is special and so able to achieve liberation from the cycle of birth and death.

John Berthrong in turn opens up a new perspective on the Confucian tradition. Confucianism is indeed taking on modern meaning, reemphasizing the moral development for individuals and a strong sense of collective responsibility. Moreover, it has played a powerful role in changing societies in recent times in places such as Singapore, Hong Kong, Taiwan, Korea, and Japan. Even in mainland China it is undergoing some revival.

The themes addressed in the chapters by Joseph Runzo, Nancy Martin, Anne Klein, and finally by Sallie McFague to some degree complement one another. Runzo's is a new perspective on those allegedly contrasting notions of *eros* and *agape*. His reconciliation of the two in what he calls "seraphic" love is important, and Nygren's old contrast should indeed be met with skepticism. It is true that there can be erotic pleasure that is self-centered, but the highest satisfaction in love-making enjoys and gives pleasure to the other. Our modern period is becoming one when love is appreciated in new ways, because of technical advances such as the provision of contraceptives, which are bound to alter our perceptions of sex. There is a greater freedom in it, and arguably it is the intensest pleasure that humans can experience. Its relationship to spiritual love is well brought out by Runzo.

Something of the same sense is found in Nancy Martin's chapter, which sets forth most poetically and movingly the varieties of accents of love in the Hindu tradition. Here we look back on some emphases alluded to by among others Julius Lipner, and forward to the imagery of Sallie McFague.

Masao Abe's chapter, as I have mentioned, remarks upon the self-consciousness of human beings. This is vital in realizing the meaning of life, for to some degree this implies standing somewhat back from it, and that in turn implies self-consciousness. Perhaps in a dim manner the horse or the cat has her values, but it is clearly the human who can reflect on the goods and evils of life. And Buddhism, among other paths, enhances that self-consciousness through the exercise known as mindfulness. That is important throughout Buddhism but particularly in Tibetan Buddhism, where Anne Klein gives us guidance in her chapter. In my view it is not only important for thinking of our deeper values in life, but also everyday in the clarification of our feelings and perceptions.

Finally, in regarding the themes of the chapters laid before us in this volume, there is a way of looking at God. Admittedly it does not cover all religions, but it can illuminate the various monotheisms of Hinduism, Christianity, Judaism, Buddhism, and Sikhism, not to mention the beliefs of Africa and elsewhere. The idea of God's body as constituting the cosmos, as being the universe, if you prefer, is a fine analogy for us to work with. For it is the body as it were in the control of the soul, and the world is completely in the control of the Lord (as Ramanuja for one would put it). This gives a sense of intimacy of the Divine without sacrificing the sense of transcendence.

In this chapter, I have tried to widen the range of phenomena we examine when we ask questions of life's meaning in the context of religion, and I have laid out what I consider to be the important dimensions of religion that must be considered – not only philosophical ideas and doctrines, but also mythic, experiential, ethical, social, and material aspects. I have, then, examined the essays of the other contributors to the volume in light of these dimensions in order to demonstrate how complex meanings actually are. I would add one final consideration to our investigation of life's meaning from the religious perspective. We must not forget science, and more fundamentally that the nature of knowledge itself is changing – something that will have a profound impact on our understanding of our world, ourselves, and life's meaning. It is only a few decades since we learned of the expanding universe. Does that not alter our perspective on the creative activity of the Lord? And it even helps to alter the Buddhist cosmology, even though the latter was much nearer to the knowledge of modern astronomy. In light of such significant changes, we need to rethink, and indeed to refeel, the cosmos and our place within it.

Part II

MEANING AND WESTERN RELIGION

Out of the desert lands of Palestine and Arabia, from among nomadic pastoralists and traders, emerged the great monotheistic religions of the world: Judaism, Christianity, and Islam. At the heart of all three religions is a belief in an all-powerful creator God who is both compassionate and just and who lives in dynamic relationship with the faithful. God's nature and God's will are revealed to human beings in a variety of ways: through creation itself, including that of humans who are made "in the image of God," and also through dreams, visions, miracles, and an inner "still small voice." God is envisioned as speaking through prophets and through the consensus of communities of the faithful and revelations recorded in sacred books: the Hebrew Bible, the Talmud, the New Testament, and the Qur'an.

Taking the latter book first, the status of the Qur'an is different from the other Western sacred texts, since it is understood by Muslims to be God's direct words in Arabic, which Muhammad, as the seal of the prophets, was directed to recite by the angel Gabriel. In contrast, for Christians Jesus is the direct revelation or Word of God as God's son and God incarnate in the world – the completion of God's self-revelation. Historically, both Islam and Christianity are intimately connected with Judaism, an ancient tradition which formed during the second millennium BCE, coalesced by around 1000 BCE in the reign of King David, and was codified in the Torah. Christianity began as a Jewish reform movement after the death of Jesus – himself a rabbinically trained Jew – in 30 CE. The experiences of his early followers were recorded over the second half of that first century in the New Testament documents which, together with the Jewish scriptures, were to become the sacred texts of Christianity. Six centuries after the rise of Christianity and three centuries after its development into a world religion with a western branch centered in Rome and an eastern branch centered in Constantinople, Muhammad was born in Mecca on the Arabian peninsula in 570 CE. Muhammad conceived of his teachings, which were to become the foundation of Islam, as continuous with those of the Judaism and Christianity he found around him. Although Judaism, Christianity, and Islam diverge over the status of the Jewish law, over the divinity of Jesus, and over the sacredness of the Qur'an, they share fundamental ideas about the nature of God, the world, and humans, and hold in common the belief that at the center of a meaningful life is a relationship with God.

To begin our examination of the answers to life's meaning that are offered by the three great Western monotheisms, Philip Quinn brings clarity to the fundamental question of what makes for a meaningful life in the first place, irrespective of religion. After clarifying the question, he goes on to demonstrate how the Western monotheistic religions generally, and Christianity specifically, imbue life with meaning. Meaning, he suggests, must be discussed both in terms of the intrinsic value of human life and of a positive purpose for living. A human life has meaning in the first sense only if "(1) it has positive intrinsic value; and (2) it is on the whole good for the person who leads it." The great monotheisms, he will show, address both requirements through the assertion that humans are created in the "image of God" and through ways of understanding even experiences of horrendous evil as potential sources of possible good. To have meaning in the second sense, Quinn suggests "human life has positive meaning only if (1) it contains some purposes the person who lives it takes to be nontrivial and achievable; (2) these purposes have positive value; and (3) it also contains actions that are directed toward achieving these purposes and are performed with zest."

In general, the great monotheisms address these requirements, defining the fundamental goal of human life as joyfully knowing, loving, and serving a God who is perfectly good, and so sharing in a beatific vision of God in an afterlife. Turning to the specific case of Christianity, Quinn suggests that the narratives of the gospels and of a cosmic salvation history unify all the aspects set out above for a meaningful life. The life of Jesus becomes a radical paradigm for a meaningful life for the Christian, a life marked by love and sacrifice. To imitate Christ is not simply to admire him but to be willing to give one's life and to be subject to the same rejection to which Jesus was subject. If taken seriously, the narrative of Jesus necessarily evokes a response of either offense or faith. Salvation history is a narrative of God's loving concern for human beings in which every person has a meaningful role because we matter to an omniscient and perfectly good God, so much so that this God incarnates in the world, suffers, and dies for its sake. However, Quinn offers two warnings. First, we should not assume that only human life matters to this God. Second, given the multiplicity of interpretations of the Christian narratives and the reasonable stories others (religious as well as non-religious) offer about life's meaning, Quinn suggests that Christians might be wise not to assume they have the whole story, although they are entitled to believe that their reading of the Christian narrative is the most compelling story available to humans.

While for Christians the salvation narrative and the imitation of Christ are at the heart of a meaningful relationship with God, Charlotte Fonrobert introduces us to the world of classical Judaism where meaning and relationship are structured by the Torah, through study and ritual practice. She delineates the fundamentally different shape a meaningful life takes in Judaism for men versus women through an analysis of textual sources (which reflect a predominantly male perspective from within the world of study traditionally closed to women) and of the ritual life of home and community (in which women have played a much greater role in creating meaning-filled lives).

On the one hand, to study Torah is to touch the mind of God, so study becomes an act not only of knowing God but of devotion to God, and as such it is the most intimate form of love. On the other hand, in practice Torah is embodied in everyday life which is imbued with sacredness through ritualization – including even such fundamental activities as eating and sex – centered in the gender-inclusive world of the home. Fonrobert argues that in both these dimensions of study and ritual Torah is said to increase life, enriching and filling it with meaning, and quite literally lengthening it.

In Islam, life's meaning is also found in the cultivation of the human–Divine relationship. To be a Muslim is to submit to God, affirming God's singular all-powerful, all-knowing, and compassionate nature and embodying that submission in acts of prayer, fasting, pilgrimage, almsgiving, and ethical and compassionate behavior. This life is only an interval on the way to the return to God, for the purpose of life is ultimately fulfilled in death and resurrection. F.E. Peters, struck by the uniformity of Muslim belief and practice, delineates the integrative power of the Qur'an and the example of Muhammad in shaping Muslim life, both individually and collectively. The system of training for interpreters of the Qur'an, both legal and theological, and the inextricable interweaving of the sacred and the secular in Islamic societies have also fostered cohesive ideals for moral and ethical living. Peters argues that in Islam two figures – the preacher and the saint – play pivotal roles. The preacher spreads Islam's moral teachings to the masses in Friday sermons (see Plate 3). The saint is the one who embodies an ecstatic and sometimes quite unorthodox relationship with God that marks the lives of the "friends of God."

The study and ritual practice of Torah, the imitation of Christ, and the submission of the faithful to the will of God are three approaches to a shared goal of intimate relationship with God. Judaism, Christianity, and Islam form a continuous, though many-branching, tree of human faith, rooted in the ancient Mediterranean deserts and seeking meaning in God for over thirty-five centuries.

Plate 1 Crucifixion mounted within the great scissor-arches at the intersection of the nave and transepts of the jewel-like Wells Cathedral, England, constructed during the thirteenth and fourteenth centuries CE. Photo: *Joseph Runzo*

3

HOW CHRISTIANITY SECURES *life's* MEANINGS†

Philip L. Quinn

When asked about the meaning of life, philosophers often express puzzlement. I think this occurs because they find the question unclear; they are unsure about what might count as an answer to it. Making some distinctions can be conducive to clarity by showing that many distinct questions have a claim to being considered questions about the meaning of life.

In this discussion, I shall understand questions about the meaning of life to concern the meaning of human life. Though some of the questions I shall consider can be expanded to apply to the lives of at least some non-human animals, I shall ignore such expansions in order to keep attention focused on the questions of paramount religious significance.

It is useful to distinguish between individual and cosmic questions about the meaning of life. One might wonder whether a particular human life is meaningful, or one might wonder whether all of human life is meaningful. It is also useful to distinguish between axiological and teleological questions about the meaning of life. One might ask whether human life is good, or one might ask whether human life serves a purpose. I shall address both individual and cosmic questions about the value of human life, and I shall also treat both individual and cosmic issues concerning the purpose of human life. In considering such questions and issues, I shall distinguish between those to which there are both secular

† I presented parts of this chapter in a paper at the 1997 APA Pacific Division Meeting where Bill Wainwright was my commentator, and I presented parts of it at the Chapman University Conference on the Meaning of Life in the World Religions where Kate McCarthy was my commentator. I am grateful to both of them for comments that helped me in revising the paper.

and religious responses and those to which there are only religious responses. Finally, I shall discuss the way in which distinctively Christian responses to both individual and cosmic questions of the value and purpose of human life are embedded in the gospel narratives of the life of Jesus and in the grand metanarrative of salvation history.

AXIOLOGICAL QUESTIONS: THE VALUES OF HUMAN LIFE

It might be thought that an individual human life has meaning if it has positive intrinsic value. As Ronald Dworkin has recently argued, religious and non-religious people can agree that human life is sacred and thus has positive intrinsic value while disagreeing about why it is sacred.[1] It would be natural for Christians to account for the sacredness of human life in terms of humans having been created in the image and likeness of God. Early in Genesis God says, "Let us make humankind in our image, according to our likeness," and the next verse tells us, "So God created humankind in his image, in the image of God he created them" (Genesis 1:26–27). Since God is intrinsically perfectly good, human beings created in his image will also be intrinsically good, but to a lesser degree. And Judaism and Islam, the other two major monotheisms, can share this explanation of the sacredness of human life with Christianity because they too take the Hebrew Bible to be authoritative.

Presumably each human being is created in the image and likeness of God, if any is thus created, and so every human life is sacred and hence has positive intrinsic value. If the intrinsic value of all of human life is the sum of the intrinsic values of all individual human lives, then the intrinsic value of all human life will also be positive, in which case a universe containing human life will *ceteris paribus* be better than a universe that lacks it. Moreover, if having positive intrinsic value is sufficient for all human life to have meaning, then human life will have cosmic as well as individual meaning if every human being is created in the image and likeness of God. But the intrinsic value a human life derives from its possessor's creation in the image and likeness of God is independent of how the life of its possessor actually goes. A human life so miserable on the whole that it would be better for the one who lives it never to have existed could have the positive intrinsic value derived from the one who lives it having been created in the image and likeness of God. This possibility gives us reason to doubt that the positive intrinsic value a human life gets from the one who lives it having been created in the image and likeness of God is sufficient to guarantee that any individual human life or all of human life has meaning.

It also forces us to confront the threat to the meaning of human life posed by certain forms of the problem of evil. This threat is portrayed with special vividness by Marilyn McCord Adams in recent work on horrendous evils. Adams cites as paradigmatic horrors the items on the following list: "the rape of a woman and axing off of her arms, psychophysical torture whose ultimate goal is the disintegration of personality, betrayal of one's deepest loyalties, cannibalizing one's own offspring, child abuse of the sort described by Ivan Karamazov, child pornography, parental incest, slow death by starvation, participation in the Nazi death camps, the explosion of nuclear bombs over populated areas, having to choose which of one's children shall live and which be executed by terrorists, being the accidental and/or unwitting agent of the disfigurement or death of those one loves best."[2] Adams herself makes the connection between horrendous evils and the meaning of human life explicit. She says that she regards the evils on her list as paradigmatic horrors "because I believe most people would find in the doing or suffering of them prima-facie reason to doubt the positive meaning of their lives."[3] And her definition of horrendous evils allows us to see a connection between the value in a human life and its meaning. The definition reads as follows: "An evil *e* is horrendous if and only if participation in *e* by person *p* gives everyone prima-facie reason to doubt whether *p*'s life can, given *p*'s participation in *e*, be a great good to *p* on the whole."[4] I think Adams is on the right track in insisting upon a link between the positive meaning of a human life and its goodness for the person who lives it. It seems to me that a human life has positive meaning only if it is on the whole good for the person who leads it. Hence if a human life is not on the whole good for the person who leads it, then it lacks positive meaning.

Horrendous evils, then, constitute a threat to the meaning of human life because they give everyone prima-facie reason to doubt that the lives of those who participate in them, either as victims or as perpetrators, have positive meaning. But it is consistent with having prima-facie reason to doubt that the lives of those who participate in horrendous evils have positive meaning to have reason all things considered not to doubt that those lives have positive meaning. If one has reason to think that horrendous evils are defeated, one's prima-facie reason to doubt will itself be defeated. Adams suggests that God could defeat horrendous evils by integrating participation in them into a participant's relationship with God. She sketches three ways in which this might come about: (1) suffering horrendous evils can be a means of identifying with the passion and death of Christ; (2) suffering horrendous evils can prompt a response of overwhelming divine gratitude; and (3) suffering horrendous evils can constitute a vision into the inner life of a passible God.[5] Though the first of these ideas is likely to seem attractive only to Christians, the other two seem to be available to other theists as well. The upshot is that theism has within its worldview the intellectual resources to rebut the claim that those who participate in horrendous evils in this life are bound to have lives that lack positive meaning by arguing that even lives that include such horrendous evils can be on the whole good for those who lead them.

It does not follow, of course, that in fact all those who participate in horrendous evils will have lives that are on the whole good for them. It seems possible that the afterlife should contain horrendous evils that are not and, perhaps, cannot be defeated, even by God, such as everlasting suffering in hell. A person who suffers everlastingly in hell in the afterlife would appear to have a life that is not on the whole good for the one who leads it and hence a life that lacks positive meaning. In other words, the traditional doctrine of hell presents a serious threat to the meaning of at least some human lives, and it does this because it is a particularly severe form of the problem of evil.[6]

There are at least two ways in which Christians and other theists can respond to this threat. Both involve a revisionary attitude toward the traditional doctrine of hell as a place of everlasting suffering. The first consists of endorsing universalism about salvation. According to universalism, even if hell is a place of suffering and some people begin the afterlife in hell, no one remains in hell forever. Eventually all humans are persuaded to desire union with God, and God then unites them with Godself in the beatific vision forever after. Once securely united with God in the beatific vision, each human is assured of a life that is on the whole good for him or her. The second way of responding to the threat consists of adopting a pure separation view of hell. On such a view, hell is nothing above and beyond the state of being separated from God by one's own choice; it does not also involve punitive physical pain or mental anguish. Even though those who choose separation from God forever forfeit the greatest of all goods, their lives are not on the whole so miserable that it would be better for them never to have existed. Their lives in hell are instead on the whole good for them, albeit not nearly so good for them as their lives might have been. Thus, if they are willing to pay the price of making revisions in the traditional doctrine of hell, Christians and other theists can with some plausibility hold that all humans will have lives that are on the whole good for them, despite the existence of horrendous evils in this life. They can thereby diffuse the threat to the positive meaning of human life, both for the lives of individuals and for all of human life, posed by the existence of horrendous evils in this life and the existence of hell in the afterlife.

What lessons are there to be learned from reflection on the connections between the value of human life and its meaning? I suggest that the chief lesson is that a human life has positive meaning only if: (1) it has positive intrinsic value; and (2) it is on the whole good for the person who leads it. The three major monotheisms are in a position to claim that satisfaction of the first of these necessary conditions for human life's positive meaning is guaranteed by the creation of human life in the image and likeness of a perfectly good God. Christians and other theists can argue that satisfaction of the second of them is insured by the combination of a soteriological doctrine that shows how God can defeat the horrendous evils that occur in this life and a doctrine of the afterlife designed to preclude any new, indefeasible horrendous evils from arising in the afterlife. May we now conclude that these two conditions are also jointly sufficient for a human life to have positive meaning? I think such a conclusion would be premature at this stage of the discussion. Many philosophers hold that the meaning of human life is somehow connected to its purposes, which may include either purposes in it or purposes for it. I next explore some of the issues to which linking meaning and purpose in human life gives rise.

TELEOLOGICAL QUESTIONS: THE PURPOSES OF HUMAN LIFE

In a discussion that has some claim to being canonical because it is the entry on the meaning and value of life in the Macmillan *Encyclopedia of Philosophy*, Paul Edwards argues that a human life can have meaning quite independently of whether there is a God or an afterlife. Edwards supposes that "when we ask whether a *particular* person's life has or had any meaning, we are usually concerned not with cosmic issues but with the question whether certain purposes are to be found *in* his life."[7] He claims that we seem to mean two things when we characterize a life as meaningful: "We assert, first, that the life in question had some dominant, over-all goal or goals which gave direction to a great many of the individual's actions and, second, that these actions and possibly others not immediately related to the overriding goal were performed with a special zest that was not present before the person became attached to his goal or that would not have been present if there had been no such goal in his life."[8] Similarly, Edwards suggests, when we characterize a life as worth living, we seem to be making two assertions: "first, that the person has some goals (other than merely to be dead or to have his pains eased) which do not seem to him to be trivial and, second, that there is some genuine possibility that he will attain these goals."[9] Drawing on but modifying these two statements, I propose to say that a human life has meaning only if: (1) it contains some purposes the person who lives it takes to be non-trivial and achievable; and (2) it also contains actions that are directed toward achieving these purposes and are performed with zest. It seems clear that many human lives would satisfy these two necessary conditions for having meaning even if there were no God and no afterlife.

It is obvious that a human life can satisfy the two necessary conditions for having meaning and yet be chock full of wicked actions directed toward evil purposes. Many of Hitler's willing executioners considered their homicidal purposes non-trivial and achievable and set about pursuing them with zest.[10] Edwards suggests responding in terms of a distinction between subjective and objective senses of a life's being worthwhile. He stipulates that "in the subjective sense, saying that a person's life is worthwhile simply means that he is attached to some goals which he does not consider trivial and that these goals are attainable for him."[11] By contrast, "in declaring that somebody's life is worthwhile in the objective sense, one is saying that he is attached to certain goals which are both attainable and of positive value."[12] In the context of the present discussion, it will prove useful to work with a related distinction between a human life having meaning and a human life having positive meaning. Hence I propose to say that a human life has positive meaning only if: (1) it contains some purposes the person who lives it takes to be non-trivial and achievable; (2) these purposes have positive value; and (3) it also contains actions that are directed toward achieving these purposes and are performed with zest. It is beyond reasonable doubt that many human lives would satisfy these three necessary conditions for having positive meaning even if there were no God and no afterlife.

Edwards recognizes, of course, that sometimes questions about the meaning of human life seek answers not so much in terms of the purposes *in* a human life as in terms of the purposes *for* human life. He observes that "sometimes when a person asks whether life has any meaning, what he wants to know is whether there is superhuman intelligence that fashioned human beings along with other objects in the world to serve some end – whether their role is perhaps analogous to the part of an instrument (or its player) in a symphony."[13] Traditional theists believe that God created the whole contingent cosmos and conserves it in existence for purposes of his own, and many of them also believe that he created human beings for special purposes. What might such special purposes be? A simple and orthodox Christian answer to this question is found in the Roman Catholic Church's *Baltimore Catechism*. The answer to question I.3 identifies a divine purpose for human life: "Why did God make us? God made us to show forth His goodness and to share with us His everlasting happiness in heaven."[14] And the answer to question I.4 tells us what to do in order to further this divine purpose: "What must we do to gain the happiness of heaven? To gain the happiness of heaven we must know, love and serve God in this world."[15] In other words, God's chief purpose for humans is that they should come to enjoy the beatific vision in the afterlife, and God's subsidiary purposes for humans are that they should in this life know, love, and serve him. Most Christians would agree that at the heart of a service to God in this life is obedience to the love commandments, which, according to Matthew, Jesus states in response to a question from a lawyer. Jesus says: "You shall love the Lord your God with all your heart, and with all your soul, and with all your mind. This is the greatest and first commandment. And a second is like it: You shall love your neighbor as yourself. On these two commandments hang all the law and the prophets" (Matthew 22:37–40).

For Christians, then, God's purposes for human life include such things as enjoyment of the beatific vision in the afterlife and obedience to the love commandments in this life. Christians are called upon to make God's purposes for human life the main purposes in their lives and to act to further them. Since God is perfectly good, his purposes for human life will assuredly have positive value. Hence, Christians who adopt the divine purposes for human life as their own and act with zest to achieve them will satisfy the three necessary conditions for a human life to have positive meaning. To be sure, some of these purposes, such as enjoyment of the beatific vision, would, contrary to what Christians believe, not be achievable if there were no God and no afterlife. However, because Christians take such purposes to be achievable, they can satisfy the necessary conditions for a human life to have positive meaning by making them their own.

Perhaps a word of warning is called for about one way in which the catechism's simple answer concerning God's purposes for human life may be misleading. Christians should not think that the only purposes God had in creating the cosmos pertain to its human denizens and their salvation. The divine providential plan encompasses the whole of creation and doubtless contains purposes for many of its non-human parts. In the biblical creation story God gave to his human creatures "dominion over the fish of the sea, and over the birds of the air, and over the cattle, and over all the wild animals of the earth, and over every creeping thing that creeps upon the earth" (Genesis 1: 26). But I do not think this grant of dominion should be construed by Christians or other theists as a divine license for the unlimited exploitation of nature. It is better thought of in terms of a divine appointment to stewardship with respect to nature. Thus Christians should be prepared, as part of their service to God in this life, to adopt as their own and act upon divine purposes for non-human parts of nature to the extent that they can discern such purposes or form reasonable conjectures about them.

The discussion so far has yielded some necessary conditions for a human life to have positive meaning stated in terms of values and some necessary conditions stated in terms of purposes. It is natural to wonder how the axiological and teleological perspectives on the meaning of human life could be unified. One proposal worth entertaining is that the axiological and teleological conditions are individually necessary and jointly sufficient for a human life to have positive meaning. However, I favor a slightly different approach to the problem of unification. Though I have no idea of how to prove it, I think the axiological and the teleological are conceptually distinct kinds of meaning, and so I hold that a human life can have more than one sort of meaning. It seems to me possible that a premortem human life should have axiological positive meaning and lack teleological positive meaning and possible that a premortem human life should lack axiological positive meaning and have teleological positive meaning. My intuitions about these matters therefore dispose me toward being a splitter rather than a lumper in the taxonomy of human life's meaning. Thus I propose the following scheme of unification:

(AM) A human life has positive *axiological meaning* if and only if: (1) it has positive intrinsic value; and (2) it is on the whole good for the person who leads it;

(TM) A human life has positive *teleological meaning* if and only if: (1) it contains some purposes the person who lives it takes to be non-trivial and achievable; (2) these purposes have positive value; and (3) it also contains actions that are directed toward achieving these purposes and are performed with zest;

(CM) A human life has positive *complete meaning* if and only if it has both positive axiological meaning and positive teleological meaning.

My argument thus far has been that Christians and other theists can make the case that human lives can have both positive axiological meaning and positive teleological meaning by mobilizing traditional or revised doctrines of creation and salvation. Theism therefore offers an optimistic worldview in which human lives can have positive complete meaning. But Christian theism, I think, packages this offer in a special way by providing at least two unifying narratives that display meaning. My final task is to say something about Christianity's narrative unification of human life's meanings.

UNIFICATION IN STORY: TWO CHRISTIAN NARRATIVES

In the heyday of logical positivism, philosophical discussion of the meaning of life fell under a cloud of suspicion. When I was younger, I more than once heard the reason for that suspicion put this way. The bearers of meaning are linguistic entities such as texts or utterances. But a human life is not a linguistic entity. Hence attributing meaning to a human life involves a category mistake. To ask what human life means is therefore to ask a pseudo-question.

In our own post-positivistic era, this argument is apt to seem too quick and dirty to produce conviction. To be sure, a human life is not itself a text or an utterance. The events that make up a human life can, however, be narrated, and narratives of human lives are meaningful linguistic entities. In addition, the history of the human race is the potential subject of a meaningful linguistic metanarrative. Of course, not all narratives of human lives exhibit them as having positive meaning in any of the senses explicated above. A narrative might, for example, portray a human life in terms of "a tale, told by an idiot, full of sound and fury, signifying nothing."[16] Or a narrative might depict a human life as lacking positive meaning of the three kinds enumerated in the previous section. Nevertheless, some narratives do present human lives that have meaning of these three kinds. The gospel stories of the life of Jesus are narratives of a human life that has special significance for Christians.

Adopting a suggestion recently made by Nicholas Wolterstorff, I think the gospel narratives "are best understood as *portraits* of Jesus, designed to reveal who he really was and what was really happening in his life, death and resurrection."[17] And like the part of Simon Schama's recent *Dead Certainties* about the death of General James Wolfe on the plains of Abraham, what they assert at some points is "not that things *did go* thus and so but that, whether or not they did, they *might well have gone* thus and so."[18] The importance of the portrait of Jesus thus narrated for his Christian followers is that it furnishes them with a paradigm to which the narratives of their own lives should be made to conform as closely as circumstances permit. The idea that the lives of Christians should imitate the life of Jesus is, of course, a familiar theme in Christian spirituality; it is developed with particular cogency in Thomas à Kempis *The Imitation of Christ.* Søren Kierkegaard spells it out in terms of a striking contrast between admiring Christ and imitating Christ in his *Practice in Christianity.*

According to Anti-Climacus, the pseudonymous author of *Practice*, "Christ's life here on earth is the paradigm; I and every Christian are to strive to model our lives in likeness to it."[19] The demand is stringent because the likeness is to be as close as possible. "To be an imitator," he tells us, "means that your life has as much similarity to his as is possible for a human life to have."[20] The Christ who is to be imitated is not the glorious Christ of the Second Coming but is instead the crucified Christ of human history. Hence the imitator of Christ must come to terms with Christ in his lowliness and abasement.

One thing this means is being prepared to suffer as Christ suffered. Anti-Climacus says that Christ freely willed to be the lowly one because he "wanted to express what *the truth* would have to suffer and what the truth must suffer in every generation."[21] Imitators of Christ must therefore be willing to endure suffering akin to his suffering. Anti-Climacus explains what this involves: "To suffer in a way akin to Christ's suffering is not to put up patiently with the inescapable, but it is to suffer evil at the hands of people because as a Christian or in being a Christian one wills and endeavors to do the good: thus one could avoid this suffering by giving up willing the good."[22] Since the Christian is not supposed to give up willing the good, however, he or she must willingly suffer evil precisely because of the endeavor to do the good.

Another thing coming to terms with Christ in his lowliness and abasement means is being "halted by the possibility of offense."[23] Anti-Climacus wittily describes how respectable people of various sorts might have been offended if they had been Christ's contemporaries. A sagacious and sensible person might have said: "What has he done about his future? Nothing. Does he have a permanent job? No. What are his prospects? None."[24] A clergyman might have denounced him as "an impostor and demagogue."[25] A philosopher might have criticized him for lacking a system and having only "a few aphorisms, some maxims, and a couple of parables, which he goes on repeating or revising, whereby he blinds the masses."[26] And others might have scoffed at him and reviled him in other ways. Yet Anti-Climacus insists that no one can arrive at mature Christian faith without first confronting the possibility of offense. He says that "from the possibility of offense, one turns either to offense or to faith, but one never comes to faith except from the possibility of offense."[27] Thus imitators of Christ can also count on being found offensive by those who have chosen to turn to offense rather than to faith.

Imitators of Christ should, therefore, anticipate suffering evils for trying to do good and expect to be found offensive. If one proposes to join Christ as a follower, one should have a realistic awareness of the conditions on which discipleship is offered. According to Anti-Climacus, they are these: "to become just as poor, despised, insulted, mocked, and if possible even a little more, considering that in addition one was an adherent of such a despised individual, whom every sensible person shunned."[28] If any imitators of Christ are not subject to such treatment, this must be the result of good fortune they cannot count on or expect. No mere admirer would want to join Christ on these conditions.

What is the difference between an imitator and a mere admirer? "An imitator *is* or strives *to be* what he admires," Anti-Climacus says, "and an admirer keeps himself personally detached, consciously or unconsciously does not discover that what is admired involves a claim upon him, to be or at least to strive to be what is admired."[29] The difference is to be seen most clearly in their contrasting responses to the stringent practical demands of discipleship. The mere admirer is only willing to pay them lip-service. According to Anti-Climacus, "the admirer will make no sacrifices, renounce nothing, give up nothing earthly, will not transform his life, will not be what is admired, will not let his life express it – but in words, phrases, assurances he is inexhaustible about how highly he prizes Christianity."[30] Unlike the mere admirer, the imitator, who also acknowledges in words the truth of Christianity, acts decisively to obey "Christian teaching about ethics and obligation, Christianity's requirement to die to the world, to surrender the earthly, its requirement of self-denial."[31] And, Anti-Climacus adds wryly, mere admirers are sure to become exasperated with a genuine imitator.

Not all Christians will accept this radical Kierkegaardian view of the demands of discipleship. There is, however, a lesson to be learned about the meanings of a distinctively Christian life if we take it to approximate the most demanding interpretation of what is involved in the call to Christians to conform the narratives of their lives to the portrait of Jesus embedded in the gospel narratives. There seems to be no difficulty in supposing that the life of a successful Kierkegaardian imitator of Christ, devoted to willing and endeavoring to do the good, will have positive teleological meaning, despite the suffering it is likely to contain. But there is a problem in supposing that every such life will also have positive axiological meaning if it terminates in bodily death, because some such lives appear not to be good on the whole for those who lead them. But, of course, the earthly life of Jesus, which ended in horrible suffering and ignominious death, gives rise to the very same problem. It is part of traditional Christian faith, however, that the life of Jesus did not terminate in bodily death but continued after his resurrection and will continue until he comes again in glory and hence is on the whole a good life for him. Like the life of Jesus himself, the lives of at least some successful Kierkegaardian imitators of Christ will on the whole be good for them only if they extend beyond death into an afterlife of some sort. Hence survival of bodily death seems required to secure positive axiological meaning and thus positive complete meaning for the lives of all those whose narratives conform as closely as is humanly possible, as Kierkegaard understands what is involved in such conformity, to the paradigm or prototype presented in the gospel narratives of the life of Jesus.

Christianity also tells a tale of the destiny of the human race through the cosmic metanarrative of salvation history. It begins with the creation of humans in God's image and likeness. The Incarnation, in which God the Son becomes fully human and redeems sinful humanity, is a crucial episode. It will culminate with the promised coming of the Kingdom of God. Christians have been divided over some questions about the details of salvation history. Will all humans ultimately be saved? If some will not, did God predestine them to reprobation? But the broad outlines of the story make manifest God's loving concern for humanity and the providential care in which it is expressed. The story's emphasis on what God has done for humans also makes it clear that they are important from a God's-eye point of view.

The narrative of salvation history reveals some of God's purposes both for individual humans and for humanity as a whole. Christians are expected to align themselves with these purposes and to act to further them to the extent that their circumstances permit. Such purposes can thus be among those that give positive teleological meaning and thereby contribute to giving positive complete meaning to a Christian's life. We may safely assume that every Christian and, indeed, every human being has a meaningful role to play in the great drama of salvation history if Christianity's view of its shape is even approximately correct.

But what are we to say abut those who refuse to align themselves with God's purposes? Mark 14:21 quotes Jesus as saying, "For the Son of Man goes as it is written of him, but woe to that one by whom the Son of Man is betrayed! It would have been better for that one not to have been born." If it would have been better for Judas not to have been born, then his life is not on the whole good for him and so lacks positive axiological meaning. This will be true of Judas on the traditional assumption that he dies fixed in his rejection of God's purposes and so suffers everlastingly in hell. On the universalist assumption, however, even Judas will eventually turn to God, align himself with God's purposes, and be saved. Were this to happen, even the life of Judas would ultimately have both positive axiological meaning and positive teleological meaning. In that case, it would not be true that it would be better for Judas not to have been born.

In a stimulating discussion of the meaning of life, Thomas Nagel argues that from a detached, objective point of view human lives lack importance or significance. He says: "When you look at your struggles as if from a great height, in abstraction from the engagement you have with this life because it is yours – perhaps even in abstraction from your identification with the human race – you may feel a certain sympathy for the poor beggar, a pale pleasure in his triumphs and a mild concern for his disappointments."[32] But, he continues, "it wouldn't matter all that much if he failed, and it would matter perhaps even less if he didn't exist at all."[33] Christians would do well, I think, to resist the seductions of this picture of the objective standpoint. For them, the objective standpoint is the point of view of an omniscient and perfectly good God. Their faith informs them humanity is so important to such a God that he freely chose to become incarnate and to suffer and die for its sake.

The snare Christians need to avoid is assuming that humanity is the most important thing or the only important thing from a God's-eye point of view. Such assumptions would bespeak a prideful cosmic anthropocentrism. Nagel claims that "the most general effect of the objective stance ought to be a form of humility: the recognition that you are no more important than you are, and that the fact that something is of importance to you, or that it would be good or bad if you did or suffered something, is a fact of purely local significance."[34] Christians have reasons to believe that facts of the sorts Nagel mentions are of more than purely local significance, but they should have the humility to recognize that such facts may well have less cosmic significance than other facts of which God is aware. Within a balanced Christian perspective, in other words, facts about what is good or bad for humans to do or suffer have some cosmic importance because God cares about them, but Christians would be unwarranted if they supposed that God cares more about such facts than about anything else that transpires in the created cosmos. Human lives and human life generally are objectively important. Their importance should, however, not be exaggerated.

Nor should Christians exaggerate the certainty about life's meanings to be derived from their narratives. The gospel narratives permit, and historically have received, diverse and often conflicting interpretations. When reasonable interpretations clash, confidence in the exclusive rightness of any one of them should diminish. What is more, other religions have reasonable stories to tell about life's meanings, as do some non-religious worldviews. Confronted with the twin challenges of reasonable intra-Christian pluralism and reasonable interreligious pluralism, Christians ought to adopt an attitude of epistemic modesty when making claims about life's meanings. They can be, I think, entitled to believe that Christian narratives provide the best story we have about life's meanings. But claims to furnish the complete story should, I believe, be advanced only with fear and trembling. When Christianity secures life's meanings, it should not offer Christians so much security that they acquire the arrogant tendency to set their story apart from and above all other sources of insight into life's meanings.

NOTES

1. See Ronald Dworkin, *Life's Dominion* (New York: Alfred A. Knopf, 1993), especially chap. 3.
2. Marilyn McCord Adams, "Horrendous Evils and the Goodness of God," in *The Problem of Evil*, ed. Marilyn McCord Adams and Robert Merrihew Adams (New York: Oxford University Press, 1990), pp. 211–212.
3. Ibid., p. 212.
4. Ibid., p. 211.
5. Ibid., pp. 218–219.
6. For recent discussion, philosophical criticism, and proposed revisions of the traditional doctrine of hell, see Jonathan L. Kvanvig, *The Problem of Hell* (New York and Oxford: Oxford University Press, 1993).
7. Paul Edwards, "Meaning and Value of Life," *The Encyclopedia of Philosophy*, ed. Paul Edwards (New York: Macmillan, 1967), vol. 4, p. 472.
8. Ibid.
9. Ibid., p. 473.
10. For historical evidence, see Daniel Jonah Goldhagen, *Hitler's Willing Executioners* (New York: Alfred A. Knopf, 1996).
11. Edwards, "Meaning and Value of Life," p. 473.
12. Ibid.
13. Ibid., p. 471.
14. *Baltimore Catechism No. 3*, with supplementary material by John A. O'Brien (Notre Dame: Ave Maria Press, 1955), p. 53.
15. Ibid., p. 54.
16. William Shakespeare, *Macbeth* V. v. 26–28.
17. Nicholas Wolterstorff, *Divine Discourse* (Cambridge: Cambridge University Press, 1995), p. 259.
18. Ibid., p. 257.
19. Søren Kierkegaard, *Practice in Christianity*, ed. and trans. Howard V. Hong and Edna H. Hong (Princeton: Princeton University Press, 1991) p. 107.
20. Ibid., p. 106.
21. Ibid., pp. 34–35.
22. Ibid., p. 173.
23. Ibid., p. 39.
24. Ibid., p. 43.
25. Ibid., p. 46.

26. Ibid., p. 48.
27. Ibid., p. 81.
28. Ibid., p. 241.
29. Ibid.
30. Ibid., p. 252.
31. Ibid.
32. Thomas Nagel, *The View from Nowhere* (New York and Oxford: Oxford University Press, 1986), p. 216.
33. Ibid.
34. Ibid., p. 222.

Plate 2 Interior of the Ben Ezra Synagogue in Old Cario, one of the oldest in Egypt, said to be built on the site of the temple of the prophet Jeremiah, recently renovated with a marble representation of the Ten Commandments. Photo: *Joseph Runzo*

4

TO INCREASE TORAH *is to* INCREASE LIFE:[†] POETICS OF THE MIND *and* POETICS OF THE EVERYDAY IN JEWISH CULTURE

Charlotte Elisheva Fonrobert

INTRODUCTION

The Life of Torah

The title of this chapter is a statement chosen from one of the prominent texts in rabbinic literature, the *Chapters of the Fathers*, an early text (second to third centuries CE) which presents the ethical lore of what could be called the "founding fathers" of rabbinic Judaism. For the purpose of this chapter, I will treat the literature of the rabbis, produced in roughly the first six centuries CE, as the foundation of most Jewish cultures that followed it. It is rabbinic literature and the institutions it creates that provided the frame for Jewish culture as we know it, rather than the biblical literature of the Hebrew Bible in and by itself. The books of what is commonly called the Bible, and what the rabbis called the written Torah, provide of course the basis of interpretation for the rabbis. But it is their particular reading of the books of the Torah, as opposed to for instance the Christian readings, that creates "Judaism."

In essence, the teachings collected in the *Chapters of the Fathers* evolve around the praise of Torah. In this treatise, the term "Torah" can be

[†] This title is a statement attributed to Hillel, perceived to be one of the founding fathers of rabbinic Judaism by the sages themselves. It can be found in a short mishnaic tract, the *Chapters of the Fathers*, which contains mostly ethical lore attributed to the major figures of rabbinic Judaism during the first two centuries CE.

understood in the narrowest as well as the widest sense of the word, as a text (i.e. the five books of Moses) or as a concept that comprises all reality. The latter is perhaps most famously expressed in a *midrash*[1] on the first verse of the Torah: "In the beginning, God created the heavens and earth" (Genesis 1:1). The rabbis read the first preposition of this verse, which is ambiguous in Hebrew, as "*with* the Torah, God created the heavens and earth." According to the *midrash*

> the Torah says: "I was the Blessed Holy One's crafting tool." In everyday experience, when a human king builds a palace he does not build it out of his own imagination. Rather, he hires a craftsman. And the craftsman does not build it out of his own imagination either. Rather, he has designs and diagrams to help him plan the rooms and doorways. So too, the Blessed Holy One looked into the Torah and created the world. (Genesis Rabbah 1:1)

According to this *midrash*, the Torah is God's blueprint of all of reality. Recently, Martin Jaffee has aptly described this conception of Torah in the terms of comparative religions as a "cosmic principle."[2]

Hence, the understanding of the term "life" in our title phrase "to increase Torah is to increase life" is dependent on our understanding of the term "Torah." The almost infinite range of meanings of the term "Torah" can perhaps best be approached from two different directions: Torah as the act of studying on the one end, and Torah as practice on the other. Let me explain.

One of the supreme values of traditional[3] Jewish culture, and – as I will claim – one of the primary ways to relate to the Divine, lies in study: study of the "written" Torah;[4] study of the oral Torah, that is, the interpretations of the written Torah by the rabbis and the legal application derived from biblical law; and study of later textual traditions, such as the commentaries and responsa literature, that has grown around the classical texts.[5] "To increase Torah" then can be understood textually: learn and study texts, and write commentaries on them. Classical (rabbinic) Judaism creates a culture with the life of the mind at its conceptual center. Within contemporary American Jewish movements this applies not just to forms of Orthodox Judaism, but to Conservative Judaism as well. Thus *Emet ve-Emunah*, the most recent Statement of Principles of Conservative Judaism, states:

> Talmud Torah (study of Torah, including all classical Jewish texts) is an essential value of Judaism. Virtually alone among all religious

> traditions, Judaism regards study as a cardinal commandment, the highest form of worship of God. Talmud Torah is the obligation and the privilege of every Jew, male and female, young and old, no matter how much or how little one knows at present. Since following the precepts of Judaism requires that one know its beliefs and practices, and since it is impossible to exhaust the Torah's meaning, each individual Jew is commanded to be a *ben* or *bat Torah* (son or daughter of Torah), studying Torah throughout his or her life.[6]

Study of Torah (*talmud torah*) is not only a form of communication with the Divine parallel to prayer, but it is indeed the equivalent of analyzing God's mind itself, or – in theological terms – the equivalent of knowing God. In the era of TV and Star Trek we can perhaps use the analogy of the Vulcan mind-meld: if the Torah is that which embodies God (or God's will) in this world, if the Torah is, indeed, the primary cultural site of the presence of God, then the highest aspiration of a Jewish life is to get as close as possible to grasping the infinite depth of the text, that is, the manifestation of God's mind in this world. A Jew should aspire to mold his or her mind into the pathways of the Torah, or – to formulate more boldly – aspire to transform his/her mind into God's mind in infinite approximation. This is what I call the poetics of the mind.

If, on the other hand, we approach the concept of Torah from the direction of practice, we find the ritual cycles that are the product of the interpretative traditions of the sages. In traditional Jewish culture, and in contemporary Jewish culture committed to "tradition," life is enhanced by rituals that define a Jewish home and the Jewish community. The rituals are elements of Torah and, insofar as they are instituted by the Torah, they expand the presence of the Divine into the space and time of the everyday. At least in theory these define the life of every Jew, even those who are less intimately involved with the culture of study per se. It is this ritualization of the everyday that has functioned as a marker of Jewish difference throughout the history of Western perceptions of Jews and that has been much more visible to non-Jews than Torah study as the center.[7]

The rituals define and reweave the fabric of life, from morning to evening, in terms of Torah. They structure time into temporal cycles that expand, circumscribing the day (prayer three times a day), then the week (*shabbat* as the climax of the week), the year (the cycle of holidays), a lifetime (life-cycle rituals such as circumcision, *bar mitzvah*), and finally the collective life of the community. Running as an axis through these cycles, we find the ritualization of food and eating, i.e., the recitation of blessings over food and the prohibition of certain foods, and of sex, i.e., rituals concerning menstruation. These rituals can be regarded as the continuous performance of Torah, which mold the pathways of living through the day into the ways prescribed by the Torah. Every aspect of life is oriented toward the Torah. This is what I call the poetics of the everyday.

In the Light of Gender

A crucial question that needs to be raised in discussing the meaning of life in Jewish culture is the question of leadership or authorship. What are the structures of authority? Who has the power or authority to imbue Jewish life with meaning and to define the ways of making a Jewish life meaningful? For whom? In Jewish culture, this is essentially a gender question or, vice versa, the gender question in Jewish discussions today is a question of authorship and leadership. In most traditional Jewish cultures learning provided and provides the basis for almost all forms of leadership, legal, mystical, charismatic, political, or spiritual. Ideally, in rabbinic tradition Jewish learning was not to be the privilege of an elite, or of a group of people distinctly set apart from and above the rest of the Jewish community by genealogical criteria (such as the priests during the existence of the Temple) nor by behavioral criteria (such as celibacy in Catholic Christianity). Rather, Jewish learning was to be the ideal of "everybody," the married man, the common Jew, the rich and the poor, the young and the old. Even the rabbi is understood in rabbinic literature as primarily a *talmid hakham*, a student of the (collective) sages and their traditions, who would himself become a teacher. He is the *primus inter pares*, the one most learned. Obviously, there is a considerable variety of forms of leadership that evolved during the long history of Jewish cultures. But generally and structurally no Jew was excluded from the hierarchies of learning, except on the basis of gender. If traditionally all men were – at least potentially – included in the hierarchies of learning, all women were structurally excluded. Women did not become *talmidot hakhamim* (students of the sages), which in turn means that women did not become teachers, which in turn means that women did not serve as religious judges (the cultural site of the production of religious law/literature), which also means that women did not produce the classic and canonic literary sources that come down to us.[8] If the basis for all forms of leadership in traditional Jewish cultures was the structures built around study, then, by virtue of having been excluded from learning, women were also excluded from all forms of leadership. In contemporary polemics between religious movements or denominations and groups in the Jewish community, therefore, the gender issue and the question of women's leadership, such as the question of ordination of women as rabbis, plays a defining role.

These observations entail this important qualification when we think about the meaning of life in Jewish culture: fundamentally, it may not be the same for men and women. The question of who defines meanings for whom can only be asked gender specifically, i.e., what is the meaning of life in Jewish culture for men and what is it for women. If the supreme way of "increasing life" is to study Torah in rabbinic culture(s), and women have been excluded from study, then what have been the ways of "increasing life" for Jewish women? And can that which has been developed as an ideal by men for men automatically be transferred or applied to women?

Obviously, this is not to say that women have not found and created avenues to define meanings of "life" within the structures of traditional Jewish cultures.[9] Occasionally, women have tried to walk along the paths of learning. This is true not only historically, but today as well, when there is an upsurge of women's traditional study in Jewish religious circles of various kinds.[10] However, we also have to consider that women have chosen different avenues to find and create meaning for their lives which are not necessarily reflected in the classic sources of Jewish culture. It is unquestionable that women have been assigned a gender-specific place in traditional Jewish cultures, defined by exclusion from places of the *production* of meaning marked as privileged by classic rabbinic texts. However, within the context of the practice of Torah, the ritual life of the Jewish home and the community, women have played a much more prominent and visible role. Both these aspects need to be viewed together when we think about Jewish culture. Therefore, the question of gender difference in constructions of "the meaning of life" in Jewish culture has to accompany the following considerations.

THE POETICS OF THE MIND

As I have stated in my introductory remarks, the study of Torah is the primary cultural site of "increasing life," since Torah – according to the rabbis – is, in fact, synonymous with "life." This needs to be fleshed out a little more now so that we can assess the range of meanings of both terms.

One of the primary metaphors for Torah in classic Jewish literature is "life" (*hayyim*), next to metaphors such as water, fire, light, or a tree.[11] These metaphors have their root in biblical poetic literature, primarily the psalms and proverbs. Probably the most well-known metaphor from biblical literature is the tree of life: "She is a tree of life to those who lay hold of her; those who hold her fast are called happy" (Proverbs 3:18). In the biblical context this metaphor describes wisdom (*hokhmah*) in general. As will become clear in what follows, the rabbis used the book of Proverbs and its Stoic praise of wisdom as a blueprint for their own praise and almost deification of the Torah. The referent is no longer undefined wisdom or abstract knowledge, but God's wisdom or knowledge as manifest in the text of the Torah in particular. Thus the verse from Proverbs in praise of wisdom as a tree of life found its way into the liturgy surrounding the weekly reading from the Torah. On *shabbat* and twice during the week Jewish congregations read from the Torah scroll containing the five books of Moses. In the setting of worship it is not just the text that is listened to, but the scroll itself becomes an object of worship, which is paraded around among the congregation before it is returned to its shrine, the ark. While it is being returned, the community chants the verse from Proverbs 3:18, "She is a tree of life . . ." with the explicit reference to the Torah scroll and the wisdom it contains.

Throughout rabbinic literature this verse is used in various interpretative contexts, such as in the following example from an early rabbinic sermon on a verse from the Psalms:

> "Let me know the path of life, the fullness of joy" (Ps 16:11). Said David[12] in front of the Holy One Blessed be He: Let me know which one is the open gate to the life of the world to come . . . The sages said: The Holy One Blessed be He said to David: David, if you want life, look towards the Torah, since it is said: "She is a tree of life to those who lay hold to her." (Vayiqra Rabba 30:2)

The art of the rabbinic sermon requires the author to correlate verses from different contexts, in this case from Psalms and from Proverbs, and to create a narrative that connects the verses. Here the connecting element is in both cases the word "life" and thus the "path of life" in Psalms is the tree of life in Proverbs which in turn is equated with Torah. The life that Torah promises includes eternal life.

The correlation of the Torah with life provides the basis for the correlation of study with the acquisition of life. The way "to lay hold to" the Torah is to study it, or – in the words of the sages – "turn it and turn it for all is in it and look in it and grow grey and old in it" (mAvot 5:25). The following teaching attributed to Rabbi Meir, one of the great sages of the second century CE, applies the language of one of the central prayers in Judaism, the Shema', to the study of Torah.

> A favorite saying of Rabbi Meir is: Study with all your heart and with all your soul in order to know My ways and to watch at the doors of My Torah. Keep My Torah in your heart and let My fear be before your eyes. Keep your mouth from all sin and purify and sanctify yourself from all transgression and iniquity, and I will be with you in every place. (bBerakhot 17a)

If according to the Shema', which is itself a composite of biblical texts arranged by the rabbis, "you shall love the Lord your God with all your heart and with all your soul" (Deuteronomy 6:5), that love of God is not merely an abstract emotional requirement. The form that the love of God is to take is to study and know God's Torah. Study and its inherent ethical refinement holds the promise of the continuous presence of the Divine in the student's life.

To strengthen the emphasis on study, the rabbis developed the concept of studying for its own sake, *torah lishmah.* One of the first blessings to be recited upon awaking in the morning is the following:

> Blessed are You, Lord our God, King of the Universe, who has sanctified us with Thy commandments, and commanded us to study the Torah. Lord our God, make the words of Thy Torah pleasant in our mouth and in the mouth of your people, the house of Israel, so that we and our descendants and the descendants of Your people, the house of Israel, may all know Your name and study the Torah for its own sake. Blessed are You, O Lord, who teaches the Torah to Your people Israel.

Further, a famous text in the Talmud here says, again in relation to the biblical "tree of life" metaphor:

> Whoever occupies himself with the Torah for its own sake, his learning becomes an elixir of life to him, since it is said "It is a tree of life to them that grasp it" (Proverbs 3:8); and it is further said, "It shall be

> healing to your navel" (Proverbs 3:8) and it is also said "For whosoever finds me finds life" (Proverbs 8:35). But, whosoever occupies himself with the Torah not for its own sake, it becomes to him a deadly poison, as it is said, "My doctrine shall drop as the rain," and *arifa* [the Hebrew word for drop] surely means death, since it is said "and they shall break (*ve'arfu*) the heifer's neck there in the valley" (Deuteronomy 21:4). (bTaanit 7a)

The interpretative method here tries to show how Torah can become deadly by connecting two verses with the help of word-play, a classic rabbinic hermeneutic move. The second verse from Deuteronomy 21:4 implies the discussion of a murder case in its context, hence the connection with death.

But what does study of Torah "for its own sake" mean? From this passage it remains ambiguous what the antonym to "for its own sake" is. In other contexts the Talmud identifies studying not for its own sake but for ulterior motives with doing something for trading, i.e., making a living from studying (bSukkah 49b), or with studying for the sake of teaching only (bPesachin 50b). Thus, the precept for turning Torah into a medicine for life is to acquire God's knowledge for its own sake, unconditionally. The weight of meaning is shifted to the act of studying itself, away from the goal of studying. The Jewish philosopher Yeshayahu Leibowitz, one of the great Jewish thinkers of the twentieth century, formulated this point in a radical manner. He emphasized that the concept of "for its own sake" also and especially excludes the expectation of any spiritual reward or satisfaction of spiritual needs. Do not study because you will find beauty and uplifting of the spirit, do not study because it makes you a better person, more beloved to your God. Study the Torah because this *is* your life. Leibowitz quotes Rabbi Hayim of Volozhin, a leader of a famous *yeshiva* in Lithuania during the nineteenth century, who wrote:

> For the reward of the mitzvah is the mitzvah [commandment, here of studying Torah] itself given to one as a reward, and that is the light enveloping him, and he truly sits in Paradise ... for he is now in the world to come as he performs the mitzvah, and this is achieved by man himself, for the mitzvah is the very reward, and the light is Paradise in the lifetime of man, and that is his reward.[13]

To revert to another concept in the preceding text, the statement that the Torah has the function of an elixir of life, can be read quite "literally" by the rabbis in the Talmud:

> Rabbi Yehoshua ben Levi stated: If a man is on a journey and has no company let him occupy himself with the study of the Torah, since it is said in Scripture, "For they [the words of Torah] shall be a fair garland [or 'accompaniment' through a word-play]" (Proverbs 1:9).
>
> If he feels pains in his head, let him engage in the study of the Torah, since it is said, "For they shall be a chaplet of grace unto your head".
>
> If he feels pains in his throat, let him engage in the study of the Torah, since it is said, "And chains about your neck."
>
> If he feels pains in his bowels, let him engage in the study of the Torah, since it is said, "It shall be a healing to your navel" (Proverbs 3:8).
>
> If he feels pain in his bones, let him engage in the study of the Torah, since it is said, ". . . and marrow to your bones" (Proverbs 3:8).
>
> If he feels pain in all his body, he should engage in the study of the Torah, since it is said, "And healing to all his flesh" (Proverbs 4:22). (bEruvin 54a)

Obviously the rabbis are playing with the biblical verses and the point of this collection of verses is to find a verse corresponding to each of the body parts. But through the play on words and verses the point is made that the act of studying the Torah has a transformative effect on life, not only the life of the mind, but the life of the body as well.

The texts we have discussed so far have addressed the praise of study of Torah primarily on a literary–imaginary level. Life lies in Torah, Torah comprises life, and one should always be engaged with it, study it, and make it become part of one's embodied mind. The rabbis in these texts explore the notion of life in its widest range: study of Torah increases life because it promises eternal life, because it promises the presence of God in this life, and because it improves the physical condition of life. God, the "author" of Torah, is not extremely prominent in this picture,[14] except indirectly in the "favorite teaching" by Rabbi Meir who applies the language of the Shema' and its commandment to love God with all one's heart and soul. But even there the love of God is translated into the love of the Torah. The reference point of devotion, or the source of meaning, is not God, but the Torah, a text.

This can perhaps also be illustrated by the famous description of God's daily schedule in the Talmud:

> Rav Yehudah said in the name of Rav: The day consists of twelve hours; during the first three hours the Holy One, blessed be He, is occupying

> Himself with the Torah, during the second three He sits in judgment on the whole world, and when He sees that the world is so guilty as to deserve destruction, He transfers Himself from the seat of Justice to the seat of Mercy; during the third quarter, He is feeding the whole world, from the horned buffalo to the brood of vermin; during the fourth quarter He is sporting with the leviathan as it is said, "There is leviathan, whom Thou hast formed to sport therewith?" (Psalms 68:18) (bAvodah Zarah 3b)

God himself is depicted as devoting himself to the Torah. Even for the author of the document his text becomes a renewable source of meaning. The author himself turns into a reader of his text. Traditionally, the point of this story has been read to be the concept of *imitatio dei.* Because God studies Torah, (Jewish) humans should also do so, and we merely imitate him. But we can push this point a little further and read the emphasis of this image as resting on the regularity and continuity of the actions. Rabbinically, study is not an act of consumption, because it is not product oriented. No matter how much one knows the text and its tradition, if even the supreme author of the text engages in study of the text every day, the emphasis lies in the ritualized nature of study. Hence, study is an act of devotion.

Here we need to move beyond the merely literary or theological construction of meaning through the elevation of study to prominence. The question is how the study of Torah (re)structures life socially. What is the institutional setting of study? The literary constructions of the importance of study in the rabbinic text provide the basis for what has dominated Jewish culture for the last two thousand years until the onslaught of modernity, and that is the *yeshiva* (the talmudic academy) culture or the culture of the *beit midrash* (the study-house). Already in talmudic times the *talmidei hakhamim*, the students of the sages, are depicted as periodically leaving their homes and their families for the sake of study. In this context, the Talmud devotes many pages of discussion to the question of whether marriage should precede institutionalized study or vice versa.[15] The problem that these discussions try to address is the tension between what the rabbis understand as the biblical obligation to procreate, to build a family as well as the obligation to satisfy one's wife, and between devotional life in the form of study.[16] This tension is intensified by the fact that study is couched in eroticized terms as well. Here we need to look briefly at the genderedness of the study of Torah.

Torah, Women, and Learning

One of the central texts for the erotic association of study in talmudic literature is perhaps the following:

> Rav Shmuel the son of Nahmani expounded: Why is it written [in the biblical text], "Loving hind and a graceful doe; let her[17] breasts satisfy you at all times..." (Proverbs 5:19)? Why is the Torah compared to the hind of love? To tell you: Just as the hind has a "narrow womb" and stays as desirable to her mate each time as she was the first time, so the Torah always stays as desirable to those who study her as she was the first time ...
>
> Why were the words of Torah compared to a breast? As with a breast, however often the child sucks it so often does he find milk in it, so it is with the words of the Torah. As often a man studies them so often does he find relish in them. (bEruvin 54b)

The symbolic structure set up in this text, which frames study as a devotional act and the desire associated with it, is that of the students of the sages as male lovers of the female Torah, or the (male) child suckling the mother's breast. The rhetorics of erotic desire here is a product of the masculinist fantasy about the eternal virgin or the mother of eternal plenitude. Study is an act of love-making between the Torah, which Ari Elon has identified as a female love goddess, and her students. As Elon phrases poetically: "This woman [the Torah] has seventy faces. The men who discourse about her know how to reveal her many faces in their studies. They know how to keep looking at her in order to find everything in her."[18] On the level of symbolic language women are structurally excluded from that which the culture holds most sacred. At the same time rhetorics translate themselves into and sustain the historical – social situation in which women are mostly confined to home-making while the men devote themselves to studying. Again, let me cite a text that illustrates this most clearly:

> Rav said to Rav Hisda: Whereby do women earn merit? By making their children go to the synagogue to learn Scripture and their husbands to the Beit ha-Midrash to learn Mishnah, and waiting for their husbands till they return from the Beit ha-Midrash. (bBerakhot 17a, bSotah 43a)

In this text, the woman is merely a part of the home which provides the material basis for the culture of learning. As indicated in the introduction, there are other texts that perhaps indicate that some women did study, but the larger trend of the classical texts as well as of the historical evolution of the *yeshiva* culture was the exclusion of women. According to Daniel Boyarin's careful analysis of the material: "The Torah-study situation was structured as a male homosocial community, the life of which was conducted around an erotic attachment to the female Torah. The Torah and the wife [at home] are structural allomorphs."[19] This symbolic and practical exclusion has led to the perception of Jewish culture as an exclusively male-dominated religious culture, rarely disrupted by the occasional Yentl.

However, even though this critique has some basis in the history of Jewish culture, especially with respect to what we have discussed so far, we have to take into consideration the other aspect of the Torah-based culture, and that is its practice and ritual performance.

THE POETICS OF THE EVERYDAY

Let me begin with a few select reflections on the poetics of the everyday life in traditional Jewish culture. This aspect of the life of Torah comprises the community as a whole and not only the elite of learning, those who have managed to arrange their lives in a way that allows them to devote themselves entirely to study. Traditional Jewish culture puts an extremely high value on the home,[20] the life of the home, and the ritualization of the home, a space in which women have central roles to play. Thus women are assigned an important role in Jewish culture as a religion of the quotidienne. The following remarks are intended to take account of the richness and complexity of traditional Jewish culture. They are not intended to be apologetic in the sense of justifying the exclusion of women from the culture of study of Torah, the most sacred activity in traditional Jewish culture, or the relegation of women to the space of the home. We need to acknowledge, however, that while operating on the basis of a cultural hierarchy with study at the top, Jewish culture also regarded the home and the institutionalization of study as complementary, because the latter could not exist without the former. The home in Jewish culture is imbued with religious significance. It is a highly visible space. One form of the visibility of the home, perhaps, is the religious quasi-obligation to invite the extended family, friends, and other guests regularly to share meals for the weekly observance of the *shabbat* or the yearly observance of the holidays. Since the celebration of these holidays is staged primarily in the family home opened to the community, the now classic juxtaposition in anthropological and ethnographic literature of public space as a male sphere and private space as a female sphere is subverted. Rather, the home is one of the important framings of Jewish life, if not the most important framing for the majority of Jews, historically and in contemporary culture. Throughout history, Jewish legislators very carefully upheld the biblical commandment to procreate as the commandment to establish a family and to guarantee the physical continuity of the community.[21] Even Jewish ascetic and pietist movements that advocated withdrawal from or denigration of the world – such as the Hasidei Ashkenaz, an early medieval group in Germany, and the ascetic movements in the Eastern Europe of the seventeenth century from which the Hasidim of the eighteenth and nineteenth century emerged – mostly remained within a *halakhic* framework and its prescription of procreation of the level of practice. There are no monastic movements in the history of Jewish culture, at least not any that would advocate celibacy and complete abandonment of the family home as a fundamental institution. Even those movements whose ideology encouraged a long absence of the husband from the home for devotional purposes did not, therefore, advocate a dismantling of the home as an institution altogether.[22]

Given this basis, the cultural importance of the space of the home provides a basis for women to play a significant role in the practice of Jewish ritual life and in providing for its continuity, in contrast to a religious culture that devalues the space of the home. This may also explain the recent attraction of many Jewish women who come from secularized homes and communities to more traditional or orthodox communities.[23]

Women play/ed a significant role especially in two areas of central importance in Jewish life: food and sex. As Joseph Soloveitchik formulated:

> It is not the spirit that is charged with carrying out the religious process but the physical-biological individual . . . The teachings of the Torah do not oppose the laws of life and reality . . . [The law that saving a life overrides all the commandments and its far-reaching effects are indicative of] the high value which the halakhic viewpoint attributes to one's earthly life – indeed, they serve to confirm and nurture that value. Holiness means the holiness of earthly, here-and-now life.[24]

Both food, the preparation of food and eating (*kashrut* as well as *berakhot*, the obligatory blessings before or after eating), and sex are inscribed with "religious" significance. That does not necessarily mean that they are unambiguously positively affirmed.[25] They are regulated and sometimes stringently so. However, at the same time this indicates that, therefore, both eating and sex are regarded as integral to life, and integral to the life of the religious person. Thus they need to be redirected but not denied altogether.

Women as traditionally the primary providers of food have an important role in the inscription of Torah into the everyday. In fact, in areas of *kashrut* (dietary laws) women have to be learned and – albeit conceptually only in connection with the space of the home – partake of the culture of learning. The same is true for the area of *taharat ha-mishpahah* (the laws of family purity), the couple's observance of abstention from marital intimacy during the wife's menstrual period and her subsequent immersion in the *miqveh*, the Jewish ritual bath. As has often been pointed out, in traditional communities the *miqveh* is one of the most important communal institutions, more so than even the building of the synagogue, since a prayer meeting can potentially be held anywhere, but a Jewish ritual bath needs to be in accordance with strict *halakhic* measurements. In fact, the ritualization of the menstrual cycle and the immersion at its conclusion did[26] and does[27] serve women as a source of enhancing their embodied lives. Hence, rabbinic culture allowed for forms of piety specific to women, ritual frameworks validated by the dominant culture through which women as women can express their devotion.

The space of the home is bound into the cycles of time marked by Torah. The life of the family moves through the cycle of the week and through the cycle of the year. Just as the space of the home needs to be prepared for the celebration of *shabbat*, the home and the family is also the major basis for its observance. Again, the wife/mother plays a crucial role in the marking of sacred time, emblematized by the ritual of the woman's lighting *shabbat* candles for the family. Likewise, the holidays that structure the year into its seasons and mark them have as their main stage the home and the context of the family.

However, here we should also, if only briefly, consider the space that complements the home, and which – aside from the halls of Torah and Talmud study – provides the other focal point for the celebration of sacred time, during the daily prayers, during *shabbat*, and during holidays. I am referring here to the synagogue which in contemporary Jewish life has ascended to central significance especially for the American Jewish community, parallel to the decline of significance of the *beit midrash* for most Jewish communities. The gendering of the space of the synagogue is extremely contested, and debates about gender boundaries here, such as the question of women's ordination as rabbis, women's participation in the worship service, or mixed versus segregated seating, are defining markers for the distinction between religious movements or "denominations" in contemporary Jewish life. Orthodox communities of various shades of religious ideology remain committed to maintaining the synagogue as a male-dominated space, even though some communities attempt to create a more meaningful space for women, such as creating separate women's prayer groups. The Conservative movement, one of the mainline liberal movements, distinguishes itself from Orthodoxy among other things by defining itself by and large as an egalitarian movement, as do the Reform and Reconstructionist movements. The intensity of the debate has grown in direct proportion to the weight of significance that has been shifted to the role of synagogue in Jewish life. The more the synagogue has become a central source of meaning in Jewish life, especially in American Jewish life and often to the disadvantage of the home, the more women have at stake to participate and be represented in the synagogue worship and to attain leadership positions in this context.

MAPPING THE WORLD

The limited space of a chapter does not allow me to lay claim to comprehensiveness in the endeavor to reflect on "the meaning of life" in Jewish culture. However, here we need to add one other framing of Jewish life, or dimension of spatial situating which is imbued with "religious" meaning and which permeates all of Jewish culture. Aside from the home, the *beit midrash*, and the synagogue it is the land of Israel that is constructed as one of the fundamental and identity-forming spaces of Judaism, whether as an imaginary space, as a utopian space, or as material space. This spatial framing of Jewish cultural practice cannot be disregarded because the land, dreams about the land, and yearning for the land are built into classical Judaism. It is in the end the dreams about the land, both as "memory" of a collective home once inhabited, then lost, and as messianic vision of a return home, whether infinitely deferred or politically concrete, that have embraced the poetics of the mind and the poetics of the everyday in classical Judaism. Suspended between the memory of having arrived once and the hope of returning again, the collective reproduction through the study of Torah and the ritualization of the home can come to its fullest fruition.

In biblical literature, as one of the foundational texts of Jewish culture, the story of the Israelites' coming into peoplehood is a process parallel to their coming into the land. However, as is pointed out by a number of scholars recently, in distinction from many tribal cultures, biblical imagination does not construct an autochthonous relationship to the land.[28]

> The land of Israel was not the birthplace of the Jewish people, which did not emerge there (as most peoples have on their own soil). On the contrary it had to enter its own Land from without; there is a sense in which Israel was born in exile. Abraham had to leave his own land to go to the Promised Land: the father of Jewry was deterritorialized.[29]

At the same time, however, biblical literature also develops a notion that in the land of Israel itself the people will be able to actualize their relationship with their God fully, or fulfill the commandments and practices stipulated in the text.[30]

If there is already a tension in the biblical fundament of Judaism, the same is true for rabbinic literature, the foundation of classical Judaism. Some scholars point to the ingenuity of rabbinic Judaism of constructing a cultural/religious/legal framework that allowed for the emergence of a diaspora Jewish culture. That ingenuity consists in the transformation of the dependence of the religious culture on the land into the collective memory of the space once inhabited and once to be inhabited again.

> Diasporic Jewish identity has been founded on common memory of shared space and on the hope for such a shared space in an infinitely deferred future. Space itself is thus transformed into time. Memory of territory has made deterritorialization possible.[31]

However, if the rabbinic ingenuity consisted in its construction of a diaspora identity, its emphasis on the land, even only as memory, focused the religious imagination of Jews for subsequent centuries until now. Rabbinic deterritorialization and refocusing on text and text study as imaginary territory did enable Jewish continuity.[32] At the same time, however, it nurtured the dream of return as its redemption. Even where this return is relegated to an infinitely deferred future, and classical Judaism as a whole discourages speculations on redemption and activism with respect to actual return, it has Jews pray at least three times a day for the quick rebuilding of Jerusalem and for the "return of God's presence to Zion," and it has Jews recite once a year at the end of the Passover Seder: "Next year in Jerusalem." The consequences often were quite concrete in terms of creating redemptive and messianic movements.

Further, this dialectic tension between deterritorialization and at the same time focus on the land as imaginary space is underlined by another tension in Jewish legal discourse which lives at the heart of its "religious" culture. At least a third of the Mishnah, the foundational document of the rabbinic movement, which also presents the fundamental legal framework for all of Jewish law to follow, is devoted to laws concerning the land. As Jacob Neusner points out, "for the Mishnah, to be Israel[33] and clean, so holy, is to live in The Land and to eat, so share in its bounty with God, the owner, in a relationship of mutuality and reciprocity."[34] He notes that two of the six orders of the Mishnah are based entirely on life in the land of Israel, both agricultural laws and laws of purity and impurity. Further, a famous passage of the Mishnah holds that "there are ten degrees of holiness. The land of Israel is holier than any other land" (mKelim 1:6), which is explained by the fact certain "divine commandments" can only be fulfilled in the land of Israel. True, the Babylonian Talmud did not bother to develop the mishnaic laws of agriculture and impurities any further, thereby signaling their insignificance for its development of a diaspora Jewish culture. But the Mishnah persists as a canonical and not just a historical development, strengthening certain strains of biblical law that emphasize the importance of the land of Israel for the full observance of God's will.

This tension in Jewish culture between diaspora and homecoming to a geographical "sacred space" is at the core of Jewish messianic or redemptive movements and of the more recent religious discourse for or against political Zionism. But Jewish concepts of the "meaning of life" are always construed with the land of Israel as their reference point, even where the land is only a space of memory or imaginary space.

CONCLUSION

At the end of this reflection the abstract terms of the title of this chapter, "to increase Torah is to increase life," should have taken on much fuller meaning. To increase Torah is to be understood both in terms of constant intellectual immersion with a textual tradition as well as in terms of permeation of the everyday life with the practice of the precepts contained in this textual tradition. The more the mind or the imagination, the way one thinks about the world and life, is becoming fine-tuned in terms of Torah, the closer a person is to the source of all meaning, and the more meaningful life becomes. Likewise, the more daily life, weekly life, and life through the year is becoming suffused by Torah, the richer its fabric. In theological terms: "Temporal life becomes transformed into eternal life; it becomes sanctified and elevated with eternal holiness."[35] That is, embodied life, suspended between birth and death, between becoming and decaying, is not transcended and thus left behind, but on the contrary, it is, as it is, imbued and infused with a new script, the Torah, which regulates it, guides it, and hence enhances it.

NOTES

1. For the purpose of this chapter, "*midrash*" may be described as creative hermenuetics of the biblical text, at least as far as narrative *midrash* is concerned. Recently the literature on *midrash* as a hermeneutic approach to text has grown enormously, because of the interest of literary criticism in searching for non-Western non-logocentric modes of readings. For a literary introduction see James Kugel, "Two Introductions to Midrash," in *Midrash and Literature*, ed. Geoffrey H. Hartman and Sanford Budick (New Haven: Yale University Press, 1986).
2. Martin S. Jaffee, *Early Judaism* (Englewood Cliffs: Prentice Hall, 1997), p. 115.
3. This term has a heuristic rather than descriptive value. I use it to avoid having to make detailed distinctions of re-valuations in each of the modern Jewish movements or denominations in contemporary America. By "traditional" I mean, then, all those formations of Jewish culture that center around biblical literature and its interpretations.
4. This is commonly known as the Old Testament in Christian and post-Christian contexts. The Torah, however, is not the same as the Old Testament. This does not merely pertain to the order of the books within the canon, but also to the liturgical status of the five books of Moses vis-à-

vis the other books of the "Old Testament," a distinction that Christians do not usually make.

5. By "classical" I refer to the rabbinic literature of roughly the first six centuries CE.
6. *Emet ve-Emunah: Statement of Principles of Conservative Judaism* (New York: Jewish Theological Seminary of America, 1988), p. 53.
7. A Greek writer as early as Hecataeus of Abdera, one of the earliest to write on Jews and Jewish culture at the beginning of the third century BCE, notes: "The sacrifices that he established differ from those of other nations, as does *their way of living*" (Menachem Stern, *Greek and Latin Authors on Jews and Judaism*, vol. 1: *From Herodotus to Plutarch* [Jerusalem: Israel Academy of Sciences and Humanities, 1974], p. 28). Tacitus, a Roman historian of the first century CE observes: "They adopted circumcision to distinguish themselves from other peoples by this difference" (Menachem Stern, *Greek and Latin Authors on Jews and Judaism*, vol. 2: *From Tacitus to Simplicius* [Jerusalem: Israel Academy of Sciences and Humanities, 1980], p. 26).
8. As in most cultures, there are, of course, exceptions to the rule, as recent scholarship on the history of women in Judaism has pointed out. Even within rabbinic literature we find one famous exception to the rule, a scholarly woman by the name of Beruriah. On the function of this woman as a token woman in the rabbinic world see Daniel Boyarin, *Carnal Israel: Reading Sex in Talmudic Culture* (Berkeley: University of California Press, 1993) and Rachel Adler, "The Virgin in the Brothel and Other Anomalies: Character and Context in the Legend of Beruriah," *Tikkun*, 3, 1988.
9. Anthropological scholarship helps us to understand this better. See, for instance, Susan Sered, *Women as Ritual Experts* (New York: Oxford University Press, 1992).
10. See Vanessa Ochs, *Words on Fire: One Woman's Journey into the Sacred* (New York: Harcourt, 1990).
11. See for instance bTaanit 7a for a discussion of these metaphors concentrated in one place.
12. In traditional Jewish interpretation David is the unquestioned author of most of the psalms.
13. Yeshayahu Leibowitz, *Judaism, Human Values and the Jewish State* (Cambridge, Mass.: Harvard University Press, 1992), p. 67.
14. This is again expressed in a fictional text cited by the philosopher Emanuel Levinas, quoting from *Yossel, Son of Yossel Rakover from Tarnopol, Speaks to God*, in *Difficult Freedom: Essays on Judaism* (Baltimore: Johns Hopkins University Press, 1990): "Yossel ben Yossel echoes the whole of the Torah: 'I love Him, but I love even more His Torah . . . And even if I were deceived by Him and became disillusioned, I should nevertheless observe the precepts of the Torah'" (p. 144).

15. For an extended analysis of these discussions see Boyarin, *Carnal Israel.*
16. Haim Grade's exquisite novel *The Yeshiva* (New York: Menorah, 1977) provides an account of this problem in the *yeshiva* world of nineteenth-century Eastern European Jewish culture.
17. The biblical verse once again refers to the words of wisdom personified which the rabbis transfer to the Torah.
18. Ari Elon, *From Jerusalem to the Edge of Heaven: Meditations on the Soul of Israel* (Philadelphia: Jewish Publication Society, 1977), pp. 53–54.
19. Boyarin, *Carnal Israel*, p. 196. The area of rabbinic textual culture that I have not touched upon here is the *halakhic* (legal) discussion of women and learning of Torah in the ritual sense. This opens a huge topic of investigation that cannot be dealt with in this context, since legal attitudes toward women need to be analyzed in the changing historical–social context.
20. The signification of the home as a central framework of Jewish life is not limited to Orthodox and so-called ultra-Orthodox circles, but translates itself into the liberal and mainstream movements.
21. On this point see Jeremy Cohen, "*Be Fertile and Increase, Fill the Earth and Master it": The Ancient and Medieval Career of a Biblical Text* (Ithaca: Cornell University Press, 1989); David Biale, *Eros and the Jews: From Biblical Israel to Contemporary America* (New York: Basic Books, 1992); and Daniel Boyarin, "Lusting after Learning: The Torah as 'the Other Woman'," in his *Carnal Israel.*
22. An exception might be the Qumran sect and a community described by the Hellenistic Jewish philosopher Philo at the beginning of the first century CE, which he calls the *Therapeutae.* Both groups withdrew into the wilderness and present forms of *anachoresis*, which was a popular form of protest in Late Antiquity. However, scholars debate whether Philo's text should be read as a descriptive or a utopian text. See Ross Kraemer, "Monastic Jewish Women in Greco-Roman Egypt: Philo Judaeus on the Therapeutrides," *Signs*, 14, 1989, pp. 342–347; Boyarin, *Carnal Israel.*
23. On this phenomenon, see for instance Debra Kaufmann, *Rachel's Daughters: Newly Orthodox Jewish Women* (New Brunswick: Rutgers University Press, 1991).
24. Joseph B. Soloveitchik, *Halakhic Man* (Philadelphia: Jewish Publication Society of America, 1983), p. 35.
25. As David Biale has shown with respect to sex in his *Eros and the Jews*, an analysis of Jewish attitudes toward sexuality throughout history.
26. As I claim in my forthcoming book, *Reading Niddah: Menstruation and the Construction of Gender in Late Antique Jewish Cultures*, which presents an analysis of the rabbinic discourse of menstrual impurity.
27. See the recent literature on the reinterpretation and resignification of the *miqveh* by Jewish female scholars and writers such as Susan Grossman,

Laura Levitt and others in Ellen Umansky and Diane Ashton (eds.), *Four Centuries of Jewish Women's Spirituality: A Sourcebook* (Boston: Beacon Press, 1992).

28. As Daniel Boyarin points out in *A Radical Jew* (Berkeley: University of California Press, 1994): "The biblical story is not one of autochthony but one of always already coming from somewhere else" (p. 252).
29. W.D. Davies, *The Territorial Dimension of Judaism* (Minneapolis: Fortress Press, 1992), p. 39, cited in Boyarin, *A Radical Jew*, p. 255. Also: "The desert is, therefore, the place of revelation and of the constitution of 'Israel' as a people; there she was elected" (Davies, *Territorial Dimension*, p. 39, cited in Boyarin, *A Radical Jew*, p. 335, n. 40).
30. See Arnold M. Eisen, *Galut: Modern Jewish Reflection on Homelessness and Homecoming* (Bloomington and Indianapolis: Indiana University Press, 1986), pp. 3–35.
31. Boyarin, *A Radical Jew*, p. 245. Eisen points out similarly that one of the achievements of rabbinic Judaism has been its "pronounced ambivalence concerning the Land's centrality – the fact that memory of and aspiration for the Land paradoxically made possible and meaningful a life lived somewhere else" (*Galut*, p. 50).
32. Eisen phrases this beautifully, with reference to a famous statement from the Babylonian Talmud: "That Torah, in fact, was not only their portable homeland, but God's. 'Since the destruction of the Temple the Holy One Blessed be He has only the four cubits of the halakhah' (bBer 8a). That was the territory which the rabbis marked, explored, and inhabited. It could by no means be limited to or by the borders of Eretz Israel" (*Galut*, p. 50).
33. He uses the term "Israel" here not as a descriptive term of the community but as a utopian term, describing the ideal community that is not yet.
34. Jacob Neusner, "Response," in Davies, *Territorial Dimension*, p. 109.
35. Soloveitchik, *Halakhic Man*, p. 35.

Plate 3 The Mosque of Muhammad Ali, or Alabaster Mosque, built between 1830 and 1848 within the walls of the Citadel, a fortress which has dominated the skyline of Cairo for 800 years. Photo: *Joseph Runzo*

5

BROADCASTING *the* WORD: PROPHET, PREACHER, *and* SAINT IN ISLAM

F.E. Peters

Islam is a member of a family, the loud and fractious and enormously self-satisfied company known as "the monotheists," or, more familiarly, as "the Children of Abraham." I refer, of course, to Judaism, Christianity, and Islam, and it is difficult to say almost anything about Islam without referring, as the Qur'an constantly does, to those other two "People of the Book," the Jews and Christians. To begin with, Islam shares the same metaphysic as the other two, that is, belief in the existence of a transcendent personal God, the creator and sustainer of the universe, and, in the end, its judge. All three possess the conviction that that same God has intervened in his creation, an intervention that has manifested itself in both deed and word. The first category, God's intervention in the world in deed, grounds the monotheists' view of history; and the latter, the intervention in word, their view of revelation.

Islam is, then, like its two Abrahamic relatives, a revealed religion, and so the Muslim understanding of the meaning of life must be sought in the book that encompasses revelation, the Qur'an. The Qur'an as we now possess it is composed of 114 *suras* or chapters which contain what was revealed to Muhammad over the course of the last twenty-two years of his life, and which he then publicly announced to his townsmen in the shrine-settlement of Mecca in western Arabia and then, after his forced departure from Mecca, to the Arabs and Jews of the nearby agricultural oasis of Medina. Atop this scriptural base is built, as there is in Judaism and

Christianity, an imposing structure of tradition, the canonical – and canonized – collection of reports from the mouth of the Prophet, the so-called *hadith*, to which has been added the only somewhat less canonical body of classical exegesis that authoritatively defines the Qur'an's teachings and explains and enlarges the scriptural base.

The Qur'an is not an easy book, either for Muslims who enjoy the illumination of faith, or for non-Muslims attempting to parse its history and contents. It itself is filled with history, though of a very special kind. Muhammad's revelations use the past to pronounce upon the present. That past is principally a biblical one and is used selectively – chiefly to demonstrate what befalls those faithless people who reject the prophets – and it is unfolded allusively and somewhat cryptically. Indeed, the allusive manner of the biblical narratives in the Qur'an has suggested to some that not only Muhammad but even his original Meccan audience had some knowledge of the biblical tradition to begin with. The prophets, at any rate, from Abraham to Jesus are all presented as teachers of monotheism, and they point forward to Muhammad, whose own message dwells emphatically upon the unity and unicity of God.

For the Qur'an, monotheism is not merely a state of mind; it is total submission to God – which is what *Islam* means – and is manifested in the heart by the assent of faith and externally by a series of acts that show forth the "submitter's" – the *muslim*'s – adherence to God's ways. These acts are chiefly liturgical prayer and the regular giving of alms to support the poor and needy of the community: what we might sum up as worship and generosity. But if the main thrust of the message of the Qur'an is clear enough, its modalities are decidedly not. The Qur'an is what New Testament scholars call a "sayings source," a collection of *logia* closer to Q or the Gospel of Thomas than to the consecutive narrative of canonical Mark.

The Qur'an's moral teachings are woven into a dense but opaque fabric of polemic against the mocking disbelief of the Meccans, the plots and strategies of Muhammad's political enemies, the derisive taunts of the Medina Jews, and the hypocrisy even of some of the new believers. But unlike the Bible and the New Testament, the Qur'an names no contemporary names, describes no places, explains no circumstances. Islam is, in consequence, rich in exegesis, much of it attempting to restore, from the available historical sources, the narrative context missing in the revealed book.

For Muslims, then, the meaning of life is certain, since it has been revealed by God, and, in the manner of all revelation, somewhat ambiguous. Eventually the Muslims would encounter – and in the end reject – the Hellenic conceit that the meaning of life had no need to be revealed at all since it was intelligible, whether understood generally or particularly, by a dialectical voyage down the well-lit *via causalitatis.* The universe's effects show forth not only the existence but the nature of the intelligent cause, to wit, God, and an investigation of human nature betrays the purpose of that nature as well as the means of achieving it. The Qur'an is not innocent of the Robinson Crusoe footprint-in-the-sand argument, or of that other version favored by Roman theologians such as Cicero: *coeli enarrant gloriam dei.* But the Qu'ran calls these traces of God's glory in the universe *ayat* or "signs." They are not vestiges of secondary causality, as they are in the philosophers' arguments, but willed and willful clues to God's creative activity spread across the natural universe.

But the Qur'an's *ayat* or signs are invoked in a limited fashion: they point to the undeniable existence of a creator God who also has a providential care for his creation; they might even suggest that the appropriate posture for the creature in the face of the creator is submission, *islam.* But the *ayat* give little or no hint of the powerful ethical imperatives that also run through the Qur'an. The *ayat* point backwards toward creation; the Qur'an's moral *kerygma* points forward toward the *eschaton.* The Last Judgment does not determine the Qur'an's ethical teaching, but it powerfully frames it.

And yet the Islamic *kerygma* is not eschatological in the same sense as earliest Christianity's was. There is eschatological watchfulness in the Qur'an but not that powerful sense of imminence that is present, say, in Paul. There is no evidence that the Qur'an was putting forth an interim ethic, as sometimes appears in the New Testament, a kind of martial law before the End comes. What the Qur'an is announcing, particularly in the Medina *suras,* is more akin to the so-called "Early Catholicism" – a long-term and institutionalized ethic – that some have proposed to find already in Luke: prayer, alms-tithing and pilgrimage, and the behavioral consequences of submission to God are already institutionalized in the Qur'an, the pilgrimage profoundly so.

The brief catechesis that later Muslims called the "Pillars of Islam" nicely catches the nuances of the Muslim community's translation of the qur'anic message. The "Pillars," which are really just five headings, are one-fifth theology – a creed that parsimoniously affirms only the unicity of God and the Prophethood of Muhammad – and four-fifths behavioral ethics: liturgical prayer, regulated almsgiving, tightly defined fasting, and highly ritualized pilgrimage. But the translation is misleading, in the manner of all catechisms. This lawyerly view of Islam, for it is surely that, is always con-textualized, that is, it is never in practice divorced from its qur'anic *Vorlage*. The qur'anic text, with all its theological and eschatological richness, floats in memory behind and informs the "Pillars of Islam." Indeed, the Pillars are best employed for the instruction of children, and probably find their most satisfying use at the hands of non-Muslims attempting to grasp, in their reductionist manner, the essence of Islam. But the essence of Islam was, and is, not in any catechetical "Pillars" but in the Qur'an – the full text in its urgency and obscurity and in all its splendid and often contradictory variety.

I hesitate, then, to characterize the Qur'an and its understanding of the meaning of life. But I too am a Western reductionist, and so I shall try. My space is limited, and so I shall ask you to supply for yourselves the usual disclaimers and caveats. Like its monotheistic relatives and counterparts, Judaism and Christianity, qur'anic Islam is based on a dichotomy between God's eternal domain on the one hand and this world on the other. But "this world" (*al-dunya*) is an interval. "What is the life of this world but play and amusement. Best is an abode in the Hereafter," says the Qur'an (6:32). This world sits like a temptingly tasty slice of *treyf* sandwiched in between the pristine state of *aeternitas ante* and "the Hereafter" (*al-akhira*), the eternity initiated by death and richly marbled with eschatological moments of fearful and exciting intensity: the trial of the tomb, the particular and general judgments. *Jahannam* for the wicked and, for the righteous, *Jannat al-'Adan*, the Bible's terrestrial paradise transformed into a vision of bedouin bliss.

If the Muslim understanding of the meaning of life is uniquely grounded in the divinely guaranteed Qur'an, its passage into the minds and hearts of people is a matter of far more varied, and human, and hence far feebler, instruments. The Qur'an calls itself the "Good News" and its first promulgator, the first evangelist, so to speak, was Muhammad himself. At the death of the Prophet the process of *evangelizein*, the spreading of the Good News, fell to others who did not, however, possess Muhammad's mantle of authority. In Christianity there was an attempt to extend something of Jesus' authority to succeeding generations through the twin concepts of the Apostolic Tradition, the conviction that Jesus imparted a special understanding of his teaching to his inner circle of the Twelve, and the Apostolic Succession, the somewhat less obvious notion that the heads of the various Christian churches, bishops as they later came to be called, shared in that understanding by reason of their designated and uninterrupted spiritual descent from the original apostles. There is no parallel, certainly not in Sunni Islam, to this Christian license to pronounce *ex cathedra* on faith and morals or, as we should say in our present context, on the meaning of life. Muslims took the Good News when and where they could get it, with results that are quite remarkably similar all over the enormous breadth of the Abode of Islam and at the same time just as remarkably diverse in local, regional, and cultural terms.

The uniformity of Muslim belief and practice is founded, obviously, in the power of that already-remarked unique text of the Qur'an, which, whether memorized in school, recited in mosques, or read off in stone, tile, stucco, paint, or embroidery from a bewildering variety of public monuments, forms the basis of every Muslim's introduction to everything from literacy to the highest moral and ethical principles. It was reinforced, fleshed out, and interpreted by the great mass of traditions professing to describe the words and deeds of that exemplar of Islamic life, the Prophet Muhammad. That much is obvious. What is perhaps less obvious is the notable uniformity over a very long period of time of the anchor institution of the Muslim high tradition, the *madrasa* or law school where for nearly a millennium the religious virtuosi, the lawyers and theologians who have shaped the Muslim understanding of life, have been trained. The methods and even the books studied in these schools, their ethos, organization, and funding has undergone very little change to the beginning of this century, and even today there are many that still bear all the telltale marks of their eleventh-century origins. The intellectual mandarins of Islam, the *'ulama* or "the learned," whatever they might have gone on to after their schooling, were all formed in the *madrasa* system, which was, like the rabbis' *yeshivoth*, a rigidly traditional but stable institution, with no challenge from either that binary node of the Western university, a Faculty of Arts, or an alternative value system imported from outside the culture – Greek ethics died at birth in Islam. The *madrasa* was philological in its textual foundation, oral–aural in its pedagogy and certification, and profoundly legal in its response to the long-unposed question of what is the meaning of life.

The trajectory of the Islamic high tradition in moral teaching is tolerably clear to us since we possess the classic texts of *madrasa* instruction, the charter documents that governed their routines down to the smallest details, and the inestimable advantage of their survival, in a not very altered state, down to the present day.[1] Attention is now being directed into a far more difficult area of scrutiny: how the literate, formalized, and institutionalized moral teaching of the specialist *'ulama* passed from the great to the little tradition, how the mass of ordinary Muslims integrated the value system adumbrated in the *madrasas* – how, in short, the society as a whole became Islamicized.

The Islamicization of society is a specific example of the larger issue of what has been called the social organization of tradition, and it is here where the Muslim perspective on life receives its regional and occasional modulations. I would like to cast what must of necessity be only a passing glance at two of the agents in this passage of values from the great tradition of the *madrasas* to the little tradition of the society as a whole, namely, the preacher and the saint.

The sermon (*khutba*) is a prescribed feature of Islamic ritual. The community is required to participate communally in the noon prayer on Friday, and the service on that occasion is accompanied by a sermon by a qualified preacher (*khatib*). It is in this setting and through the agency of the preacher that most adult Muslims receive their moral education – more accurately, most adult male Muslims, since female attendance at the mosque for prayer services is neither required nor even much encouraged. Where then did the Muslim woman receive her moral instruction in traditional societies? The subject has not been much studied, but it seems safe to conclude that most if not all of it was imparted by her father or uncles and later by her husband.

There have been a number of studies of the work of the Islamic preacher, in both medieval and modern Islamic societies, but that done by the anthropologist Richard Antoun in Jordan is the most germane to our present purpose. Antoun observed, for example, that while standard or *'ulama* teaching on the modesty of women, all solidly underpinned with qur'anic and *hadith* citation, was a standard pulpit theme, in the everyday life of the village considerable restraint was shown by both the preacher and others when these norms were violated, on the assumption, Antoun concluded, that "as long as the most elevated interpretation of the law and ethics prevailed at the cognitive level, toleration of deviance at the behavioral level was permitted."[2] This is but one example of the constant local accommodations that seem to go on between the "idealized" norm of the catholic *'ulama* and what most people in any given community regard as proper behavior, which is by no means the same thing.

From as far back as we have evidence, which is far indeed, the Muslim Friday sermon has been devoted both to this world and the next; its message was, as has been said, both social and soteriological. Unlike the Christian sermon, where the preacher is bound by both prescribed scriptural readings and a liturgical calendar with its tightly packed round of seasonal holy days and daily saints' days, either of which generally provides the point of departure for a homily, the Muslim *khatib* may occasionally feel bound to preach on a current liturgical theme, the end of the Ramadan fast, for example, or the *hajj* in season, but by and large he enjoys a great discretion in the choice of his topics. Antoun analyzed a half year of Friday *khutbas* in a traditional Jordanian village of today, and though a great variety of matters – ritual, theological, and social – was touched upon, the primary emphasis was notably upon ethical questions: justice, equality, obligations toward the family, respect for parents, asking forgiveness, observing modesty, the reconciliation of estranged friends.

The preacher is the talking head of Islamic morality; the saint is its embodiment. The first is stable, conservative, attuned to the *madrasa* orthodoxy of the high tradition; the Islamic saint is labile, eccentric, unique. What I have just called a "saint" is never addressed as such in Muslim terms, where the Arabic equivalent of *sanctus, qaddis* or *qaddus* is limited to Allah: the Muslims are much stricter interpreters of Jesus' dictum that God alone is holy. The "saints" are rather the "friends of God," *awliya Allah,* a good qur'anic name (Qur'an 10:63): they are God's friends; He is their patron and protector.[3]

The first of the Muslim saints is, of course, the Prophet himself. The pattern of his life, his *sunna,* served not only as a ground for the extraction of a good deal of Islamic *halakha* but as a paradigm for more generalized Muslim behavior from style of dress to tone of voice, and as such was, as has already been remarked, one of the principal factors that has contributed to the uniformity of Muslim praxis over the centuries. But for all his virtue Muhammad was, after all, a mere mortal, a man like other men. The Qur'an insisted on this in the face of the Meccans' demands for something higher, more supernal, in a prophet. But what the Qur'an denied, later Muslim piety granted in abundance. Not long after his death

Muhammad's biography was being adorned with the very miracles he refused in the Qur'an to perform and in the end he achieved a status that, if it was not professedly divine – Islam is stout in its monotheism – was considerably more than mortal.[4]

It was perhaps the very exaltation of Muhammad that rendered him less accessible to ordinary Muslims. But Islam knows other "friends of God" who are more localized and available to ordinary popular veneration and emulation. Like its Jewish counterpart, Muslim orthodoxy railed against the cult of the dead: a corpse is unclean and so a tomb is a place of impurity. This has not, however, prevented the proliferation of tomb cults across the entire length and breadth of the Abode of Islam. "Any hamlet," it has been remarked, "without a saint's tomb is a place without a center or a soul." The simple or elaborate domed tomb shrine (*qubba*) is the final resting-place and cult center of the dead saint; what more concerns us here is the living saint, the Muslim who was recognized in life as possessing God's blessing and so might legitimately be regarded as a paradigm of Muslim behavior.

Not all were ideal Muslims, however. In Christianity saints enjoy an institutional cachet. The increasingly stringent process of canonization has weeded out of their number not only those of dubious historicity but, more pointedly, those of dubious sanctity and dubious orthodoxy. Islam knows no such screening of the "*friends* of God" and hence their company generously includes notorious examples of men and women who were the subject of great veneration and at the same time proponents of some highly radical theology – pantheism was a popular theological theme – and others whose observance of Islamic law was what one might term, only by the most extravagant generosity, lax. Indeed, the comparison of the Muslim holy man and Christian saint is highly misleading. The prototype of the latter was the martyr, whose death, echoing Christ's own, presented the Christian world with its ethos of suffering, which has no Muslim counterpart, at least in Sunni Islam. Later, the Christian martyr was transformed into the confessor, the man or woman whose heroically blameless manner of life was, in fact, a sort of living martyrdom. The Muslim "friend of God" was a far more charismatic notion, an individual who enjoyed a special "blessing" or *baraka*. The Muslim saint may indeed have been an ascetic, but if so he was generally a highly publicized one and almost never the self-effacing monk or nun beloved of the Christian tradition. The Western Church in particular regulated its holy men and women through the institution of monasticism, and while there were Sufi communities in Islam they were notoriously unregulated by anything except their own traditions and inclinations.

The "friends of God" were, then, only rarely exemplars of the high ethical tradition of the *madrasas* and their moral theologians. But they were, for all that, highly visible Muslims, with their own practices, prayers, and rituals, who offered a somewhat alternative view of Islam, somewhat as Hasidic Jews did to the conventional Judaism of the *yeshiva* rabbis. But though something of their *baraka* might rub off on the ordinary Muslim, or induce a few to take up the Sufi manner of life, the saint's intercession counted for nothing with God, and so they are not prayed to, iconized, or integrated into the liturgy.

To what degree did the Sufis affect the ordinary Muslim's understanding of Islam? As an institution we may guess the Sufis' influence was considerable since Sufi sodalities and their convents were once widespread in the urban areas of the Muslim world, and they were regarded as potent enough, though perhaps, like the Jesuits, politically rather than spiritually, to merit widespread suppression at the beginning of the modern era. But it is a considerable stretch from everyday Sufism with its rather mild asceticism and communal prayers to the mystical transports we associate with the Sufi poets. On the one hand, mysticism is rather more easily explained and even described than it is experienced. But by the same token, Sufi poetry, where those transports are depicted in rather graphic detail, has worked its way deep into popular consciousness in some parts of the Islamic world. I speak particularly of Iran, where long passages of such poetry seem often to punctuate even the most ordinary conversations. One cannot help but think, however, that what are being waved about are not so much the emblems of a transformed religious sensibility as the banners of cultural pride.

To conclude, I offer some personal observations. I am struck, as have been many others, by the unity of the Islamic message and experience. There are local modulations, as one might expect in a body of such size and extent, but they are tied together by, and subsumed into, the powerful integrative force that is the Qur'an. And it is a unity supported by only the barest of prescribed rituals: Muslim daily prayers are quite direct and simple and remarkably free of symbolism, while the most complex of Muslim rituals, the pilgrimage to Mecca, is in fact made by only a tiny fraction of the planet's one billion Muslims, and then generally only once in a lifetime.

The other personally striking element of Islam is its totalizing effect. At Mecca Muhammad was not unlike Jesus, a Jesus, that is, with a wife and a family: he was a local preacher trying to bring his people to a new understanding of God and the divine plan, but at Medina he had perforce to become something else. Somewhat aphoristically, perhaps, Muhammad had to become his own Constantine. And Islam became, willy-nilly, what we would now call both a church and a state, and with Muhammad as the head of each, Muhammad was now not merely a prophet but a prayer-leader, preacher, tax-collector, general, and bureaucrat. There was at Muhammad's Medina not here a City of God and a City of Man but a single seamless society. Those days have long passed – perhaps they already began to pass at the death of the Prophet – but the ideal of a unitary society, which is simply assumed in the Qur'an – we cannot imagine that book saying "Render to Caesar . . ." – a society in which the values are pervasive and not compartmentalized, has never quite vanished from Muslim consciousness, though it has been much battered by quite different modernist convictions.

NOTES

1. For how the *madrasa* system functioned in medieval society, see Michael Chamberlain, *Knowledge and Social Practice in Medieval Damascus, 1190–1350* (Cambridge: Cambridge University Press, 1994); and for its survival into modern times in some venues, Brinkley Messick, *The Calligraphic State. Textual Domination and History in a Muslim Society* (Berkeley: University of California Press, 1993).
2. Richard Antoun, *Muslim Preacher in the Modern World. A Jordanian Case Study in Modern Perspective* (Princeton: Princeton University Press, 1986), p. 4.
3. For an excellent treatment of saints and sainthood in Islam, see Frederick M. Denny, "God's Friends: The Sanctity of Persons in Islam" in *Sainthood: Its Manifestations in World Religions*, eds. Richard Kieckhefer and George Bond (Berkeley: University of California Press, 1988), pp. 69–97.
4. The depth and extent of this veneration of Muhammad is traced by Annemarie Schimmel, *And Muhammad is His Messenger. The Veneration of the Prophet in Islamic Piety* (Chapel Hill: University of North Carolina Press, 1985).

Part III

MEANING AND ASIAN RELIGION

When we turn from Western monotheism to the religious traditions of Asia, we find a whole new range of understandings of the nature of time and space, of ultimate reality, and of the human predicament. These alternative worldviews radically impact the understanding of life's meaning. How might our understanding of the meaning of life differ if instead of having one life to live, we felt ourselves caught in a seemingly unending round of rebirth governed by the law of karma? And what if time, too, moved in great cycles of creation and destruction, with the world winding down from a pristine state, only to be destroyed and recreated anew at regular intervals? How might our perspective change if we saw the fundamental human problem not as sin or rebellion against God, but as ignorance? And what if there were no God?

All these possibilities and more emerge within the fertile religious soils of the Indian subcontinent – birthplace of Hinduism, which arose during the time of the earliest Pharaonic dynasties in Egypt, centuries before the origins of Judaism in the West. India further added to this richness of religious life in South Asia when, in the mid-sixth century BCE Mahavira, a Hindu, founded Jainism and by the end of the century Siddhartha Gautama, another Hindu, had founded Buddhism. At the same time in East Asia during the global religious "axial age" six centuries before Jesus of Nazareth, Lao Tzu initiated Taoism and K'ung fu-tzu instituted Confucianism in China. Finally, around the time of the death of Jesus and the rise of the early Christian communities, Buddhism moved north from

India through the Himalayan passes into China, took root, and developed distinctly Chinese forms, only to be further transformed as it was carried into Cambodia, Vietnam, and Korea, reaching the latter in the fourth century CE, and from there finally reached Japan by the sixth century CE, only decades before the birth of Muhammad in Mecca. China is also the home of the Ch'an tradition in Buddhism, which traveled to Japan in the eleventh century and became the basis for Japanese Zen Buddhism.

On closer inspection "Hinduism," the crucible of religion on the Indian subcontinent, is a problematic idea. As Julius Lipner makes clear, "Hinduism" refers more to the religions of the people of this geographic region than to any specific set of beliefs and/or practices, and it encompasses a broad range of religious perspectives, some seemingly quite contradictory. The artifacts of the ancient cities of the Indus Valley date back to approximately 2500 BCE and suggest a world marked by respect for ancestors and the past, concern for purification and fertility, the practice of sacrifice and possibly also meditation, and the worship of deities, especially goddesses. During the middle of the next millennium BCE, Indo-Aryans migrated from the central steppes of Asia to the fertile plains of India. The interaction of the indigenous Indian traditions and the introduced Indo-Aryan worldview produced the hymns of the Vedas, dating to perhaps 1500 BCE. Unlike the ancient Indus Valley tradition, the Vedas are highly articulate and reflect a shift in perspective from that of settled farmers to nomadic herdsman. The religion they speak of includes a pantheon of gods (with few goddesses), an understanding of the cosmos as fundamentally ordered, and an interchange between the human and divine mediated by sacrifices. Though the hymns express desires primarily centered around life in this world – sufficient food, longevity, healthy children, strong warriors, and abundant cows and horses – we also find the beginnings of philosophical speculations about what lies beyond this world of multiplicity and what existed before the gods.

With time, the sacrificial rituals became more and more complex and their enactment the purview of priestly castes (Brahmins) and their wealthy patrons. Eventually, the inner meaning of the rituals and of life was questioned, and from about 800 BCE this questioning conversation of teachers and disciples was recorded over the next three centuries in the Upanishads. Here Hindu thinking about the ultimate oneness of reality (Brahman) and the ultimate unity of the true self of all beings (Atman) was articulated. Some spoke of that One as personal, as God, while others suggested that Absolute Oneness is necessarily beyond relationality and thus beyond personhood. Various spiritual disciplines of meditation and asceticism were developed to aid in the full realization of this Reality. Spanning the last centuries before the Common Era and the first few centuries CE, the great religious epics, the *Mahabharata* and the *Ramayana*, were compiled and the *Bhagavadgita* composed. Philosophical and theological speculation reached an apex in the medieval period with the non-dualism of Shankara in the eighth century, the more theistic qualified non-dualism of Ramanuja in the eleventh century, and the full-blown dualism of Madhva in the thirteenth century. Concurrently, devotional or *bhakti* movements arose beginning in the sixth century CE, focusing on intense personal relationships of love between devotees and God (manifest in various forms including Shiva, Vishnu, and his avatars – especially Krishna – and the Great Goddess) (see Plates 9 and 10).

Julius Lipner suggests that this extraordinary complexity of Hinduism might be understood through the image of a banyan tree which, though starting from one trunk, becomes a forest, dropping new roots from extended branches that grow to be additional trunks. In the end there is no identifiable central trunk for the banyan, just as there is no clear center for Hinduism. There is no one Hindu view of life or meaning, but rather multiple centers of meaning, belief, and practice, all legitimately called Hinduism, and all connected yet radically different. However, within this great diversity, Lipner is able to identify common threads of these connected worldviews. Fundamentally, life and self-identity are seen as fluid, marked by impermanence, while ultimately there is an Absolute Oneness into which all the distinctions between multiple forms of the divine, the world, and human beings dissolve. If everything is in constant flux but is really all the same anyway, this might seem to lead to a sense of meaninglessness. Lipner suggests instead that this double perspective both gives life a sense of serious playfulness and generates an inward-looking focus, a desire to touch Reality beneath the shifting surface. For the playfulness of life (the *lila* of the gods) is structured by deeply rooted systems of ordering – dharma. One must know these "rules of the game," this dharma, to live a purposeful and meaningful life. Later understandings of dharma as a kind of moral truth marked by justice and compassion emerged to guide the lives of great men and women such as Mahatma Gandhi.

Let us turn now to Jainism, a tradition which began as one trunk of the "banyan" of Hinduism. Jainism shares many of the characteristics enumerated above for Hinduism, and the idea that Jainism is "not Hindu" has only recently become a matter of discussion in India, as once-fluid religious boundaries harden in today's identity politics. Christopher Chapple begins his discussion of Jainism with the Indus Valley, demonstrating the continuity with earlier South Asian religious traditions, and then compares Jainism to Yoga and explores Jain influence on Gandhi, thus showing the continuity and contemporary significance of this tradition. Jainism describes a world without a creator God in which human beings' true nature as "energy, consciousness, and bliss" has been tarnished by karma. This karmic dust clings to the pure *jiva* (life-force or soul) and must be burned away and prevented from reaccumulating through a combination of asceticism and ethical action. Once this purification process is complete, each *jiva* floats up to the top of the cosmos to exist eternally with others similarly purified, each remaining distinct yet all fundamentally of the same blissful and omniscient nature (see Plate 5). The free movement of life force toward its fulfillment in purity is the supreme value, upheld by an ethic of radical non-violence (*ahimsa*), characterized by a respect for the life force of all beings and a recognition of the fundamental interconnectedness of all. Chapple ends by suggesting that there is a plausibility to the Jain perspective, given what we know about the global environment today and the consequences of our disregard for other beings, and to ignore this truth about life's interconnectedness endangers ourselves and the planet, whether we subscribe to the Jain worldview or not.

Buddhism too shares common threads with Hindu traditions – notions of rebirth and karma, of cosmic cycles of time, and of the impermanence of this world, for example. Young Siddhartha Gautama, a minor North Indian prince and Hindu living in the foothills of the Himalayas, encountered the transient nature of the world in an abrupt and harsh way. Having been sheltered all his life from suffering by his wealthy, powerful, and protective father, his world came crashing down around him when he finally traveled outside his "pleasure palace" at the age of twenty-nine and abruptly discovered old age, disease, and death. He abandoned the life of hedonistic indulgence to which he was accustomed and went off in search of inner peace after seeing a serene holy man in the midst of this world of suffering. He studied with the greatest Hindu teachers in the Upanishadic style, learned yogic disciplines, and practiced severe asceticism, but all without achieving his goal. Extreme self-denial, it seemed, was no more conducive to religious progress than the excessive self-indulgence of his youth. Finally he came to an enlightening realization while meditating alone under a sacred pipal tree near present-day Bodhgaya.

The Buddha, that is the now "Awakened One," diagnosed the human condition in the following way. Life is out of balance and characterized by suffering because all things are impermanent, and yet we desire things as if they were permanent. We each view our own self as if it too were permanent and completely independent from other selves, and so we think of our self as competing for those things with other discrete selves. Everything that we desire will ultimately pass away – we cannot hold on to anything in the end, not even our own bodies and minds – so our inappropriate desires are frustrated and we suffer, only to be reborn again into a new life of desire and suffering. To break the cycle of rebirth (*samsara*), we must overcome our ignorance about the true nature of things, cut the root of desire, and give up attachment to self, for we are *anatman*, no-self.

The path to achieve this goal includes ethical guidelines for living a moral (and incidentally non-violent) life and teachings about the nature of reality, which can be fully realized only through stages of meditation that transform our consciousness. Fundamental to the Buddha's teachings is the idea that nothing exists independently. Rather, we are all constituted in a web of interrelationships, which in turn are arising and ceasing every moment, giving us and the world a fluctuating kind of existence. There is no absolute ground of "God" or "Brahman" underneath to stand on. Rather than *Being*, ultimate "Reality" is the fullness of emptiness.

Masao Abe, a Japanese Zen philosopher, offers a compelling description of the experiential realization of these Buddhist teachings. His very words reflect the cadence of a meditation master's instruction, using Zen's repetitive patterns designed to produce mindfulness. He gives us a view from "inside" and seeks to invoke in us the experience both of the co-arising and co-ceasing of all things in each moment – which is called "dependent co-origination" – and of our own emptiness. We cannot, he suggests, address the question of life's meaning until and unless we also face the reality of death. We cannot from a Buddhist perspective be one hundred percent living until we also realize that we are one hundred percent dying in every moment. Life and death are not oppositional states but non-dual and simultaneous, even as are nirvana and this world of *samsara.* Indeed, this interrelational reality, living and dying in each moment, is all that is real. With this realization, we are liberated to live fully, for our goal is no longer to liberate ourselves from *samsara* into nirvana, but to work without attachment within *samsara-cum-*nirvana for the liberation of all beings out of compassion, seeing clearly the interdependence of things.

When Buddhism entered China, during the first century CE, well-established traditions were already in place. During the earlier axial age of the sixth century BCE, when the Buddha, Mahavira, and the Upanishadic teachers were active in India, great religious leaders also appeared in China. It was a time of social and political chaos, and many pondered how order and harmony might be reestablished. Some said universal love was the solution, others that only force would keep people in line. The Taoist solution was to get oneself in harmony with the Way or Tao of the universe, to learn to move through the world with flexibility and fluidity according to the nature of things, rather than fighting it, ourselves, or other people. K'ung fu-tzu (whose name is anglicized as Confucius) suggested instead that the deliberate creation of tradition and the infusion of ritual and the sacred into social life would bring about a harmonious world. He insisted that individuals must be educated in order to become fully human and to be qualified to be virtuous leaders of society.

John Berthrong takes us into this complex world of Chinese religion, where threads of popular or folk religiosity are interwoven with the developing traditions of Taoism, Confucianism, and Buddhism as they challenge and inspire each other across the centuries. Underlying these traditions is a common Chinese way of thinking, Berthrong suggests, that might at first make understanding them difficult for a Westerner. He argues that the Western proclivity to try to achieve precise thinking by grouping things into definable categories is in tension with the Chinese tendency to see the world in terms of associations and analogies. (In fact, the same tension exists between Western approaches and Hindu traditions with their fundamentally oral character which, as Julius Lipner observes, thrive on multiple tellings of myths and narratives and the multivalency of symbols.) Chinese "correlative" thinking, while different from typical Western analytic thinking, is not, therefore, sloppy or inaccurate. One way to mark the distinction Berthrong is making is that Western thinking tends to be atomistic, breaking things down into constitutive parts, and Chinese thinking relational. But as the Austrian philosopher Ludwig Wittgenstein has pointed out, many of our Western categories of thought are actually "family resemblances," grouping items in a relational way. And this is much like "correlative" Chinese thinking – pragmatic and not inaccurate.

When we begin to ask about the meaning of life within Confucianism, we do not simply find propositional answers but rather a mixture of ethical teachings, expressive traditions, and embodiment in the actions and life of the sage. An individual is defined in profoundly relational terms (even as is the case in Haitian Vodou as we will see in the next section), and self-actualization – the Confucian goal – can only be realized in a social context through humane interactions with and service to one's fellow humans. There is a place for gods and spirits, but meaning is found in the fulfillment of human nature, a fulfillment that becomes "meaning filled" only through living in the world with "truthful sincerity."

Though differing in many ways from Hinduism and Buddhism, the Confucian idea of a true order of all things resonates with Hindu notions of dharma, and the Confucian emphasis on relationality parallels Buddhist dependent origination. Finally, the Confucian sage, who is both living exemplar and teacher and acts as a transformative presence in the society guiding others to self-actualization, seems very much like a Mahayana Buddhist Bodhisattva, although Confucian and Buddhist understandings of the precise nature of human self-actualization differ radically (see Plate 7). These Asian traditions thus offer a wide array of different yet related ways to approach life's meaning.

Plate 4 Sunrise at the holy Ganges River with *Sadhus* (holy men) and others performing ablutions praising the rising sun and the river Goddess Ganga, at the shoreline *ghats* (steps) in Benares, India. Photo: *Nancy M. Martin*

6

A HINDU VIEW *of* LIFE

Julius Lipner

METHODOLOGICAL CONSIDERATIONS

The Problems of an Essentialist Approach

In 1927, S. Radhakrishnan (1888–1975), the well-known Hindu philosopher, comparative religionist, and statesman published a famous book entitled *The Hindu View of Life.* This work has seen numerous reprintings and continues to be popular as an introduction to Hinduism.[1] It is short, concisely written, and presents a clear point of view. The essence of Hinduism, it is claimed, indeed of religion itself, is the Vedanta. As Radhakrishnan says without embarrassment: "The Vedanta is not a religion, but religion itself in its most universal and deepest significance."[2] By "Vedanta" Radhakrishnan means Advaita Vedanta, that is, the non-dualist or monist standpoint elaborated out of the Upanishads and the corresponding teaching tradition (*sampradaya*), by the great theologian Shankara (*c.* eighth century CE). Radhakrishnan, like his famous advaitic predecessor a generation earlier, Swami Vivekananda (1863–1902), brings this viewpoint up to date in dialogue with contemporary Western thought. In short, notwithstanding different formulations of Shankarite Advaita, its basic teaching is that there is only one reality that is lastingly real, called Brahman. All the differentiation in existence, from planets to plasma, from deities to demons, from the multiplicity of the outside "object-world" to the multiplicity of our inside "subject-world," is only phenomenally real, a more or less transient appearance, the result of *avidya* – the congenital spiritual unknowing that we must ultimately overcome – and is underpinned by the reality of Brahman. In this sense, Brahman is identical with our deepest self, the Atman. The goal of life is to realize, on the basis of the appropriate ethical lifestyle, the underlying identity of everything in, or rather as, Brahman. Then will all division and boundary of being become utterly transparent to the one, true Real, Brahman, and at death will dissolve away in that state of final liberation called *moksha* – liberation, humanly speaking, from all suffering, pain, strife, divisiveness, egoity, limitation. This is a state of unutterable and undivided being, consciousness and bliss (*saccidananda*). This, according to Radhakrishnan, is, in brief, *the* Hindu view of life.

If only it were that simple to formulate. I am not speaking of the task of trying to encapsulate Advaita, difficult enough though that is. I am speaking of the task of seeking to summarize basic Hindu teaching about the meaning of life. Elsewhere,[3] I have likened the religious traditions we are pleased to group under "Hinduism," *phenomenologically*, to a vast banyan tree that has lost every trace of the original trunk;[4] that resembles a widespread thicket of trees (the banyan has a way of dropping aerial roots from its extensive branches to the earth below so as to make them look like separate banyan trunks), interlinked by a continuous tracery of leaves and branches. Here, however, instead of a uniform whole, we must imagine an interrelated complex of botanic diversity. One yet many! A *polycentric* rather than monocentric unity, wonderfully rich in the variety of its fruits, flowers, foliage, and arboreal forms.

To reduce this variety to one particular expression of Hinduism would be to deny *a priori* a distinctive identity to the different forms subjected to the reductive process. Any desired relationship of true "identity-in-difference" between these forms within the religious tradition as a whole becomes impossible. One could say that in the attempt to make of every reduced form a "brother" if you like, or more properly a kind of clone, of the normative form, the sense that each may also be some genuine "other," is irretrievably lost. Important relational and ethical consequences for the Hindus involved follow from this. But the reductive process here also imposes evaluative distinctions of "outer" and "inner" (the other forms are "outer" or "external" expressions of their "inner" norm), "primary" and "secondary," and, possibly, "higher" and "lower"). So it comes as no surprise that Radhakrishnan can say (though he universalizes the argument even beyond the boundaries of Hinduism):

> Hinduism accepts all religious notions as facts and arranges them in the order of their more or less intrinsic significance. The bewildering polytheism of the masses and the uncompromising monotheism of the classes are for the Hindu the expressions of one and the same force at different levels. Hinduism insists on our working steadily upwards and improving our knowledge of God. "The worshippers of the Absolute are the highest in rank; second to them are the worshippers of the personal God; then come the worshippers of the incarnations like Rāma, Kṛṣṇa, Buddha; below them are those who worship ancestors, deities and sages, and lowest of all are the worshippers of the petty forces and spirits."[5]

Again, to seek to assimilate the other forms of a tradition to some putative normative form of that tradition is not only to swallow up the separate identities of the former, but to introduce a hegemonic relationship that cannot but have important, and usually undesirable, consequences for the adherents of the so-called lesser forms. It is not a good basis for genuine interreligious understanding or dialogue.

In effect, Radhakrishnan has been seduced by the modernist fallacies of essentialization ("Hinduism has an essence"), homogenization ("This essence manifests in different secondary forms"), totalization ("There is one normative form which makes sense of all others"), and reification ("There is such a thing as Hinduism which can be spoken of in this way") – a pretty kettle of fish! I do not think that today, in post-modernist times, when particularity, distinctiveness, contingency, and context have come into their own as constituents of the "other's" identity, we can seek the meaning of life in Hinduism on what is a prescriptive rather than descriptive basis. We must acknowledge the truly diversified phenomenon that Hinduism is and adopt a different approach.[6]

THE MEANING OF HINDUISM

But first some further clarifications. "Hinduism" is generally taken to be coextensive with religious forms of life. By "religion" here I mean a more or less disciplined ethical path of self-realization pursued in the context of a relationship with some irreducibly transcendent being or state. This ethical path may be more or less individualistic, more or less institutionalized. Whilst it may well be true that most persons we would describe as "Hindu" historically have been religious in this broad sense, it is another thing to say that to be Hindu is *necessarily* to be religious. The origins of the term "Hindu" may indicate why. "Hindu" started life as a geoculturally descriptive term. It is derived from *sindhu*, a Sanskrit term for "river" found in the most ancient Hindu scriptures, the Veda, and applied *par excellence* to that river, now called the Indus, that acted as a natural north-western boundary against invasion of the subcontinent. "Hindus," in the language of the ancient Persians, were those who lived on the other, i.e. subcontinental, side of this riverine boundary. No doubt religion was an implied part of this description, but its thrust was not primarily religious. Later, for the Arabs, "al-Hind" was the place where these particular non-Muslim peoples lived. So an obvious religious connotation now entered this use of the term. Toward the sixteenth century or so, the word became increasingly appropriated in some regions as a self-description by those who wished to distinguish themselves from Muslims living in their midst, and who followed a dharma or code of life that in some way could be based on or derived from the Veda. "Hindu" now became a specifically "religious" description.

In modern India, particularly in the India of the twentieth century, the cultural connotations of the term have once again come to the fore without however suppressing its religious meaning, in the hands of ideologues who wish to totalize the use of the term. In other words, they wish to use "Hindu" to refer to a monolithic rather than plural reality. This represents another, but now sinister, attempt at homogenization: "sinister" because "Hindu" is being used in an exclusivistic, marginalizing sense, in contrast to Radhakrishnan's inclusivist intentions. So Veer Savarkar (1883–1966), a founding father of the modern exclusivist political ideology of Hindutva or "Hinduness," can write in his tract entitled "Essentials of Hindutva":

> A Hindu is one who feels attachment to the land that extends from *Sindhu* to *Sindhu* (sea) as the land of his forefathers – as his Fatherland; who inherits the blood of the great race whose first and discernible source could be traced by the Himalayan altitudes ... and which, assimilating all that was incorporated and ennobling all that was assimilated, has grown into and come to be known as the Hindu people; and who ... has inherited and claims as his own ... the Hindu civilisation, as represented in a common history, common heroes, a common literature, a common art, a common law and a common jurisprudence, common fairs and festivals, rites and rituals, ceremonies and sacraments.[7]

Homogenization, from the point of view of race, territory, history, culture, and religion, and its marginalizing implications, could hardly go further than this. If we are to be faithful, at the very least to the plurality and pluralism of Hindu religious history (and we shall confine our comments in this chapter to religious Hinduism, the Hinduism of the vast majority of Hindus past and present), we cannot pander to this ideology in talking about life's meaning in Hinduism.

A CRUCIAL SYMBIOTIC RELATIONSHIP

There is another issue to which we must advert here, one which sociologists and others raise in terms of the distinction between "great" and "little" traditions, or between "orthodox," "official," and/or "elite" forms of religion and its "unorthodox," "popular," or "unofficial" forms. For our purposes, this would seem to correspond to the distinction between the Sanskritic tradition in Hinduism and the latter's popular expression. Sanskrit – an anglicization of the term *samskrita*, which means "polished," "perfected" – is the ancient language of the Veda, a voluminous body of sacred texts which were compiled over many centuries (*c.* 1200 BCE–200 CE) and which has functioned as canonical scripture in more or less direct ways for what we may loosely term "orthodox" Hinduism. It was on this basis that Sanskrit developed into the language that the Hindu intelligentsia generally used to codify ritual, rites of passage, worship, domestic practice, and social relationships, to preserve and formulate narrative and folklore, to articulate their theories about language and the various arts, and to express their views about the human person, the good life, and its goals, both this-worldly and post-mortem. As such, the Sanskritic tradition was given a regulative function by the elite for Hindu living.

It was only in the early eighteenth century or so, in the context of expanding British rule, that this position was challenged by new ideas, socially, politically, and religiously, about human rights and ends, entering from the West. The ensuing interactions were one of the main components in fashioning what we may generalize as the modern Hindu mentality. But many aspects of the pre-modern Sanskritic tradition continue to exercise all sorts of hidden and more overt regulative influence, both proactively and reactively, in contemporary India. So-called popular Hinduism was the other major component that fed into this modernizing process, and this too continues to develop and grow in new forms.

Popular Hinduism has been characterized as spontaneous (depending as it does on an oral tradition of myth and narrative which makes religious commitment accessible and relevant), emotional, adaptable, itinerant (in that it is given to processions and pilgrimage) and thus transgressive of boundaries, down-to-earth in its understanding of deity, decentered and accommodating of the role of women, holistic, celebratory (it revels in feasts and festivals), and communitarian, in contrast to the intellectual formalization, inflexibility, remoteness, sobriety, and heightened androcentrism of its orthodox counterpart.[8] No doubt descriptions of and introductions to Hinduism have often stressed the Sanskritic tradition to the detriment of popular religion,[9] thus running the risk (in the absence of the appropriate disclaimers) of significantly misrepresenting the reality of Hindu forms of life. We must guard against this pitfall in our own articulation.

The problem is, however, that the Hindu Sanskritic tradition on the one hand, and forms of popular Hinduism on the other, cannot be dichotomized in the hard-and-fast way suggested by the distinction made above. For what have been identified as features of popular religion characterize with disconcerting regularity much of the Hindu Sanskritic tradition, whilst for its part, popular Hinduism can be amazingly hidebound in important respects.

Thus the Sanskritic tradition has in fundamental ways been constitutively an oral tradition, strongly valuing the role of narrative, symbol, and mnemonic. As such it shares in the "fluidity" (Anand's expression) of popular religiosity. This feature is particularly visible not only in epic and folkloric (i.e. puranic) Sanskrit literature,[10] but also specially in those "Sutra" texts that ground so many of the classical artistic and scientific disciplines of the tradition and which require ongoing interpretation and contextualization. The Sanskritic tradition (like popular Hinduism) also fosters emotionalism and holism, not to mention a plural and hence flexible approach to authority, in many of its devotional and medical texts, for example, while its celebratory, even carnivalesque, traits emerge in its descriptions and endorsements of festivals and similar ceremonies. All this gives Sanskritic Hinduism a profoundly decentering thrust which tends to encourage open-endedness in its conceptual and behavioural expressions.[11] Popular Hinduism, on the other hand, can be fiercely closed, e.g. in its implementation of caste and a wide range of ritual.

The truth is that like popular Hinduism, the Hindu Sanskritic tradition can itself be highly plural and pluralistic, endorsing an open approach to belief and practice. The Sanskrit *Mahabharata*, a seminal repository of the classical understanding of the protean concept of dharma or righteous living, is often quoted as saying: "The Vedas are varied and the traditions are varied: one is not a sage if his view is not varied."[12] So too the orthodox, classical Sri Vaishnava theologian Ramanuja can with fine tolerance quote scripture as follows: "Sāṃkhya, Yoga, the Pañcarātra and the Vedas, as well as the Pāśupata system, are sound sources for the knowledge of the Self. They must not be dismissed through [specious] reasoning."[13] And a number of stories are told with pride by his followers about his religious commitment that conform to the liberality and spontaneity of the "popular" approach.[14] Indeed similar examples pertaining to representatives of the Sanskritic tradition can be multiplied indefinitely.

Hinduism, both in its so-called official and unofficial forms, then, tends to resist neat, absolute categorization. What have been described as characteristics of orthodox religion regularly find expression in popular forms, both negatively and positively. Popular religion, on the other hand, similarly has a number of key formalized characteristics. To some extent this is understandable; after all, spontaneity, if it is not to degenerate into chaos, must have an adequate degree of structure, not least if certain patterns of belief and practice are sought to be consolidated and transmitted. Difficulties arise, as we have pointed out, when this structure becomes, as it often is, unduly formalized and inflexible. In other words, there is a great deal of ongoing symbiosis in Hinduism across the divide of official and unofficial religion, and this is a reality that any understanding of life's meaning in Hinduism must acknowledge.[15] To summarize then, the Hinduism we are considering is a family of religious traditions – a plural and pluralizing phenomenon – with its various orthodox and popular forms often existing in close symbiotic relationship. We must understand that it is within the parameters of such a Hinduism that life's meaning is to be devised.

TOWARD FORMULATING LIFE'S MEANING IN HINDUISM

This symbiotic interaction in the great and ancient banyan accommodates a tremendous range of belief and practice: from stark monism to pure pantheism, from forms of agnostic ritualism to an apparently rampant polytheism, from ardent theisms to a dispassionate spiritual atheism.[16]

These variants would alternately inform and be informed, of course, by the full gamut of human relationships, individual and social, devotional and/or ritual, domestic and/or communitarian, and so on. We have suggested that there are a number of daunting procedural problems in seeking to identify a putative normative form of belief or practice from among this range as the basis for arriving at the meaning of life in Hinduism. The way ahead, I believe, is rather to look at some of the key features that result pervasively from the symbiotic relationship mentioned above, for it is these that would shape alternative formulations of the meaning of life in religious Hinduism. We cannot, of course, claim to be exhaustive in this inquiry, but at least a guideline will emerge for the task at hand. Any non-idiosyncratic formulation of life's meaning in Hinduism will tend to be governed by the constituents detailed below.

The Influences of Orality

We have seen that a pervasive feature of Hinduism is the oral mode of communication and transmission. This does not mean, of course, that non-oral modes of discourse have not also become established in much of the tradition. It means, rather, that orality and its formal implications are constitutively embedded in the Hindu *mentalité*, even to the present day. Orality implies a deep-set reliance on the role of myth, narrative, and hence symbol; it is also the most apt medium for a sense of drama and the figurative use of words. As such it is a pliant form of transmission and communication, favoring an open-ended rather than closed mode of conceptualization. Hindus are not likely to seek out some *Ur*-form of a myth or story so as to "straighten out" the variants. On the contrary, they would instinctively understand that it would not only be futile, but also undesirable, to do so, for it is the very pliability of myth and narrative, their tendency to proliferate into variants, that allows their content to become relevant to one's present circumstances. Hindu sacred texts, Sanskritic or otherwise – and even when committed to writing, these texts tend to be constitutively oral – are replete with myth, story, parable, narrative, illustration, and polysemy, not only as a literary form but as a key mode of conveying their content. Hindu sacred teaching tends to work in and through the oral textual mode, the flexibility of language, the dramatic color of metaphor. This explains why some form of guru–disciple relationship – not only in religion, but also in vocal and instrumental music, sculpture, traditional architecture, and a host of other artistic and technical disciplines[17] – continues to be profoundly viable, even if only residually among Westernized urbanites, in Hindu ways of life.

The Idiom of "Identity"

By the idiom of "identity" I mean the widespread tendency within the Hindu religious enterprise to valorize as a set religious objective the dissolution or submerging of one's everyday identity ("the empirical ego") in some higher Self ("a divine or transcendent Self"). This pervasive idiom expresses itself in various ways and at different levels, through conceptualization, imagery, and behavior. The monistic theology of Shankara, with its goal of identity with Brahman, the ultimate Reality, and its range of fertile images for the realization of this identity, i.e. the light of knowledge dissolving the veil of illusion, superficial differentiation (gold ornaments), masking oneness of substance (the gold mass), and so on; the systematic identity-in-difference of Ramanuja (eleventh–twelfth century CE) in which the world is described as Brahman's "body," the various theories of "non-difference in/and difference" (*bhedabhedavada*) of other Vedantins, are but well-known examples of the high theologies of this idiom. There are many more. But there are also endless variations on this theme at more down-to-earth and behavioral levels. The rhetoric and practice of Hindu devotionalism, in the myriad *bhakti* cults, also illustrate this tendency. Here is one expression of it from an early canonical scriptural text, the Shvetashvatara Upanishad (*c.* second century CE) which describes God in his creative omnipresence thus:

> You, the indigo bumble-bee,
> The green parrot coppery-eyed,
> The cloud with lightning in its belly,
> The seasons and the seas.
> Without beginning, you abide in omnipresence,
> You – whence all worlds are born. (4.4)

The *Bhagavadgita*, another more or less contemporary seminal devotional text, has numerous passages expressing the idiom of identity in different ways between features of the world and Krishna, the supreme being who has become visible in embodied form. Here are some examples: "I am taste in the waters, light in the moon and sun, the sacred syllable in all the Vedas, sound in the air, manhood in men. Also I am the pleasant fragrance in the earth, the radiance in the fire, the life in all beings, and in ascetics I am austerity" (7.8–9). The point being made is that in traditional, cosmological terms Krishna is the very essence of all these items. Again, "I am the ritual, I am the sacrifice, I am the offering to the ancestors, I am the herb, I am the mantra, I am the clarified butter, I am the fire, I am the oblation" (9.16). The point here is that Krishna comprehends and consummates the traditional sacrificial ritual. To this we may add: "For the man who sees me in everything and everything in me, I am not lost for him and he is not lost for me. That yogin grounded in oneness, who honours me as being in all creatures, whatever his mode of life otherwise, exists in me" (6.30–31).[18] Here Krishna is saying that if he is perceived as the ground of the unity of all things, the yogin, i.e. the dedicated spiritual aspirant, will achieve his goal of oneness with the deity. The language of identity takes different forms as end and context vary, and this theme can be multiplied in countless other examples from Hindu religious texts.[19]

But the idiom of identity does not stop at texts, of course. It is poured equally distinctively and abundantly into practice and experience. To take an ubiquitous example, consider the practice and intentionality of *prasada*, the offering, in Hindu worship. The phenomenon has been described as follows:

> *Prasada* is the indispensable sequel to all acts of worship in popular Hinduism. There are several different types of *prasada* ... *Prasada* is the material symbol of the deities' power and grace. During *puja* [worship] ... different substances have been ritually transmuted to become *prasada* imbued with divine power and grace, which are absorbed or internalized when the *prasada* is placed on the devotee's body or swallowed. Whenever *puja* is concluded by waving a camphor flame, taking in the *prasada* is a process that replicates and consolidates the transfer of divine power and grace through the immaterial medium of the flame. Hence the flame and *prasada* together divinize the human actor to *achieve the identity between deity and worshipper (including non-participatory devotees)*, which completes the transformation initiated by the offerings and services made during *puja*.[20]

Let us give one more pervasive example of what I have called the idiom of identity from "popular Hinduism," whether of urban or rural contexts. This refers to the phenomenon of "possession" by a deity, a very common form of which is Goddess-possession.

> The most dramatic way in which the Goddess manifests herself to her devotees is through possession of human, usually female, vehicles [p. 105] ... From the theological point of view, it is the Goddess herself who controls the possession. She chooses it as her means of self-revelation and manifestation in the world of humans ... *A milieu in which the line between human and divine is seen as permeable and in which the individual self is not seen as an inviolable fortress is favourable to the acceptance of possession as a phenomenon* [p. 133] ... In the cases we have outlined, a common pattern emerges: the vehicle participates in the power of the deity ... In some virtuosi, possession is used as a spiritual practice ... similar to yogic practices aimed at merging oneself with the divine [p. 134].[21]

As the last excerpt intimates, the idiom of identity is predicated on an inherently porous if not fluid sense of self (and self-identity) at its deepest level. This provides, for instance, one basic explanatory factor for the tenacity of the doctrine of karma and rebirth in Hindu views of life.[22] This teaching entails the belief that one's present self and its parameters of experience are, to a significant extent, causally determined by a series of selves in previous lives, and, under certain conditions, will determine "one's" subsequent self and its context in the next life. It is a porous or fluid sense of self that helps give this belief, which implies a causal nexus between individual selves in an indefinite series of lives, the wide-ranging explanatory power it has in Hinduism. As a counterweight, this sense of self has given rise to distinctive modes in which Hindus seek self-preservation and self- or community-perpetuation, an instance of a particular search for order, in an unstable world.

A Distinctive Search for Order (Dharma)

The word dharma comes from the Sanskrit *dhṛ*, the verbal root referring to that which upholds, or bears up to scrutiny, to the defining characteristics of something. As such dharma has both a prescriptive and a descriptive connotation. Traditionally one's dharma is what one has to do to live an upright life, because one *ought* to do it (the moral aspect) and because that is the way one is (the natural aspect). For example, traditionally a woman, as human, must practice *sadharana* or "general" dharma – the ethics of honesty, patience, wisdom, self- and sense-control, kindness, and so on; as a woman (*stri*), she must be attentive to her husband and caring for her children and domestic duties, and observe the rules of her gender as regards the expression of her sexuality, of ritual purity, etc. (*stri-dharma*); as a Brahmin of a particular birth-group (*jati*) perhaps, she must live within certain allowances and restrictions of status and social relationships, as well as of ritual and worship (*varna-* and *jati-dharma*); there will be further dictates deriving from clan (*kula-dharma*) and religious faith (*sampradaya-dharma*), and so on. In modern times, a number of these distinctions are breaking down, though residually they still exercise considerable influence depending on context and circumstance. Another modern phenomenon has been to give dharma the connotation of "religion"; even then, it signifies more a way of life than a set of beliefs. In short, dharma most aptly intimates the structuring of order out of chaos, and in its culturally and historically most embedded form, it is distinctively Hindu. This means that even the changes to this system of patterns are taking place in a specifically Hindu manner. Articulating the meaning of life within Hinduism must come to terms with dharma's traditional boundaries and its modern expressions and transformations.

THE DHARMA OF HIERARCHY

A pervasive feature of this distinctive search for order is a tendency toward hierarchization in various kinds of religious relationships, often associated with grades of ritual purity. Let us take just two wide-ranging examples those of the perceived manifestations of divinity and of the structure of caste

DIVINE EXPRESSIONS. In Hinduism, the supreme being tends to manifest itself in progressive order, from higher to lesser forms. This can be expressed not only conceptually, in high theology for instance, but also iconically. As to high theology, we can give an example from Shankara's gloss on Aitareya Upanishad 3.1.3. In a statement purporting identity, the Upanishad says: "[Atman: the Self] is *brahman*; it is Indra; it is Prajāpati; it is all the gods. It is these five immense beings – earth, wind, space, the waters, and the lights; it is these beings, as well as those that are some sort of mixture of trivial beings, living beings of various sorts – those born from eggs, from wombs, from sweat, and from sprouts. It is horses, cattle men, and elephants. It is everything that has life – those that move, those that fly, and those that are stationary."[23] Shankara glosses as follows:

> This Self, of the form of consciousness, is the lower Brahman, abiding in all bodies ... It is Indra, the king of the gods on account of his

> prowess. It is Prajāpati, who is the first-born as the embodied one. That Prajāpati whence were produced fire etc., the presiding gods, ... is this Self. All these gods, fire and the rest, are just this Self, as are these five great elements, earth and so on, which exist as the basic material of every body and are characterized both as food and the eater of food. [The Self is] even the beings consorting with low forms of life ... snakes etc., as well as those kinds of life that have eggs as causes ... namely creatures produced from shells (birds etc.), from wombs (human beings and so forth), from warm vapour (lice etc.), and from sprouts (trees and so on); horses, cattle, people, elephants, and any other living thing... This [supreme being] which is in itself bereft of the specification of every limitation (*pratyastamitasarvopādhiviśeṣa*), which is spotless, without stain, actionless, serene, one, non-dual ... to be known by eliminating every distinction, beyond the bounds of all thoughts and words, becomes known, through relationship with the superimposition of infinitely pure knowledge, as the inner controller (*antaryāmī*) insofar as it is the ruler, the one who guides the seed of the undifferentiated world which is the basis of everything, the all-knowing God. After this, it becomes known as Hiraṇyagarbha, who is characterized as identifying himself as that Wisdom which is the seed of the manifest world. Next it is known as Prajāpati or Virāṭ, who takes on the form of the first body arising from within the [cosmic] egg. It is then known as the gods in the form of fire and the rest, who spring from that egg. Finally [the supreme] Brahman takes on different names and appearances in the forms of various bodies, from [the highest god] Brahmā right down to tufts of grass. (Author's translation)

So here is the hierarchy of being, from the highest to the lowest – all expressions of the ultimate One – according to Shankara. This sense of hierarchy, often as progressive expressions of the same one Source, is common in Hindu theologies, whether these be monistic or theistic, etc. But it is also manifest in iconic representation, especially in Hindu temples. Thus it is not uncommon to find in a temple "lesser" or more subordinate forms of the chief iconic focus of a deity, situated at points progressively further away from that focus, in descending order of a bestowed priority or superiority. These progressively lower forms are usually located in correspondingly less and less ritually pure temple-zones.

CASTE. We come now to the hierarchy of caste. As is well known, this is an inherently hierarchical form of order. "Caste" is a broad term, generally used to refer to two kinds of structure. The first, *varna*, of which traditionally there are four, is really an ideal form; the second, *jati* or "birth-group," of which in fact there are thousands, refers to the reality on the ground. In theory, *jati* derives from *varna*, and is locatable within *varna*; in practice, the connection between the two orders is often unclear. The four traditional *varnas* are the Brahmin or priestly, the Kshatriya or warrior/ruler, the Vaishya or mercantile, and the Shudra or servant order. The earliest significant expression of *varna* can be found in hymn 90 of the tenth book of the Rig-Veda, the so-called Hymn of the Cosmic Person (*c.* 1000 BCE). This hymn tells how the Cosmic Person was sacrificially apportioned by the gods "in the beginning" to produce different features of our universe. For our purposes verse 12 is particularly significant. It declares: "[The Person's] mouth became the Brahmin, his arms became those who protect and rule (*rājanya*),[24] his thighs became those who trade (*vaiśya*), from his feet those who serve (*śūdra*) were born." We have here a clear organic hierarchy, the prototype of caste, according to which the Brahmins are the ritually purest group, associated with the mouth of the primeval Person (for their proper function is to utter, explain, and propagate the sacred texts), next in purity are the Kshatriyas who spring from the arms and thus protect the social order; they are followed by the Vaishyas or traders who, in the role of thighs, support the body politic, while the Shudra or servant is born at the bottom from the feet or ritually most impure part. So impure are the Shudras that they were not regarded as *dvija* or twice-born like the others; they could undergo only one birth in this life, namely the birth common to every creature, physical birth. They were not permitted to undergo the purifying ritual second birth of initiation into the study of the Veda which would have opened the world of saving Vedic knowledge to them. In time, soon after the beginning of the Common Era, new paths to salvation became available to them as to everyone else, paths that turned on the reciprocal relationship of the deity's graciousness to his/her devotee, on the one hand, and the quality of the devotee's love (*bhakti*) for the deity on the other. Yet the Shudra never managed to shake off the stigma of ritual impurity. In addition to special contexts of traditional worship and ritual, this was specially telling in the realms of marriage, commensality, and occupation.

Jati refers to the myriad birth-groups that actually exist among Hindus and are supposed originally to have derived either directly from one *varna* or other, or from their more or less reprehensible intermingling (*varna-samkara*). *Jati* is generally formidably hierarchical – different areas can have a descending hierarchy of Brahmin *jatis*, for example, which correspond to a decreasing degree of ritual purity – and traditionally has been tied to occupation, location within a village, and other restrictive measures. The most degraded *jatis* in terms of ritual impurity are the so-called untouchables, now acquiring for themselves the general designation of *dalit* ("the oppressed"). Under the influences of enlightened reform stemming mostly from within the umbrella of Hinduism itself, especially in the last two centuries, and ratified by appropriate current legislation, many discriminatory practices of the caste hierarchy in modern India have fallen into desuetude or have been abolished; but a great many continue, either residually or not far below the surface. The constitution of a modern democracy such as India cannot tolerate socio-religious discrimination on grounds of birth. On the other hand, caste has been said to bestow a sense of stability, order, purpose, and regulated change in society. This dialectic of dharma, the continuing dialectic, that is, between positive and negative aspects of caste, is a potent factor of which individuals must take account, each in his or her own particular context, in shaping sense out of their lives.[25]

A special word about women, especially where caste-dharma is concerned. As in the other major religious traditions of the world, women in Hinduism have traditionally been subjected to the articulation of their self-identity in terms generally imposed by men who, wittingly or unwittingly, have sought to maintain their dominant status quo. Though socially women have had to abide by the regulative impositions of their caste (*varna* and *jati*), religiously as women they have had to submit to a further set of restrictions. Thus traditionally, except in early times, they were forbidden to study the saving knowledge of the Veda (irrespective of their caste status). However, as in the case of the Shudras, the religiously saving paths of numerous *bhakti* or devotional traditions became open to them. Women in Hinduism were generally cast in an ambivalent role: as mothers and wives they were to be subject to their menfolk, but by that token were to be respected and protected in those roles, and could act as helpmates to salvation. Outside these relationships they were less controllable and hence potentially hazardous, liable to seduce men and lead them to perdition unless kept at arm's length. In any event, one way or the other, they were powerful ambivalent symbols of life and death, joy and sorrow, tenderness and destruction, purity and impurity. On the one hand they gave birth and nurtured, and were the means of perpetuating the line (generally valorized as patrilineal); in thus expressing their sexuality (invariably ratified through religious norms) they gave joy and satisfaction. But as such, they were also the agents *par excellence* of ritual impurity as the locus of various biological discharges (menstrual blood, semen, and so forth), and the harbingers of the inevitable suffering and death that follows birth. As the means of sexual pleasure for men, on the other hand, they were symbols of potentially spiritually destructive pleasures. Here again much has changed in modern India, especially in urban contexts; but a great deal of this stereotypical symbolism continues to profoundly influence the psyches of Hindu men and women, with its behavioral consequences. Women have special difficulties in trying to give meaning to their lives in Hinduism.

THE DHARMA OF SPACE AND TIME

Within the parameters of dharma, bounded as it is by an equally protean sense of *adharma* (sin, disorder), there are other significant features in a variable landscape that religious Hindus must come to terms with in living their lives. The underlying constitutive features here would include a particular religious sense of space and time. Philosophical theories apart – and these have varied over the ages from school to school – religious space tends to be viewed as distinctively recapitulative, its focuses being subsumed and re-presented to each other in a characteristic way. This has had distinctive repercussions for such manipulations of space as temple architecture, the disposition of deities not only physically (e.g. as icons) in holy places but in the theologies of sects and denominations, and making pilgrimages and undertaking sacred crossings (*tirtha*). I have given the following excerpt elsewhere,[26] but it is worth repeating since it illustrates typically what I am trying to say.

> Among India's *tīrthas*, Kāshī [Benares] is the most widely acclaimed. Pilgrims come from all over India to bathe in the Ganges at Kāshī and to visit her temples, and they come from all sectarian groups ... From one perspective, Kāshī is a single *tīrtha* among others ... At the same time, Kāshī is said to *embody* all the *tīrthas*. One may visit the far-off temple of Shiva, high in the Himālayas at Kedāra – right here in Kāshī. And one may travel to the far South to Rāmeshvaram ... right here in Kāshī. And even if one does not visit the sites of these *transposed tīrthas* in Kāshī, the power of all these places has been assimilated into the power of this one place, and the pilgrims who visit Kāshī stand in a

> place empowered by the whole of India's sacred geography ... A place such as Kāshī is important, even *supreme, without being unique* ... To celebrate one god or one *tīrtha* need not mean to celebrate *only* one. Far from standing alone, Kāshī, like a crystal, gathers and refracts the light of other pilgrimage places. Not only are other *tīrthas* said to be present in Kāshī, but Kāshī is present elsewhere. In the Himālayas ... the pilgrim will come to a place called the "Northern Kāshī" ... This kind of "*transposition of place*" is a common phenomenon in Indian sacred topography ... the affirmation is that the place itself, with its sacred power, *is present in more than one place.* In addition to the northern Kāshī, there is a southern Kāshī and a Shiva Kāshī in the Tamil South ... In a similar way, the River Ganges is a prototype for other sacred waters, and her presence is seen in countless rivers and invoked into ritual waters all over India.[27]

The expressions "embody," "transposed," "supreme, without being unique," "transposition of place," "is present in more than one place," which I have emphasized, bring out particularly in the context of the whole what I mean when I say that religious space in Hinduism is recapitulative (or polycentric). The focuses of that space, physical or spiritual, coexist in a continuously interactive grid, the potency of one being an expression of the potency of all simultaneously, each one focus being able to recapitulate, radiate, crystallize, and replace, when the occasion demands, the potency of the whole system. Thus the "original" Kashi or the original Ganges, or for that matter, Vishnu or Shiva or the Goddess herself, relocate in multiple manner, as potent and functional in each new location as at source. Indeed, it is not always easy to identify the source, for the source expresses itself anew in each focus of its nodal web. You can benefit from the spiritual power of Kashi or the Ganges at different nodal points in Hinduism's sacred geography, but you can benefit from the spiritual power of Rome or Mecca only if you travel to a particular physical location. There is a subtle but profound difference here.

Sacred time too tends to be experienced by the Hindu in a distinctive way. Thus cosmic time is also cyclic, but not as simplistically as it is often depicted to be. Sacred cosmogony in the Sanskritic tradition, though this has filtered down into popular Hinduism, functions as continuously degenerative and regenerative. From one perspective of this process, the start represents the most perfect era (*yuga*) of four; it is called the *satya* age, is the longest in duration and is characterized by the perfection of human powers and relationships. But owing to moral frailty, the perfect dharma of this situation begins to wane, and in due course the second age or *treta yuga* takes effect. This age is shorter and physically and spiritually less perfect than its predecessor, and as time passes turns into the *dvapara* age. This period is proportionally shorter and is characterized by further deterioration of dharma in general. Finally, the *dvapara* age gives way to the shortest and most degenerative era of all, the *kali yuga*, in which dharma is in dire straits. It may come as no surprise to know that according to this symbolic scheme, our own time is a short way into this final stage. When the *kali yuga* runs its course, the whole universe dissolves (it is thought generally into the supreme Spirit or God), conscious souls exist in a kind of suspended animation, and then a new *satya* age begins, repeopled by the now activated souls. It is important to note that though the structure of the universe remains the same in each cycle, its particular events and individuals do not. Personalities and world events come and go in accordance with the strictures of the progressive maturation of karma, individuals die and are reborn, and some achieve salvation never to reappear again.

The stretch of time of each *yuga* may be vast, so there is plenty of scope in the system for linear understandings of time and its consequences of contingency, urgency, and unrepeatability. So there is scope for the construct of history, though this is undermined by the belief of the porousness of self-identity and by the influence of the idiom of identity. From another perspective, however, humans in our own period can look forward to a new era of hope for their descendants in the fullness of time. All is not lost, not only for each of us individually (the doctrine of karma and rebirth implies the continued functioning of free will[28]), but also for the collective and our world. For by our efforts we can contribute to limiting the degenerative effects of dharma in our present *kali* age, and to the making of a perfect world in the next *satya* age. This is not hope for some *eschaton*, the final culmination of "salvation history" in a beatific state of all the righteous as in Christianity, but it does offer a positive vista for the future for which each of us can be held accountable.

We can mention briefly here the role of the *samskaras* or rites of passage in Hindu views of life. In contrast to the cosmic, we have here an individual recapitulation of time, again neither simplistically linear nor cyclic. It is not to our purpose to give the varying lists of *samskaras* in the codes; they include the usually expected ones that deal with birth, initiation into religion, marriage, and death. Traditionally they were intended generally for twice-born males (women, however, were specially included in birth, marriage, and death rites), though there is precedent, even in modern times, for some *samskaras* or *samskara*-substitutes being administered to Shudras. The point is again that the *samskaras* are meant to be recapitulative in the sense that they bind up the Hindu's life, make it whole as well as *a* whole. As the Sanskrit term *samskara* indicates, they "complete" and sustain the individual by delivering the body from the accretions of particular forms of ritual impurity and by warding off adverse influences (including sickness and hostile powers such as ghosts and curses) so that the recipient becomes a fit agent to strive for salvation in his or her due place in society. So the *samskaras* tend to mark a social rather than simply individual process, and as a group (inclusive of the death rites) characterize the life they ratify as a completed, public event. Further, the *samskaras* are a way of endorsing the importance of the human body in the passage through life; besides socializing the body and highlighting key interpersonal relationships, they intimate that the body is the vehicle and mark of the soul, requires protection and regular purification during the stages of life, and must be helped on its way into a suitable postmortem existence. Religious (or socially minded) Hindus today in general will endorse the administering of at least some *samskaras* for themselves and members of their families.[29]

Our discussion so far has led cumulatively to the final feature of a Hindu view of live that we shall consider.

The Rhetoric of Transience

Hindu religious discourse is pervaded by the rhetoric of impermanence. There are a great many theories, no doubt, about the origins and nature of impermanence; what these share is the perspective that things are not what they seem, that the world and social relationships are passing away, that there is a deeper and more enduring reality behind the scenes, whether in the microcosm (the individual) or in the macrocosm (the world at large). This perspective tends to generate distrust in the promises and ends of the visible world. This world is a deceptive kind of reality, indeed something that trifles with us and in which we may, in turn, sit lightly. The teachings of countless gurus, past and present, in much of the length and breadth of Hinduism, testify to this. As a corollary, it is not uncommon for divine figures to be depicted, especially in narrative, as agents who can dazzle or fascinate us, and who are skilled at using the pliability of the world to teach us eternal truths. So the fury of a storm might be described as "Mother's (i.e. the Goddess') play (*khela*);" a friend or superior may characterize an excessive or unwarranted display of grief as indulging in the *maya* or delusion of this world.

This approach must not be misunderstood; it does not diminish or undermine the overriding graciousness of God, or the felt seriousness of life. But it makes of life a game (*lila*) – a serious game, if you will, with its full complement of joys and sorrows, but nevertheless a trackless and hazardous landscape unless subject to the following rules. To have a chance of reaching your goal, whether this be prosperity and equanimity in this life or salvation in the next, you must abide by the rules. The law of karma, worship of God, the guru–disciple relationship, the discipline of yoga, the spiritual paths of knowledge (*jaana*), action (*karma*) – gainful and selfless, and devotion (*bhakti*), the build-up and release of spiritual power (*tapas*) through ascetic discipline, the practice of astrology and sorcery, the dictates of fate, various forms of "homology," namely seeking correspondences between features of the microcosm (the body) and of the world at large in order to exercise some control over one or the other, the pursuit of dharma – all represent, from sublime to mundane, from high to low, a distinctive and ceaseless quest for discerning rules in life in order to achieve purposeful and stable paths in an unstable world. These are to be followed if one's determinate goal is to be achieved. Many times these rules may be hard to discern, but they are believed to exist and are disregarded at one's peril. So play the game, and win the prize. Religious Hinduism expresses a great hankering for accredited reference-points in life. For without these one runs the risk of becoming hopelessly lost in this shape-shifting, deceptive universe. And underlying this bewitching arena of instability, out of sight, deeper even than the invisible tiers of multiple heavens and hells, dwells the ultimate Ground of all being, the unshakable, beckoning, gracious core of truth and bliss, call it whatsoever you will (Brahman, Vishnu, Shiva, the Goddess, and magnanimously by extension today, Trinity, Allah, Adonai . . .).

So, theologically, we have come full circle to the multi-tiered perception of reality mentioned earlier. This generates in very many Hindu lives, where religious experience is concerned, an appeal to the language of *interiority*. At the crudest level, body is different from mind;[30] but on a more reflective basis, body is the outer tier on a continuous path to the spirit dwelling within. This is where the supreme being – by whichever name – is to be sought, for it indwells the body and the world. Even the path of action in Hinduism, of the *karmayogi* or selfless activist, requires, if it is to be effective, its complement of reflection, a contemplative mood. This penchant came out powerfully among exponents of Hindu nationalism seeking freedom, *svaraj,* from British rule, not least in the life of "Mahatma" Gandhi. For *svaraj,* which means self-rule, could only be attained if one first learnt to rule oneself. This reflective mood seems to be conspicuously absent in the behavior of most Hindu politicians today.

CONCLUSION

There is an underlying tendency, in all that we have discussed so far as characterizing a Hindu view of life, that I refer to as *polycentrism.* This is the tendency to structure one's religious landscape, from the point of view of a particular focus – whether of worship, or scripture, or pilgrimage, or virtue (dharma), and so on – in such a way as to set up a network of nodal points in which any one node is empowered or valorized in terms of its interaction with the others. One's parameters of experience with regard to the focus under consideration then become a continuously interactive grid of decentered and recentering nodal points. Thus from the point of view of pilgrimage, for example, we have seen how the power of Kashi is recentered synchronously in other "Kashis" physically located elsewhere, without the "original" Kashi being undermined in any significant way. On the contrary, the power of the original Kashi is refracted in its multiples; functionally each of them becomes Kashi too. Similarly for the Ganges, whose spiritual significance is relocated simultaneously in chosen multiple locations.[31] This polycentric phenomenon is repeated in many other contexts – of the worship of icons, the valorizing of scripture, the pursuit of dharma or virtue, and so on.[32] It is this pervasive tendency, I suggest, that binds the various determining features we have considered in this chapter into a distinctive whole which can then be characterized as a particular "Hindu" view of life. Its open-endedness allows for an endless variety of individual lifestyles; its binding quality makes them "Hindu." There will always be exceptions, dubious instances, ambivalent examples: that is the nature of such an exercise. Nevertheless, a case has been made, I believe, for characterizing the rich yet elusive phenomenon we call Hinduism in a non-essentialist, informative, and useful way.

NOTES

1. First published by George Allen & Unwin, London; I have the Unwin Paperback edition, London, first published in 1980.
2. Ibid., p. 18 (emphasis added).
3. See J. Lipner, *Hindus: Their Religious Beliefs and Practices* (London and New York: Routledge, 1994), esp. pp. 5–6.
4. *Chronologically* "Hinduism" may well be described differently, e.g. on the basis of Vedic origins. How far such a description may be said to comprehend the gamut of religions that can be called "Hinduism" would be a matter for debate.
5. *Hindu View of Life*, p. 24. It appears that the section within quotation marks in the original is meant to encapsulate the hierarchy of religion from the Hindu point of view.
6. I am not saying that it is illegitimate to use abstractions and generalizations in the course of discussion. One can hardly avoid doing so, and I myself have resorted to a number in the course of this chapter (e.g. "the Sanskritic tradition," "popular Hinduism," and so on). The point is that one must distinguish between using such expressions as an unavoidable literary device, on the one hand, and as encapsulating an essentialist approach, on the other. The context and content of discussion will indicate which is which, and it is this distinction that lies at the basis of our critique of an essentialist approach.
7. "Essentials of Hindutva" in *Samagra Savarkar Wangmaya, Hindu Rastra Darshan*, (Poona: Maharastra Prantik Hindusabha, 1964), vol. 6, p. 64.
8. See, for example, Subhash Anand's stimulating contribution, "The Liberative Potential of Popular Religious Traditions," in *Re-visioning India's Religious Traditions: Essays in Honour of Eric Lott*, ed. David C. Scott and I. Selvanayagam (Bangalore: ISPCK, 1996).
9. Radhakrishnan's book is a blazing example of this tendency.
10. See, e.g., the work of G.M. Bailey where this is brought out.
11. To demonstrate this is the principal aim of my article "Ancient Banyan: an Inquiry into the Meaning of 'Hinduness'," *Religious Studies*, 32, 1996, pp. 109–126.
12. "Vedā vibhinnāḥ smṛtayo vibhinnā nāsau munir yasya mataṃ na bhinnaṃ." There is a variant of this in the so-called critical edition of the *Mahābhārata*, in Appendix 1, no. 32, of vol. 4 (*Āraṇyakaparvan*, part 2). It reads: "*tarko'pratiṣṭhaḥ śrutayo vibhinnā naiko ṛṣir yasya mataṃ pramāṇam. dharmasya tattvaṃ nihitaṃ guhāyām, mahājano yena gataḥ sa panthāḥ*," i.e. "Reason is unfounded, the scriptures are varied, there is no one seer whose view is the norm. The essence of dharma lies hidden; the path to be taken is that of the great man." At the end of the preface to the

translation of the *Sarvadarśanasaṃgraha* (Chowkhamba Sanskrit Series, vol. 10, Varanasi, 1961), by E.B. Cowell and A.E. Gough, Cowell writes: "Well may some old poet have put into the mouth of Yudhishṭhira [a righteous king] the lines which one so often hears from the lips of modern pandits – *Vedā vibhinnāḥ smṛtayo vibhinnā, Nāsau munir yasya mataṃ na bhinnaṃ, Dharmasya tattvaṃ nihitaṃ guhāyām, Mahājano yena gataḥ sa panthāḥ.*" To this there is the following footnote: "Found in the Mahābh.iii.17402, with some variations. I give them as I have heard them from Paṇḍit Rāmanārāyaṇa Vidyāratna," p. xi.

13. "*Sāṃkhyaṃ yogaḥ pañcarātraṃ vedāḥ pāśupataṃ tathā, ātmapramāṇāny etāni na hantavyāni hetubhiḥ*"; *Śrī Bhāṣya*, 2.2.42.
14. See J.B. Carman, *The Theology of Rāmānuja: An Essay in Interreligious Understanding* (New Haven: Yale University Press, 1974), esp. pp. 31, 39–40.
15. This does not mean, of course, that much injustice and restriction may not have been perpetrated on women and "dalits" (including the so-called untouchables) through the agency of Sanskritic Hinduism, or that numerous Sanskrit (and vernacular) texts do not exist which idealize an extreme form of orthodox religion. For a good example of such a Sanskrit text, see *The Perfect Wife: The Orthodox Hindu Woman according to the Strīdharmapaddhati of Tryambakayajvan*, ed. and trans. by I. Julia Leslie (Delhi etc.: Oxford University Press, 1989).
16. Classical Samkhya inculcates belief in the reality of the spirit but not in God.
17. See, for example, J. Alter, *The Wrestler's Body: Identity and Ideology in North India* (Berkeley: University of California Press, 1992), for the role of the guru in traditional wrestling.
18. These translations are taken from Will J. Johnson, *The Bhagavad Gita* (Oxford and New York: Oxford University Press, World's Classics edition, 1994).
19. See, for instance, Nancy Martin's contribution to this volume (chap. 11).
20. C.J. Fuller, *The Camphor Flame: Popular Hinduism and Society in India,* (Princeton: Princeton University Press, 1992), p. 74; emphasis added.
21. Kathleen M. Erndl, *Victory to the Mother: The Hindu Goddess of Northwest India in Myth, Ritual, and Symbol* (New York and Oxford: Oxford University Press, 1993) (emphasis added).
22. There are many variants of this doctrine in Hinduism, ranging from philosophical explanations (see e.g. R.N. Dandekar's article "The Role of Man in Hinduism," in *The Religion of the Hindus*, ed. K.W. Morgan [New York: The Ronald Press Co., 1953] to *explanationes ex machina*, i.e. ad hoc or partial explanations when other kinds do not seem to do (see e.g. Susan S. Wadley and Bruce W. Derr, "Eating Sins in Karimpur," *Contributions to Indian Sociology*, vol. 23, 1 [New Delhi/Newberry Park/London: Sage Publications, 1989]; see also Fuller, *Camphor Flame*, esp. pp. 245 ff.). The

variants notwithstanding, it is both the nature of the belief and the fact that it is so instinctively and ubiquitously accepted to which I am pointing. It seems to entail a "soft" notion of self in contrast to the firmer notions of self in the Abrahamic traditions of Judaism, Christianity, and Islam.

23. I have used P. Olivelle's translation from *Upaniṣads* (Oxford and New York: Oxford University Press, 1996), pp. 198–99. "Indra" and "Prajāpati" are names for the supreme god(s) of the time.
24. Generally understood to mean the same as *kṣatriya.*
25. Hierarchies in Hinduism need not be straightforwardly linear; they can accommodate variable peaks and crests. For example the traditional *ashrama* configuration can be viewed as a variable hierarchy. An *ashrama* is a staging-post in life; in the early formation of religious norms in Hinduism (that is by about the fourth or fifth century BCE), four *asramas* developed as a kind of unit in the Sanskritic tradition. These are often enumerated as follows: first, *brahmacharya*, the stage of celibate studenthood during which the twice-born (male) studies the Vedic way of life under an accredited teacher. This is followed by *garhasthya* or married life in which children are produced, proper social relationships affirmed, and tradition acknowledged. Next comes *vanaprastha.* In this *ashrama*, the male householder begins to withdraw from worldly transactions and pleasures – in the company of a willing wife, if he so chooses. The fourth *ashrama* is *samnyasa* or renunciation, in which, all ties with the world having been severed, the renouncer wanders about alone, the living symbol of the view that life is but a pilgrimage to post-mortem immortality. Some traditional law codes see the householder's stage as the most important, for without it as a basis, the whole social order and everything else that it makes possible (even renunciation), collapses. Others valorize *samnyasa* as the liminal horizon of the other three, continually posing pivotal questions about life's true goals and values. Sometimes the *ashrama* code is set alongside another ancient variable hierarchy, that of the four *purusharthas*, or "goals of life." These may be listed thus: *artha*, or wealth (originally wealth to enable one to act as patron of Vedic sacrifice), *kama* or enjoyment (to include all forms of aesthetic appreciation), dharma or the single-minded pursuit of virtue proper to one's caste, gender, and stage of life along spiritual paths appropriate to one, and *moksha* or spiritual liberation. Here too there is discussion about degrees of importance, with *moksha* acting as the questioning horizon of the other three. In essence, both the *ashrama* and *purushartha* codes are meant to be regulative norms rather than a universal blueprint for actual implementation, though Hindus have always felt free to interpret and live out these ideals in the varying circumstances of their lives. These two schemes, by the tension they posit between their fourth

and preceding members, confront the Hindu with the overarching tension between *pravritti* (involvement, engagement with the world) and *nivritti* (withdrawal from the world) in their lives. On the *purusharthas*, see G. Flood, "The Meaning and Context of the *Puruṣārthas*," in *The Fruits of Our Desiring: An Inquiry into the Ethics of the Bhagavadgītā for Our Times*. ed. J. Lipner (Calgary: Bayeux Arts Inc., 1997).

26. See Lipner, *Hindus*, pp. 276 f.
27. Quoted from D. Eck, *Banaras: City of Light* (London: Routledge & Kegan Paul, 1983), pp. 39–41.
28. Notwithstanding a tendency among many Hindus to conflate this doctrine to some degree with a more or less vague belief in "fate," which acts as a kind of causal check on actions and events.
29. For more detailed information on the *samskaras*, see K. Klostermaier, *A Survey of Hinduism* (Albany: State University of New York Press, 1989), chap. 11, and R.B. Pandey, *Hindu Saṃskāras: Socio-Religious Study of the Hindu Sacraments* (Delhi: Motilal Banarsidass, 1976; repr. of 2nd rev. edn.).
30. The frequent charge leveled at Hindus of espousing a kind of Cartesian dualism can survive only at this level.
31. How "these" rather than "those" instances become the active nodal points of a particular grid of a particular focus is a separate question in which sociological considerations play a leading role.
32. I have elaborated on what I mean by "polycentrism" with reference to some of these examples in the article cited in note 11.

Plate 5 The famous Ranakpur Jain temple, constructed in the fifteenth century in Rajasthan, India, is among the largest of its type and is intended as an earthly mirror of the celestial assembly hall of the Jinas. Photo: *Nancy M. Martin*

7

LIFE FORCE *in* JAINISM *and* YOGA

Christopher Key Chapple

INTRODUCTION

Jainism and Yoga constitute two important renouncer traditions of India that emphasize adherence to a strict code of ethical behavior emphasizing respect for life. They arise from within the Indian subcontinent as part of the broader Shramanical or renouncer movement that also includes Buddhism. Both Jainism and Yoga affirm views of life that value the intrinsic vitality of reality, and both advocate non-violence as a consequence of this view.

The renouncer movement in India can be traced back several thousand years to the Indus Valley civilization. From the ruins of this civilization, which extend from the cities of Mohenjadaro and Harappa in modern Pakistan to Lothal in southern Gujarat and beyond, archaeologists have determined that starting approximately 3000 BCE these people practiced irrigation and agriculture, engaged in trade with Egypt and Mesopotamia, and developed a distinct (though as yet undeciphered) system of writing. Various artifacts from these cities, including statues and seals, depict meditating figures, animals, and women. One motif in particular appears frequently: a meditating figure in a variety of what are later called Yoga postures surrounded with cattle, antelope, and other animals.

Around the year 1500 BCE, the people of South Asia ceased crafting cities, statues, and seals from stone. For a period of approximately 1,200 years, India left virtually no physical record of its civilization. The wood-based world written of in the *Mahabharata* and *Ramayana* has vanished without leaving a physical imprint. We know for certain that the great literary and religious traditions of the Vedas, the Upanishads, and the epics developed during this period, as well as the philosophies of Mahavira and the Buddha. But stone artifacts do not appear again until 300 BCE, this time far to the east of the Indus Valley in the city of Mathura, located in the Gangetic plain. These stone remains, perhaps inspired by a wave of Hellenistic art introduced by Alexander's generals, include motifs associated with the Jaina tradition as well as a prototype for the pan-Indian goddess Sarasvati.

Despite the lack of strong historical support for assessing the precise moments of origin for India's many philosophical schools, we know that many aspects of Indian religious culture extend back into the Indus Valley period. Four major features characterize this earliest known civilization of India: knowledge of and respect for water, intimacy with and reverence for animals, mastery of meditation and yogic postures, and veneration of the reproductive powers of women. Each of these early themes finds expression in later forms of Indian civilization and culture, up to the present day. Water tanks flank Hindu temples. Cows continue to be adorned and worshiped. The Yoga tradition itemizes scores of yogic postures, many in imitation of animals, and meditation is widely practiced. The goddess or Devi plays a prominent role in the Hindu pantheon through her power or *Shakti* as expressed in Sarasvati, goddess of learning; Lakshmi, goddess of wealth; Kali, the ferocious mother; and many others. Over a period of several centuries, these ancient traditions merged with and complemented the brahmanical Vedic ritual, philosophical thought, and social practices to form the expansive tradition known as Hinduism. However, independent from this mainstream aspect of Indian culture, meditators and renouncers seeking to escape societal norms have persisted to the present day in India, including the Jaina monks and nuns, and various groups of yogins and yoginis, whose contemporary practices and rigors can be seen in India's earliest artifacts.

JAINISM AND RESPECT FOR LIFE

The Jaina faith, a tradition that does not draw its inspiration from the Vedas, Upanishads, the Dharmashastras, or the Hindu epics, finds its voice several centuries before the Common Era. The earliest surviving mention of Jainism can be found in Buddhist texts[1] that criticize various aspects of Jaina asceticism, indicating that Jainism was recognizable as a well-established tradition at the time of the Buddha (*c.* 400–350 BCE, according to the recent analysis of Heinz Bechert). The *Kalpa Sutra*, a Jaina text of the first or second century BCE, traces the origins of the tradition to the great teacher Parshvanatha, a Tirthankara or liberated being who lived approximately 250 years before the Buddha. Parshvanatha advocated the protection of forms of life and perhaps systematized the observance of four religious vows that include non-violence, truthfulness, not stealing, and non-possession. According to the *Kalpa Sutra*, Parshvanatha lived thirty years as a householder, attained *kevala* or liberation eighty-three days after renouncing the world, and taught for seventy years as a Kevalin, an enlightened being, gathering 16,000 male monastic followers, 38,000 nuns, and thousands of lay disciples. He conducted his work in north-east India, primarily around the city of Varanasi or Benares. During his lifetime, thousands reportedly attained perfection.

The twenty-fourth and most recent Tirthankara is Mahavira Vardhamana, also known as the Jina or "victor," from which the term Jaina derives. The Jina most likely lived around the time of the Buddha. According to the *Kalpa Sutra*, Mahavira, whose parents followed the teachings of Parshvanatha, renounced the world, observed strict ascetic vows, attained the state of *kevala* or spiritual perfection, and taught for several years. During his lifetime he assembled a large community of followers, including 14,000 monks, 36,000 nuns, 159,000 laymen, and 318,000 laywomen.

The earliest textual material we have for the Jaina tradition is the first part of the *Acaranga Sutra*, recorded within several decades of the death of the Jina.[2] Several passages from this text attest to the hallmark Jaina commitment to non-violence toward all life forms, providing the earliest complete articulation of this cardinal principle of Shramanic religiosity in India. The following verse specifies that no living beings may be harmed or abused:

> All breathing, existing, living, sentient creatures should
> not be slain, nor treated with violence, nor abused,
> nor tormented, nor driven away.
> This is the pure, unchangeable, eternal law. (I.4.1)

Indicating a continuity with other life forms, this next passage suggests that human beings are not different from one another, nor do they fundamentally differ from other living beings. As the later tradition specifies, all life forms are interchangeable through the process of reincarnation and hence all life forms must be regarded as past or future family members:

> To do harm to others is to do harm to oneself.
> "You are the one whom you intend to kill!
> You are the one you intend to tyrannize over!"
> We corrupt ourselves as soon as we intend to corrupt others.
> We kill ourselves as soon as we intend to kill others. (I.5.5)

Consequently, Mahavira exhorted his followers to abstain from harming all beings, stating that the mark of wisdom can be found in the one who becomes a shelter for all:

> With due consideration, preaching the law of the mendicants,
> one should do no injury to one's self,
> nor to anybody else,
> nor to any of the four kinds of living beings.
> A great sage, neither injuring nor injured,
> becomes a shelter for all sorts of afflicted creatures,
> even as an island, which is never covered with water. (I.6.5.4)

Mahavira advised against causing pain to any being in any of the three realms:

> Knowing and renouncing severally and singly
> actions against living beings in the regions
> above, below, and on the surface,
> everywhere and in all ways –
> the wise one neither gives pain to these bodies,
> nor orders others to do so,
> nor assents to their doing so.
> We abhor those who give pain to these bodies
> (of the earth, of water, of fire, of air, of plants, of
> insects, of animals, of humans).
> Knowing this, a wise person should not cause
> any pain to any creatures. (I.7.1.5)

This last quotation points out one of the most remarkable features of the Jaina worldview. Jainism proclaims that life pervades nearly all aspects of reality. The term used for life in Sanskrit is *jiva,* derived from the verb root *jiv,* which means to live. Some scholars have chosen to translate this term as "soul." However, in Jainism, not only do human beings possess this life force or soul or spirit, not only do animals possess this *jiva,* not only do plants possess *jiva,* but this life force also pervades the basic constituents of physical reality. Jainism asserts that the earth, the water, fire, and the air itself consist of countless bodies, each suffused with *jiva.*

Furthermore, the Jaina worldview states that each *jiva,* in its pure state, consists of energy, consciousness, and bliss. However, due to the obscurations of karma, the true nature of life becomes obscured. The story of life becomes a saga of taking on and expelling countless varieties of karmas through a repeated process of birth, death, and rebirth, referred to as *samsara.* As long as the karmas continue to adhere to the life force, the soul remains in bondage.

To illustrate the nature of karma, a traditional story narrates how the personality types are associated with each of the primary five colors (*leshya*) of karma:

> A hungry person with the most negative black lesya karma uproots and kills an entire tree to obtain a few mangoes. The person of blue karma fells the tree by chopping the trunk, again merely to gain a handful of fruits. Fraught with gray karma, a third person spares the trunk but cuts off the major limbs of the tree. The one with orangish-red karma carelessly and needlessly lops off several branches to reach the mangoes. The fifth, exhibiting white or virtuous karma, "merely picks up ripe fruit that has dropped to the foot of the tree."[3]

The process of Jaina religiosity, for both laypersons and monks and nuns, involves adhering to a strict ethical code designed to lessen the grip of all karmas. This code includes five vows or *vratas* to be observed by all Jainas: non-violence (*ahimsa*), truthfulness (*satya*), not stealing (*asteya*), sexual restraint (*brahmacharya*), and non-possession (*aparigraha*). Some of the rules that were developed to support this code include vegetarianism, employment in life-friendly trades, sweeping the ground in front of one's feet, drinking only filtered water, and the wearing of masks over the mouth to protect insects.

Additionally, Jainism developed a rigorous tradition of fasting. During the course of abstention from food and water, a person renounces injury even to plants and water, thus preventing the accrual of any additional karmas. Late each summer, pious Jainas attempt a fast that can last up to seven days. Furthermore, in the Jaina tradition, the most honored death involves the voluntary rejection of food and eventually water in an attempt to invite and consciously move from one life form to the next embodiment. This fast unto death, referred to in India as *sallekhana* or *santhara*, according to Jaina tradition, expedites the diminishment of karma and, in a sense, polishes the soul as it prepares for transit.

Umasvati, a second-century Jaina thinker, systematized the theory of karma found in the *Acaranga Sutra* and other early Jaina texts. His *Tattvartha Sutra* provides both a physical and metaphysical rationale in support of the practice of non-violence out of respect for the integrity of life forms. According to this text, countless beings (*jiva*) inhabit the universe, constantly changing and taking new shape due to the fettering presence of karma, described as sticky and colorful. The presence of karma impedes the soul on its quest for perfect solitude and liberation. By first accepting this view of reality and then carefully abiding by the five major vows (non-violence, truthfulness, not stealing, sexual restraint, and non-possession), the aspirant moves toward the ultimate goal of untrammeled spirituality. At the pinnacle of this achievement, all karmas disperse and the perfected one (*siddha*) dwells eternally in omniscient (*sarvajna*) solitude (*kevala*).

This framework outlined by Umasvati grows to include the articulation of 148 distinct karmic configurations or *prakritis*, to be overcome through a successive progression through fourteen stages of spiritual ascent or *gunasthanas*.[4] Success in this process rests in the careful observance of *ahimsa*, through which one gradually dispels all karmas. Although it is said that no Jaina has achieved the highest state of *ayogi kevala* for several hundred years, thousands of Jaina monks and nuns in India practice a lifestyle that seeks to restrict and eliminate karma through the observance of monastic vows.

The goal of peeling back the layers of karma to reveal the core of one's life force inspired Haribhadra, an eighth-century Brahmin convert to Jainism, to describe the enlightened state as follows in his *Yogadrishtisamuccaya*:

> When the clouds of destructive karma
> are destroyed by the winds of Yoga,
> that is the escape.

> Then the glory of singular knowledge arises.
> With faults diminished, omniscient,
> endowed with fruits of all that can be accomplished,
> with things done now only for the sake of others,
> such a one attains the end of Yoga. (184–85)

The prime practice for purifying one's karma requires scrupulous observance of the five vows listed above, all of which require respect for and avoidance of injury to all life forms.

The Rite of Veneration, a standard practice observed by Jainas in the performance of temple worship, includes homage to all living beings and expiation of sin for any harm caused to living beings:

> For injury in the course of walking, in going and coming, in treading on living things, in treading on seeds, in treading on green plants, in treading on dew, insects, mold, mud, clay, spiders, and cobwebs, whatever living beings have been injured by me – one-sensed, two-sensed, three-sensed, four-sensed, five-sensed, have been hurt, knocked down, squashed, struck, collided with, oppressed, fatigued, frightened, displaced from one spot to another, deprived of life – for all those, may the wrong action be of no karmic consequence. For those, as an additional effort, as penance, as purification, in order to be without the thorns of sinful karmas, for the destruction of sinful karmas, I stand in the body-renouncing pose (*kayotsarga*).[5]

This ritual practice reinforces the Jaina commitment to avoid harm to life in all contexts throughout daily life.

Jainism and its advocacy of *ahimsa* continues to exert an influence on Indian culture today, and leaders of both Jainism and Hinduism actively engage in the animal rights and environmental movements. The Mughal ruler Akbar (r. 1556–1605) became deeply influenced by Jaina teachings on non-violence and declared certain regions of India sacred to Jainas as cruelty-free. Mahatma Gandhi (1869–1948) grew up in Gujarat, a region of India where many Jaina reside. Although born into a Hindu family, Gandhi was deeply influenced by the Jaina layman Raychandbhai Mehta, who advised Gandhi extensively on the practice of non-violence. Non-violence (*ahimsa*) and holding to truth (*satyagraha*), the cornerstones of Gandhi's resistance movement against British colonialism, come directly from the first two vows of the Jainas. In his ashram residence, he assiduously observed austerities and attributed his success to these practices.

The lay Jainas of India have long been associated with trade in materials that require a minimum of violence in manufacture and transport, such as quarried rock, gems, vegetable-based fabrics, and books. Jainas worldwide continue to support the small but important monastic communities, carefully observe vegetarianism, and monitor their business affairs with close attention to non-violent precepts.

Throughout world history, various movements have embraced values similar to those upheld by the Jainas. Within Asia, the upper-caste Hindus eventually adopted a vegetarian diet. Similar to Jainism, Buddhism puts forth non-injury to life as its first precept and many communities of Buddhist monks, particularly in China, traditionally practice vegetarianism. In medieval Europe, vegetarianism became part of many Christian movements, including the Paulicians, the Bogomils, the Patarenses, and the Cathars. Many modern Christian monastic orders observe vegetarianism, including the Trappists, the Camaldolese, and the Carthusians. Within American religious movements, the Church of the Latter Day Saints advises eating meat only sparingly and Seventh Day Adventists practice vegetarianism.[6]

In the twentieth century, two significant figures taught a philosophy of life that resonates with some of the basic principles of Jainism: Martin Buber and Albert Schweitzer. Buber (1878–1965), although best known for his Jewish existential humanism, also regarded animals as possessing a spiritual being or power. Buber scholar S.N. Eisenstadt has noted that for Buber, "Animals, especially domestic animals, are capable of regarding a man in a 'speaking' way; they turn to him as one to whom they wish to announce themselves."[7] This insight anticipates the current scientific research on animal ethology and cognition[8] and accords well with the Jaina perception that animals possess spirit, will, and emotion.

The great humanitarian, theologian, and physician Albert Schweitzer (1875–1965) promulgated teachings on reverence for life that included both animal advocacy and anti-nuclear activism. In his many writings, he urged humans to extend their network of concern to the animal realm:

> We feel that it is not right to be permanently preoccupied with our own well-being; the welfare of others and of human society in general must become part of our responsibility. The first step toward a development of this ethical principle is marked by an extension of this solidarity with our fellow creatures ... We must never permit the voice of humanity within us to be silenced. It is man's sympathy with all creatures that first makes him truly a man.[9]

In one passage reminiscent of the *Acaranga Sutra,* he wrote:

> The friend of nature is the man who feels himself inwardly united with everything that lives in nature, who shares in the fate of all creatures, helps them when he can in their pain and need, and as far as possible avoids injuring or taking life.[10]

In an essay entitled "The Ethics of Reverence for Life" he wrote:

> We are born of other lives ... We possess the capacities to bring still other lives into existence. So nature compels us to recognize the fact of mutual dependence, each life necessarily helping the other lives which are linked to it.[11]

This attitude toward life for Schweitzer extended even to insects, for whom he implicitly advocated protection:

> The poor fly which we would like to kill with our hands has come into existence like ourselves. It knows anxiety, it knows hope for happiness, it knows fear of not existing any more. Has any man so far been able to create a fly? That is why our neighbor is not only man: my neighbor is a creature like myself, subject to the same joys, the same fears, and the idea of Reverence for Life gives us something more profound and mightier than the idea of humanism. It includes *all living beings.*[12]

Although in his book *Indian Thought and its Development* (1935), Schweitzer was quite critical of various aspects of India's thought and culture, he clearly embraced an ethic of non-violence similar to that practiced by the Jainas, Buddhists, and Yogis.

LIFE FORCE (*PRANA*) IN YOGA

The Yoga tradition, as noted earlier, can probably trace its roots back to the Indus Valley civilization, whose artifacts include figurines and images of yogic poses. The Upanishads, the *Mahabharata,* and other texts dating from the first millennium BCE mention a variety of yogic practices.[13] The tradition becomes fully articulated in the *Yoga Sutras* of Patanjali, which probably date from the first or second century of the Common Era.[14] Patanjali's Yoga shares with Jainism several key features: purification through observance of the vows of non-violence, truthfulness, not stealing, sexual restraint, and non-possession; karma theory; and *kaivalyam*: isolation from karma. According to Patanjali, the practice of non-violence (*ahimsa*) results in the alleviation of ill will in one's presence. Patanjali urges the Yogi to practice non-violence in its broadest sense of the great vow (*mahavratam*), unrestricted by caste (*jati*), place (*desha*), time (*kala*) or circumstance (*samaya*), not unlike the manner urged by the Jainas. Beyond the strong ethical and philosophical emphasis found in the classical texts, in the medieval Yoga treatises such as the *Hatha Yoga Pradipika* and the *Gheranda Samhita*, we see an emphasis on physiology and the vitality of the breath.[15] For the purposes of exploring the yogic approach to "life force," we will now discuss the role of breath in the Yoga tradition.

The significance of breath can be traced to the term *atman*. Used extensively in the Upanishads to refer to one's highest self or soul or spirit, this term derives from the verb root *an*, to breathe. The *Chandogya Upanishad*, which possibly dates from approximately 800 BCE, tells the story of a contest between the various components of the body. One by one the faculties of speaking, seeing, hearing, thinking, and breathing contend that they are superior and that without the particular skill they possess the body would collapse. One by one, each withdraws: first the ability to speak, then sight, then hearing, then thinking withdraw, each for one year. In each instance, the body absorbs the jolt, but continues to live, though dumb, blind, deaf, and mindless in sequence for a year at a time. Finally, life breath or *prana* begins to pull away from the body. The body creaks and twitches and moans. The senses and the mind cry out to the breath, begging it to return. Supreme yet not arrogant, the breath returns, assuring continued life for all the other faculties (*Chandogya Upanishad*, V.I.1–15).

The significance of the breath as the energizing force of life can also be found in the cosmology of Samkhya, the root worldview outlined in the Upanishads and embraced by the Yoga system, the Puranas, and, in revised form, by both Buddhists and Jainas.[16] The Samkhya system lists out the various components of reality or *tattvas*, ranging from the base elements of earth, water, fire, air, and space; through the five senses and the mind; up through the ego and emotions and intellect to the highest self. In one important verse, Ishvarakrishna, the author of the *Samkhya Karika*, specifies that breath (*prana*) enlivens the operations of the life process from the senses and mind to the ego and intellect (*Samkhya Karika* 29).

Patanjali lists "expulsion and retention of breath" (I.34) as a means to overcome "sickness, dullness, doubt, carelessness, laziness, sense addiction, false view, nonattainment of a stage, and instability" (I.30). He also discusses three forms of controlling the breath, emphasizing the inbreath, the outbreath, and the retention of breath (II.49–50).

The *Hatha Yoga Pradipika* and *Gheranda Samhita,* which date from the late medieval period, list various means for achieving mastery of breath. The *Hatha Yoga Pradipika,* a text written probably in the fifteenth century by Svatmarama Svamin, states that "if the breath is disturbed, then the mind becomes disturbed. By restraining the breath, the Yogi gets steadiness of mind" (II.2). In addition to listing several specific breathing exercises such as alternate nostril breathing and rapid inhalation and exhalation, Svatmarama writes that when *pranayama* or control of breath is performed properly, it eradicates all diseases (II.16). The *Gheranda Samhita* lists even more complicated breathing exercises, and says that mastery of breath makes one like a god (V.1), awakens the *shakti* (spiritual energy), calms the mind, causes bliss, and brings happiness (V.56).

Breath plays a vital role in the yogic tradition. It is associated with consciousness and activity; without the breath, neither *purusha* nor *prakriti* could survive. In addition to being the vehicle for life and the senses, breath is also the pathway for purification. The performance of yogic breathing exercises or *pranayama* brings one into direct connection with life force.

CONCLUSION: LIFE BREATH AND THE WORLD

Life as breath as respiration as spirit leads us into a recognition of the interconnectedness between the breath within our body, the air outside our body, and the very definition of life itself. Several years ago, NASA hired James Lovelock, a biochemist, to develop a system through which scientists could determine whether life exists on other planets. To do so, Lovelock began with the obvious: how might, from afar, life be detected on our own planet, on Earth? He discovered that the atmosphere of Earth differs radically from the atmosphere of nearby planets, and that these planets cannot support life as we know it. He then began to investigate the origins of our particular atmosphere and confirmed some earlier hypotheses: millions of years ago, bacteria on Earth ate and digested rocks. They removed carbon dioxide (which exists in abundance in other planetary atmospheres) from the atmosphere, produced limestone, and released nitrogen and oxygen into the air, allowing new life forms to develop by feeding off this new mixture. He writes:

> The air we breathe, the oceans and the rocks are all either direct products of living organisms [think of the chalk cliffs of Dover, just one gigantic pile of shells] or else they have been greatly modified by their presence, and this even includes the igneous rocks coming from volcanoes. Indeed organisms are not just adapting to a dead world determined by physics and chemistry textbooks alone, they live with a world that is the breath and the bones and the blood of their ancestors and they themselves are now sustaining.[17]

The simple process of respiration, lauded in the Upanishads and minutely studied and controlled by the Yogis, in fact demonstrates the interconnectedness of life itself. Each particular manifestation of earth reality, including the rocks, the water, warmth, and the air itself, relies upon the dynamic, vital process of inhalation and exhalation. Each particularity, in this vision, shares a common process. Livingness pervades all things, as the Jainas have suggested. Furthermore, we can all be assured that after the particularity of this specific life form expires, the process itself will continue.

What are the practical consequences of a worldview that emphasizes such an expansive relationship between life forms? For the Jainas, it entailed the development of a scrupulous non-violent ethic. The teleology of Jainism involves the ascent to a state of spiritual perfection. This ascent of the life force takes place through the observance of vows designed to lessen one's karmic accretions. This process of gradual purification considers all forms of life, even the elements themselves, to be sacred. Jaina and yogic observances mandate lifestyle and occupation choices that minimize violence to living beings. Such a stark commitment to a non-violent ethic influenced the political thinking and action of Mahatma Gandhi, Martin Luther King, Jr., and, more recently, Nelson Mandela. For the Jainas, the Yogis, and these modern activists, the meaning of life lies in valuing life forms in their particularity. The valuing of life results in altering behavior, through self-effort, working at self-purification. This purification ideally results in a lessening of violence and an openness to the needs and realities of other life forms, a sense of respect for the lives of all beings.

At this particular phase of world history, the juxtaposition of Jaina ritual concern for not harming spiders and the contemporary ecologist's concern about ecosystems out of balance make for interesting contrast and comparison. On the one hand, the Jaina might be criticized for being overly concerned, not with the welfare of others, but with the status of his or her own soul. In the same vein, the environmentalist might be criticized for ignoring pressing human economic issues. But the intimacy of the practicing Jaina with minute life forms and the distance or "big picture" view of the contemporary environmentalist intersect in a very interesting way. To the extent that we can care for our immediate self and its surroundings, life can be protected. To the extent that we can be aware of and sensitive to the impact of our collective lives on the greater biosphere, a lifestyle can emerge that will help heal the damage done by chemical pollutants to the earth, water, and air. A temple ritual need not be seen as irrelevant to adherence to automobile emissions standards. Both of these recognize the delicacy of the life forms upon which our world is built. In the case of Jainism, the philosophy of non-violence helped develop rituals to remind and encourage its adherents not to kill. This ritual attitude has led to broader orthopraxy that governs the mores and taboos of Jaina culture. Similarly, Schweitzer's reverence for life and Martin Luther King, Jr.'s commitment to non-violence led to social movements that have changed the course of modern history. Today, scientists have notified the world that the human environment has been imperiled by human waste and careless consumption. Entire species have been obliterated; forests have been cut; waters have been fouled. Further destruction will take place which in several generations might spell disaster for our planet unless a philosophy takes hold that encourages a lifestyle respectful of life.

Non-violent respect for life leading to lifestyle changes might be the key to human survival. Mahavira advised his nuns and monks to "change their minds" about things; rather than seeing big trees as "fit for palaces, gates, houses, benches . . ., boats, buckets, stools, trays, ploughs, machines, wheels, seats, beds, cars, and sheds," they should speak of the trees as "noble, high and round, with many branches, beautiful and magnificent" (*Acaranga Sutra* II.4.2.11–12). In other words, Mahavira advised his followers to see natural resources not in terms of their ability to enhance human comfort but to respect them for their own majesty and beauty. These same words might be used today to encourage people to change the way they see the world. Rather than seeing the world as an object for human exploitation, the non-violent vision encourages humans to acknowledge the pervasive and sacred nature of life in all its myriad forms.

NOTES

1. Adelheid Mette, "The Synchronism of the Buddha and the Jina Mahāvīra and the Problem of Chronology in Early Jainism," in *When Did the Buddha Live? The Controversy of the Dating of the Historical Buddha*, ed. Heinz Bechert (Delhi: Sri Satguru Publications, 1995), p. 183.
2. See Hermann Jacobi, trans., *Jaina Sutras Translated from Prakrit: Part I: The Akārānga Sūtra, The Kalpa Sūtra* (Oxford: Clarendon Press, 1884).
3. Jagmanderlal Jaini, *The Outlines of Jainism* (Cambridge: Cambridge University Press, 1916), p. 47.
4. Nathmal Tatia, trans., *That Which Is: The Tattvārtha Sūtra of Umasvati* (San Francisco: HarperCollins, 1994), pp. 279–285.
5. John Cort, "The Rite of Veneration of Jina Images," in *Religions of India in Practice*, ed. Donald S. Lopez, Jr. (Princeton: Princeton University Press, 1995), p. 328.
6. See Christopher Key Chapple, *Nonviolence to Animals, Earth, and Self in Asian Traditions* (Albany: State University of New York Press, 1993), pp. 112–115.
7. S.N. Eisenstadt, ed., *Martin Buber: on Intersubjectivity and Cultural Creativity* (Chicago: University of Chicago Press, 1992), p. 86.
8. Christopher Key Chapple, "Animals and Environment in the Buddhist Birth Stories," in *Buddhism and Ecology: The Interconnectedness of Dharma and Deeds*, ed. Mary Evelyn Tucker and Duncan Ryuken Williams (Cambridge, Mass.: Harvard University Center for the Study of World Religions, 1997), p. 132.
9. Albert Schweitzer, *Reverence for Life: The Words of Albert Schweitzer*, comp. Harold E. Robles (San Francisco: Harper San Francisco, 1993), pp. 141, 143.
10. Ibid., p. 27.
11. Ibid., p. 30.
12. Ibid., p. 31.
13. See Robert Ernest Hume, trans., *The Thirteen Principal Upanishads* (Delhi: Oxford University Press, 1931).
14. See Christopher Key Chapple and Yogi Ananda Viraj (Eugene P. Kelly, Jr.), trans., *The Yoga Sutras of Patanjali* (Delhi: Sri Satsang Publications, 1990).
15. See Rai Bahadur Srisa Chandra Vasu, trans., *The Gheranda Samhita* (Delhi: Sri Satguru Publications, 1979) and Pancham Sinh, trans., *The Hatha Yoga Pradipika* (New Delhi: Oriental Books, 1980).
16. See Gerald J. Larson, *Classical Sāṃkhya* (Delhi: Motilal Banarsidass, 1979).
17. James Lovelock, "The Gaia Hypothesis," in *Gaia, the Thesis, the Mechanism, and the Implications*, ed. Peter Bunyard and Edward Goldsmith (Cornwall: Wadebridge Ecological Centre, 1988), p. 38.

Plate 6 Sculpture of the feet of the Buddha, a traditional way to illustrate the notion of impermanence, on a lotus pedestal at the entrance to a temple for the Bodhisattva Jizo dedicated to commemorating the death of infants, Toyama, Japan. Photo: *Nancy M. Martin and Joseph Runzo*

8

THE MEANING *of* LIFE *in* BUDDHISM[†]

Masao Abe

Buddhism does not understand human existence as a form of life that has death as its inevitable end. Rather, human existence is a continuous living-and-dying. The understanding of human existence that sees life as having death as its inevitable end presumes that life is lived only in opposition to dying and seeks the conquest of death – immortality, or eternal life. Here, death is always seen as something alien to life, something to be overcome. In contrast to this, the understanding of human existence as a continuous living-and-dying does not view life and death as objects in mutual opposition but as two aspects of an indivisible reality. Present life is understood as something that undergoes continuous living-and-dying. Therefore, Buddhism, which is based on this realization, seeks liberation from living–dying (*shoji*) rather than the mere conquest of death alone. Buddhism's aim is not immortality and eternal life through a resurrection that conquers death, but the unborn and the undying (*fusho–fumetsu*) state of nirvana realized directly in and through living–dying by liberation from living–dying itself. Herein lies the fundamental standpoint of Buddhism.

Understanding human existence as something consciously aware of inevitable death implies much about the beginning and the end of human existence. Understood thus, human existence is grasped as something

[†] This chapter is largely based on Masao Abe's previously published works *Zen and Western Thought,* ed. William R. LaFleur (Honolulu: University of Hawaii Press, 1985) and *A Study of Dôgen: His Philosophy and His Religion,* ed. Steven Heine (Albany: State University of New York Press, 1992). The author is greatly appreciative to James Fredericks for careful revision at the last stage of preparation.

uniquely human and distinct from the existence of other animals. The fact that a human is something that must die suggests that there is a definitive beginning and end of human existence. In contrast to this view, the understanding of human existence as something that continuously undergoes living–dying does not recognize any special significance to the beginning and end of human existence. By interpreting human existence in terms of living–dying, or as something that undergoes arising–ceasing (*shometsu suru mono*), Buddhism does not necessarily view human beings as distinct from other animals. Rather, it sees humans as part of the radical impermanence of all and undergoing the vicissitudes of arising–ceasing which is a dimension of life for all "sentient beings" (*shujo*). Thus, human existence needs to be grasped in the dimension transcending the limits of "human" reason.

Buddhism talks about the vicissitudes of birth-and-death in terms of *samsara* and transmigration through the six realms: hell, hungry ghosts, animals, fighting spirits, humans, and gods. Buddhism also recognizes that karma, the root of transmigration for all sentient beings, not merely humans, penetrates the six realms of the "triple world." Therefore, Buddhism transcends humanism and anthropocentrism; it can be referred to as being "beyond humanism." Buddhism, which understands human existence as a form of life that undergoes continuous living–dying rather than merely as life facing inevitable death, sees human beings as sentient beings originally transcending anthropocentrism. And it also discloses the way to a fundamental emancipation of human existence based upon this transcendent dimension. The standpoint of what is called the "Dharma" (*ho*) in Buddhism is grounded on this "way."

Accordingly, in Buddhism life and death or birth and death are not understood to be two different entities. They are inseparably interconnected. This is why Dogen, the thirteenth-century Japanese Zen master, emphasizes that "it is a mistake to think that you pass from birth to death."

In such an understanding of birth and death, a person who "understands" in this mistaken way not only sees death as an object over there while standing within life, but also, by interpreting the relation of birth and death in terms of "passing away," looks upon death and the present life of the self from a standpoint removed from both. The person who understands in this way grasps the relation of living–dying while standing outside it and thereby lapses into a standpoint that is the opposite of the existential reality of the self's continuous living–dying. In this case, anxiety about death is not addressed experientially; and the meaning and reality of life is never investigated truly. One should not regard the relation of living–dying objectively *from outside.* This relation needs to be awakened *from within.* In this manner, the living–dying relation is not seen as a sequential change from the former to the latter. Rather, we are living–dying at each and every moment. This does not mean, however, that we are 50 percent living and 50 percent dying. Not so! Rather we are 100 percent living and 100 percent dying at each and every moment. We are undergoing "living–dying" in each and every moment. The understanding of human existence as something constantly undergoing "living–dying" is the fundamental standpoint of Buddhism.

The Buddhist view can be clarified by contrasting it with Christianity, which sees human existence not as "something that undergoes living–dying" but as "something that must die." In the Christian interpretation of human existence as something that must die at some particular time, terminating life, dying and the conquest of death are regarded as a serious issue for which the contrast between life and death is presupposed. At least, in Christianity, the ultimate root of human life as part of creation is clear. Our human lives originate and develop by virtue of a Creator-God who dwells eternally. But even in Christianity, life is never simply presupposed. Christianity teaches that since Adam, the primordial person, committed the sin of disobeying the command of God, the human being, in punishment for this sin, became something that must die. Life's original connection to the Creator was cut off. In Christianity, the human attempt to establish themselves as separate from God and therefore as autonomous beings is regarded as sin in defiance of God. For this reason, humans, while originally deriving from the eternal life of God, become something that must die. Thus humans are seen in Christianity as something that must die, not simply as a matter of natural necessity but as a consequence of sin.

As the Genesis story shows, Christianity assigns to human beings the task of ruling over all other creatures and reserves for humans alone the *imago dei* through which they, unlike other creatures, can directly respond to the word of God. Human death is understood as the "wages of sin," the result of one's own free acts, that is, rebellion against the word of God. Here, one can see Christianity's homocentrism. Accordingly, Christianity makes a clear distinction between humans and other creatures regarding their nature and salvation, with the former having priority over the latter. This homocentric standpoint is intimately related to Christianity's personalism in which God is believed to disclose himself as personality and in which a dialogical I–Thou relation between human and the divine is essential.

Does Buddhism establish any distinction between humans and other creatures? In Buddhism, do humans have any special significance among creatures? To answer these questions one must first get beyond the limitations of the homocentric perspective and realize that human birth–death is an essential part of a wider problem, that is, the generation–extinction problem common to all living beings. This transcendence of the human perspective is impossible apart from the "self-consciousness" of human beings. Animals, *asura*, and so on, like human beings, are all undergoing transmigration, equally confined within the realm of generation–extinction. Unlike human existence, however, other living beings cannot know transmigration as transmigration. Since only a human, who has self-consciousness, can realize the nature of generation–extinction as such, for a human this becomes a "problem" to be solved rather than a "fact." When a "fact" becomes a "problem," the possibility of solving the problem is also present, that is, the possibility of being liberated from transmigration. Because of this characteristic peculiar to humans, Buddhism emphasizes the need for us to practice Buddhist discipline and attain enlightenment while each of us, though transmigrating endlessly through other forms of life, exists as a *human*. "The rare state of a human" is, in Buddhism, highly regarded; one should be grateful one is born human, for it is more difficult to be born a human being than for a blind turtle to enter a hole in a log floating in an ocean. Unlike other creatures, a human is a "thinking animal," endowed with the capability of awakening to the Dharma. Here one can see the Buddhist notion of the human being's special position among all living beings.

It should be clear that while both Christianity and Buddhism are concerned primarily with the salvation of human existence, the *ground* of salvation recognized by each of these religions differs: in Christianity it is personalistic, whereas in Buddhism it is cosmological. In the former, the personal relationship between a human being and God is axial, with the universe as its circumference; in the latter, personal suffering and salvation reside in the impersonal, boundless, cosmological dimension that encompasses even the divine–human relationship.

How then does the truly subjective and existential realization of living–dying as the original experience of "moment-to-moment living–dying" take place? The first thing is to realize that life, which is itself living–dying, is none other than nothingness. Or to put it another way, life which is itself living–dying is none other than death in essence. In the mode of attachment described above, life that is itself living–dying is grasped as being. But when living–dying is realized in terms of the original moment-to-moment living and dying, there cannot be substantialization or objectification. That is because moment-to-moment living and dying is the living and dying directly realized right here and now in subjectivity. Therefore, our living–dying is "nothingness" in that it cannot be substantialized by any means. Further, this is the nothingness of subjectivity itself realized at the root of the subject in that it is non-objectifiable by any means – that is, it is death. In the realization of moment-to-moment living–dying, our life that undergoes living–dying is indeed realized as death.

This is the realization of the "Great Death" rather than a simplistic view of death. In thoroughly realizing the death of life, that is itself our living–dying in the realization of the Great Death, the root of the living–dying of the self is attained. To undergo the Great Death is to die a death in the authentic sense by realizing that the root of living–dying is none other than death in its authentic sense. But to undergo death by realizing the root of living–dying as death is none other than to be liberated from living–dying in the root and precisely thereby to live life in its authentic sense. Therefore, in the realization of the Great Death, when we thoroughly die the death of life that is itself living–dying, the realization of *life* that is itself no-life-and-death is manifested. The realization of life that is itself no-life-and-death, that is, the realization of nirvana, is inseparable from the realization of the Great Death. Indeed, it is precisely the realization of the Great Death itself. This is the principle that living–dying itself is nirvana.

The second implication contained in a truly existential realization of living–dying moment-to-moment is the insight that life is life and death is death. In the existential realization of moment-to-moment living–dying, the oneness of living–dying never means that life and death are seen in an immediate identity. When life is lived as living–dying in the primordial, nonsubstantial nothingness, one realizes that life is bottomlessly life and death is bottomlessly death. Life does not change into death, and death does not take away life. That is why Dogen writes that "life does not obstruct death, and death does not obstruct life." In the existential transcendence of living–dying, we realize that in the present moment that life is absolute and at the same time death is absolute. Of course, although life is absolute, this does not mean that life should be interpreted only as a substantive being. Rather, to realize life as absolute is to be existentially emancipated from life itself in that very realization, which understand that life is not life. The same applies to death. That is why Dogen writes:

> Being a situation of [timeless-] time (*hitotoki no kurai*), birth is already possessed of before and after. For this reason, in the Buddha Dharma it is said that birth itself is no-birth. Being a situation of [timeless-] time as well, cessation of life also is possessed of before and after. Thus it is said, extinction itself is non-extinction. When one speaks of birth, there is nothing at all apart from birth. When one speaks of death, there is nothing at all apart from death.

Mahayana Buddhists take *samsara* (endless transmigration of living and dying) in itself as "Death" in its authentic sense. Death in its authentic sense is not death as distinguished from life, just as the real Nothingness is not the nothingness as distinguished from somethingness. If we grasp the process of transmigration, not from the outside (objectively), but from within (subjectively or existentially), then we are always living and yet always dying at every moment. Without living, there is no dying; without dying, there is no living. Living and dying are non-dualistically one in our existential realization. Since living and dying are two opposing principles, this antinomic oneness of living and dying itself is the greatest suffering: Death. In this existential realization, the endless transmigration of living–dying as such is realized as the Great Death.

This implies that the process of transmigration, insofar as it can be said to be a continuity, must be grasped as a continuity of endless living–dying in which every moment of living from the past toward the future is radically severed by dying both from what went before and what comes after. It is a dynamic continuity which is marked by discontinuity at each point. Since this dynamic "continuity of discontinuity" of the process of living-dying is endless, it is realized as the Great Death. However, with this realization of the Great Death as a turning-point, the endless process of living–dying is re-grasped in an entirely new light. It is no longer a negative "continuity of *discontinuity*" (*samsara*), but a rather positive "*continuity* of discontinuity" (nirvana). This "turning over" takes place through the radical reversion at the depth of our existential realization. Through the realization of the Great Death, the realization of the Great Life opens up.

The view that "this present birth and death itself is the life of Buddha" represents the realization of the "unborn" (*fusho*) in Dogen. Therefore, it is mistaken both to detest birth-and-death as something separate from nirvana and to seek nirvana as something different from birth-and-death. Since, as Dogen writes, birth-and-death is the "practice of the Buddha Way" or the "place of the Buddha Dharma," "to think that birth-and-death is something to be eliminated is a sin of hating the Buddha Dharma." At the same time, if one clings to nirvana while seeking nirvana, that is not genuine nirvana. Genuine nirvana is realized in entering into nirvana yet not abiding in nirvana; being liberated from birth and death, yet playing in the garden of birth-and-death. That is also genuine birth-and-death. Thus Dogen can say, "Just understand that birth-and-death itself is nirvana" and "The coming and going of birth-and-death is the true Person." It is also the principle of birth-and-death in the true sense. Dogen writes, "Although the birth-and-death is the vicissitudes of the average person, it is the liberated place of the great sage." This explains why "the coming and going of birth-and-death is the true Person." That is, we may vacillate lost in the delusion of everyday living–dying, but if we penetrate the principle of living–dying, abandoning all illusory views, there is a detachment from living–dying while undergoing living–dying.

As the above discussion implies, the realization of Great Death has a double connotation: negative and positive. On one hand, the Great Death is negative in that it entails the antinomic oneness of living and dying as the greatest suffering – the most serious existential problem which must be solved to attain emancipation. On the other hand, the Great Death is positive in that it entails the resolution of the problems of suffering and the realization of the Great Life. This double connotation and the accompanying shift from the negative to the positive connotation are possible because the Great Death is a total, holistic, and existential realization of the endlessness of living–dying in which one becomes identical with the Great Death and thereby overcomes the endlessness of living–dying. Once we come to this existential realization, we can say with justification that *samsara* and nirvana are identical. Thus the realization of the Great Death is the crucial point for the seemingly paradoxical

Mahayana doctrines. This is simply another expression for the above statement that the realization of absolute Nothingness is indispensable for attaining the Mahayana notion of Emptiness which is no other than Fullness.

Ethically speaking, Buddhists clearly realize that good should conquer evil. However, through the experience of their inner struggle, Buddhists cannot say that good is strong enough to overcome evil. Good and evil are completely antagonistic principles, resisting each other with equal force, yet inseparably connected and displaying an existential antinomy as a whole. However imperative it may be from the ethical point of view, it is, according to Buddhism, illusory to believe it is possible to overcome evil with good and thereby to attain the highest good. Since good and evil are mutually negating principles with equal power, an ethical effort to overcome evil with good never succeeds and results in a serious dilemma. Realizing this existential dilemma innate in human existence and characterizing it in terms of original sin, Christians have propounded the necessity of faith in God who delivers humans from sin through redemptive activity. From a Christian perspective, God is Good with a capital "G," as can be noted in the biblical statement "no one is good, but God alone" (Mark 10:18; Luke 18:19). Since the law is the expression of God's will, obedience and disobedience to the law constitute human good and evil. Moreover, it is emphasized, "Do not be overcome by evil, but overcome evil with good" (Romans 12:21).

In Buddhism, on the contrary, what is essential for salvation is not to overcome evil with good and to participate in the supreme Good, but to be emancipated from the existential antinomy of good and evil and to awaken to Emptiness prior to the opposition between good and evil. In the existential awakening to Emptiness, one can be master of, rather then enslaved by, good and evil. In this sense, the realization of true Emptiness is the basis for human freedom, creative activity, and ethical life.

Thus, the following two aspects of Buddhist salvation must be noted: (1) Buddhism is primarily concerned with salvation of a human being as a person who, unlike other living beings, has self-consciousness and free will and thereby alone has the potential to become aware of and emancipated from the transience common to all things in the universe. This is the existentialistic and personalistic aspect of Buddhism. However, (2) a cosmological dimension is the necessary basis for this Buddhist salvation, because in Buddhism salvation is not from sin as rebellion against God, but emancipation from the cycle of birth and death which is part of the transience of the universe. This is the cosmological aspect of Buddhism. These two aspects are inseparable – the more cosmological the basis of salvation, the more existentially thoroughgoing the salvation. In this sense, the Buddhist cosmology that is the basis of nirvana is an existential cosmology, and Buddhist existentialism or personalism may be called "cosmo-existentialism" or "cosmo-personalism."

Mahayana Buddhism has always emphasized "Do not abide in nirvana" as well as "Do not abide in *samsara*." If one abides in so-called nirvana by transcending *samsara*, it must be said that one is not yet free from attachment to nirvana, and is confined by the duality of nirvana and *samsara*. It must also be said that one is still selfishly concerned with one's own salvation, forgetting the suffering of others in *samsara*. On the basis of the idea of the Bodhisattva, Mahayana Buddhism thus criticizes and rejects nirvana as the transcendence of *samsara* and teaches true nirvana to be the returning to *samsara* by negating or transcending "nirvana as the transcendence of *samsara*." Therefore, nirvana in the Mahayana sense, while transcending *samsara*, is nothing but the realization of *samsara* as *samsara* – no more, no less – through the complete returning to *samsara* itself. This is why, in Mahayana Buddhism, it is often said of true nirvana that "*samsara*-as-it-is is nirvana." This paradoxical statement is again based on the dialectical character of true nirvana which is, logically speaking, the negation of negation (that is, absolute affirmation) or the transcendence of transcendence (that is, absolute immanence). True nirvana is, according to Mahayana Buddhism, the real source of both *prajna* (wisdom) and *karuna* (compassion). It is the source of *prajna* because it is entirely free from the discriminating mind and thus is able to see everything in its uniqueness and distinctiveness without any sense of attachment. It is the source of *karuna* because it is unselfishly concerned with the salvation of all others in *samsara* through one's own returning to *samsara*.

For the sake of wisdom, do not abide in *samsara*; for the sake of compassion do not abide in nirvana. This is the meaning of life in Buddhism.

Plate 7 The ideals of the Confucian sage and the Buddhist Bodhisattva merge in this figure found at the Tzuen Temple complex in Xian, China, originally built in the seventh century CE. Photo: *Nancy M. Martin*

9

CONFUCIANISM: HOW TO SERVE THE SPIRITS *and the* GODS

John Berthrong

When we consider the broad sweep of the history of Chinese religion, there are all kinds of answers to the question of the meaning of life provided by the various cumulative spiritual and philosophic traditions. Many of these answers have close analogs with other great world religions, such as Taoist self-cultivation and Buddhist meditation practice. There are concurrently plenty of spirits and gods to give advice, provide admonitions, and demand worship. The higher speculative regions of Taoism and Buddhism generate sophisticated regimens of mystical teachings that reform the adept on the road to union with the Tao. These mystical paths guide the student to a profound encounter with the Tao or even nirvana. In the Taoist tradition there have been great chiliastic reform movements and revolutions that promised to bring high heaven down to the world, often at the cost of great suffering caused by intense civil unrest. All of these varieties of Chinese religion provide definitions of meaning and practice for the lives of their followers.

The great family of Chinese religion has many streams – folk or popular religion, Confucianism, Taoism, and Buddhism. Like a great river, it has carved out new channels over time; old beds have sometimes become dry. Nonetheless all Chinese religious and philosophic thought is derived from a pan-Chinese religious and cultural sensibility that is distinctive. No one would mistake Confucius for Jeremiah, the Buddha, Plato, or Shankara. Here the image of a prototype metaphor is apt. It is impossible to give a perfect definition of Confucianism, but we can recognize its distinctive style especially when we compare and contrast it with Judaism, Christianity, Islam, Buddhism, and Hinduism. Moreover, rather like the written Chinese language, it has been a remarkable stable human project, albeit protean, over thousands of years. In fact, the consistent use of graphs from their archaic Hsia and Shang origins to the present has allowed for uniformity of conceptual imagination unique among the great religious traditions of the world. Alphabets may be easier to learn, but they fracture the historical continuity of language over time, whereas Chinese characters assume different pronunciations but are still intelligible to any educated person regardless of phonetic transformation.

For instance, in general cultural terms, the role of the family has always remained a key metaphor for Chinese religious life. But even the meaning of family is more protean than it might appear at first glance. The genealogical mode suggests not a fixed or given nature but rather a complex inheritance that is ramified from generation to generation in the act of creation. Following the work of David Hall and Roger Ames,[1] this is a focus (the person) within a field of potential (the extended family) and is not an organic model such as we find in Aristotle where final causes tend to dominate the metaphor. The phrase *tzu-jan* (spontaneity), although identified with the Taoist tradition, works just as well in the Confucian context in pointing out that things become what they are out of a complex of influences and inheritances and not as some preordained outcome or artifact fashioned by a unique creator.

Even Buddhism, in its transformed Chinese guise, made use of family metaphors to describe the work of the monastic communities, such as the image of the abbot as the father of all his students. Furthermore, more specific relational concepts such as yin and yang pervade the thought patterns of every Chinese religion. For comparative purposes, scholars suggest that Chinese religion in its folk or non-elite form shows remarkable regional and temporal variations and persistence. This is the world of the family and village, of the spirits of ancestors, and gods of the rivers and mountains. Contemporary Communist administrators worry just as much about these folk traditions as did their Confucian ancestors. Resting on this common folk heritage are the great elite traditions of Taoism, Confucianism, and Buddhism.

The elite traditions have always called the folk tradition gross superstition, but this need not blind anyone to the massive continuity between the basic forms of Chinese religious life and its elite manifestations. In terms of intellectual orientations, scholars such as Marcel Granet, A.C. Graham, Joseph Needham, David Hall and Roger Ames, have called this pan-Chinese form of thinking "correlative cosmology." These astute students of Chinese thought contrast the Chinese proclivity for metaphorical, analogical, and correlative thinking with what Graham called Western causal, logical, and propositional styles of thinking. Such second-order Western causal thinking often includes an understanding of the cosmos as a single-ordered world with a priority of rest or substance over movement or process. It is a world that can be defined in terms of first principles and the rules of logical thinking. It is an intellectual world that loves analysis, logic, and the dialectical definition of clear and distinct ideas.

The Chinese fundamental intellectual sensibility moves in different directions. It is a form of correlative or analogical thinking that involves "the correlation of significances into clustered images which, though they could by no means yield univocal definitions, could nonetheless be treated as meaning complexes ultimately unanalysable into any more basic components."[2] Marcel Granet went as far as to suggest that Chinese thought could be understood as an extended analogical system based on metaphor/metonym.[3] As the recent work of George Lakoff and Mark Johnson in linguistics, cognitive science, and philosophy has shown, there is nothing necessarily sloppy, vague, or mystical about correlative thinking based on metaphor. In fact, Lakoff and Johnson argue, based on modern linguistics and cognitive science, that good metaphorical, correlative thinking is the basis for second-order analytical thinking.[4]

The reason for setting up such a sharp contrast between Western causal and Chinese correlative thinking is to indicate that the way the Confucian tradition defines the meaning of life is not always parallel to the Western desire for providing a set of definitions of the good life or human flourishing. The Confucians use narrative and what Lakoff and Johnson call metaphorical prototype thinking. We learn the meaning of life by looking at prototypes of superlative behavior. We seek to model ourselves on the sages of a process of self-cultivation. Are there strict definitions of such ethical standards for the meaning of life? There assuredly are such definitions, but the Confucians, in contradistinction to the Mohist logical tradition that did believe strongly in accurate logic and paying attention to correct definitions, were vigilant in reminding their students that definitions as mere verbal propositions are not enough to establish human flourishing. A model or exemplary person provokes a better metaphor for life that actually guides our conduct and the formation of character than any formal definition of meaning and character. The narrative structure of this kind of analogical patterning is presented in detailed genealogical constructs that rest upon the metaphor of the family. While it is true that families have stability, they do change, grow, diminish – they are alive and almost never at rest.

However, the Confucian tradition in China and the rest of East Asia has always presented a problem to Western historians of religion. Confucianism never quite seems to fit in with the other religions, and in fact many serious scholars have questioned whether or not Confucianism is really a religion at all if the model of religion is based on the great traditions of West Asia such as Judaism, Christianity, and Islam. Often it is asserted that, at best, the Confucian tradition is agnostic in its worldview. Confucianism, in terms of Western intellectual taxonomies, is viewed as a social ethics or political ideology. The *locus classicus* for this agnostic reading of the Confucian Way is found in *Analects* 11.12: "Zilu asked how to serve the spirits and gods. The Master said: 'You are not yet able to serve men, how can you serve the spirits?' Zilu said: 'May I ask about death?' The Master said: 'You do not yet know life, how could you know death?'"[5] Generations of historians of religion have been perplexed by this statement, which implies an unwillingness of the Master to talk about things normally considered within the purview of religion such as divine beings and the ultimate destiny of human life. But surface readings are deceptive. What Confucius urged on his students was not the necessity for speculation about spirits and gods but rather that the proper duty of humanity was to cultivate the person so that a society permeated by humaneness could flourish. Real meaning for human life comes on the road as a metaphor for the Tao in service to humaneness and civility rather than in reflection on some hypothetical afterlife or divine spirit. Only with proper self-cultivation can we talk about the meaning of life.

This reticence on the part of Confucius and many later Confucian teachers to talk about the spirits, gods, and afterlife actually opens the gate for the distinctive sensibilities of Confucian spirituality. Rather than ignore this hard saying, it is better to explore just what it meant within the vast mansion of the Confucian Way. It is important to note that Confucius does not deny that the spirits and gods exist or are important in their proper place; he merely insists that thinking about them in a wrong order for proper human self-cultivation is a terribly misguided way to become a human being. Clearly there is nothing like a full-blown monotheism at work here, nor any kind of Western ecclesiastic structure save for the most elevated imperial cult; however, there is a distinctive Confucian sense of spiritual transformation although what is transcended and the destination of the effort are radically different from the West Asian monotheisms. For instance, there is no central focus on divinity and hence the need to transcend mundane reality to become one with or obey the supreme will of God. Nor is this a tradition with a carefully crafted meditation system, such as we find in early Buddhism, designed to escape the toils of this world and to overcome human emotion. As Herbert Fingarette so perceptively noted, the secular is the sacred for the Confucians.[6]

One of the real tasks of comparative religion and philosophy is to allow for a tradition to speak for itself, to unfold its own taxonomies of structure and metaphors of meaning. What is precisely not surprising is that the Confucian tradition does not resemble the linked religions of West Asia. Why in the world should it? It would have been surprising if Confucianism had mapped onto the common taxonomies of Judaism, Christianity, or Islam.

Nonetheless, scholars are gradually accepting the argument that there is a distinctive Confucian spirituality or religious dimension that has informed the growth of the entire tradition across East Asia. The language of dimension needs to be stressed. Clearly, there are many elements of the Confucian tradition that are not overtly spiritual or religious. Confucians are interested in history, linguistics, civil engineering, mathematics, medicine, poetry, military theory, and social ethics, just to mention some perennial Confucian concerns. On the other hand, with a cross-culturally sensitive appreciation of the religious variability of humanity, it is impossible to read the classical tradition after Confucius without sensing its religious dimension. The second sage of the tradition, Mencius, is famous for his careful delineation of humanity and the cultivation of human excellence. Slightly later Chou dynasty texts such as the *Doctrine of the Mean,* especially as interpreted in the neo-Confucian period from the eleventh century on, provided the spiritual capstone for any worthy Confucian life.

In this constellation of Confucian spiritual witnesses, Hsun Tzu (fl. 310–213 BCE) has always been an anomaly.[7] He had the audacity to suggest that Mencius, the beloved second sage after Confucius, was wrong about the goodness of human nature. If Hsun Tzu is remembered for anything, it is for his doctrine that human nature is evil and for being the great secularizer of classical Confucianism. The standard account is, if there was any vestigial Confucian religious piety before Heaven and the spirits, that Hsun Tzu debunked the earlier forms of Confucian piety and replaced them with a rationalistic natural account of the way of the world and the heavens. Of course, there are reasons for the durability of this image of the third sage. Hsun Tzu said things like "One who is adept at study exhausts the principles of rational order. One who is adept at putting things into practice examines problems."[8]

Yet there is another side to Hsun Tzu that was probably more important to him than his rigorous commitment to critical thinking. This is the Hsun Tzu who defined the sage in most spiritual terms and who characterized the development of the sage in terms of the truthfulness of self-realization. In fact, it is in the notion of *ch'eng* as sincerity, truthfulness, and self-realization that the distinctive prototype of Confucian religiously shines forth. Critical reason was important to Hsun Tzu, but no more so than when it helped the student of the Confucian Way make progress toward becoming a sage. Here is his definition of a sage as put in the mouth of Confucius as he responds to a question from Duke Ai.

> Those who are called great sages are persons who have an awareness that extends to the Great Way, who are limitlessly responsive to every transformation, and who discriminate between the essential and the inborn natures of each of the myriad things. The Great Way is what is employed to alter and transmute and then in consequence to perfect the myriad things. The essential and inborn natures of things provide the natural principles of order whereby one determines what is so and what is not so of them and whether one should select or reject them. For this reason
>
> Their undertakings are great and comprehensive like Heaven and Earth, brilliant and illuminating the truth like the sun and moon, and essential and important to the myriad things like the wind and rain. With their formless majesty and their profound and pure mystery, their activities cannot be grasped. It is as though they were the successor of Heaven whose undertakings cannot be recognized.[9]

This is hardly the image of a completely rational bureaucrat at work in a dully mundane secular world. This is a world of mystery, heavenly power, and ceaseless creativity. This is the sage as charismatic religious leader of humanity and the whole of creation. How does the sage achieve all of these wondrous things?

> Though the sky does not speak, men can infer that is it high; though the earth does not speak, men can infer that is thick; though the four seasons do not speak, the Hundred Clans anticipate their proper sequence. This is because having attained perfect truthfulness, they possess a constant regularity.[10]

The term that Knoblock translates as truthfulness is *ch'eng*, perhaps the most religious of Confucian ethical norms. For Hsun Tzu, along with humaneness and ritual, truthfulness gives perfection to human nature. It is this perfected human nature, as the *Doctrine of the Mean* teaches, that links human beings with the creative and divine power of heaven and earth.

Hsun Tzu writes an almost Pauline hymn to the power of *ch'eng*. St. Paul argues that if the Christian does not have love, then she or he really has nothing at all and becomes a noisy cymbal. Hsun Tzu writes:

> For a gentleman to nurture his mind, nothing is more excellent than truthfulness. If a man has attained perfection of truthfulness, he will have no other concern than to uphold the principle of humanity and to behave with justice. If with truthfulness of mind he upholds the principle of humanity, it will be given form. Having been given form, it becomes intelligible. Having become intelligible, it can produce transmutation. If with truthfulness of mind he behaves with justice, it will accord with natural order. According to natural order, it will become clear. Having become clear, it can produce transformation. To cause transmutation and transformation to flourish in succession is called the "Power of Nature."[11]

This ability to manifest actualized truthfulness and sincerity of purpose is a profound spiritual power for the sage. Hence it is fair to say that even the most secular and rationalistic of the classical Confucians had a place for the spiritual meaning of life in his philosophy. As with so many other Confucian reflections on the meaning of life, the religious dimension of the tradition focuses attention on the proper cultivation of the self. The virtue par excellence for self-cultivation remains *ch'eng* for the development of the Confucian Way in East Asia. In one strong sense the Confucian tradition and the Christian tradition, at least as defined by St. Augustine in the West, do share one major commonality. This shared feature is their concern with the weakness of the will and the necessity for moral and spiritual self-cultivation such that true humanity can be restored. Both the early Christian thinkers and Hsun Tzu were concerned with the weakness of the will that keeps us from doing what we should to promote human flourishing.

While the Confucian tradition developed in fascinating ways over the centuries, it is commonly recognized that the second great phase arrived with the rise of the neo-Confucian movement in the Northern Sung dynasties, especially in the eleventh century. The great masters of the Northern Sung created a full-fledged revival of the tradition from the 1060s and charted the course of the Confucian Way until the end of the nineteenth century. The main stimulus for the revival came not from internal reform or innovation, but because of the massive impact of Buddhism on all aspects of Chinese social and intellectual life. Confucians responded to the Buddhist challenge by reformulating many of their traditional positions and adding new dimensions to previous achievements. For instance, the most signal intellectual response to the Buddhist challenge was the creation of a number of specific and comprehensive Confucian philosophic syntheses.

The most important and far-reaching creative response to the Buddhist challenge was made by Chu Hsi (1130–1200) during the Southern Sung dynasty. Chu wove the work of his beloved Northern Sung masters into a tapestry of commentary, ritual texts, history, classical studies, and independent philosophic treatises that became the benchmark for all later Confucians. In this respect Chu melded a Buddhist philosophic desire to define one's terms with a persistent Confucian proclivity to respect the authority of the past. In fact, in terms of disputation, Chu mixes appeals to tradition with a willingness to define what Confucian terms mean. In the examples below we will deal with the definitional side of Chu's work because it expands the range of Confucian discourse.

Chu was also, as were all the great neo-Confucians, passionate about his role as teacher. They saw their task as the revival of what they called "this culture of ours." In order to do so they provided their students with the best possible education in terms of basic texts and commentaries. Along with their ambitious research and printing program was a personal commitment to the cultivation of the role of teacher, as living examplars of what they taught. Through teaching they sought to assert the truth as they knew it in propositional philosophic discourse, to express their metaphoric feelings in their poetry and paintings, and to live the truth as action in their lives as teachers and servants of the state and the common people. Neo-Confucianism was a total package wherein the meaning of life was asserted, exhibited, and acted out through proper moral teaching, personal conduct, and social service.

The concept of *ch'eng* was as central to Chu's synthesis as it had been to classical texts such as the *Doctrine of the Mean* and philosophers such as Hsun Tzu. Chu would have hardly been willing to move beyond the classical canon even though he, and the other Sung thinkers, were willing to make use of overlooked timber for the elaboration of their new intellectual habitats. Typical of the Sung achievement was to take what had been latent philosophic metaphors for truthfulness/sincerity in the classical tradition and give them a full-blown systematic exposition. The most systematic of these expansions of the classical metaphorical prototypes were assembled by Chu and his students.

The method that Chu used was based on his appropriation of the Ch'eng brothers' concept of *li* (principle). The trait of principle was devised by the Ch'engs and adopted by Chu to try to show the recurrent patterns of the world and of each and everything in the world. From the perspective of the *li* theory, the world was normed by principle as the Supreme Ultimate, and each thing itself also had a principle that was its particular norm. For instance, human beings should be humane, and in order to be fully humane, that is, to be in sync with principle, a person must be truthful and sincere. *Ch'eng* is a normative or perfecting function, and principle of humaneness as authenticity and truthful self-actualization. The use of principle by Chu allowed him to mine the rich legacy of the classical Confucian lexicon and to respond to the Buddhist metaphysical challenge to the Confucian Way.

Of course, Chu ramified *ch'eng* in subtle ways. For instance, Ch'eng I (1033–1107) defined *ch'eng* as the not false, and Chu added that it was not false and true. Chu's most astute philosophic student, Ch'en Ch'un (1159–1223), provided this definition of his master's idea. "In every flower or leaf, the veins and grains have been arranged the same for all time without the slightest error. Even with perfect arrangement by human effort, the organization and arrangement cannot be equal to them. All of this is so according to the concrete principle and is so naturally."[12] *Ch'eng* is the very true ordering of all elements of the world. Of course, Ch'en goes on to note that this form of truthfulness is manifest in human life as a search for the harmonious and good as its final goal. Speaking of *ch'eng*, Ch'en argues that "As to perfect *ch'eng*, it is on the level of the sage's moral nature. Only when all principles are perfectly true and real without an iota of insincerity can one deserve the description."[13]

Chu Hsi tied the concept of *ch'eng* into his interpretation of how the way of heaven and the way of humanity are to be conjoined in true human flourishing.

> *Ch'eng* is the way of heaven. *Ch'eng* is the principle that is self-determining without being falsely ordered. How to achieve *ch'eng* is the way of humanity. It is to carry out this real principle and therefore to make an effort to achieve it. Mencius said: "All things are complete in us" – this is *ch'eng*. "[There is no greater] delight than to be conscious of *ch'eng* upon self-examination" – this is how to have *ch'eng*. Self-examination is merely to seek in oneself. *Ch'eng* refers to the fact that all things are complete without any defect.[14]

This was to be done by being faithful to the principle of how things ought to be, in this case, the fulfillment of humanity, and by manifesting this principle of humanity through truthfulness and self-actualization. *Ch'eng* is both the process and a quality of humanity that creates human meaning.

Wing-tsit Chan, the great translator of neo-Confucian texts, glosses Ch'en Ch'un's rendering of Chu's theory of *Ch'eng* by calling it "realness." The reason for this is that "*ch'eng* is a description of natural principle, whereas loyalty and faithfulness have to do with human effort."[15] In a later section, Ch'en likens the perfection of *ch'eng* to the ordered sequence of the seasons and day and night. For human beings, this order is manifest in the functioning of the mind–heart when it is cultivated in a correct fashion. "Although the most evil person has been muddled by material to the highest degree, as soon as these desires stop for a moment, the true substance of his innate mind naturally shows itself."[16]

In one famous imperially sponsored anthology of Chu's work from the Ch'ing dynasty, the opening sentence in the section devoted to *ch'eng* shows how Chu was influenced by the logical style of his Buddhist partners in disputation and how difficult it is to translate even a four-character sentence into intelligible and faithful English.[17] To paraphrase, *ch'eng* is to make real (*shih*) principle or express the reality of principle. This is a fascinating definition because it embraces the neo-Confucian doctrine of principle as a norm of existence and tries to define such existence as reality or concrete norms as manifested in human life. The term *shih* is Chu's favorite term used to differentiate the Confucian Way from the ways of Taoism and Buddhism. *Shih* means the real, the concrete as opposed, in Chu's interpretations, to the empty and pathless ways of Buddhism and Taoism respectively. From Chu's viewpoint, real self-cultivation was based on a real world with real norms. In fact, to achieve the highest form of self-cultivation was to actualize the norms of the sages in real life as measured by a timely response to present circumstances. In a short explanation of the opening sentence, Chu goes on to say that truthful self-actualization means being honest, prudent, or guileless – someone who is both personally transparent to the truth and who allows the truth to shine through for anyone else who would care to observe their behavior.

In the passage that immediately follows this short definition of the meaning of *ch'eng* as the truthful conformation of life to ethical principle, Chu gives a homely analogy for the functioning of principle and truthful self-actualization. One of Chu's favorite illustrative items was the fan. The nature of the fan would be like seeing the fan itself as a model, as the abstract fan in the sense that we notice the fan but do not yet use it to fan ourselves; if the fan does a good job cooling us, then this is like *ch'eng*. One assumes that Chu invited his students to look at his fan, seeing its general shape and that it was in the form of a fan as a common household object in Sung China. But only when the object, which itself is merely concrete in the sense of being actual, functions well can we say the fan is a good fan.

Heretofore we have reviewed the Confucian meaning of life in terms of truthfulness in the Chinese context. However, Confucianism is an international movement. Vietnam, Korea, and Japan have, in varying ways, all been impacted dramatically by Confucian thought and forms of social organization. There were times when the most creative work being done in Confucian thought was in Korea or Japan. For instance, the sixteenth century was a grand period for Korean Confucians. In the late fourteenth century, the young founders of the new Choson dynasty decided to "confucianize" Korea by replacing Buddhism and other traditional Korean social patterns with models derived from the new neo-Confucian philosophy they observed in Ming China.

One of the greatest of the sixteenth-century Korean thinkers was Yi Yulgok (1536–1584). Although he based his thought on Chu's great synthesis, Yi Yulgok actually expanded the range of Chu's work and refined what we had received from his acknowledged Sung master. The specific genius of Yi Yulgok's philosophic contribution was in ramifying Chu's concept of principle and showing how this could be effectively connected to the notion *ch'i* (matter–energy). The problem for the Korean Confucians was, how could something as abstract as principle be understood as the engine of life and generativity itself? The context of the question was based on Chu's understanding that principle gives directions and norms to the dynamic aspects of the world as thematized by the notion of *ch'i*. Of course, the question of how principle and matter–energy were cosmologically related was one of the key questions for the followers of Chu. For anything to be or become, according to Chu, there had to be a principle that gave shape and direction to matter–energy. As is commonly known, *ch'i* was the other cosmological building-block for Chu's interpretation of the concrete world.

As one of the great Chinese critics of Chu had asked, how could a dead principle ride upon and direct a live *ch'i* (material force)? How can the abstract direct the living, moral reality of the world? Yi Yulgok provided a subtle answer to this question that owed a great deal to one of Chu's major Northern Sung masters, Chang Tsai (1020–1077). Chang was the preeminent Sung philosopher of *ch'i*, and Yi Yulgok used Chang's insights into the dynamic and living nature of a principled world to express a very sophisticated interpretation of the interpenetration of principle and matter–energy. However, like most Confucians, Yi Yulgok was not interested in metaphysics as a purely academic sport. Yi Yulgok wanted to show how Chu's synthesis provided meaning for life. And like Chu, Yi Yulgok fixed on *ch'eng* to articulate this aspect of the Confucian Way. Yi Yulgok considered the learning of truthfulness/sincerity to be the essence of the teaching of the sages.

Yi Yulgok understood *ch'eng* to be the essential feature of self-cultivation, the glue that bonded principle and the dynamic side of the person together as a student of the teaching of the sages. Truthfulness is situated between the nourishing of matter–energy and practical learning for the service to society and self. In short, truthfulness is the virtue that allows the cultivation of matter–energy to come to fruition as a social virtue. According to Yi Yulgok's moral anthropology, one must pay special attention to matter–energy because it is the dynamic, emotional, and passionate complex of human nature. It could be either good or evil, and in order to make sure that the good prevails, it is necessary to cultivate the restless matter–energy. Truthfulness is the trait that helps to bring balance and harmony to the emotional life of the disciple. It cannot be highlighted too strongly or often that for the neo-Confucians there was nothing ontologically evil about the emotions. In fact, for true human flourishing human emotion was essential, but only when it was in a proper pattern. Hence, emotion was subject to the cultivation of principle itself in a truthful fashion.

Yi Yulgok also suggested that truthfulness/sincerity was the best way to understand Confucian moral pedagogy by means of a three-step process. The first stage was that of a student, someone at the beginning of the path. This is the initial stage of critical thinking and is a difficult and painful beginning for the student. Any success at this stage, focused on the investigation of things, the extension of knowledge, and the rectification of the mind–heart, was only achieved at the price of great and painful applied effort on the part of the student. At the second stage, that of the superior person, the student of the Way still must think and labor at knowledge, but this becomes a much more fluid, effortless process. In this second stage the learner "investigates things and extends knowledge, and makes the will sincere and corrects the mind, but does not yet reach [these things in their] utmost." At the third stage, the effort that thinking and investigating requires drops away.[18] Yi Yulgok's favorite image is that of Confucius' famous young disciple, Yen Hui. In fact, Yen Hui functioned as a paradigmatic student of the Way, almost a patron saint for the neo-Confucian philosophers. "Yen-tzu [Hui], was not exempt from 'thinking' and 'laboring'; but he did not have to make an effort. The learner, however, cannot avoid the mental pain and extreme effort [of 'thinking' and 'laboring']. In general, I consider understanding without thinking to be the utmost knowledge, and being in the right without effort the utmost action."[19]

For Yi Yulgok, all of this learning is for the pragmatic generation of meaning, of what he called in Korean "sincere reality." From Yi Yulgok's point of view, this was the true foundation of the meaning of life. Here the mind–heart is conformed to the real principles by means of efficacious ethical action. Only such a living engagement with the world can be considered truly meaningful and meaning giving. Yi Yulgok is clear that mere academic learning as something abstract is not what he intends. "If there are things to be taken care of, take care of those things and then read books. Reading books without taking care of things is useless learning."[20] The seventh of his eleven articles on self-cultivation states the pragmatic turn as "Carry out good work with a sincere heart."[21] However far Confucian doctrines of meaning and self-cultivation wander, they inevitably return to the secular world, the concrete reality of the secular as the sacred.

In essence Yi Yulgok's theory of *ch'eng* achieved two different tasks within Confucian moral discourse. First, Yi Yulgok used truthfulness as a means of linking normative principles with the dynamics of matter–energy. *Ch'eng* was the way he conjoined *li* and *ch'i* into a meaningful metaphor for life. Second, it was also the means by which Yi Yulgok demonstrated the essential unity of the religious dimension of his tradition with concrete self-cultivation. It was by means of truthfulness that humanity can be joined with heaven and earth as the source of cosmic generativity. As is the case with many other Korean Confucians, the religious dimension of the notion of truthfulness is particularly prevalent. Such obvious spiritual concern is not always manifest in the neo-Confucian tradition, but in Yi Yulgok's treatment of *ch'eng* it is impossible to miss.

Yi Yulgok's theory of *ch'eng* as providing the meaning of life is a beautiful example of how a profound Confucian teacher illustrates three dimensions of the human communicative act. If cognitive science is at all correct, we now know that human speech and communication are constituent aspects of the emerging human reality. While speech does not entirely define the human species, it goes a long way to giving human beings their distinctiveness among other natural complexes. These human speech acts are ranged along the continuum of assertion, exhibition, and action. The assertive dimension most commonly seeks to convey meaning in terms of propositional discourse. In the West it is taken to be the paradigmatic form of philosophic discourse as propositional assertion and dialectical confrontation. The exhibitive mode is more aesthetic in nature. Perhaps this is why the Confucians were so concerned about their poetry and art as well as their philosophic treatises. They realized that they needed to exhibit as well as define their way. The active dimension illustrates the moral coherence of human life as manifested in the moral conduct of the sage and cannot be reduced to the other two communicative dimensions of human meaning making.

All three elements of the assertive, exhibitive, and active dimensions of human communication are illustrated in the thought of the three great Confucian teachers briefly reviewed in this chapter. Yi Yulgok essentially summarizes the message of Hsun Tzu and Chu Hsi in his elaboration of *ch'eng* as truthful sincerity. Truthful sincerity, for Yi Yulgok, asserts the truth, exhibits the marks of sagely wisdom, and gives meaning to the ordinary conduct of human life. *Ch'eng* provides the bond that holds the human, earthly, and heavenly in a proper balance. It can never be reduced to mere theory or art, or a static form of morality. It is living order in a dynamic world and as such, its meaning is truthful sincerity but only as constituted within the full genealogy of the Tao. Truthful sincerity is the meaning of a life in service of self and others.

NOTES

1. David Hall and Roger Ames, *Anticipating China: Thinking Through the Narratives of Chinese and Western Culture* (Albany: State University of New York Press, 1995).
2. Ibid., p. 123.
3. Marcel Granet, *La Pensée Chinoise* (Paris: Editions Albin Michel, 1968; first publ. 1938).
4. George Lakoff and Mark Johnson, *Metaphors We Live By* (Chicago: University of Chicago Press, 1980).
5. *The Analects of Confucius*, trans. and with notes by Simon Leys (New York: W.W. Norton, 1997), p. 50.
6. Herbert Fingarette, *Confucius: The Secular as Sacred* (New York: Harper & Row, 1972).
7. The translations of Hsun Tzu (Xunzi) are all taken from the exemplary modern annotated translation by John Knoblock, *Xunzi: A Translation and Study of the Complete Work*, 3 vols. (Stanford: Stanford University Press, 1988–1994).
8. Ibid., vol. 3, p. 225.
9. Ibid., vol. 3, p. 261.
10. Ibid., vol. 1, p. 178.
11. Ibid., vol. 1, pp. 177–178.
12. Ch'en Ch'un, *Neo-Confucian Terms Explained: The Pei-hsi tzu-i*, ed. and trans. and with an introduction by Wing-tsit Chan (New York: Columbia University Press, 1986), p. 98.
13. Ibid., p. 99.
14. This is a translation taken from what are commonly called *The Dialogues of Master Chu.* See Li Ching-te, ed., *Chu-tzu yu-lei ta-cha'üan* [The Complete Dialogues of Master Chu], 8 vols. (Tokyo: n.p., 1973), vol. 4, pp. 3287–3288. For scholars using other editions, this is found in the traditional format in *chuan* 64:5a–b.
15. Ch'en, *Neo-Confucian Terms Explained*, p. 97.
16. Ibid., p. 99.
17. See Li Kuang-ti, ed., *Chu-tzu ch'üan-shu* [The Complete Works of Master Chu], 2 vols. (Taipei: Kuang-hsüeh she yin shu kuan, 1977). This is really a very fine later imperial anthology that makes use of all of Chu's extensive publications.

18. The translation and my interpretation of Yi Yulgok relies on Young-chan Ro, *The Korean Neo-Confucianism of Yi Yulgok* (Albany: State University of New York Press, 1989), p. 98.
19. Ibid.
20. Ibid., p. 109.
21. Ibid., p. 6.

Part IV

LOVE, RELATIONSHIPS, AND RELIGION

As we traverse the terrain of meaning across the great monotheisms of the West and the diverse traditions of Asia, we find again and again that the meaningful life is intimately tied to relationships, whether defined primarily in terms of human–divine or human–human relationships. Keith Ward suggested in the opening chapter that among the common characteristics of religions is a prescribed movement away from self-centeredness – and, we might add, a movement toward relationships. In Judaism, Christianity, and Islam that relationship is first and foremost between humans and God, and though it is many faceted, its deepest current is love, a bond with God which is echoed in Hindu devotional traditions of *bhakti*. Importantly though, that love necessarily flows out to other human beings, as those devoted to God make manifest God's love and concern for justice in the world. Buddhism, too, speaks of compassion (coupled with wisdom) as characteristic of the enlightened being and of the Bodhisattva's vow to remain in the world until all sentient beings attain enlightenment. Jain teachings of *ahimsa* or non-violence also affirm that our own liberation is tied to and affects our relations with all other beings. In its own way, Confucianism arrives at this same conclusion. Individuals are constituted by a complex of social relations, and it is in this nexus that they become fully human. The meaningful life in these Confucian terms is profoundly social, and therefore relational. Following out this common theme in the world religions, this section will explore in more detail the connection between love and relationships and religious perspectives on life's meaning.

Joseph Runzo argues that relationality is the fundamental ground of morality, of religion, and of meaning in human life. All religion, he suggests, is fundamentally about relationship with the Transcendent and the concomitant treatment of other persons as spiritual beings who are also in potential relation with that Transcendent (see Plate 8). (The Transcendent is often but not necessarily a personal God – the Buddhist Dharmakaya has this quality of being in some sense "beyond" or "greater than" the human individual, society, and the material world as well.) But what is the precise nature of this "religious point of view" and of the relationship between humans and the Transcendent? Focusing on theistic conceptions, Runzo argues against Christian understandings of God's love (and therefore ideal human love) as disinterested and unconditional – "love that asks nothing in return," which is a traditional interpretation of *agape* – and also against the denigration of *eros* or erotic love as self-interested and base. Pointing to the widespread use across the world religions of the language of human erotic love to describe human–divine relations, he first suggests that there is strong support both within Christianity and elsewhere for an understanding of the human–divine relation as one of passionate interest and desire for relationship, both on the part of the human being and on the part of God. Such love is not selfish but other-focused, wanting the best for the beloved. Yet it is not disinterested either – there is a strong desire to be with the beloved. Drawing on a wide range of religious traditions, Runzo works to enrich our understanding of human–divine love, claiming that this love, which he names "seraphic love," has two poles: *eros* and *agape*. For seraphic love has certain characteristics associated with erotic love rather than with *agape*: reciprocity, vulnerability, surrender, integration or wholeness, union, and equality. And, he argues, it is the relationship of seraphic love which includes *eros* – both with the Transcendent and ultimately with one's fellow human beings – that is the ground of life's meaning. These are radical claims, but they recur in the writings of great lovers of God from multiple traditions, as his many examples reveal.

In the next chapter we have the opportunity to look more deeply into one such tradition – devotional Hinduism or *bhakti*. Nancy Martin offers us a window on the experiential world of Hindu devotees of Vishnu, Krishna, Shiva, the Devi, and God beyond any form or characteristic, poured out in poetic songs that have become the primary religious texts of this branch of Hinduism (see Plate 9). We hear a chorus of voices spanning a thousand years, of women and of men, of high and low social standing, both ordinary people and royalty, from very diverse regions of the subcontinent. They speak of the painful experience of seemingly endless rebirths, of the mystery of the One being all in all yet taking particular forms and loving the individual devotee, of the joy of union and the heart-wrenching sorrow of separation from God, and of the difficulty of following the religious path. The Hindu idea that all multiplicity is in the last analysis really One takes a particular form here. Yes, we are all "sparks of the divine" as it were, but our separation from the One, as painful as it may sometimes be, makes relationship and thus love possible – we who are of God can only love God because we are apart from God. Martin argues that according to devotional Hinduism, this relationality is the source of meaning in human existence, our reason for being: to manifest love and to become and fulfill bliss, the bliss that, together with being and consciousness, *is* God.

The Buddha also spoke of a fundamental relationality between all beings, though not in the form of a unifying personal divine presence. Rather, Buddhist dependent co-origination asserts the co-arising and co-ceasing of all beings in an interconnecting web of relationships, without beginning or end. In this Buddhist view we are fundamentally constituted by our relationships, having no independent and separate existence as individual selves unrelated to others. Though Buddhism posits no God, it does speak in its Mahayana forms of these constitutive relationships as including other beings akin to gods and of a Transcendent that encompasses them all – the Dharmakaya. Anne Klein takes us into this relational Buddhist world via the practice of mindfulness within Tibetan Buddhism, which includes exercises focusing on one's guru and on deities. But before we turn to Klein's chapter, let us look at how the originating teachings of Shakyamuni Buddha evolved into its later Tibetan tantric forms.

Spreading rapidly across India, Buddhism was on its way to becoming a world religion within two centuries of the Buddha's death when Emperor Ashoka unified the subcontinent in the third century BCE and sent emissaries far and wide to promulgate its teachings. Major reforms around the beginning of the Common Era led to the development of two distinct strands, Theravada (the Teaching of the Elders) and Mahayana (the Great Vehicle). While Theravada stressed meditation, the monastic life, and the attainment of individual enlightenment, claiming to follow the original teachings of the Buddha, Mahayana came to emphasize compassion, the equality of laity and monastics in the spiritual pursuit, and the Bodhisattva ideal of one who vows to remain in the world and work for the liberation of all beings rather than pursuing working for individual enlightenment alone. A third major strand, Vajrayana (the "Diamond" or "Thunderbolt" way), became established around the middle of the first millennium of the Common Era. Though sharing many doctrines with Mahayana, this tantric form of Buddhism promises the possibility of enlightenment in a single lifetime, using alternative meditative practices of transformation. Mahayana had spread quickly into East and Southeast Asia although Theravada took hold in Thailand, Sri Lanka, and Mayanmar (Burma). Vajrayana became strongly established in Tibet although strands of this esoteric path also can be found in East Asia.

Anne Klein writes from the perspective of the Vajrayana Tibetan tradition although much of what she has to say about Buddhist mindfulness applies to all forms of Buddhism. She begins with meditations that cultivate mindfulness, designed to bring one to full realization of the basic Buddhist teachings of impermanence and dependent co-origination, which cannot be fully known through the intellect alone. Only through the cultivation of mindful attention and the proper silencing of the mind can we come to understand the nature of the fundamental relationality of the world posited by Buddhism. Compassion for all beings arises from such practices as well, generated by awareness of their pain in life and of their deep suffering brought on by both their ignorance of their true nature and by impermanence. Compassion informed by wisdom is the guiding light of meaning in the Buddhist life – to work to end the suffering of other beings is the purpose of human life in Mahayana Buddhism, Klein asserts.

Yet how does one develop the highest level of compassionate wisdom? Klein introduces us to another Buddhist practice, one particularly important to Tibetan tantric traditions: Guru Yoga. This practice involves the cultivation of relationship and encounter with one's guru (or enlightened spiritual guide, often understood to be the reincarnation of an earlier guru) and with Bodhisattvas or deities who embody universal principles such as compassion or wisdom. A rich world of narrative and visualization supports these practices. But in this meeting the boundaries between self and other become permeable. And it is his or her own primordial consciousness that the practitioner meets at the same time he or she meets the very human guru, and the universal principles embodied by the Bodhisattvas or deities are cultivated within the individual as he or she "becomes" the divinity. The Great Bliss Queen is such a figure, embodying "the essence of all Buddha wisdom" and in meeting her, becoming her, we cross over into wholeness and into a life of ever deepening meaning, according to Klein. (For the importance of the Goddess in Indic thought see Plate 10.)

Though coming from a radically different perspective – that of Haitian Vodou – Karen McCarthy Brown also speaks of a tradition fundamentally grounded in relationships that cultivate encounters with spirits embodying aspects of human nature. Like other world religions, the traditions of Africa have become global, though they did so in part through the horrendous violence of the slave trade. There is no singular African tradition, but the various traditions originating in Africa do share common assumptions about the nature of the world, much as the immense varieties of Hindu religiosity do, and when they take new forms in the Americas, many different strands of tradition are woven together to produce new yet ancient forms such as Haitian Vodou.

In Karen McCarthy Brown's description of contemporary Haitian tradition, we find a religion that is ostensibly monotheistic and whose adherents participate in Catholic ritual life but that also acknowledges human life lived in "a complex weave of relationships" extending across the fluid boundaries of life and death to include ancestors and spirits. And it is in this latter context that life's meaningfulness is deeply challenged and reaffirmed and that healing and spiritual transformation occur. Haitian tradition affirms this life and the social nature of human beings (in a way paralleling Confucianism) and acknowledges that no individual can live a meaningful and productive life in this world apart from others (echoing the Buddhist emphasis on interdependence).

Basic survival remains a fundamental issue for many Vodou practitioners, and life-enhancing healing lies at the center of religious ritual – the unblocking of the free flow of life energy and the making of right relationships. Those relationships may be with other human beings, but they may also be with ancestors or with spirits (the *lwa*). The spirits embody human types (not necessarily ideals as in the Buddhist case) and forms of life energy, and through their behavior and character demonstrate the multiple facets, both positive and negative, of power, sexuality, death, and family loyalty. They are also givers of these types of life energy, according to Haitian tradition, and people with similar personality types are recognized as having special associations with them, cemented in ritual "marriages" to these spirits.

Karen McCarthy Brown suggests that meaning and morality converge in Haitian tradition with a powerful affirmation of life, upholding mutual care and respect for self and others with an acceptance of conflict and difference and enhancing life energy, and working for mutual survival even while looking death squarely in the face. Once again, we find religion and meaning resting on a foundation of relationship. A meaningful life cannot be lived in isolation; a meaningful life is fundamentally marked by relationship, both with other beings and with a Transcendent Reality, which is greater than our individual and collective selves.

Plate 8 Jesus and the Twelve Disciples above the altar on the ceiling of the presbytery, 1220 CE, in the fine Norman Cathedral at Peterborough, England. Photo: *Nancy M. Martin and Joseph Runzo*

10

EROS AND MEANING *in* LIFE *and* RELIGION†

Joseph Runzo

> Know that the Lord is God!
> It is God that made us, and we are God's; . . .
> For the Lord is good;
> God's steadfast love endures forever.
>
> Psalm 100:3, 5[1]

The Hebrew Psalmist conjoins God's goodness and God's love, expressing the idea that it is through God's love that God's goodness is present in the world. When we say that something is "good," we are saying that it has meaning and value for us. What, then, does it mean to say that divine love causes – or is the source of – all meaning and value in human lives? And what kind of love is this divine love?

I will develop an answer to these questions in several stages. To begin I will need to say something about how I shall be using the terms "meaning" and "value." I will then use these two ideas to develop a key notion – the notion of what I shall call "the religious point of view." Understanding the religious point of view will bring us to an integrated understanding of both divine love and of the meaning of human life. I shall argue that divine love includes the dimensionality of *eros*. But since human love, in a religious conception, properly reflects divine love – as the writer of 1 John puts it, "we love because God first loved us" (1 John 4:19) – the highest human love will also include the dimensionality of *eros*. In sum, divine love, and

† I presented portions of this chapter at Cambridge University and Oxford University in the spring of 1998. I am grateful to Julius Lipner and Keith Ward for those invitations to speak and for their comments which helped me refine the ideas in this chapter.

so the highest human love, is erotic. As I develop this view, I shall assess not only the place of erotic love within Western monotheism but also the wider place of erotic love in the world religions.

MEANING AND VALUE

In *The Examined Life* Robert Nozick suggests that something has intrinsic value to the degree it is "organically unified."[2] The organic unity of something depends upon two things: the degree of diversity[3] and the degree of unity to which that diversity is brought. So, the greatest value comes from the greatest integration of the greatest diversity. Thus, a human life has greater value and an even greater potential value than a tree, say, or a painting, because of the greater complexity and integration of the mental and physical aspects of the human being.

On the other hand, meaning comes from a thing's connectedness to other things outside itself. Thus our lives have meaning through our connectedness to other persons. However, ultimate meaning will only result if there is an eventual connection with something outside us which is unlimited in value. Since meaning comes from an integrative connectedness with things of value outside ourselves, meaning enhances value. Obviously, any connection with unlimited value is itself valuable. But the degree of value derived from our connection to unlimited value will be proportionate to the degree of integration resulting from that connection.

Now, divine love is (1) intrinsically valuable; (2) unlimited; and (3) maximally integrative. For those who think in Western, Aristotelian terms, God – as supremely intrinsically valuable – is conjointly the material, efficient, formal, and telic cause of meaning and value in human lives. That is, in every respect, God is the source of the good within Western monotheism. Within the Hindu tradition, to take an example from Asian religions, this is captured in the evaluative notion that somehow atman (the self) *is* Brahman (the fullness of Being). Through manifestation, rather than intentional creation as in the West, Brahman gives atman ultimate meaning. In the conception of the world religions generally, to the extent that there is a lived connection with the Transcendent, the religious life has meaning because it brings one into contact with ultimate value. The religious life serves as, so to speak, a "connective bridge" to ultimate value.

THE MORAL POINT OF VIEW

It is universally held that to be religious is in part to be moral. While being moral is not sufficient for being religious, to be genuinely religious entails being moral. Since the moral life is one component that gives meaning and value to the religious life, let us first ask what it means to take the moral point of view.[4]

Particular moral imperatives and values vary amongst individuals and cultures. But the salient feature and the crux of taking the moral point of view is taking others into account in one's actions because one respects them as persons.[5] The obligation to take the moral point of view and take others into account because they are persons is an ultimate obligation, but where does this obligation come from?

One often-recognized characteristic of moral agency is autonomy – the ability to make rational and responsible decisions on one's own. Autonomy alone obviously does not produce a moral point of view or a sense of obligation: the amoral sociopathic person is, unfortunately, all too autonomous. But persons are social beings, and relationality – the willingness to relate to others – is a further defining characteristic of moral agency. As a fundamental characteristic of taking the moral point of view, relationality supports Immanuel Kant's ethical dictum to "always treat others as ends in themselves and not merely as means to an end" (the sociopath treats people as merely means to his/her ends). And it is reflected in the Jewish thinker Martin Buber's justly famous notion of the "I–Thou" perspective: "When I confront a human being as my You and speak the basic word I–You to him, then he is no thing among things nor does he consist of things."[6] For relating to persons *as persons* is different in kind from treating something as an "it," and as Buber insists, whoever lives only by treating everything as an "it" "is not human." Thus relationality, insofar as it is a defining characteristic of one's autonomy, is the wellspring of the obligation to take the moral point of view.

THE RELIGIOUS POINT OF VIEW

Now just as religion supervenes on morality – that is, just as religion encompasses but is more than morality – I propose that there is a religious point of view which supervenes upon the moral point of view. I do not mean that there is only one religious perspective, for of course religious values are variant and relative to each particular religious worldview. But variety presupposes commonality. A variety of things is a variety of some common kind. Thus one does not have a specifically religious perspective unless one shares a fundamental "religious point of view" with others having quite different specific religious perspectives. Just as the moral point of view functions as the wellspring and the point of commonality and universality for moral value and truths, so too the religious point of view is the wellspring, the point of commonality, and the manifestation of universality, in religion.

Regarding the moral point of view, in his innovative book *Relationship Morality* James Kellenberger argues that "the ultimate grounding of obligation, and finally of all morality, is a single but universal relationship between each and all." For it is a realization of this "person–person relationship" to others, says Kellenberger, that creates "a sense of duty grounded in a recognition of the intrinsic worth of persons."[7]

To be genuinely religious is to realize the person–person relationship Kellenberger identifies, with the added or supervening dimension of relating to the Transcendent. That is to say, the ultimate grounding of spirituality is the realization of a single universal relationship among all persons as spirits and the Transcendent. Clearly, this universal relationship is particularized in different ways for different people. For each person has a unique set of personal relations, and a unique relation to the Transcendent. Still, to take the religious point of view is to so conform one's life – through prayer and meditation, creed and text, ritual and social practice – so that one is directed toward a felt Transcendent – whether Allah, or Shiva, or Yahweh, or God or the Dharmakaya – and in so doing, one treats other persons as spiritual beings. This means that one treats others as persons, as having the same spiritual value as oneself, as being on the same spiritual quest as oneself and with the same potential for salvation/liberation.[8]

As we have seen, meaning is relational, the result of our connectedness to other things, especially other persons. Our "spirit–spirit" relationships are not only extrinsically meaningful, they are intrinsically valuable for they connect us to other persons *and* to the Transcendent. As Buber nicely puts it: "As soon as we touch a You we are touched by a breath of eternal life . . . the lines of relationships intersect in the Eternal You."[9] But I want to go beyond this conclusion about meaning and value to make a point about metaphysics: the interconnected web of personal relations is part of the fundamental structure of the universe. As Nammalvar, the ninth-century CE Indian poet-saint, writing about Krishna, says:

> lative.
> ves relate,"

of view; it is the path of wisdom, w reflects the underlying structure cendent. Consequently, taking the mate value to life, for to do so vith the structure of reality: this is na in Hinduism and Buddhism.

, as I am doing here on the basis of re amenable to personalistic than Transcendent. It will be more u theism or to a devotee of Krishna Vedantist such as Shankara, more a Buddhist. But that is O.K. What the religious point of view; what relationship. The accuracy of one's his (which is a good thing because it is a path for the blind). For even view of the Transcendent – such as and Japanese Rinzai Zen Buddhism do treat all persons as spirit, and compassion for all living things.

LOVE

the spirit–spirit relationship and relationality is encapsulated in the Golden Rule, the moral imperative to do unto others as you would have them do unto you, found in all the world's great religious traditions.[11] So for example Jesus, citing the Levitical injunction (Leviticus 19:18), said:

"You shall love the Lord your God with all your heart, and with all your soul, and with all your mind" and then adds: "You shall love your neighbor as yourself" (Matthew 22:37–39). But what kind of love is this?

The Second Commandment is an extension of the First. The only appropriate object of this sort of unconditional love is the Transcendent, and therefore anything made, or manifest, in the "image" of the Transcendent – i.e. other persons as well as ourselves – is also to that extent an appropriate object of unconditional love. In Paul Tillich's words, "faith as the state of being ultimately concerned implies love, namely, the desire and urge toward the reunion of the separated."[12] But this kind of love has the dimensionality of *eros*. The thirteenth-century Islamic poet Rumi writes of the *eros* God imparts to creation:

> As God put desire in man and woman to the end that the
> world should be preserved by their union,
> So hath he implanted in every part of existence the desire
> for another part.[13]

In *eros* is the desire to be with the beloved. Further, *eros* contains the passionate desire to, in a sense, even be the beloved. As the Hindu poet Nammalvar, portraying the devotee's relation to Krishna, vividly writes:

> While I was waiting eagerly for him
> saying to myself,
> "If I see you anywhere
> I'll gather you
> and eat you up,"
> He beat me to it
> and devoured me entire.[14]

Consequently, John Hick's well-known definition of religion as the concern to move "from self to Reality centeredness" can be misleading – for to be Reality centered is to be – through *eros* – not only centered on the Transcendent but, at the same time, self- and other-centered.

However, we need to consider three possible objections to this emphasis on *eros*. First, how can the highest human love be, if only in part, self-directed? Unbridled self-centeredness is destructive. But appropriate self-interestedness can be transformative. As C.S. Lewis explains about falling in love:

> ...in one high bound [*eros*] has overleaped the massive wall of our selfhood; it has made appetite itself altruistic, tossed personal happiness

> aside as a triviality and planted the interests of another in the center of our being. Spontaneously and without effort we have fulfilled the law... It is an image, a foretaste, of what we must become to all if Love Himself rules in us without rival.[15]

A second objection to *eros* is this: surely the carnal/corporeal elements usually associated with erotic love will inevitably misdirect one away from the pure spirit of the Transcendent. Several responses can be made here.

1. Genuine love is neither solely nor excessively sexual, for then it would be just a form of retractive self-love. Genuine love is expansive; it is integrated with the whole of one's love – in genuine love one loves others through one's love for the beloved.
2. The greater the possible benefits of any type of relationship, the greater the risks. To relate to the Transcendent through *eros* involves the greatest risks of all. But it also has the greatest potential meaning. As the tantric Buddhist tradition observes:

> (Erotic) Love (Kama), enjoyed by the ignorant,
> Becomes bondage.
> That very same love, tasted by one with
> understanding,
> Brings liberation.[16]

3. Most significantly, consider the astonishing idea – found in some form in all the world religions – that humans reflect the image of the divine. Proceeding from God to humans, we have the language of the Hebrew scriptures: "So God created humans in God's own image, in God's image God created humans; male and female God created them" (Genesis 1:27). And proceeding from the human to the Divine, this idea is reflected in both the anthropomorphism and incarnation of various divine personae: Yahweh and Shiva and Krishna and the idea of a Bodhisattva. Even Christians, though often reluctant to see the body as holy, proclaim that God so loved the world that God incarnated Godself. The message is that the Divine seeks embodiment and that spirit only develops in the context which the Divine grants humans – the context of embodiment.

   Perhaps the holiness of embodiment was better recognized in the seminal traditions of both Western and Asian religion, namely, in the Hindu and Hebrew traditions. And perhaps we have become too serious (and too Greek?) in the West to accept the gift, for as Hinduism understands, the manifestation of the Divine is *lila* or the delightful play of incarnation.

Thus, the world is imaged in early Indic thought as created by the sweat that falls from Shiva's brow in the great cosmic dance, and Yahweh is imaged by the Hebrews as making humans from the "clay." These images make sense because the physical is how the Divine becomes manifest and the body is how we in turn and, in the image of the Divine, manifest ourselves. For the body is essential for the expression of love. As we saw in the opening quote from the Psalms, God's goodness is expressed in God's love by means of creation.[17] God finds fulfillment in the manifestation or embodiment of Godself, for the body makes love affective – it makes love vivid and intense. For the greatest of all loves is passionate; the greatest of all loves is erotic love.

Even Tillich – for whom the Transcendent is the impersonal "Ground of Being" – borrows from Kierkegaard to declare that "ultimate concern is passionate concern; it is a matter of infinite passion," and he concludes that "passion is not real without a bodily basis, even if it is the most spiritual passion."[18] This is captured in the Hindu notion of *darshan*, the passionate reciprocity of physically both seeing the Divine and being seen by the Divine. When we radically separate spirit from body, the result is a desiccated, intellectualist view of the Transcendent. The notion of Divine embodiment offers a richer understanding of the plenitude, the as it were "ocean," of the Transcendent.[19]

Finally, a third objection might still be raised against *eros*, at least in the Christian tradition. Isn't *agape*, or altruistic love, rather than *eros* the foundational type of Christian love? Again several responses can be given.

1. During the rise of Christianity within the first-century Roman Empire, the licentious Dionysian cults and the salacious idea of the god Eros gave the Roman use of the Greek term *eros* a negative connotation for the new Christian communities. This nascent moral/religious community fastened on another Greek term – *agape* – to identify "Christian" love. And while it is true that the Pauline epistles emphasize *agape*, it must be remembered that Paul is writing in a time of persecution for the new church, when the joys of marriage are set aside for the rigors of discipleship. The resultant narrow focus in the first century on only one of the Greek terms for "love" proves too restrictive.

2. After the fourth century the Christian tradition in the West was heavily influenced by the Manichaean doctrines of Augustine, with their dichotomy between the bad, which resides in the body, and the good – the spirit. However, if I am right, the later theological dichotomy between spirit and body is mistaken, and there is a related false dichotomy between *agape* and *eros.*

Divine love is interested, not *dis*interested. So too for human love. To capture both the feature of *eros* that is passionate interest as well as the other regarding features more commonly associated with *agape,* we might refer to the ultimate love of both God and humans as "seraphic love." "Seraphim" comes originally from a Hebrew root for "burning," which is why Christian theologians named the highest order of angels the "seraphs," the angels with the greatest ardor, those burning with the most intense love of God.

We might think of *agape* and *eros* as the two poles of seraphic love, two poles in a dynamic tension. On the one side, the motive for *agape* is the passionate love of *eros.* And on the other side, true *eros* is not manipulative – for *agape* is the counter-balancing pole within seraphic love. To be controlling obviates the agapistic pole of seraphic love, and so distorts *eros.* But of the two poles of seraphic love, the most active love, *eros,* is the most dangerous. Yet this is no reason to avoid *eros,* for to avoid risk is to avoid both life and spirituality. And ultimately, to avoid *eros* is to fail to achieve the unity of *eros* and *agape* which is seraphic love.

SIX CHARACTERISTICS OF EROTIC LOVE

To see better the role of *eros* as a dynamic pole of seraphic love, consider the appropriateness of the traditional bridegroom metaphor for God (shared in the Hindu tradition by the role of Krishna as lover/bridegroom of all devotees.[20]) The Hebrew text declares:

> For your Maker is your husband,
>   and the Lord of hosts is his name; . . .
> For the Lord has called you
>   like a wife forsaken (Isaiah 54:5–6)

> and as the bridegroom rejoices over
>   the bride,
> So shall your God rejoice over you. (Isaiah 62:5)

We see this communal Hebrew understanding mirrored in the more individualized Christian reading of the twelfth-century saint Bernard of Clairvaux. Bernard says that in the "loving descent of God into the soul," the soul

> will be far from content that the Bridegroom should manifest Himself to her in the manner which is common to all ... She desires that He whom she loves ... should be, as it were, impoured into her; that He should not merely appear to her, but should enter into and possess her.[21]

So why conceive of God as a husband or a bridegroom? The purpose is centrally not to convey a sense of power or control over Israel or the individual Christian. The notion of God as king or shepherd would be sufficient for that. Rather, what this metaphor brings out is the relational/erotic dimension of the love of God. In response, the devout are to love God with their whole mind, soul, and strength – and body. Thus the evocative erotic marriage metaphor for divine–human love is fitting. To see this more fully, consider six salient elements of *eros*: relationality, surrender, vulnerability, integration, union and equality.

First, *eros* is important because it fundamentally involves the reciprocity of relationship. Indeed, in the Hindu tradition this is made explicit through the iconography of the divine couple – Shiva and Parvati, Krishna and Radha, and so on. Within Buddhism, the fundamental doctrine of dependent co-origination is clearly relational. And the *bhakti* tradition of Hinduism and the tantric traditions of Hinduism and Buddhism are also only more explicit ways of expressing the elemental relationality of Indic tradition.

Second, *eros* involves vulnerability. This is important because being "loved" by someone who does not know our weakness and faults does not tell us that we ourselves are, even so, lovable and desirable; it does not tell us that we are the one desired. Here is Mahadeviyakka, the twelfth-century CE Indian saint, writing about Shiva:

> Finger may squeeze the fig
> to feel it yet not choose
> to eat it.
> Take me, flaws and all.
> O Lord[22]

Third, *eros* requires surrender. Karen Lebacqz, in arguing for the importance of vulnerability as a God-given purpose for sex, describes *eros* as an "antidote to the human sin of wanting to be in control."[23] This is why the later developments of the devotional *bhakti* tradition in Hinduism and the development of Christianity out of Judaism have the virtue of moving away from the obedience of ritual and sacrifice to the vulnerability of love and surrender. Erotic love both reflects and is reflected by this spiritual surrender to the Other.

Fourth, *eros* is integrative. Thus the self is actually integrated through *eros* toward God. As Tillich says:

> Ultimate concern is the integrating center of the personal life ... the center unites all elements of man's personal life, the bodily, the unconscious, the spiritual ones. Faith ... is the centered movement of the whole personality toward something of ultimate meaning and significance.[24]

Fifth, *eros* brings union. St. Bernard argues that "Man and God ... are with strict truth called 'one spirit' if they adhere to one another with the *glue of love.* But this unity is effected not by coherence of essence but by concurrence of wills."[25] The elemental religious drive to make one's will congruent with – rather than opposed to – the will of the Divine is at least one feature of the *bhakti* Hindu poet Allama Prabhu's description of union with Shiva:

> If it rains fire
> you have to be as the water;
> if it is a deluge of water
> you have to be as the wind;
> if it is the Great Flood,
> you have to be as the sky;
>
> and if it is the Very Last Flood on all the worlds,
> you have to give up self
> and become the Lord.[26]

Lastly, this characteristic of union in *eros* leads to a sixth feature.

In erotic love, two are as one, for in *eros* is the equality of acceptance. Here is St. John of the Cross regarding mystical union with God: "For the property of love is to make the lover equal to the object loved. Wherefore, since its love is now perfect, the soul is called Bride of the Son of God, which signifies equality with Him."[27] Yet spiritual growth, the struggle to arrive at a concurrence of wills, is messy. To get "down and dirty" with the self, to wrestle with your own spirit and that of an other, to admit that you hurt others – this struggle is absent from *agape*; this struggle is the glory of *eros.*

Relationality, vulnerability, surrender, integration, union, and equality – with these six characteristics God dwells among humans, and no person has greater love than is captured in these six qualities. And to take the religious point of view, to treat others as spirit, to enter fully into a spirit–spirit relationship which is the very structure of reality, is to be genuinely open to seraphic love.

FAITH AND COMMITMENT

But is this postulation of a universal religious point of view, a universal ethos, justified? I do not believe that an argument can be given either for the universality of, or the obligation to take, the religious point of view.[28] Rather, I think that the recognition of the religious point of view and of the significance of relationality is a matter of intuition, whereby "intuition" I mean what G.E. Moore intended in *Principia Ethica*: "When I call ... propositions 'Intuitions,' I mean *merely* to assert that they are incapable of proof; I imply nothing whatever as to the manner or origin of our cognition of them."[29]

When relationality is the defining characteristic of one's autonomous actions, relationality will become the wellspring of the felt obligation to take the moral point of view and, supervening that, the religious point of view. However, this requires the willingness and the courage to act relationally. No argument can of itself affect this kind of attitude and action. In the words of the Sufi poet Rumi:

> The way of love is not
> a subtle argument.
>
> The door there
> is devastation.[30]

One must struggle to make hard choices to be a certain kind of person, to have a certain karma (character); one must take the risk of making transforming choices against self-centeredness, the risk of cultivating attitudes and habits that will eventually enable one to better act relationally.

I do think humans have an innate disposition, like our disposition to be moral, to recognize spirit–spirit relations and the religious point of view. However, one cannot recognize anything without the relevant conceptual resources, and one cannot choose freely unless one knows what choices there are to make. Therefore, in order to acquire the conceptual resources for the religious point of view, we must develop a commitment to at least some rudimentary religious worldview.[31] We must cultivate in ourselves religious habits of action and learning if we are to achieve a religious outlook.

This is why wisdom is meant to be coupled with virtuous action and meditation in the Buddhist Way; why in the fourth gospel Jesus says: "If you continue in my word, you are truly my disciples, and you will know the truth and the truth will make you free," adding "I am the way, the truth, and the life" (John 8:31–32 and 14:6). One cannot see the truth, and so follow the way that brings freedom from false self, unless one is willing to commit to take the religious point of view – to have ultimate concern not for the transitory, but for spirit–spirit relations and for the Transcendent. For only then are we in a position to accept that meaning is found in our reflection of the Divine. Only then do we see that Divine love (and our highest love as an image of that divine love) is love characterized by relationality, vulnerability, surrender, integration, union, and equality – it is seraphic love with the passionate dimensionality of *eros.*

NOTES

1. All biblical references are to the text of the Revised Standard Version, but put into gender-neutral language.
2. Robert Nozick, *The Examined Life* (New York: Simon & Schuster, 1989), p. 164.
3. As Leibniz put it, not just the quantity but the variety of goodness makes for the "best of all possible worlds."
4. See Joseph Runzo, "Ethics and the Challenge of Theological Non-Realism," in *Ethics, Religion, and the Good Society: New Directions in a Pluralistic World,* ed. Joseph Runzo (Louisville, Ky.: Westminster, 1992), p. 90, n. 45.
5. In "Ethical Universality and Ethical Relativism," in *Religion and Morality,* ed. D.Z. Philips (London: Macmillan, 1996), I argue that there are at least four identifiable characteristics of the moral point of view: (1) taking others into account in one's actions because one respects them as persons; (2) the willingness to take into account how one's actions affect others by taking into account the good of everyone equally; (3) abiding by the principle of universalizability – i.e. the willingness to treat one's own actions as morally laudable or permissible or culpable only if similar acts of others in comparable circumstances would be equally laudable or permissible or culpable; and (4) the willingness to be committed to some set of normative moral principles.

6. Martin Buber, *I and Thou*, trans. Walter Kaufmann (New York: Scribner's, 1970), p. 59.
7. James Kellenberger, *Relationship Morality* (University Park, Penn.: Pennsylvania State University Press, 1995), pp. 42 and 53.
8. This can also be put in terms of two other features of the religious point of view which parallel the moral point of view: recognizing the spirit of everyone equally and accepting the universalizability to others of one's own treatment of oneself as spirit.
9. Buber, *I and Thou*, pp. 113, 123.
10. A.K. Ramanujan, trans., *Hymns for the Drowning: Poems for Viṣṇu by Nammāḻvār* (1981; New York: Penguin, 1993), p. 75.
11. For a persuasive argument for this see John Hick, "The Universality of the Golden Rule," in Runzo (ed.), *Ethics, Religion, and the Good Society*, p. 158.
12. Paul Tillich, *Dynamics of Faith* (New York: Harper & Row, 1957), pp. 113–114.
13. Jelaluddin Rumi, *Love is a Stranger*, trans. Kabir Helminski (Battleboro: Threshold Books, 1993), p. 123.
14. Ramanujan, trans., *Hymns for the Drowning*, p. 69.
15. C.S. Lewis, *The Four Loves* (New York: Harcourt, Brace and World, 1960), p. 158.
16. From the *Cittavisuddhiprakarana*, verse 42, as cited in Miranda Shaw, *Passionate Enlightenment* (Princeton: Princeton University Press, 1994), p. 140.
17. And looking to the other end of time, this is why the Christian scriptures speak of a "new heaven and a new earth." See Isaiah 65:17 and Revelation 21:1.
18. Tillich, *Dynamics of Faith*, p. 106.
19. See Lee Seigel, *Fires of Love, Waters of Peace* (Honolulu: University of Hawaii Press, 1983), p. 95.
20. Krishna as lover is the common metaphor; Krishna as bridegroom is less common.
21. St. Bernard of Clairvaux, "Sermons on the Canticles," 30: 5–6, quoted in Nelson Pike, *Mystic Union* (Ithaca: Cornell University Press, 1992), p. 81.
22. A.K. Ramanujan, trans., *Speaking of Śiva* (New York: Penguin, 1973), p. 133.
23. Karen Lebacqz, "Appropriate Vulnerability," in James B. Nelson and Sandra P. Longfellow, eds., *Sexuality and the Sacred* (Louisville, Ky.: Westminster 1994), p. 259.
24. Tillich, *Dynamics of Faith*, p. 106.
25. St. Bernard of Clairvaux, "Sermons on the Canticles,' 71, quoted in Pike *Mystic Union*, p. 36.
26. Ramanujan, trans., *Speaking of Śiva*, p. 162.

27. St. John of the Cross, "Spiritual Canticles," 2, quoted in Pike, *Mystic Union*, p. 81.
28. The conviction that one should act so as to respect others as spirit in relation to the Transcendent, while it might be supported by reasons as I have tried to do, is, it seems to me, itself a basic belief, and in the right epistemic circumstances, a properly basic belief. That is, while a justified belief, it is not based on other beliefs as reasons. Hence, belief in the religious point of view is, in this regard, like belief in God.
29. G.E. Moore, *Principia Ethica* (Cambridge: Cambridge University Press, 1965), p. x.
30. Rumi, *The Essential Rumi*, trans. Coleman Barks (San Francisco: Harper, 1995), p. 243.
31. This would constitute a fourth element of the religious point of view.

Plate 9 Painting of Krishna with Mirabai cradled in his arms, on the wall of the Charbhuja Temple in Merta, Rajasthan, India, where this popular woman saint is said to have begun her renowned devotion to the flute-playing god. Photo: *Nancy M. Martin*

11

LOVE *and* LONGING IN DEVOTIONAL HINDUISM

Nancy M. Martin

As Julius Lipner has so eloquently stated in his chapter earlier in this volume, Hinduism is stubbornly multiform, a tapestry of interwoven worldviews, practices, and beliefs characterized by a fundamental and irreducible orality, a movement from multiplicity and outward appearance toward identity and interiority, and a search within a constantly shifting world for ordering principles and centers of meaning around which to shape meaningful lives. I would now like to explore one current within this broad river of tradition – the devotional or *bhakti* path. The passionate love shared by devotee and God that is the driving force of this current yields a distinct perspective on life's meaning and offers a compelling example of a tradition marked by the fundamental relationality which, Joseph Runzo has argued in the previous chapter, lies at the ground of the religious life.

When and where does this strand of Hinduism emerge? Though the roots of devotion to God can be traced from the Upanishads through the *Bhagavadgita*, *bhakti* truly flowered only after the development of temple worship and the elaborations of myth and iconography that occurred during the fourth to sixth centuries in north India under Gupta rule. At that time deities became associated with kings and kingdoms, and regional gods and goddesses began to be absorbed into pan-Indian figures.[1] Then in the Tamil-speaking region of south India during the period from the sixth to ninth centuries, a new type of religiosity emerged. At its center was an intimate relationship of love between devotee and deity, articulated in the language and idioms of classical Tamil lyrics of love and war. Vishnu was the focus of one group, the Alvars or those immersed in God, and Shiva the focus of another group, the Nayanmars. Myth was inscribed in the regional landscape and celebrated in pilgrimage and song, and religious authority was no longer a question of birth and purity but of experience and direct encounter with God (at least in the initial stages of this and subsequent devotional movements).[2]

Devotion to Shiva swept across the Kannada-speaking region in the tenth to twelfth centuries with an emphasis on religion not as making or doing things but rather as being a particular kind of person in a particular kind of relationship with God, something open equally to all, regardless of wealth or birth.[3] The body became the temple, the wandering poet-saint the image of God present in the world, and the familiar language of home and family the language of religious expression, displacing Sanskrit. (Many of the critiques and changes introduced by these movements parallel those of the Protestant Reformation in Christianity.) Called the Virashaivas, these radical devotees sought to establish a society truly based only on a hierarchy of spiritual experience, rejecting caste- and gender-based systems of dominance – an experiment that the wider society ultimately would not tolerate.

In the Marathi-speaking region another movement arose, founded in the thirteenth century by the four socially ostracized children of a Brahmin renouncer who returned to the householder life. As with the earlier movements, its saints included men and women of low castes, and its followers, called the Varkaris, were and are devoted to a particular manifestation of God, Vitthala or Vithoba, who resides at Pandharpur and is said to be an incarnation of Krishna (although iconographically he also has characteristics associated with Shiva). According to Varkari tradition, God longs for the devotee like a cow pining after her calf, and steps in to help devotees in many ways, even becoming a servant woman to assist the saint Janabai in her backbreaking domestic labor.[4]

By the fifteenth century such movements also swept across north India. Some saints, such as Surdas and Mirabai, sang of the full range of love a devotee might have for an incarnate Lord, and the stories of Krishna's incarnation among the cowherding people of Vrindavan (a modern-day pilgrimage center) became the specific context for articulating and experiencing such love as devotees took on roles within this eternal drama. The founding figures of the two major branches of Krishna devotion,

Chaitanya and Vallabhacharya, were considered incarnations of Krishna and their associates identified with his various companions.[5]

Other saints turned away from the rich world of myths, images, and temples and advocated a devotion exclusively to the *nirgun* Lord, the Lord beyond form. Kabir, who spoke out vehemently against all hierarchies of birth and outward forms of religion (Hindu or Muslim), and Nanak, the founder of the Sikhs, are among the saints dedicated to this formless Lord.[6] Devotion to the Great Goddess or Devi emerged as well, crystallized in the *Devi Mahatmya* and eloquently sung by Ramprasad Sen, the eighteenth-century Bengali saint.[7] These movements grew up in a fertile religious milieu, influenced by Sufi and Ishmaeli forms of Islam, Nath traditions, and through them Hindu and Buddhist tantric traditions. Their religious competitors included Buddhists and Jains as well as others within the Hindu fold who saw devotion to a personal Divine as an inferior religious path.

Although there is no singular perspective on life and its meaning that can be identified even within this series of movements that form a subset of Hindu traditions, *bhakti* lies at the heart of them all. Though "devotion" may be used as a shorthand translation of this term, *bhakti* implies a multifaceted relationship with the Divine that involves much more than simple adoration, bringing the lover of God into contact with the Divine through an array of different types of love relationships and through every form of touch, employing metaphors of sight, sound, taste, smell, and the most intimate of all touching, the sexual.[8] Beyond even this, the beloved takes over the lover in a kind of possession that leaves the devotee speaking as if he or she were God. It is a passionate and intoxicating love that may be utterly spontaneous but which is also cultivated through ritual and song, practiced as well as received. The religious movements that are the vessels for such love are characterized by a shift away from ritual performance mediated by a priest to a personal relationship between the individual and the Divine, sometimes facilitated by a guru whose love affair with God is advanced to the point that he or she has become transparent to the Divine and a channel of grace.

From this devotional perspective, what is the nature of this world we live in, and what is its relationship (and ours) to Ultimate Reality? Theological and philosophical discussions of these questions are extensive and elaborate in texts that inform and are generated by these movements. Shankara, the eighth-century expounder of Advaita Vedanta, suggests that the One Reality, Brahman, of which the Upanishads speak is ultimately impersonal and that the multiplicity of the world is fundamentally *maya* or illusion. The eleventh-century theologian Ramanuja on the other hand suggests that the world is the embodiment of God and that Ultimate Reality is fundamentally personal.[9] In his view the world of multiplicity, though we may misperceive it, is not fundamentally illusion but *lila*, the play or sport of God, an outpouring of divine enjoyment and creativity. Vallabhacharya follows in the line of Ramanuja, expanding on earlier upanishadic notions. The personal Brahman or God, he claims, is *sat*, existence, choosing to limit or conceal aspects of Brahman's totality so that manifest existence might come into view. Brahman is also *chit* or consciousness manifest in souls, and *ananda*, the capacity to experience bliss or enjoyment. Yet we fail to know ourselves as fragments of Brahman and as fundamentally constituted out of God's body of bliss. Our role in God's divine play or drama is precisely to cultivate our capacity to experience bliss and to act in love for the greater One Reality of whom we are a part.[10]

This all seems a bit abstract, however. How does one actually live with this understanding of Ultimate Reality or God and human existence and shape a meaningful life within it? To find this out, we must look to the primary texts of these traditions – the songs composed by its poet-saints, songs of love, complaint, and praise to their chosen forms of God in the language of everyday life. At the heart of communal and individual religious practice, these songs continue to be sung today, and within their passionate verses we find articulated the most intimate struggles of the heart and mind with issues of meaning. An authentic core of songs originally composed by a specific saint almost always remains elusive in these predominantly oral traditions, and instead we have many people composing in the names of saints across the centuries as the voices of women and people of lower castes blend with those of men and Brahmins.[11] Stories of the saints' lives are also told, embodying meaning in story, in hagiography and specifically religious contexts, but also in a host of other narrative genres including folk epics, novels, comic books, films, and dramatic performances.

In their songs, these poet-saints struggle to express their experiences of God and to evoke them in others, and explore the contours of meaning and meaninglessness that mark life in this world. When the ninth-century Tamil devotee Nammalvar sings of his beloved Lord, he marvels that God is at once what the "Good Old Books" describe as the subtle essence of all that is, both form and formlessness, and the very specific iconographic form of Vishnu, concluding:

> [W]henever we say
> whatever we say
> it becomes you
>
> however we say it.[12]

God is all in all, immanent yet transcendent, beyond human description yet fulfilling and becoming all that we might imagine or ever have glimpsed in our limited experience. At the same time God appears to us in multiple forms as manifest Lord – for Nammalvar as Vishnu and his avatars.

The movement toward a meaningful life in relation to this God entails first that we wake up to the meaninglessness of the lives we are currently leading. Awash with delusion, in the snare of ignorance, we pursue the desires of the senses with abandon, expecting that wealth, a constant stream of surprise and delight for the senses, or the possession of objects or persons will satisfy the thirst that lies within. Yet, in the first moments of spiritual awakening we find ourselves caught in an endless and meaningless round of rebirth and redeath, fueled by karma, the consequences of our actions in the past yet to be played out.

The saints speak eloquently of the pain and struggle of this endless cycle. Mahadeviyakka, a beautiful young devotee of Shiva living in the twelfth century in the Kannada-speaking region, cries out in a plea for mercy:

> Not one, not two, not three or four,
> but through eighty-four hundred thousand vaginas
> have I come,
> I have come
> through unlikely worlds, guzzled on
> pleasure and on pain.[13]

She concludes her song with a plea for mercy. Her elder contemporary Basavanna asks "Was it wrong just to be born, O Lord?" and in another song he cries out to Shiva, "Why, why did you bring me to birth, wretch in this world, exile from the other?"[14] Ramprasad Sen, too, complains about the cycle of rebirth to the Devi in eighteenth-century Bengal:

> How many times, Mother, are You going
> To trundle me on this wheel like a blind-
> Folded ox grinding out oil? You've got me
> Tied to this old trunk of a world, flogging me
> On and on. What have I done to be forced to serve
> These Six Oily Dealers, the Passions?[15]

Enslavement to the passions is clearly the epitome of the meaningless life.

Yet in our blindness we fail to see our situation. The fifteenth-century north Indian weaver saint Kabir compares the forgetful self to "a frantic dog in a glass temple bark[ing] himself to death" or a lion who leaps into a well after his own reflection.[16] "Who has caught you?" he asks. The mind as well as the passions shackle us, and the saints admonish their own minds, challenging the mind's tendency to run off on meaningless pursuits and to cultivate self-deception rather than realization.

Yet the passions and the mind are stubborn and not easily redirected. Mahadeviyakka likens embodied existence to a snake: "If one could draw the fangs of a snake and charm the snake to play, it's great to have snakes," she says. Even so with the sensual body – untamed it is a poisoning influence on life.[17] And Kabir with another twist of the image describes the double bind of embodied existence as:

> A raft of tied-together snakes
> in the world-ocean –
> Let go and you'll drown
> Grasp, and they'll bite your arm.[18]

If simply to live is not enough, and the pursuit of beauty and sensual pleasure or of wealth and security (*kama* and *artha*) do not in themselves bring lasting satisfaction, then, grasping for meaning, we might turn to other things – the ordering principles of social dharma or even religious actions – fulfilling caste and family obligations and social responsibility or building temples, going on pilgrimages, making offerings of flowers and sweets, practicing asceticism and yogic postures, disputing with those of other religious persuasions, maintaining ritual purity, and the like. While many followers of devotional Hinduism acknowledge such practices as provisional sources of meaning, social hierarchies are relativized by the radical equality of all before God and by shifting identities across rebirths, and religious practices are explicitly linked to the cultivation of a personal relationship with the Divine. Other devotional voices are more iconoclastic, renouncing all such sources of meaning and identity as empty distractions and misperceptions of the true nature of the world. Clearly there is more invested in such outward forms for those who gain status from them. In any case, we humans are so easily seduced by our own accomplishments, proud of what we have made and done, sure of our own religious path, and ready to condemn others. In all this God is easily forgotten, but for a *bhakta* or devotee, in losing sight of God all meaning slips through our grasp. Our accomplishments fade from memory; temples crumble; the body decays. Wealth is exhausted, relationships broken. Death comes knocking at the door – another human life wasted, and the cycle continues.

"Death is standing on your head. Wake-up friend," Kabir shouts.[19] "Human birth is hard to attain; you don't get a second chance," he says, though he does not claim to know precisely "who gets caught and who goes free."[20] There is an urgency to the search for liberation as well as a real possibility of finding life's ultimate meaning, but only if we wake up in time to act upon this potentiality. Kabir says "Plunge into Ram!" Plunge into God!

Turning toward God does not automatically end our difficulties, however, as Ramprasad Sen makes clear, crying out:

> Five elements, Six Passions, Ten Senses –
> Count them – all scream for attention.
> They won't listen. I'm done for.
> A blind man clutches the cane he's lost
> Like a fanatic. So I clutch you, Mother,
> But with all my bungled karma, can't hold on.[21]

Basavanna likens us to rabbits pursued by hounds – the lusts of body and mind – hoping against hope to reach God before they catch us, and to cows mired in the mud whose only hope is to be "pulled out by the horns" by God.[22] In this embodied human existence, we are desperately in need of God's grace.

Yet if this world really is the manifestation of God and God offers Godself as a refuge to the devotee, why then is it so difficult for us to overcome our ignorance and enslavement? Is not God in some sense responsible? The tenth-century Virashaiva saint Dasimayya sings to God, noting that his body seems neither to belong to himself nor to God because it follows neither his will nor God's. He concludes:

Obviously, it is neither your body
nor mine:
it is the fickle body
of the burning world you made.[23]

And in frustration Ramprasad Sen cries out:

Kali, You've got me so hooked
To the things of this world, I can't cut loose.[24]

You lured me into this world,
You said: "Let's play," only to cheat
My hope out of its hope with Your playing.[25]

If God is the *lila* master, then why does He/She seem to play with us, deceive us?

After describing the way in which God plays master of ceremonies in a game of deception that seduces us all, Kabir concludes:

The magic is false,
the magician true –
to the wise it's clear.
Kabir says, what you understand
is what you are.[26]

God's creative manifestation in this world is mysterious, baffling to human comprehension at times. If we believe the "magic" is real, we live in delusion, completely caught up in it. But if Kabir is right and the "magic" is false, then why bother with this world? Seemingly in complete rejection, Mahadeviyakka cries out:

Why do I need this dummy
of a dying world?
illusion's chamberpot,
hasty passions' whorehouse,
this crackpot
and leaky basement?[27]

Why, indeed?

These are not the last words on the world, however, and rejection not the only stance the *bhaktas* take. For the world is also the body of the Divine, manifest simultaneously through concealment and abundance. And an embodied life in the world *is* the site of liberation and love. To reject the world and embodied existence entirely, then, would be to reject

God. Although the world is in some sense a hostile environment (both sociopolitically and religiously) and the senses and desires of embodied existence tend to draw us into meaninglessness and delusion, manifest existence – embodiment in some form – is essential to relationality, to the love that lies at the heart of *bhakti*, of God, and of a meaning-filled existence.[28] We must learn to look at the world with new eyes, the kind of eyes that Krishna gives to Arjuna before revealing his true nature in the *Bhagavadgita* but even more, eyes which simultaneously see the All, both transcendent and immanent in the world, and the manifest Lord, beloved of the devotee.

Looking at the world with the eyes of a devotee, we might see as Nammalvar does. Overwhelmed by God manifest as a particular deity, yet also as the forces of nature, every dimension of the moral realm, and as death itself, he sings, "how fantastic can you get?"[29] But how, Nammalvar asks, can we establish a relationship with this fantastic Lord embodied in all that is? Describing God as "the three worlds in all their beauty," as each of the gods in turn, as the image before him, he asks "just where shall I reach you?"[30]

Mahadeviyakka, too, speaks of the hiddenness of a God who is present everywhere, asking her Lord who is forest, trees, and all creatures that dwell in the forest, who is "filling and filled by all," to reveal his face to her.[31] Not only is God manifest in the world's multiplicity, but even as Atman and Brahman are ultimately one, so too God dwells equally in the human heart. To this mysterious indwelling Divine, she says:

> When I did not know myself
> where were you?
>
> Like the colour in the gold,
> you were in me.[32]

In a similar kind of bewilderment, Nammalvar acknowledges further that this God who is beyond compare and in all things, their very "breath and form," is also intimately involved in his own life:

> becoming mother and father
> you made me know
>   what I couldn't know
>
> I do not even know
>   the things you've done for me.[33]

What is the human response to such a God? – *bhakti* in all its multiple meanings.

From a devotional point of view, we are fundamentally lovers of God, and our life is a journey of ever-deepening love, marked also by intensified longing. Separation between self and God is absolutely essential for love and relationality to be possible, but it leaves us pining for complete union. The language of servanthood applies when we understand this separation to be based on God's greatness and our own comparative insignificance and dependence. Other types of human relations, however, also become an emotional training-ground and mirror, metaphor and model for the human-divine encounter – the love of parents for children, children for parents, siblings, and friends. But it is the language of erotic love and the most intimate human experience of the meeting of embodied human hearts that most clearly articulates the longing that is so characteristic of the interested pure love between humans and the Divine. And more than this it is the language not of *kama*, the erotic love of marriage with its attendant responsibilities and obligations, social acceptance, and resulting procreation, but rather *prema*, the delight of hearts that meet freely, risking social sanction, with no end but love itself.[34]

The whole range of emotions surrounding erotic love come into play, reinscribed with devotional meaning in the songs of the saints, and the devotee finds meaning in cultivating his or her capacity to love – fiercely, gently, with abandon, with tenderness, and with a depth that is only possible by tapping into the infinite wellspring of love that is the Divine itself. The saints' songs, expressions of their intimate encounters with God, evoke this multifaceted love (albeit based on particular constructions of the feminine and of romantic love). Nammalvar speaks often in the voice of a woman, as the feminine soul approaches God manifest in male form. Separated from her beloved, she addresses the wind and the moon asking if they too miss the Lord, and she asks birds to go in search of him, carrying her heart's message. "Without him here," she says, "what shall I say? how shall I survive?"[35] In other songs the lover of God speaks of devouring and being devoured, of possessing and being possessed by God. She even speaks at times as if she were God, losing awareness of anything but God. Addressing a friend she articulates the paradox of union and separateness in intimacy – separation brings pain but makes the joy of union all that much more intense yet also transient, rare, valuable, and tinged with longing. Time itself changes, moving infinitely slowly in times of separation but flying when they are in each others' arms. "So," she says, "I suffer even when my lover joins me many nights in a row, and suffer again when he goes away."[36] What other language, what other human experience could approach the experience of loving God with one's total being? Nammalvar's songs also suggest that there could be no greater separation than that of human and divine, and no greater depth of love than that which bridges this chasm with intimacy.

Of Shiva, Mahadeviyakka says simply:

> He bartered my heart,
> looted my flesh,
> claimed as tribute
> my pleasure,
> took over
> all of me.[37]

No ordinary love is this, but a raging fire that utterly transforms life and the individual. While Nammalvar sang of the separation and sadness at the heart of union, Mahadeviyakka sings of the intensification of love and union after separation:

> Better than meeting
> and mating all the time
> is the pleasure of mating once
> after being far apart.[38]

But she wants both the intensity that only separation makes possible and the constant joy of her divine lover's presence, wanting both to "be with Him" and "not with Him" at the same time. In some deep sense we *do* have it both ways, though we may not realize our true situation. We are both other than and inseparable from the Divine, so that longing remains in the heart of union, union in the heart of separation.

The love of which *bhakti* speaks is not simply a love of the devotee for God but also of God for the devotee. Attentive to human struggle, God intervenes. Devotional songs speak of God coming to work side by side with devotees, especially those of low castes and women, and taking on their suffering and their socially outcaste status. In a song attributed to the seventeenth-century Varkari saint Tukaram, he celebrates the love of God for the saints. Has not God acted freely to "dye skins with Rohidas, weave silk with Kabir, sell flesh with Sajana, garden with Samvat, carry away dead cows with Chockha, gather cow-dung with Janabai, ... drive

Arjuna's chariot, ... absolve Eknath's debt, take poison for Mira," and more?[39]

And even as we might love God, so God pursues us, woos the human heart, makes love to the human soul. It is a two-way street even as is *darshan* (seeing but also being seen by God when one visits a temple, for example).[40] There is an equality and consequent vulnerability in this love between lover and beloved that no other language can articulate so well, no other form of intimacy approach. Devotional songs of Bengal trace each step in the process of falling in love through the love of Krishna for the cowherding women (*gopis*) and especially his lover Radha – the first stages of the girl's innocence on the brink of womanhood, Krishna's infatuation, the utter absorption in each other that marks first love. A question takes hold – can we really ever know the other or does he or she remain ever-deepening mystery even as he/she becomes utterly essential to our being? A devotee sings:

> [A]s wing to bird,
> water to fish,
> life to the living –
> so you to me.
> But tell me,
> Madhava, beloved,
> who are you?
> Who are you really?[41]

Though in loving God intimately we in one sense internalize and possess God as two become one, we also find God perpetually beyond our grasp, never confined to a specific form or to our preconceived notions and never belonging to us alone in the freedom of love.

It is an embodied being whom God loves. A devotee, taking on the persona of an old woman, speaks of her body no longer young, and yet she says "on this withered body the God of Love plunges and rolls."[42] The physical body provides the material base and ground for our emotional response to the Divine, both in the experience of bliss and the agony of separation, and is a fundamental level of God manifest.

The shades of love – regret at having surrendered to another, anger when abandoned for another love, jealousy, the fear of losing the beloved's love, the physical agony of longing and unreciprocated love, the utter delight of union – all are explicitly described and ascribed to both soul and God. God makes love to the devotee and the devotee to God. In another song a devotee describes Radha and Krishna – the human soul and God – thus:

> How beautiful the deliberate, sensuous union of the two;
> the girl this time playing the active role
> riding her lover's outstretched body in delight.[43]

To know such love, to encounter God in this way, then, is life's goal. Leaving behind modesty and shame, Mahadeviyakka cries out,

> O Śiva
> when shall I
> crush you on my pitcher breasts?[44]

We find in these words a celebration of true meeting, of growing familiarity, of the sacrality of embodied beings conjoined in bliss. Devotees might be quick to point out that such language is not about physical bodies or lust – this is not *kama* but a form of *prema,* a full-bodied love that encompasses every kind of human love and brings, in the erotic context, continuous rather than momentary pleasure. Clearly these songs are very much about embodiment and the liminal space where the boundary between self and other dissolves, where human and divine are both one and two, and where passion flows free and pure and we know at the depths of our being why we are here.

What more meaningful life could there be than to be the lover of God, beloved and loving, seeing God in all that is. *Bhakti* would suggest that we and the Divine are most fundamentally and most completely relational, and it is the fulfillment of this relationality that constitutes a meaningful life. The separation and difference of lovers that make the experience and enjoyment of love possible, however, leaves the human heart filled with an irrevocable longing, a loneliness, because the final resting-place of our desire for God (and God's desire for us) is union. Yet this experience of love is the goal rather than some permanent and impersonal merger with Ultimate Reality. Ramprasad Sen says, "Sugar I love but I haven't the slightest desire to merge with sugar."[45] In the end this life is about tasting – love, bliss, the Divine – and absence and hunger intensify the experience. From a *bhakti* perspective, then, it is in this ever-deepening dance of love and longing for God that life proves to be most meaningful.

Embodied existence makes possible this love, and each birth is a chance to love yet again and to deepen one's own capacity to love. It is also a chance to lead others into that love and show them the way home. Devotees speak both of finally leaving the cycle of rebirth, of "crossing over the ocean of existence," through love and grace, and of a love that is "many lives long" carrying over in birth after birth. In each lifetime we can only offer all that we have, all that we do, all that we are to God, coming as we are with all our "bungled karma," missed opportunities, enslavements, and infidelity. In a poem uncharacteristically describing Rama, the sixteenth-century Krishna devotee Mirabai sings of a poor, uneducated tribal woman who broke all purity rules in her desire to give her Lord only the sweetest fruit. She tasted each one before offering it. Her gift should have been rejected, but Mirabai exclaims:

> Ram took that fruit – that touched, spoiled fruit –
> for he knew that it stood for her love,
> This was a woman who loved the taste of love,
> and Ram knows no high, no low.
> ... You are the Lord who cares for the fallen;
> rescue whoever loves as she did![46]

And so we offer the sweetest yet tainted fruit of our own lives and find God waiting to enfold us in his/her embrace. And we, like Mahadeviyakka, must ask for divine release, bound up in love yet not quite knowing the way to God.[47] Only then will we see God everywhere we look and the Divine at the heart of all our relationships as love moves out from that center across our lives. For the Hindu devotee, this love is life's essence.

NOTES

1. A.K. Ramanujan provides an excellent introduction to *bhakti* and its origins in the Tamil region in his afterword to *Hymns for the Drowning: Poems for Viṣṇu by Nammāḻvār* (1981; New York: Penguin, 1993), pp. 103–169.
2. For further details on the Alvars in addition to Ramanujan's book on Nammalvar, see John Carman and Vasudha Narayanan, *The Tamil Veda* (Chicago: University of Chicago Press, 1989) and Vidya Dehejia, *Āṇṭāl and her Path of Love: Poems of a Woman Saint from South India* (Albany: State University of New York Press, 1990) and for the Nayanmars, see Indira Viswanathan Peterson, *Poems to Śiva: The Hymns of the Tamil Saints* (Princeton: Princeton University Press, 1989).
3. A.K. Ramanujan, trans. with intro., *Speaking of Śiva* (New York: Penguin Books, 1973).

4. R.D. Ranade, *Mysticism in India: The Poet-Saints of Maharashtra* (1933; Albany: State University of New York Press, 1983).
5. John Stratton Hawley and Mark Juergensmeyer, *Songs of the Saints of India* (New York: Oxford University Press, 1988); John Stratton Hawley, *Sūrdās: Poet, Singer, Saint* (Seattle: University of Washington Press, 1984); Kenneth Bryant, *Poems to the Child-God: Structures and Strategies in the Poetry of Sūrdās* (Berkeley: University of California Press, 1978); A.J. Alston, *The Devotional Poems of Mīrābāī* (Delhi: Motilal Banarsidass, 1980).
6. Linda Hess and Shukdev Singh, trans., *The Bījak of Kabīr* (1983; Delhi: Motilal Banarsidass, 1986); W.H. McLeod, *Gurū Nānak and the Sikh Religion* (1968; Delhi: Oxford University Press, 1996).
7. Thomas Coburn, *Encountering the Goddess* (Albany: State University of New York Press, 1991); L. Nathan and C. Seeley, trans., *Grace and Mercy in Her Wild Hair: Selected Poems to the Mother* (Boulder: Great Eastern, 1982); Malcolm McLean, *Devoted to the Goddess: The Life and Work of Ramprasad* (Albany: State University of New York Press, 1998).
8. Ramanujan discusses all these multiple facets of the relationship between the human and the Divine in much greater detail in his afterword to *Hymns for the Drowning*, pp. 103–69.
9. Carman and Narayanan, *The Tamil Veda*; John Carman, *The Theology of Rāmānuja* (New Haven: Yale University Press, 1974); Julius Lipner, *The Face of Truth: A Study of Meaning and Metaphysics in the Vedāntic Theology of Rāmānuja* (Albany: State University of New York Press, 1986).
10. Richard Barz, *The Bhakti Sect of Vallabhācārya* (1976; Delhi: Munshiram Manoharlal, 1992).
11. The reasons why a saint's name might be attached to a song not actually composed by the saint are many. For example, people might improvise on songs previously associated with the saint, try to claim the saint's authority for their own creations, acknowledge with the name a particular style of devotion associated with the saint, or attach the name of a well-loved saint to a well-loved song.
12. Nammalvar, in Ramanujan, trans., *Hymns for the Drowning*, p. 42.
13. Mahadeviyakka, in Ramanujan, trans., *Speaking of Śiva*, p. 117.
14. Basavanna, ibid., pp. 68, 71.
15. Ramprasad Sen, in Nathan and Seeley, trans., *Grace and Mercy in Her Wild Hair*, p. 24.
16. Kabir, in Hess and Singh, trans., *The Bījak of Kabīr*, p. 67.
17. Mahadeviyakka, in Ramanujan, trans., *Speaking of Śiva*, p. 131. Dasimayya uses the same venomous snake image for the hunger that encompasses not only the insatiable desire for pleasuring a falsely conceived isolated individual self but also the very real demands of the physical body for sustenance (ibid., p. 98).

18. Kabir, in Hess and Singh, trans., *The Bījak of Kabīr*, p. 103.
19. Ibid., p. 101.
20. Ibid., pp. 102, 63.
21. Ramprasad Sen, in Nathan and Seeley, trans., *Grace and Mercy in her Wild Hair*, p. 25.
22. Basavanna, in Ramanujan, trans., *Speaking of Śiva*, p. 69.
23. Dasimayya, in ibid., p. 98.
24. Ramprasad Sen, in Nathan and Seeley, trans., *Grace and Mercy in Her Wild Hair*, p. 22.
25. Ibid., p. 23.
26. Kabir, in Hess and Singh, trans., *The Bījak of Kabīr*, p. 68.
27. Mahadeviyakka, in Ramanujan, trans., *Speaking of Śiva*, p. 133.
28. Theologians wrestle with this issue of embracing embodiment and yet rejecting the world or some part of it and offer various resolutions, reflecting the larger tension within Hindu traditions between the values of asceticism and renunciation and the celebration of the joys and responsibilities of the householder life. Within the Pushitimarg, Vallabhacharya's followers speak of *laukika* versus *alaukika* realms, perceptions, and attitudes (Barz, *The Bhakti Sect of Vallabhācārya*, pp. 10 ff). The common ordinary everyday world perceived in material terms is the *laukika* realm, and a process of spiritual purification is required to move from *laukika* to *alaukika* perception of and attitudes toward the world and the body. The followers of the Gaudiya *sampraday* or sect of Chaitanya distinguish clearly between the physical (and ultimately illusory body) and the true body or *siddha-rūpa*, and between the realm of ordinary life and the divine drama of the soul's love affair with God, played out in the eternal realm of Krishna's incarnation in Vrindavan. See David Haberman, *Acting as a Way of Salvation* (New York: Oxford University Press, 1988), pp. 72–73. In some sense these theological formulations express a retreat from the deeply rooted ambivalence surrounding sexuality and the conflictual world of everyday life and an interiorization of religion.
29. Nammalvar, in Ramanujan, trans., *Hymns for the Drowning*, p. 18.
30. Ibid., p. 28.
31. Mahadeviyakka, in Ramanujan, trans., *Speaking of Śiva*, p. 122.
32. Ibid., p. 119.
33. Nammalvar, in Ramanujan, trans., *Hymns for the Drowning*, p. 55.
34. Frederique Apffel Marglin, "Types of Sexual Union and their Implicit Meaning," in *The Divine Consort: Radha and the Goddesses of India*, ed. John Stratton Hawley and Donna Marie Wulff (Boston: Beacon Press, 1982), pp. 298–315.
35. Nammalvar, in Ramanujan, trans., *Hymns for the Drowning*, p. 33.
36. Ibid., p. 64.

37. Mahadeviyakka, in Ramanujan, trans., *Speaking of Śiva*, p. 125.
38. Ibid., p. 140.
39. Tukaram, trans. in Ranade, *Mysticism in India*, pp. 335–36. This is a slightly revised form of Ranade's translation, with the verb tenses changed.
40. Diana Eck, *Darśan: Seeing the Divine Image in India*, 2nd ed. rev. and enl. (New York: Columbia University Press, 1996).
41. Vidyapati, trans. in Edward C. Dimock, Jr. and Denise Levertov, *In Praise of Krishna: Songs from the Bengali* (Chicago: University of Chicago Press, 1967), p. 15.
42. Unspecified Bengali poet, trans. in ibid., p. 37.
43. Unspecified Bengali poet, trans. in ibid., p. 56.
44. Mahadeviyakka, in Ramanujan, trans., *Speaking of Śiva*, p. 136.
45. Ramprasad Sen, in Nathan and Seeley, trans., *Grace and Mercy in Her Wild Hair*, p. 62.
46. Mirabai, trans. in Hawley and Juergensmeyer, *The Songs of the Saints of India*, p. 137.
47. See Mahadeviyakka's wonderful poem in which she likens herself to a silkworm caught in a cocoon of its own making, in Ramanujan, trans., *Speaking of Śiva*, p. 116.

Plate 10 Sculpture of MahaDevi (The Great Goddess) with her many powers and attributes represented by multiple limbs and emblems, Sri Srinivasa Perumal Temple, Singapore. Photo: *Joseph Runzo*

12

MINDFULNESS *and* MEETING *the* GREAT BLISS QUEEN

Anne C. Klein

Postmodernist narratives about subjectivity are inadequate.

Jane Flax, *Thinking Fragments*

If you hold yourself dear, watch yourself well.

Dhammapada 157

Refracted through Buddhist lenses, our lives' meanings are a rainbow arc of many colors. Our purpose is at once to overcome suffering and to acknowledge it fully, to be wholly present in ourselves and openly compassionate to others, to know the illusory nature of things and maintain ethical behavior, to accomplish spiritual goals by practicing intensely and give up all goal orientation.

These apparent paradoxes lose all tension in the face of the knowledge of "how things are" as this is understood in Buddhist traditions. What I would like to suggest here is how certain practices and their underlying logic lead toward that place of understanding within which, according to particular traditions, the meaning of all things is most fully possible.

I will begin by briefly surveying how mindfulness functions in the Theravada and Tibetan traditions, then consider the cultivation of compassion and *bodhicitta* in Tibetan Geluk contexts, and move from there to discuss the practice of Guru Yoga, here regarded in a Nyingma context. All these practices, I will suggest, are intended to bring one to the point where the potential of one's being is most dynamically experienced. This is a core meaning throughout Buddhist and many other traditions, often forming part of the "cosmic optimism" invoked by John Hick. It is in the specificity of how this is understood and accomplished that we come face to face with certain elements uniquely Buddhist.

MINDFULNESS[1]

> Without mindfulness there will be no reconstitution of already acquired knowledge and consciousness itself would break to pieces, become fragmentary.
>
> Soma Thera[2]

A subjective experience that is not primarily a function of language is central to Buddhist understanding. Buddhists are keenly aware of the profound intertwining of language and subjectivity; indeed this issue has been deeply considered from the earliest days of Buddhist philosophy in India. Nevertheless, these traditions also maintain, both implicitly and explicitly, that the mind is not only its linguistic associations, but has a depth and dimension neither wholly governed by language nor accounted for in constructionist discussions of subjectivity.

Rather, classic descriptions of mindfulness and associated states depict mind as a kind of immaterial plasticity, to be molded or toned in certain ways. These ways are described in words such as "clarity," "stability," and "intensity"[3] – terms which, familiar though they are, have not been incorporated into dominant Western discourse on mind. Nor are they descriptive of merely cognitive functioning.

For example, in ancient India, would-be surgeons were presented with a leaf floating on water and a sharp cutting instrument. Their challenge was to sever the leaf without sinking it. Too strong a stroke and the leaf is submerged; too timid an effort and it remains uncut. "[O]ne who is clever shows the scalpel stroke on it by means of a balanced effort."[4] The balance of the surgeon models the balance of mindfulness. Mindfulness, which participates in both insight and concentration, moderates both insight's tendency toward "agitation" or "excitement"[5] and concentration's tendency toward "idleness" or "laxity."[6]

In these ways, mindfulness facilities a focusing capacity beyond the level of ordinary flickering attention. Theravada, the earliest Buddhist tradition still extant (in Sri Lanka, Thailand, Mayanmar [formerly Burma], and, increasingly, among new Buddhists in India and the West), makes the *Foundations of Mindfulness Sutra*, central to its practice of insight meditation. This text teaches mindful observation first of the breath, in order to train and stabilize attention, then of the body, mind, feelings, and existential attributes of these, such as impermanence.[7] Such cultivation increases clarity and concentration. Less famously but equally importantly, it also affects how objects are experienced. When one places keen attention on breath, body, or mind itself, that object seems to dissolve and "having seen the dissolution of that object, one contemplates the dissolution of the consciousness that had that as its object."[8] As Buddhaghosa expresses it,

> all formations [e.g. the person's mental and physical constituents] which keep on breaking up, [are] like fragile pottery being smashed, like fine dust being dispersed ... Just as a man with eyes standing on the bank of a pond or on the bank of a river during heavy rain would see large bubbles appearing on the surface of the water and breaking up as soon as they appeared, so too he sees how formations break up all the time.[9]

For example, the arm usually feels solid and constant. With practice it comes to feel, at least during a meditation session, like an ongoing flux of mini-sensations with no overarching "arm" except as a name given to these myriad sensations. If one turns attention to other mental processes, including that of perception itself, the mind too is experienced as only flux, only "a cognizing function," according to Piyadassa Thera.

It might sound, from such a brief explanation, that mindfulness leads to a hopelessly particularized experience of objects and processes, perhaps even to insufferable perceptions like those of a young man known as Funes the Memorius in Jorge Luis Borges' story of the same name. After an injury to his head, Funes found every moment to be "almost intolerable in its richness and sharpness."[10] His was not an enviable situation for "Funes remembered not only every leaf of every tree of every wood, but also every one of the times he had perceived or imagined it... He was, let us not forget, incapable of ideas of a general, Platonic sort. Not only was it difficult for him to comprehend that the generic symbol *dog* embraces so many unlike individuals... it bothered him that the dog at three fourteen (seen from the side) should have the same name as the dog at three fifteen (seen from the front)."[11] Though Buddhaghosa's description might seem to suggest such a tendency toward the particular, this is not the case.

It is the case that when mindfulness is brought to bear on the body or mind, one has a powerful experience of the incurable flux that characterizes them. It is also the case that the more one's mindful concentration develops, the clearer one is about the fragile and constructed nature of mind and body. It becomes clear that mind and body are nothing but a great disappearing act. At the same time, the more grounded one is in present experience and in the steadfast flow of consciousness itself, the more one develops a physical sense of centeredness. No matter how intense the insight into flux, steady continuity of one's own mindfulness functions as a visceral voucher of meaningful continuity. Thus, in addition to its capacity to discern particularity, mindfulness is also a unifying dynamic, lending coherence to the subject even as it vividly reveals the inalterable flux of self and world. This is not a thematic or conceptual coherence; it is unified in the sense that the flow of attention, like the steady motion of a wave, is elegantly coherent.

Mindfulness simultaneously demonstrates the self's constructedness and its fully viable agency. This is not just a theoretical issue; it is perhaps the fundamental existential oxymoron: all my life I am changing (getting older, dying) and at the same time remaining the same (retaining a sense of identity). Professor Abe put this eloquently in describing our situation as 100% living and 100% dying.

All these qualities of mindfulness have to do with characteristics of mind other than knowledge. Such qualities depend on the possibility of a subjective dimension inhabited by silence. They suggest a subjective dimension which is not primarily governed by language, and which can therefore offer a form of coherence that is not necessarily a *narrative* or cognitive coherence. Mindfulness, in contrast to the intellect with its thematic ways of making connection, has the possibility of what we may call a *collateral* coherence, meaning a unifying dynamic that is an integral, or collateral, part of the functioning of continuous attention.[12]

Therefore mind is not to be understood only as a data-bearing instrument.[13] In its function as a witness, mindfulness is a silent observer, saying nothing itself. In this it resembles the "evenly hovering attention" of a psychoanalyst.[14] During meditation, as much attention is paid to one's state of the mind – distracted, soporific, peaceful, clear, intense – as to its contents. Silence in the face of thoughts and psychological distance from them are important aspects of internal processes as Buddhism understands them.

The difference between experiencing the state of mind and its contents is an important difference in Buddhism that has no real parallel in contemporary theory. Nor is there a parallel to the related and equally crucial internal difference between mindless distraction or laxity and mindful intensity. Probably only a tradition that acknowledges the significance of internal silence can feature its ontological analog, the unconditioned emptiness, as part of a path to liberation. Buddhism must have categories of mind that are not linked with language since it does not find all epistemological error to be a function of language.[15] It is not only language that splits us into object-observing subjects. The senses do this also. But all silences are not the same.

I have just suggested that the silent mind has its analog in the world of objects as well. This is what Buddhists variously call emptiness, selflessness, or the unconditioned. Buddhism recognizes the unconditioned as a category compatible with this endless flow. Here we can understand "unconditioned" simply to mean that any person or thing is qualified by an absence of existing independently of causes and conditions. The absence of independence from causes and conditions is not a factor created by anyone, and is therefore itself unconditioned. Yet this unconditioned makes possible all conditioning, causality, and change. The unconditioned is also often called "inexpressible," but to understand the significance of this in a Buddhist context, we need to recognize that all things are inexpressible. Inexpressibility alone does not signify the unconditioned.

Gelukba and much of Indo-Tibetan Buddhism understands language to be a system of imperfect and indirect representation. Words do not elicit the actual emptiness, any more than the word "table" elicits a complete table. The unconditioned emptiness cannot be communicated fully through language, but neither can ordinary things be fully expressed by language or known by thought. When emptiness is known directly, however, thought is absent. At the same time emptiness, the absence of inherent existence, is fully present to one's experience. Nothing about emptiness is deferred or differentiated from one's mind. Yet, there is nothing particular in emptiness to be assumed present in the first place. It is a mere absence.

So we have moved from the silence of mindfulness to the absence of emptiness. Does this mean that nothing happens in a meaningful life? Of course not. To explore this, we can consider the cultivation of compassion and its relation to both mindfulness and the wisdom of emptiness.

COMPASSIONATELY KNOWING EMPTINESS

In about the sixth century, Candrakirti wrote a text that was to become central to the subsequent development of Madhyamika in India and fundamental as well to Madhyamika scholarship in Tibetan traditions down to the present day. This was of course the *Entrance to the Middle Way (Madhyamakavtara, dbU ma la 'jug pa),*[16] a commentary on the only work that may claim priority in the field of Madhyamika, Nagarjuna's *Root Verses of the Middle Way (Mulamadhyamakakarikas, dbUma rtsa ba).*[17] It is widely understood that the full meaning of these works may ripen, if one is fortunate, after a lifetime of study and practice. However, we can touch on one aspect significant for our discussion.

In the fourth verse in his root text, having praised compassion, non-dual understanding, and altruism as the core conditions giving rise to Bodhisattvas, Candrakirti considers compassion more specifically. He attributes all the suffering of cyclic existence to an erroneous sense of self. This deeply ingrained error inevitably produces craving based on an unrealistic sense of ownership; hence, the mistaken sense of "I" and "mine" is the ultimate cause of suffering. Those of us who have not yet been freed of this inborn error are in Candrakirti's words "powerless like a bucket in well" – yanked willy nillly up and down the uninviting parameters of cyclic existence.[18] Candrakirti eloquently pays homage to the arc of compassion Bodhisattvas extend to such persons. He further suggests that there are three styles of compassion that are distinguished, not by their subjective aspects, which is always a wish to relieve suffering, but are distinguished by how they understand the objects of their compassion. He says:

> [Homage to that compassion for] beings
> Seen as evanescent and empty of inherent
> Existence like a moon in rippling water.[19]

In his own commentary on this verse, Candrakirti notes that there are three styles of compassionate understanding. The first arises through having observed the manifest pain of living beings, from which derives a wish to protect them. Candrakirti bows down to this great compassion.[20] The second and third types of compassion, Candrakirti continues, are even clearer about the situation, or nature, of those for whom they have compassion. The second compassion is nourished not only by an awareness of how beings suffer, but through understanding as well as their impermanence and consequent instability, likened to the movement of rippling water. The third type of compassion is an understanding that, just as the moon reflected in water looks like the moon but is in fact devoid of even the slightest vestige of moon-nature, so living beings who look so substantial, self-sufficient, and self-possessed are in fact devoid of even the slightest vestige of a real or true nature, meaning a nature that is wholly independent of causes and conditions. This ignorance about their own nature is described as a vast blue ocean of ignorance in which beings wander continually.[21]

This three-fold way of structuring the growth of wisdom in compassion became central to numerous traditions in Tibet. Gampopa, the famous eleventh-century student of Milarepa, names them in his *Jewel Ornament of Liberation*, a classic primer of Tibetan Buddhism by one of the father figures of the Kagyu lineage. In the fourteenth century, Tsongkhapa, the teacher of the first Dalai Lama and founder of the Geluk or Yellow Hat order of Tibetan Buddhism, also elaborates on these in his commentary to Candrakirti's work, *Illumination of the Thought (of Candrakirti's Middle Way)*.[22]

This suggests, among other things, that knowledge of the specific ills of individual beings' condition is compatible with, and indeed amplified by, knowledge of the universal conditions to which all life is subject. Everyone born dies. Moreover, between birth and death there is not a single moment of changlessness, of stability. Subtle impermanence pervades our existence, as well as the existence of the universe and its insentient contents. Yet despite the incontrovertible fact that all these things and beings are subject to moment-by-moment disintegration, they appear quite differently. They look solid, and often seem altogether independent of the causes that gave rise to them, or even the parts on which they depend in this very moment. To see beyond this illusion of independence is to begin to move in the direction of the famous wisdom that finally liberates one from that blue ocean of delusion and suffering. This wisdom is aware of, and inseparable from, that which is variously called emptiness, Buddha-nature, the unconditioned, primordial purity, the nature of things, or the natural condition. Whatever exists is suffused by this nature. In other words, the specificity that goes along with compassionate reflection brings one to this vast arena of unity, known in some traditions as the single sphere.[23] This is the ultimate sea from which even the ocean of ignorance springs, and into which it is meant to dissolve.

For the Mahayana traditions in particular, gifting others with kindness is the central purpose of practice and life in general. Fully flowered, such compassion is imbued with and sustained by the all-encompassing embrace of wisdom. This expansive wisdom arena can be approached by seeing thoughts dissolve in the face of mindfulness, and by experiencing the singularity expressed in the multiplicity of life as we know it.

GURU YOGA AND THE GREAT BLISS QUEEN

The process of dissolution, and the relationship between the particularity of conditioned things and the expansive breadth of the unconditioned, is also announced through the practice of Guru Yoga, a ritual meditation central to all the Tibetan traditions.

There are three main configurations of disciple–guru relations. The first is human to deity, such as Tsongkhapa's living vision of Manjushri; the second and perhaps most significant for our discussion is the ritualization of human-to-human as well as human-to-divine student–teacher relationships in a practice known as Guru Yoga; the third and most difficult to ascertain is what actually goes on between human beings who are students and teachers. I speak here primarily of Guru Yoga, with some allusion to other elements involved in the connection between guru and students.[24]

Guru Padmasambhava, the great guru of the Nyingma tradition, is understood to have promised always to be present to anyone who has faith. "In my life, death does not exist. For this reason, I shall always be present to every individual who has faith." And the fifth Dalai Lama who, despite being the ranking master of the Geluk order was known to have great faith in Guru Rinboche, was sometimes teased by a servant, who claimed he had great difficulty entering His Holiness' room at night because Guru Rinboche was sitting in the doorway.[25] This in fact describes the archetypal activity of the guru – being there. Guru Rinboche promised:

> For men and women who have trust [faith] in me
> I, Padmasambhava, have never gone anywhere, but am standing at their door.
> There is no birth or death in my life.
> In front of every person there is a Padmasambhava.[26]

Guru Yoga is the culminating practice of a liturgical recitation and meditational training known as the preliminary practices (*sngon 'gro*). All the preceding practices (refuge, compassion, Vajrasattva purification, and mandala offering) are seen as preparing the ground, mentally, physically, spiritually, and ethically, for the encounter with the guru. For the Nyingma tradition explicitly, and in much of the Tibetan tradition as a whole, including the more esoteric rituals of tantra which require initiation and formal commitments, some aspect of Guru Yoga is *the* central practice.

The principle of Guru Yoga is that one is tuning in to, connecting with, one's own guru; hence the heart-to-heart – or sword-to-heart – connection between Tsongkhapa and Manjushri. The efficacy of this practice depends to a great extent on the heartfelt connection with a particular teacher as well as an idealized universal – hence the conflation of mythos and image with one's own personal teacher. Guru Yoga therefore also depends on the practitioner's ability to see the teacher as enlightened, utterly pure, unsullied by illness, anger, or any other limiting factor. Only in this way can one's own consciousness come into harmony and fully resonate with the mind of enlightenment embodied in the lama.

This methodology may include, but also expands upon, what Western psychology calls idealization. The practice of pure appearances (*tag snang*) involves cultivating a felt sense that one's environment and the persons encountered in it are all composed of light, unsullied in any way by solidities such as flesh or any other kind of solid matter. This sensibility is cultivated in relation to most practices. Sustaining such a sense of pure appearance is considered, in the words of the modern Lama Khetsun Sangpo, to actually bring the student more closely in touch with what is really there. It is explicitly not a case of covering over reality with something prettier, but of uncovering a pristine reality behind the appearance that would obscure it.

To speak about one's relation to reality is to point in the direction of the subject, not the object; to the self, and not the guru. This suggests the most subtle and, from the perspective of many traditions, the most wondrous aspect of the guru–disciple relationship, and one that takes place in the distinctly human realm. It has to do with understanding that the guru is a manifestation of one's own most excellent, primordial consciousness (*ye shes*). This term is a standard Tibetan gloss for what is often translated as wisdom, thereby suggesting something more like a finished product than a beginningless and utterly natural dynamic.

It is very clear, both in tantric and in Dzogchen presentations, that ultimately the divine deity, the great guru, is to be understood as oneself. There are different ways of approaching this remarkable understanding; to speak of them would be to open the virtually endless catalog of practices and narratives associated with Tibetan and many other forms of Buddhism. For the Tibetan imagination, the human guru, male or female, dwells in a matrix of vibrant space, peopled by extrasensory beings, some of whom the guru actually embodies. The guru may also be understood – in a crucial cultural difference only briefly alluded to above – as the representative *qua* reincarnation of previous renowned figures in the lineage he now imparts to the student.

Yet, the same Tibetans who fully regard His Holiness the Dalai Lama as the enlightened Bodhisattva Avalokitesvara also pray on a regular basis for his long life. The invisible presence of Avalokitesvara, and his manifestation in the human body of Tenzin Gyatso the fourteenth Dalai Lama, are wholly identified, and at the same time not confused. This makes it possible to engage in extraordinary "idealization" without at the same time losing the human dynamic.

In 1973 I visited the residence of Geshe Wangyal, the first Tibetan-trained teacher to come to the West, who was then living in rural New Jersey with a few American students. I had no idea how to behave, but I had heard a little bit about Guru Yoga so the one thing I was sure of was that, since I would of course regard him as omniscient, I need not say anything. He would know what I was thinking, recognize who I was, and act accordingly. I played my part by waiting quietly. Before too long he was loudly declaring his assessment of me to the other students: "What is wrong with her? She doesn't say anything." It was clear that, in order to pass lunch with the guru, I was going to have to interact with him like an ordinary human being. At the same time, I could choose to enrich that interaction by knowingly pretending that I was experiencing a Buddha's presence presiding over the pizza.

Like the Tibetans who pray for the Dalai Lama's long life while still seeing him as the deathless Avalokitesvara, like the monk whose anger arises but dissolves into the vast ocean of the mind, like the bestower of compassion who has infinite concern for a world she fully understands as illusory, any student of Buddhism trains in uniting two realms into one the ocean and its waves, the empty and its appearances, the ultimate and the conventional it makes possible, the pervasive and the particular.

This infinitude proceeds along spatial as well as temporal dimensions. In a particular form of Guru Yoga associated with the female figure of enlightenment known as Yeshey Tsogyal, the Great Bliss Queen, one proceeds to this infinitude through finite imagery, using one's sustained awareness of her magnificent iconographic detail to cultivate a measure of mindful concentration. This stable focus facilitates compassionate understanding of the spacious dimension that such awareness reveals. Simultaneously, this special subjective state that is present to the conflation of the visible and invisible, manifest and secret, is also at the heart of the dynamism of the Buddhist philosophy, practice, art, and ritual. It is exemplified as well in the prayer of refuge to the Great Bliss Queen:

> Never having parted from you or met you, I take refuge in
> you
> Sky Woman's[27] unborn, primordial wisdom dimension.

These words are uttered in, and usher forth, a state of focused exaltation in which one recognizes and honors one's own oneness with all gurus, here manifest as the Yeshey Tsogyal, the Great Bliss Queen. She is now experienced as identical with oneself, an expression of the primordial purity and spontaneous excellence of one's own mind, even if the actual experience and nature of that identity is presently obscure. This is why meeting the Great Bliss Queen – the essence of all Buddha wisdom – is in a very specific sense meeting the most primal part of oneself. If one does not yet know that aspect of oneself, other practices – compassion, purification – which are initially based more on the particular than the universal, are required.

But one is finally meant to recognize, at least ritually, that you, the invisible and pervasive, are one with me, the all-too-visible, limited, and ordinary. Philosophically and practically, this kind of endeavor only makes sense if we consider that there is a dimension of our being not governed by the specific, not governed by language, emotion, and image. Then, the movement toward Yeshey Tsogyal in Guru Yoga is not approaching a boundary waiting to be crossed, but a wholeness ready to be encountered, already replete with meaning. The pervasive unconditioned gives dynamism to the localized conditioned, and the latter offers the seeker a way to the universal unconditioned. The open dimension of specific expressions of mindfulness, compassion, and wisdom becomes accessible though any or all of these intersuffusing pathways.

NOTES

1. Much of this section is condensed from my *Meeting the Great Bliss Queen: Buddhists, Feminists, and the Art of the Self* (Boston: Beacon Press, 1995).
2. Soma Thera, *The Way of Mindfulness: The Satipaṭṭhāna Sutta and Commentary* (Candy, Ceylon, [Sri Lanka]: Buddhist Publication Society, 1941, reprinted 1967), p. xviii.
3. Clarity, *gsal ba, samprakhyāna*; also, Tibetan treatments, "factor of subjective clarity" (*drang cha*); intensity (Tib. *ngar*). For discussion of these in relation to calm abiding see Geshe Gedun Lodro, *Walking Through Walls*, trans. Jo Hopkins (Ithaca: Snow Lion Publications, 1992), pp. 166 ff.
4. Buddhaghosa, *Path of Purification* (*Visuddhimagga*), trans. Bhikkhu Ñyāṇamoli (Berkeley and London: Shambala, 1976), IV. 68 (vol. I., p. 141).
5. *Auddhataya, rgod pa.*
6. *Laya, bying ba.* "Mindfulness protects the mind from lapsing into agitation through faith, energy, and understanding, which favor agitation, and from lapsing into idleness through concentration, which favors idleness" (Buddhaghosa, *Path of Purification*, IV. 49 [vol. I, p. 136]. Buddhaghosa also notes that "balancing the faculties" is one of eleven activities that lead to the arising of concentration (specifically, that concentration known as a "limb of enlightenment") (IV. 61 [vol. I, p. 139]).
7. For a translation of this sutra see Nyanaponita Thera, *The Heart of Buddhist Meditation* (London: Rider & Company, 1962, reprinted 1980), pp. 117–135; for further discussion of mindfulness by modern Theravadins see Ibid., and Walpola Rahula, *What the Buddha Taught* (New York: Grove Press, 1980).
8. Buddhaghosa, *Path of Purification*, XXI. 23.
9. Ibid., XXI. 27.
10. In Jorge Luis Borges *Labyrinths* (New York: Modern Library, 1983), p. 63
11. Ibid., p. 65.
12. This use of the term "collateral" derives from Gregory Bateson' formulation in *Mind and Nature: A Necessary Unity* (New York: Dutton 1979), p. 108. My use of the term is further developed in *Meeting the Grea Bliss Queen*, esp. pp. 66–69, 194–199.
13. As is the case for Bakhtin or in Rorty's reading of Freud. See Jane Flax *Thinking Fragments: Psychoanalysis, Feminism, and Postmodernism in th Contemporary West* (Berkeley: University of California Press, 1990), p. 21

with reference to Richard Rorty, "Freud and Moral Reflection," in *Pragmatism's Freud: The Moral Disposition of Psychoanalysis*, ed. Joseph H. Smith and William Kerrigan (Baltimore: John Hopkins University Press, 1986).

14. This is also the goal of the person in analysis. This is a kind of mental silence that allows the analyst to listen closely and clearly to the analysand, and the analysand to be aware of what is coming to her own consciousness. (Thanks to Meredith Skura for this observation in the course of a seminar sponsored by the Rice Center for Cultural Studies, Fall, 1990.)
15. This is especially true in the Gelukba Consequentialist (Prasangika) school which regards the errors it seeks to correct as not only mental or conceptual but as pervading sensory perception as well. Moreover, sensory perception can, at least in Buddhist theory, operate without conceptual overlay. For a discussion of Buddhism's claim to deal with a level of error more primal than language, see Elizabeth Napper, *Dependent Arising and Emptiness* (Boston: Wisdom Publications, 1989), pp. 92ff.
16. For a French translation of the root text and Candrakirti's own commentary (up to VI. 165), see Louies de la Vallee Poussin; in *Museon*, 8, 1907, pp. 2249–317; *Museon*, 11, 1910, pp. 271–358; and *Museon*, 12, 1911, pp. 235–328. For English translations see C.W. Huntington and Geshe Namgyal Wangchen, *The Emptiness of Emptiness* (Honolulu: University of Hawaii Press, 1989).
17. For English translations see Frederick Streng, *Emptiness: A Study in Religious Meaning* (Nashville, New York: Abingdon Press, 1967) and Jay Garfield (trans.), *The Fundamental Wisdom of the Middle Way: Nagarjuna's Mulamadhyamakakarika* (New York: Oxford University Press, 1995).
18. 3c (the third line "c" in the third stanza), Hopkins, p. 117; *Rang 'grel* (Candrakirti's own commentary) 8.13 ff.
19. 4abc (the first, second and third lines of the fourth stanza); 14.1 in the original Tibetan text; Hopkins, p. 120.
20. *Rang 'grel* 9.11.
21. *Rang 'grel* 10.5.
22. *DbU ma la 'jug pa'i rgya cher bshad pa dgongs pa rab gsal* (Sarnath: Pleasure of Elegant Sayings Press, 1973). English translation of first five chapters in Jeffrey Hopkins and Kensur Ngawang Lekden, *Compassion in Tibetan Buddhism* (Ithaca: Snow Lion, 1980). Oral commentary and translation of opening section of chapter in *Path to the Middle: Oral Madhyamika Philosophy in Tibet, The Spoken Scholarship of Kensur Yeshey Tupden*, trans. and ed. Anne Klein, Tsonkhapa's text trans. Jeffrey Hopkins (Albany: SUNY Press, 1994).
23. *Thigle nyag bcig* is a well-known phrase in the Dzogchen traditions of Nyingma and Bon.

24. This section is condensed from my "Gurus and Disciples in Tibet: Worlds Visible and Invisible," forthcoming as part of the proceedings of the NYU Conference "Rending the Veil: Concealment and Revelation of Secrets in the History of Religions."
25. Khetsun Sangpo, *Tantric Practice in Nyingma,* ed. and trans. Jeffrey Hopkins, co-ed. Anne Klein (London: Rider, 1982).
26. Tulku Thondup, *Enlightened Journey: Buddhist Practice as Daily Life* (Boston and London: Shambala, 1995), p. 158.
27. Ngawang Denzin Dorje, *Ra tig.* 12.1 (*The Ra Commentary on the Great Bliss Queen Practice*). This paragraph is drawn from Klein, *Meeting the Great Bliss Queen,* p. 172.

13

HAITIAN VODOU: THE DISTINCT SELF *and the* RELATIONAL WORLD[†]

Karen McCarthy Brown

In this chapter, I discuss the meaning of life in Haitian Vodou, arguably the most maligned and misunderstood religion in the world. As "voodoo" the word is often used as a synonym for evil, but it actually means "spirit" or "deity" in the language of the Fon of the former kingdom of Dahomey, now the People's Republic of Benin. Haitian Vodou was born from the turmoil occasioned by transatlantic chattel slavery, and it thus represents a primary response to some of the worst exploitation and cruelty in human history. These are the philosophical and moral credentials with which Haitians configure a world in which people emerge as distinct individuals only to the extent that they respect and nurture their relationships with family members, friends, ancestors, and spirits. This is not the paradox that it might seem from the individualistic perspective of Euro-America. In Vodou, it is accepted that no individual can accomplish anything truly worthwhile without calling on the help of others. The dense nexus of relationships among Vodou spirits, the living, and the dead defines, sustains, and even creates each individual human being.

The chapter begins with a description of a healing ceremony performed by Brooklyn Vodou priestess Mama Lola. This ritual provokes a larger and more general discussion of the worldview and ethics of Haitian Vodou. My chapter ends with a decentering move in which I

[†] This chapter is a slightly revised portion of Karen McCarthy Brown's previously published essay "The Moral Forcefield of Haitian Vodou," found in *In the Face of the Facts: Moral Inquiry in American Scholarship*, ed. Richard Wightman Fox and Robert B. Westbrook (1998) and is reprinted here with the permission of Cambridge University Press.

suggest that we read current public moral debates in the United States against the views of person and community operative in Vodou.

MORALITY AND HAITIAN VODOU

In the fall of 1994, Mama Lola, a Vodou priestess living in Brooklyn, produced a *mare djòl*, a charm called "shut the mouth," for one of her clients.[1] Inside a terracotta pot, roughly the size of a bulging milk bottle, she put *sabilye* leaves (to foster forgetting), salt (a prophylactic), molasses (a sweetener), the name of an electronics company on Long Island, and the name of a female employee of that company. She completely covered the pot with a white cloth ("you tie the mouth with a white cloth") and then wrapped yard after yard of white cotton string around the pot until it came to resemble a small, fat mummy. Having produced a wide loop with the last few feet of string, she suspended the *mare djòl* from a heating pipe that crossed the ceiling of her small basement altar room. Whenever she thought of it in the course of a day's work, she would reach up and set the charm swinging.

My intention is to the use the *mare djòl* as a road into Vodou morality. In the process of evoking a religious context and then focusing on the operation of values within that context, I will quote Mama Lola and refer often to her style of practicing Vodou. I have worked with Mama Lola since 1978, and it is largely to her that I am indebted for what I know of the intricacies and intimacies of Haitian Vodou, the religion of the great majority of Haitian people.[2]

A Web of Relationships

Mama Lola's *mare djòl* was created for a man having trouble with his supervisor at the electronics plant where he worked. The supervisor was jealous of him because he attracted favorable attention from those higher up in the firm. So, she gossiped about Mama Lola's client in ways that damaged his reputation and, he feared, threatened his job. Healing work (one-on-one treatment sessions for problems of health, family, job, love, and money) is the most time-consuming part of the work of a *manbo*, a Vodou priestess, or a *oungan*, a Vodou priest. And yet it is more than metaphoric speech to claim that all Vodou, even elaborate public ceremonies, is about healing. All healing orchestrated by Vodou priests and priestesses concerns the healing of relationships.

Mama Lola practices the "science of the concrete" in her healing work; she objectifies complex relational situations.[3] She turns them into objects in the physical world and then changes them, in this instance, by introducing more desirable ingredients into the social–emotional mix. Into the red clay pot containing the names of the supervisor and the electronics firm, Lola put *sabilye* leaves to make the supervisor and those she influenced forget the entire affair. Salt and molasses were also added; the first as a cleanser and the second as a sweetener of the office atmosphere.

There were several distinct African religious traditions practiced among the people who made up Haiti's slave population. Haitian Vodou originated as the blending of these traditions with a number of eighteenth-century European spiritualities represented in the French colonial population. Of the latter, Catholicism was by far the most important influence, although by no means the only one. Freemasonry, for example, has also left a significant mark on Haitian Vodou. Despite the bouquet of detectable influences in Vodou, it remains at the core an African religion displaced to and transformed by the Caribbean.[4] The assumptions about the nature of personhood in Vodou make this judgment clear.

In the Vodou view of things, human beings are not only defined by the web of relationships that surrounds them; it is more accurate to say that they are created out of those relations. This relational web has both temporal and spatial dimensions. It connects persons to living family members of all ages, as well as to ancestors, and through ancestors, to the many *lwa,* Vodou spirits.

On the plane of the living, the dense relational web may be stretched by the creation of honorary "mothers" and "fathers," "aunts" and "uncles," and innumerable ad hoc "sisters," "brothers," and "cousins." These are persons who, through social influence, relative wealth, exceptional wisdom, or the goodness of their hearts, have come to play the role of a family member. When considering this somewhat cumbersome fictive family, it is good to remember that Haiti is one of the poorest countries in the world. Adding members beyond blood kin to one's exchange network provides extra strength in the social safety net, something that is important to impoverished Haitians.

Ideally, all relations within the web are reciprocal. It is easiest to grasp this point in relation to the living family where reciprocity entails not only the respect and service the young are expected to give their elders as a matter of course, but also the shelter, food, and general care due to children from those same elders. From this perspective, biology is not sufficient to establish the parenthood of the parent; acting like a father or mother is. Theoretically, a Haitian who neglects the responsibilities of the parental role, or abuses the power that comes along with it, can be shamed into compliance by a respectful speech in which the offender is frequently referred to as "father" or "mother."[5]

There are other ways in which the Vodou ethos reinforces the ties and responsibilities among the living. For example, Vodou underwrites the influence of children and of the poor, the least powerful of society's creatures. It designates both as exceptional sources of blessing and of luck. For example, to ensure the continued good fortune of the family, every family with the means to do it is expected to host a *manje pov*, a ritual feeding of the poor. The *manje pov*, which ideally should be held every few years, begins with a highly stylized feeding of the spirit children, the *mawasa* or divine twins. This special pre-meal is presented to the stand-ins for the *mawasa*, the children of the poor people who have been invited to the patron's temple or home for the feast. Being both children and poor, this is a group doubly empowered to dispense blessings. When everyone has eaten, the poor – children and adults – wash their hands in an infusion of basil leaves and wipe them on the clothing of the patron of the feast, thus passing on their blessings to their host.

Like the poor, the ancestors are both dependent and powerful. Mama Lola recently remarked: "When you die you have more power than when you alive. When somebody die he can help his children." Yet she has also told me more than once that *vivan-yo*, the living, do not envy the condition of the dead. In Vodou the dead do not go to heaven; instead they descend to the bottom of the water, a place of chill and dampness. Furthermore, after a year or more has passed, it is up to the living to rehabilitate the souls of the dead, or at least those that had important spiritual connections during their lives. The *rele mò nan dlo*, calling the dead from the waters, is a lengthy and expensive Vodou ceremony without which these ancestors can do nothing more constructive than harass their descendants. This ceremony warms the dead, raises them up from the water (they emerge complaining of cold and hunger), feeds them, and finally installs them in consecrated *govi*, pots, on Vodou altars.[6] Periodic feeding is necessary after the ancestral spirits have taken their place on the family altars. Without attention from the living, the ancestors could not continue to work for the living by warding off danger, countering malevolence, giving advice, and enhancing luck.

The *lwa,* spirits who were brought to Haiti from Africa, are central to the religion of Vodou, and they are not to be confused with the ancestors, or with God. God is called Bondye by those who serve the Vodou spirits, and it is Bondye who created and sustains the world. But as Mama Lola frequently observes: "He is too busy." A person cannot plead with Bondye or demand from him; if it is determined that a disease "comes from God," the Vodou healer can do nothing about it. The *lwa* are different. The *lwa* enjoy the song and dance performed for them. They need the food prepared for them, the candles that are lighted for them, and the libations that are poured.

Some *lwa* are like intimate family members who can be coaxed and cajoled. Others are fiercer. But if the one who serves the spirits knows how to treat the fierce *lwa,* they too will deliver healing, luck, and even money. Sometimes the *lwa* can even be told what to do. The living occasionally explode in anger at the spirits and threaten to cut off the flow of gifts and honors if they do not come through with the desired help. (Haitian Vodou is a religion that values self-confidence more than humility.) *Lwa* interact with the living mainly through possession-trance, during which they take over the body and voice of an adept in order to sing and dance with the faithful, as well as give them advice and, when necessary, chastisement. Interaction with the *lwa* by means of possession-trance is frequent, powerful, intimate, and central to Vodou.

The living, the dead, and the spirits are all caught up in this dense relational web, and furthermore, it is not always easy to mark the boundaries among the three important groups. Just as the line between persons and their spirits is blurred during possession, so the dividing line between spirits and ancestors can sometimes appear less than distinct. One example demonstrates both of these types of boundary blurring equally well. People speak of Mama Lola's major spirit as "Lola's Ogou," and when she dies, the family member who takes over her altar, and therefore her spiritual obligations, may well be possessed by a spirit identified as "Lola's Ogou." Such an occurrence would be both a return of the ancestor and a visit from the spirit. Also, both spirit and ancestor would manifest by possessing the body of the living family member.

The intermingling and overlapping of the living and the dead, the human and the divine, is beautifully captured in a song often sung at the opening of Vodou ceremonies. It begins:

Anonse o zanj nan dlo,
Bak odsu miwa . . .

Alert the angels down in the water,
Back beneath the mirror . . .

Vodou's Ginen, or Africa, is the watery home of the spirits, who also are called "angels," and of the dead as well. Ginen lies under the sea, "back beneath the mirror." With sparse language this song evokes the image of devotees gazing into the calm, mirroring surface of the sea, a boundary that separates them from Africa, and seeing there faces composed from transparent layers: their own reflections in the mirror; beneath their reflections, the faces of the ancestors; and, deeper still, those of the spirits themselves.

When Mama Lola made the *mare djòl*, she sought to clear blockage in the relational network that sustains her client – most immediately, a constriction in the relationship between him and his supervisor at the place where he worked. (Note that the problem was not conceptualized as an essential flaw in either one of the persons involved; it was located in the space between them.) Yet the blockage in that relationship was indicative of other, more serious, blockages. It was understood that for Mama Lola's client to have a problem of this sort there must be parallel problems in his relationship with the spirits. If all had been well with them, they would have prevented his problem with the supervisor from developing in the first place. Because of this two-tier diagnosis, treatment for the problem proceeded on two levels as well. Mama Lola told her client what to do in his own home, on a daily basis, that would feed and strengthen his spiritual protectors. Then, turning to the more immediate symptom of the problem, Mama Lola made the *mare djòl* to "tie up the mouth" of the gossiping supervisor. Several months later, when her client told Mama Lola that his supervisor had been promoted and, at the same time, transferred to another branch of the company outside New York, both he and Mama Lola pronounced the healing work successful.

The Spirits in and around the Head

It is generally assumed in Vodou circles that the character of a person is largely composed of the various spiritual influences playing in and around that person, including but not limited to spirits inherited within the family.[7] Each person has one spirit called the *mèt tèt*, master of the head, and this spirit is thought of as residing in the head of the person, as well as being a free-moving spirit in the larger social world. ("The spirit is a wind," Mama Lola is fond of saying.)

The Vodou system of identifying each person's *mèt tèt* amounts to a method for personality typing, and this system is of great significance for understanding the moral force field of Haitian Vodou. For example, one whose *mèt tèt* is Ogou, the warrior spirit, can be expected to have a life larded with issues of justice and power. Since each Vodou spirit is not so much a moral examplar as a moral catalyst, both the constructive and destructive dimensions of the spirit's particular domains are likely to surface in the life of the person served by that spirit. Again, consider Ogou. He is connected to the soldier-liberators of Haiti's slave population, Toussaint L'Ouverture and Jean-Jacques Dessalines, but there are other manifestations of Ogou as well, ones that mirror him back to the devotee as braggart, drunkard, and liar.

Ogou's possession-performances act out a wide range of possible outcomes from the aggressive use of power. For example, military power can liberate, but it can also betray, and even become self-destructive.[8] Ogou thus preserves, in highly condensed form, the lessons of Haitian history, a history that includes not only the single successful slave revolution in the history of transatlantic slavery, but also brutal dictators drawn from the Haitian population, as well as two occupations by the U.S. armed forces. In all layers of this dense history, themes of pride and liberation are interwoven with those of shame, anger, betrayal, and self-destruction. By extension, Ogou also explores the many kinds of metaphoric "war" a person is faced with in a place like New York City, home of the largest Haitian diaspora community. At the same time the various personae of this warrior spirit present an almost clinical analysis of the beneficial uses of anger and aggression, as well as their attendant pathologies.[9]

Vodou is a system able to configure considerable nuance and complexity in the character of individual persons because of its recognition of secondary spirit influences. The dominance of the *mèt tèt* over a person's character and consciousness is significantly modulated by the counterweights of a small number of other spirits (usually two or three) also said to "love" that person. These coteries of personal *lwa* vary from one individual to another and cause the Vodou community to have somewhat different behavioral expectations of persons who "serve," that is observe ritual obligation to, different configurations of *lwa.*

For example, Mama Lola serves two of the Ezili sisters, Freda and Dantò, in addition to Ogou. Ezili Freda is a spirit of wealth, beauty, and sexuality whose destructiveness emerges as self-involvement and an insatiable hunger for attention and affection. Dantò is stronger, more effective, and also potentially more destructive. She is the woman who bears children, something Freda cannot do, and the mother who raises them on her own, as most poor women in Haiti do. Ezili Dantò's ability to endure in the midst of great hardship is paramount to her character. Equally pronounced is her willingness to defend her children at all costs, but, when her anger-driven persistence skids off track and runs amok, she can quickly transform into the kind of mother who might well attack her own children.[10]

Ogou energy is individualistic; it takes risks and has adventures. The character traits Mama Lola shares with Ogou are those that pushed her to take the risk of leaving Haiti and trying life in the United States. Yet, were it not for almost equally strong Dantò energy, Mama Lola would not be who she is, the mother of four and the head of a lively multigenerational Brooklyn household. Similarly, without a visible though subtle Freda presence, Mama Lola would be less of a playful vamp than I know her to be, and she probably would not be taking on a new "boyfriend" as she approaches her sixty-third birthday.

The matrix of spiritual energies within a single individual provides important moral flexibility for the one who serves the Vodou spirits. Consider the issue of abortion. As a Catholic, Mama Lola feels that abortion is wrong. As one who serves Ezili Dantò, the quintessential mother, she is also opposed to abortion. Nevertheless, she tells two quite different stories about the spirits' influence in relation to this issue in her own life. In one story Ezili Dantò came in a dream and told Lola to stop trying to abort a pregnancy. Even though Lola had been deserted by the father of the child and, at the time, was so poor she had to struggle to feed the two children she already had, she bowed to the wishes of Dantò. Her third child was born. Some years later, while in a stable relationship with a man, she became pregnant again. Both Lola and her partner wanted the child, but long after discovering her condition, Lola got word that she had been granted a visa to emigrate to the United States. If the pregnancy had been discovered, she would have lost the visa. So Ogou, the adventurer and risktaker, gave support to Lola's decision to have an abortion in order to take advantage of what might have been her only chance to escape Haiti.[11]

Wande Abimbola, a Nigerian Ogun priest and an internationally known scholar, once described the central moral energy of traditional Yoruba religion as helping people "ride their horses in the direction they are going."[12] In other words, he described a religion that recognizes that people are different from one another, with different talents, different strengths and weaknesses. Living a good life will then mean different things for different people. Thus knowledge of self becomes a prerequisite for knowing how to live a good life, a life of responsibility to the community. The Vodou attitude toward persons is similar.

The Yoruba and the Haitian religious traditions are historically related. Both traditions have elaborate divinatory systems designed to diagnose character, as well as to assess the particular problems in people's lives. What each person who serves the Vodou spirits learns through this divination process is the pattern of spirit influences peculiar to them. Once this is known and a Vodou adept has been given the tools to consult and feed these personal spirits, that person has also garnered some leverage in the moral world and has done so by gaining self-knowledge. The adept can lean into her strengths and anticipate where life's problems are likely to arise.

Along with this dynamic view of personhood, one constituted from several distinct spirit energies, comes considerable appreciation for diversity within the individual. In Vodou communities there is no high premium placed on maintaining a smooth facade or on behaving consistently. In a related way, there is also a high tolerance for diversity within the community at large. For example, in the context of a quite homophobic larger society, gay men and lesbian women are welcomed into the Vodou temples. While this is generally true in all Vodou temples, there are some temples that specifically cater to Haiti's gay population.

Balanse

"Why did you hang the *mare djòl* from the ceiling in your altar room?" I asked Mama Lola. "So I could *balanse* . . . You know, make it go like that," she replied, swishing her hand from side to side. The word *balanse* in Haitian Creole is one of those words that is used in everyday discourse but takes on added meaning in a Vodou context. In ordinary speech a person might reply, in response to a question about what she is doing that evening, "I am balancing between going to see a movie and staying home." In other words, she is undecided and is weighing her options. The image conjured up is that of a pair of scales, a mechanism on which one thing is weighed against another. Such a pair of scales, called a *balans*, is in fact a central image in Vodou iconography, just as it is in American jurisprudence. But in the Vodou temple the scales do not signify the quest for evening scores, balancing punishment against crime, and achieving equilibrium. On the contrary, in Vodou settings the *balans* (the scale) signals a quest for dynamism, movement, energy.

A set of scales signals the process by which the static can be reanimated. For example, when certain objects are taken off a Vodou altar, they cannot be introduced into the ritual action until someone has swung them from side to side, or has turned themselves around and around while holding the objects in their hands or on their heads. To move thus with a ritual object is to *balanse.* But there are other layers to the word as well.

The well-known Haitian painter André Pierre once used the word *balanse* in a way that was both shocking and revealing. When I stopped by to visit one day, I referred to the recent death of someone we had both known. The grizzled old painter, who is something of a trickster, gave a loud laugh, slapped his thigh, and hooted: "Bawom Samdi te rive la. Ah! Li te balanse kay sa." (Bawon Samdi came there. Oh! He balanced that house.)

Bawon Samdi is the head of the Gede, the spirits of death. So André Pierre seemed to be saying that death arrived and set the house reeling. That seemed true enough. The troubling part was his laughter. It suggested that, despite the pain, this confrontation with death might be the source of new life energy for the family of the man who died. The Gede are the perfect ones to deliver such a hard, contradictory message. The domain over which the Gede preside comprises sexuality, fertility, and social satire, as well as death. The Gede are irrepressible tricksters. They often wear dark glasses with one lens missing. One Vodou priest told me this was because they can see into the lands of the living and the dead simultaneously. He also suggested that this was the source of their humor.

The shared use of the verb *balanse* in the Vodou ritual context and in André Pierre's story puts the innocuous swinging of a sacred object on the same spectrum of signification with treating the living to a sudden terrifying look into the face of death. What these two actions have in common is that they both use conflict or contradiction to *chofe,* heat things up or raise energy. In general, the Vodou ethos is one that accepts conflict, works with it, and ultimately orchestrates it to produce something life enhancing. In European and American culture we typically fear that our instinctive energies will get out of hand; in Haiti the fear is that life energy will diminish and go out, like a candle.

The practitioners of Vodou have never been able to kid themselves about death and suffering. They do not have either the power or the resources to sustain the kinds of fictions about mortality and pain (e.g. cosmetics, plastic surgery, the mortuary arts) that are commonplace among wealthier peoples. The sickness and death of a family member is still a hands-on experience in most parts of Haiti. Since they cannot directly distance suffering, those who serve the Vodou spirits laugh in its face.

They call on Gede for the transformation of death into humor. This alchemical moment is captured for me in a familiar, oft-repeated scene. Bawon Samdi has possessed someone; the person's immobile body lies stiff on the temple floor beneath a white sheet. Suddenly a crude bit of sexual slang slips from the mouth of the ritual corpse, moments before the figure throws off his sheet, jumps up, and grinds his hips lasciviously. Bawon has gone; one of the trickster Gede has taken his place. This is the way Vodou deals with the very human fear of death and of suffering. There is no attempt at theological rationalization. A popular Haitian proverb, one often accompanied by a shrug of the shoulders, says it all: "*Moun fèt pou mouri*" (People are born to die.) The following comments, necessarily broad and suggestive, are intended to hint at what the practitioners of such a religion might bring to a dialogue on morality with North Americans in the late twentieth century.

THE UNITED STATES FROM THE VANTAGE POINT OF HAITI

The moral orientation of Haitian Vodou rests on the assumption of complex, substantive interconnections among people, as well as among people, their ancestors, their spirits, and God. Yet the same moral system also places a premium on self-knowledge and values self-confidence over humility. Those who enter the Vodou system find out that they must know themselves, and what they are made of, before they can learn how to live with others with integrity. Vodou thus presents a provocative alternative to traditional North American individualism.

Vodou is centrally concerned with healing. Vodou healers address problems of love, family, job, and money, as well as problems of health. As a result they inevitably deal with issues of morality. Yet there is no essential good or evil in the Vodou worldview. The closest thing in the Vodou system is the primary contrast between what is "tied," "chained," or "bound," and that which is "open" and "free flowing." Vodou healing is directed at the relations between parties, and the main method of healing is to untie, or unblock, relationships so that reciprocity between persons, and among persons, ancestors, and spirits can flow freely in all directions. Of course, untying one person may mean tying up another, as Mama Lola tied the mouth of her client's supervisor at the Long Island electronics plant. The point here is that there is no utopian drive in Vodou. Those who serve the spirits accept that as human beings we live in an imperfect world, one in which we can never have perfectly clean hands. So, if securing one person's freedom means temporarily tying up another, it may not represent a perfect solution, but it will nevertheless have to be done. Haitian Vodou thus represents a viewpoint instructively different from the polarities of "right" and "wrong" that often structure discussions of morality in popular U.S. media.

Vodou morality is dynamic, and values cannot be reduced to a set of universal and timeless principles. Yet Vodou morality has stable ways of being and acting at its core and cannot justifiably be called either radically relativist or radically contextual. Furthermore, in its focus on self-knowledge and self-respect, it adds a particular emphasis to a discussion of moral education that is largely missing in North America.

In the Haitian Vodou moral system, survival is a moral goal.[13] Honesty about the nature of human life is a moral requirement. A comparison between popular American morality and Haitian morality, or the morality of any people for whom survival has been a basic issue, could help us North Americans gain perspective on our moral claims. Living in a nation as powerful as the United States in the late twentieth century, while knowing what we do about global economic, ecological, and political interconnections, leaves many of us with a sense of guilt about things we cannot control. Some North Americans appear to be developing a brittle moral fanaticism in an effort to reassert control over their moral well-being.

In a country as privileged as the United States of America, people have trouble accepting the limitations of the human condition. We want to think that moral responsibility extends only to those areas of life over which we have control, and furthermore, we think we should be able to keep ourselves morally pure. Sadly, we tend to articulate awareness of our inevitable failures at perfection in metaphors of dirt, rot, and disease. These notions work against the basic self-respect that systems such as Vodou assume are integral to living a moral life. Haitian Vodou offers us the intriguing possibility of thinking about morality in quite a different way, one that keeps such metaphors at bay.

By locating problems in the relations between people, rather than in individuals themselves, and by understanding goodness as a temporary achievement in the midst of life's movement – much as a ballet dancer temporarily achieves beauty – Haitian traditional culture places itself in what could be a productive tension with pervasive moods and motivations in American culture. Vodou offers the intriguing suggestion that moral progress might well be understood as the refinement of a talent called "moral style" or "moral imagination," rather than as increasingly consistent adherence to rules or laws.

Vodou morality is a collection of attitudes and practices that encourages the acceptance of conflict and suffering; the celebration of plurality, both in the group and within the person; and the search for the good through whatever preserves life and enhances life energy. In Vodou, as in many other religious systems, life energy and sexual energy tend to flow together. The Vodou spirit Gede is a prime example of that tendency. The suspicion of sexuality that has long characterized European and American Christian culture can easily flow over into a repression of general life energy. The disembodied character of much of white Euro-American culture is striking. As adults, we do so little dancing, and it scarcely occurs to us that this has anything to do with the frequently brittle character of public moral discourse.

In sum, those of us in the United States who are interested in the revival of moral inquiry ought to consider taking Haitian Vodou on as a conversation partner – not to become like it, something we could never do anyway, but to see ourselves from a different angle in relation to it.[14] The challenge of the postmodern age is centrally about hegemonic power or, more precisely, the loss of it. Haitians would be good conversation partners for North Americans precisely because they have never had the money, the power, or the weapons to be tempted to think that they possessed universal truths or that they could speak with authority for the rest of the world. Haitians have lots of experience, however, living in a troubled relationship with the United States, where such assumptions have been routine. Haiti, a country that has long been the target of the most stubborn of U.S. racist projections,[15] might be a very interesting interlocutor for the conscience of the United States. The records, oral and written, of United States–Haiti interaction span more than two centuries, starting during the period of transatlantic slavery and running continuously through the end of the cold war. As such, they provide a rich resource for exploring the parameters of moral vision. As Haiti has come increasingly under the sway of U.S. popular culture and political economy during the last century, all of the learning has tended to flow in one direction – from the United States toward Haiti. The time may be right to test what can flow in the other direction.

Notes

1. *Mare djòl* translates literally as tie the lips; the same type of charm can also be called *mare bouch*, tie the mouth.
2. Vodou – spelled according to the phonetic orthography of Haitian Creole most widely used in Haiti today – usually combined with Roman Catholicism, is the religion of 85 percent of the Haitian population. Since participation in Vodou is not a matter of formal membership, but of practice that can include anything from an occasional consultation with a priest to structuring one's entire life around obligations to the spirits, others put the figure closer to 100 percent.
3. Claude Levi-Strauss, "The Science of the Concrete," in his *The Savage Mind* (Chicago: University of Chicago Press, 1966).
4. In my classes I have often compared Vodou to an amoeba. When confronted with a foreign substance, the Vodou amoeba does not recoil and cry "heresy;" instead it sends out its pseudopods, surrounds the new spirituality, absorbs it, and turns it into fuel for the maintenance of *its own system.*
5. Consider this event in a different sort of fictive kin relationship. In 1986, just after Jean-Claude Duvalier abdicated the presidency of Haiti and left the country, Haitians were wary about how the United States, which had long backed the Duvalier family, would respond to the power vacuum. During that time, a hardscrabble farmer in northern Haiti was quoted in the *New York Times* as saying something like: "Uncle Sam is a good uncle and we know he will help us." The reporter mistook this for evidence of Haitian affection for the United States. A Haitian hearing this line would have known that whatever else was being communicated, this was also a pointed suggestion that the United States ought to refrain from being abusive in its relations with the small island republic of Haiti.

6. At the *rele mò nan dlo,* calling the dead from the water, the spirits of the dead seem to speak from the water-filled jugs in which the spirits are housed and later carried back to the family altars. This same type of possession, involving throwing the voice, can be used subsequently when the spirits are called after the *govi* have been installed on the altars.
7. For a creative essay on the spiritual diversity within the self, see Jim Wafer, *The Taste of Blood: Spirit Possession in Brazilian Candomble* (Philadelphia: University of Pennsylvania Press, 1991).
8. The following passage is from Karen McCarthy Brown, *Mama Lola: A Vodou Priestess in Brooklyn* (Berkeley and Los Angeles: University of California Press, 1991), pp. 94–95. It describes a ceremony in 1979 during which Mama Lola was "ridden" by Ogou.

> Ogou's possession-performance began with a series of familiar gestures. Taking his ritual sword in his hand and slicing the air in broad aggressive strokes, Ogou first attacked an invisible enemy. Then he took more controlled, menacing jabs at those members of [Mama Lola's] . . . Vodou family standing nearest him. Finally, in a gesture full of bravado that also hinted at self-wounding, Ogou turned the sword on himself. Lodging the point in one hip, he bent the rapierlike blade into an arc. Ogou performs his dance with the sword at nearly every public occasion on which he makes an appearance. Its elegant gestures are to body language what proverbs are to spoken language, a condensation point for complex truths: power liberates, power betrays, power turns on those who wield it.

9. For further discussion of Ogou and his relation to the lessons of Haitian history as well as to contemporary struggles in Haiti and in the New York diaspora community, see Karen McCarthy Brown, "Systematic Remembering, Systematic Forgetting: Ogou in Haiti," in *Africa's Ogun: Old World and New,* ed. Sandra T. Barnes (Bloomington: Indiana University Press, 1989), pp. 65–89; and Brown, *Mama Lola,* pp. 94–139.
10. Ezili Freda and Ezili Dantò, like Ogou, reflect part of the Haitian social terrain. They also map the complex psychodynamics of women's sexuality and childbearing. Freda, with her pale skin and love of luxury, mirrors the women of the Haitian elite who set the standards for female beauty in Haiti. Dantò, almost always identified as exceptionally black, makes visible the lives of the majority of poor women who raise children without the help of a man. See Brown, *Mama Lola,* pp. 220–257, for a more detailed discussion of the Ezili in Haitian Vodou.
11. For a lengthier discussion of this material, see Brown, *Mama Lola,* pp. 241ff.
12. Wande Abimbola, unpublished talk given at the Liederkranz Club in Manhattan, 1981.

13. On this issue see Katie Geneva Cannon, *Black Womanist Ethics* (Atlanta: Scholars Press, 1988).
14. Much of what is attractive about Vodou morality could not be replicated in the United States. Eighty percent of the Haitian population lives on the land, in small communities where everyone knows everyone else. This circumstance reinforces tolerance for behavioral diversity within each person and among people in general. Such small agricultural communities also foster the strong spirit of cooperation, even communitarianism, that is at the heart of Vodou. Yet, at the same time, rural life where people depend so much on one another also inevitably feeds the more dysfunctional aspects of Vodou, for example, the tendency of the group to accuse talented or wealthy individuals of sorcery.
15. See Robert Lawless, *Haiti's Bad Press* (Rochester: Vt.: Schenkman Books, 1992).

Part V

GLOBAL VIEWS

We have seen that religions in general offer a distinctly "religious" perspective on life's meaning while each tradition offers more particular formulations of the meaning of life. Diversity within commonality marks the variety of religious traditions, from the great monotheisms of the West and the deeply African traditions of Haitian Vodou, to the great Asian religions of Hinduism, Jainism, Buddhism, and Confucianism. Having examined the nature of the relationship between humans and the Transcendent which lies at the foundation of all religious perspectives, it now remains for us to conclude with some global perspectives on religion and the meaning of life. Huston Smith, John Hick, and Sallie McFague each offer us global perspectives which honor and respect particular world religions.

Huston Smith presents the position of "perennial philosophy," mapping out a four-part cosmos, made up of the visible world, the invisible world, God's knowable aspects, and God's unknowable transpersonal nature, all four described in various ways by different religious traditions. In this context, our purpose as human beings is to experience and embody within ourselves all four of these levels of reality and thus, in Smith's words, to "flesh out God's infinity." Within each religion, different spiritual personality types experience these different levels and life's meaning in different ways (see Plate 11). To explain this, Smith uses the four Hindu paths popularized by Vivekananda. Followers of two of the possible paths he calls "esoterics": those whose religious experience comes either through intellect or through realization, made possible by meditation. Followers of the other two paths are "exoterics" and include those who cultivate devotional relationships and those who pursue compassionate and selfless actions in the world, according to their individual gifts.

Having established this general understanding of the religious meaningfulness of life, Smith then asks whether it is true. He suggests not only that we cannot objectively prove that it is true, but also that we would lose our dignity if we did. However, we can examine its potential impact on life. Smith asserts that life burns with the greatest intensity if it is lived from the religious perspective. By addressing life's most fundamental problems and most profound suffering, and by offering the greatest possible hope, religion provides the highest motivation to solve these problems and posits the unequaled support of divine grace. The religious perspective must be taken on faith, Smith concludes, but offers the greatest possible meaning and thus a deep joy in just being alive.

John Hick, too, speaks of the optimism of the religious perspective. Even though the world religions operate with radically different views of the world, Hick asserts that they all share a fundamental optimism about the ultimate nature of reality and about the human predicament. Though they see this life as in need of transformation, the world religions speak very positively about the potential for human liberation or salvation or change. Hick admits that what religions teach and what people feel on a day-to-day basis may be different. We may not always be able to be optimistic in the face of life's events. Nor are all subsets of all religions entirely optimistic. Some teach an exclusivity that may be optimistic for their own community, but they may be practicing a form of cosmic pessimism with regard to the larger world. Hick identifies two definitive aspects to this religious cosmic optimism. The Transcendent or ultimately Real as well as the structure of the universe are understood to be benign in human terms. He then offers us a detailed case in point, taking up the tradition of Buddhism, beautifully explicating its ultimate optimism (see Plate 12). Afterward, he shows briefly how other traditions – Judaism, Christianity, Islam, and Hinduism – also fit this definition of religion. With regard to life's meaning and the human project, then, religions offer the greatest degree of optimism, according to Hick.

Hick points to exclusivist claims as examples not of cosmic optimism but of pessimism regarding all those who do not share one's beliefs. Sallie

McFague confronts the exclusivist claims of Christianity head on, suggesting that exclusivity may not be essential to Christian claims. Instead she offers an alternate and much more optimistic view of Christianity, shifting the focus to incarnation and embodiment and suggesting that the universe *is* the body of God and what is critical is God's choice to be embodied among us as a human being (see Plate 13). Drawing on an understanding of all reality as interconnected and thus as "the body of God," she suggests that Christianity's special message is that the poor and the oppressed of every kind also constitute a part of God's embodiment and have intrinsic value. She includes nature among the "oppressed" and insists that Jesus' ministry of parables, healing and feeding of the multitudes highlights the pressing need to address multiple levels of oppression and the physical needs of the body of God. "Survival of the fittest" is not the Christian model, but rather solidarity with the oppressed working for the betterment of all and sharing in the suffering of all. This model approaches that of the Buddhist Bodhisattva.

Further, creation is the site of salvation (not unlike the Hindu devotional understanding of embodiment as a necessary condition for loving God) and salvation the trajectory of creation – a clear statement of Hick's cosmic optimism and Smith's hope. McFague offers us a view of a cosmic Christ and a Christianity that is radically inclusive and embodied, affirming this life and sacralizing the world. She suggests that no religious tradition may or need claim to have the whole truth. Each offers a unique perspective and contribution, and she seeks to uncover Christianity's message for the world today, taking into account both science and our increasing global awareness of the perspectival nature of knowledge and the interconnectedness of life (see Plate 14).

What can the world religions offer for the understanding of life's meaning? Smith, Hick, and McFague suggest that they offer the greatest hope, the most profound motivation, and the paramount value to life. There is no objective proof of their truth, but they point to paths into meaning, calling us to transformation and promising fulfillment grounded in the Transcendent. In the end we must choose whether or not to embrace their optimism and lay claim to this ultimate meaning in life.

Plate 11 Modern mendicant Zen Buddhist in traditional dress undertaking a pilgrimage to temple sites, receiving alms on the streets of Kyoto, Japan, below the great Kiyomizu Temple, which was completed in 798 CE. Photo: *Joseph Runzo*

14

THE MEANING OF LIFE *in the* WORLD'S RELIGIONS

Huston Smith

The meaning of life is the most urgent question.

Albert Camus

In the following chapter, I shall address the topic of the meaning of life in the world's religions from what I take to be the generic religious standpoint, alluding to individual religions only to ground and illustrate the points I will be making. The first half will be descriptive. Taking off from the assumption that the basic religious posit is that life is meaningful, I shall, first, attempt an objective account of its meaning – a God's-eye account, to speak presumptuously – and go on to note the chief ways that human beings access that meaning. The second half of my chapter will be given to assessment. Is the religious posit concerning life's meaning true?

THE RELIGIOUS POSIT

That life is meaningful is religion's basic posit, and the claim can be elucidated both subjectively and objectively, the difference being whether we are thinking primarily of life's meaning for us or, alternatively, trying to determine its meaning in the total scheme of things. I begin with the latter.

Life's Objective Meaning

Considered from the standpoint of the whole of things, the significance of human life consists in the way it bodies forth – fleshes out, we might say –

God's infinity. That we are here proves that we are possible, and if we were possible but not here, God's infinity would be compromised. There would be a hole in the cheese of God's plenitude (to put the matter crudely), and God would be incomplete. In short, without us God would not be God.

This reading of things gives stature to our lives, but its argument is compact, so I will elaborate it. I agree with Ernst Cassier, Arthur Lovejoy, and proponents of the perennial philosophy generally, that all traditional philosophies and religions took for granted some version of the Great Chain of Being which envisions reality as an inverted triangle – the *yiggisdril* of Nordic lore, and the *asvattha* tree in the Upanishads whose roots are in heaven and whose branches extend downward to form the *samsaric* world.[1] The upper base of that triangle is the *ens perfectissimum* which filters through every level of intermediate being down to the meagerest existences at the bottom that barely escape non-existence.

Astronomers tell us that the center of the universe is where the astronomer happens to stand, and metaphysically too we find ourselves situated in the middle of things with heavens above and hells below, however we gloss these metaphors. Looking out on things from this center, we find that four regions of the ontological hierarchy are so important for human purposes that they turn up in every known collectivity, though there are wide differences in the degree to which they are explicitly articulated. The four derive from an initial central "cut" that divides existence into halves – "this world" and "another world" – and then subdivides both of those halves.

For the West, Plato provided the presiding metaphor for the distinction between "this world" and "another" in his allegory of the cave, where the shadow world within the cave contrasts unfavorably with the sunlit world outside it. In their own ways, every religion turns on a distinction like this, so much so that the presence of the distinction can be said to be what makes a worldview religious. Mircea Eliade assumed this by titling his survey of religious history *The Sacred and the Profane*, and Carlos Castenada alluded to it when he titled one of his books *A Separate Reality*. As for the subdivisions of the two worlds, "this world" divides into its visible and its invisible sectors, and the "other world" into God's personal and transpersonal aspects. Each of these four divisions of the world must now be described.

Prior to the invention of the magnifying glass, the visible part of this world consisted of what our physical senses report, but the invention of microscopes, telescopes, and other modes of amplification have driven our senses deeper into nature, so to speak. This makes it better now to think of the visible world as the physical universe – what our senses pick up as supplemented by science.

As for the invisible or immaterial part of "this world," we encounter it directly in our thoughts and feelings, but the traditional and modern views differ radically on how far into the objective world immaterial things extend. In the traditional worldview, consciousness – obdurately invisible – was fundamental, and matter obtruded from it like icebergs in the sea. Modernity reverses that image. Matter is now considered fundamental, and consciousness is generally regarded as an epiphenomenon which, like steam from a boiling teakettle, is generated by biological organisms and has no existence apart from them. In traditional societies angels, demons, patron saints, shamanic allies, woodland sprites, and discarnates of innumerable variety peopled the world as routinely as do mountains and rivers. Today's conventional wisdom banishes them. It withdraws invisibles from the world at large into the province of biological organisms and their feelings, to which human beings add thoughts.

As for the "other world," we find it everywhere subdividing into God's external, personal, knowable aspects on the one hand, and on the other, God's inmost, transpersonal, unfathomable depths – the Divine Abyss as it is sometimes called.

To arrive at the personal God, we need only begin with our human virtues and elevate them as far as our imaginations can carry us. Strain out the dross that tarnishes those virtues as they appear in us, pin the resulting unblemished virtues onto the X of God's unfathomable infinity, and *voila*, the personal God. Human beings can love. They can know. They can create. They are in ways beautiful. In God's personal mode, she is the archetypal constellation of all of these virtues and more: the Ninety-nine Beautiful Names of Allah.

The personal God is not a fiction; archetypes are more, not less, real than their earthly reflections. Still, as long as we stay with God's knowable aspects, we fall short of what God truly is. There being no commensurability between the finite and the infinite, all of our thoughts about God are as fingers pointing to the moon; they can direct our gaze, but they fall light years short of their object. The transpersonal – not impersonal! – ineffable God is the moon toward which the personal God points. Theologically speaking, it is the domain of *apophatic* as distinct from *kataphatic* theology, the *via negativa* that comes after the *via positiva*. The distinction is ubiquitous, as a glance at the three main families of historical religions will suggest. In East Asia we find Confucianism's *shang ti*, the supreme ancestor, and beyond him *tien*, or Heaven. In Taoism, there is the Tao that can be spoken, and the Tao that outdistances speech. In South Asia, Hinduism presents us with *saguna* Brahman – God with attributes or qualities; *sat*, *cit*, and *ananda* – and *nirguna* Brahman, the *neti, neti* of God beyond qualities. Buddhism presents a special case because of its ambiguous stance toward God, but though the personal God is absent in early Buddhism, it could not be excluded indefinitely and comes pouring in via the Mahayana in the person of the Goddess of Mercy or Amida Buddha of the Pure Land sect whose name, if sincerely uttered even once in one's lifetime, carries the believer to the Western Paradise. The transpersonal God is, of course, solidly ensconced in Buddhism in *shunyata* and nirvana. Finally (and reversing the situation in Buddhism) the western or Abrahamic family of religions pulls the stops on the personal God – the God of Abraham, Isaac, and Jacob; Christianity's Father of our Lord and Savior Jesus Christ; and Allah with his Ninety-nine Beautiful Names – but the transpersonal God is not lacking. We catch glimpses of it in the *'ein sof* of the Kabbalah; in *The Cloud of Unknowing*, Eckhart's *Gottheit*, and Tillich's God-beyond-God in Christianity; and, in Islam, in Allah's Hundredth Name which (because it is unutterable) is absent from the Sufi rosary.

With the four most important levels of reality now in place – important for us as human beings; the rest is not our business – we can get back to the question of life's meaning. As far as we know, human beings are the only ones that intersect all four of these regions of God's infinity. That we have visible bodies and invisible minds is obvious, and to those religion adds soul. Most people stop there, but esoterics in every tradition add spirit, causing the complete inventory of ourselves to read body, mind, soul, and spirit. And objectively, from God's perspective this is human life's meaning: to flesh out and complete God's infinity by including within it a species of creatures who, despite their finitude, include within themselves in decreasing obviousness all four of the major levels of reality and are capable of experiencing them all.

Accessing Life's Meaning

As a *jnana yogi* whose primary access to God is through knowledge or intuitive discernment, I find this account of life's meaning completely satisfying. What greater importance for our lives could we ask than derives from doing our part to make God God? When someone asked Charles Hartshorne for the purpose of life, he said, "To make the world more beautiful." That's not bad; in fact it's true, given the fact that as in Indra's net all of the beautiful names of God take on the colorations of the others. Contrary to Hartshorne, esoterics would say that nothing that we can do can mar the beauty that the Godhead finds perpetually in the world, but that is an in-house theological difference that does not concern us here.

As I say, *jnana yogis* are satisfied with this account of life's meaning, but proportionally their numbers are few, and for other spiritual types their answer cuts little ice – it comes to little more than a head trip and playing with words. Most people are exoterics, which means that feeling (or experience as they would say) counts for more than thought. And that in turn means that they need to feel/experience life's meaning, not just acknowledge what sounds to them like its abstract rationale. So how do people experience life's meaning? And what are the religious portals to that experience?

There are times when all of us, esoterics and exoterics alike, feel completely happy and so at peace with the world that we sense not the slightest lack. Wallace Stevens alludes to these as "times of inherent excellence":

> As when the cock crows on the left and all
> Is well, incalculable balances,
> At which a kind of Swiss perfection comes.[2]

Such epiphanies can arrive even in the midst of long marches. In the novel I am currently reading, Charles Frazier's *Cold Mountain*, set against the backdrop of the Civil War, its heroine suffers hardships that never seem to let up; yet even they brook interruptions. "On a day such as this, despite the looming war and all the work she knew had to be done, she could not see how she could improve her world. It seemed so fine she doubted that it could be done."

In moments such as these we don't ask for life's meaning, for it comes through to us transparently in the way that romantic love at its best explains why we are male and female. Since philosophers have found no more precise definition of explanation than "an account that leaves us satisfied," in the times when we feel completely at home in life, that feeling is itself life's explanation – its best possible explanation for being intrinsic and self-contained. But as we know all too well, such moments cannot be stabilized – they can recur, but not be retained. That is so obvious that it hardly needs to be documented, but the Old Adam in us resists accepting its truth, so I will quote two masters to fix the point in place. "Whoever thinks that in this mortal life a man may so disperse the mists of bodily and carnal imaginings as to possess the unclouded light of changeless truth, and to cleave to it with the unswerving constancy of a spirit wholly estranged from the common ways of life," St. Augustine wrote, "he understands neither what he seeks, nor who he is who seeks it." St. Teresa's formulation is similar: "If anyone told me that after reaching this state [of union] he had enjoyed continual rest and joy, I should say that he had not reached it at all."[3]

So, since we cannot keep life's meaning always in direct view, extrinsic and articulated explanations are required. I have already sketched the esoteric *jnanic* explanation, and turn now to Hinduism's other yogas to round out my typology. The move is reasonable, for the four yogas have proved to be so useful that they now belong to the world. Like *jnana yogis*, *raja yogis* are esoterics, but instead of intuiting life's meaning intellectively through the *buddhi* (or *intellectus* in the technical, scholastic sense of that word which yields *gnosis*), *raja yogis* meditate to find life's meaning through experiencing the Atman directly.

The two remaining yogas, *bhakti* and karma, are tailor made for exoterics. For them, selfhood is always in full view, and they would not have it otherwise, for – to paraphrase the title of a mid-century book on Eastern European Jewry, *Life is with People* – life for them is in relationships. *Bhakti yogis* find the meaning of life in cultivating an ever-deepening love affair with the Divine, for if even love between humans can retire the need to look beyond it, how much more is this the case when the beloved possesses superlatively everything we love in human beings. *Karma yogis* find the meaning of their lives in serving God; things need to be done, and life acquires significance by responding to their call. "Learning to live consists of learning what one has to offer to the world and then learning how to make that offering," Thomas Merton wrote;[4] to which we can add the Buddhist parable of the bird that, until it dropped dead from exhaustion, carried water from a distant lake to drop it, beakful by beakful, on a raging forest fire that was killing millions of sentient creatures. That its efforts were no match for the task never entered its mind, for under the circumstances that was the only thing it wanted to do.

ASSESSMENT

What I have thus far attempted is one way of summarizing what I take that the world's religions say about life's meaning, but is their posit of its meaningfulness true? To paraphrase John Betjeman:

> Is it true? Oh, is it true,
> This most astounding claim of all:
> That glory reigns above earth's pall
> Untarnished even by the Fall?[5]

Objectively there is no way to decide that question. There are things to be said in favor of life's meaning, the chief being that it is the seasoned answer to the question, the one that has presided over every known human collectivity, but that is not enough to insure its truth. The hermeneutics of suspicion is always waiting in the wings, ready to challenge the existence of religion's "other world" by claiming that it is only wishful thinking – a projection of the human mind to compensate for the world's lacks. "There is no other world," Malinowski intoned, and neither reason nor experience can prove him wrong. Rationally, there are as many reasons for thinking that "life is a tale told by an idiot, full of sound and fury, signifying nothing" as for believing that it is shot through with meaning. As for experiential proof, although New Agers, envious of scientists' ability to prove their points, like to claim that religious hypotheses can likewise be tested – do X and Y will follow; meditate X number of years and you will be enlightened – the claim is exaggerated. Luther practiced his own version of X assiduously, and Y didn't follow. After twenty years of meditation as a Tendai monk, Shinran had to face his absolute failure to change from self-centeredness to non-ego, from attachment to non-attachment; from blind passion (*klesha*) to clear-eyed dispassionate calm, from ignorance to enlightenment. John Wesley led a devout and pious life while working relentlessly for the poor, but in his later years he had to confess that his Aldersgate experiences declined. Even Jesus felt abandoned on the cross. I am not devaluing spiritual endeavors, nor taking sides on the *tariki–jiriki* dispute – which is more important, grace or self-effort? What it does not set right is the thought that life can be brought under control – that our thumbs can pin down its mercury ball. I have great empathy for a friend of mine who confesses to feeling left out. Most of his friends, he reports, seem to be seeking enlightenment, whereas he in his later years finds himself increasingly caught up in damage control, trying to cut his losses.

Irredeemably ambiguous to public gaze, life and the world come to us not tagged, but like Rorschach inkblots which everyone must interpret individually. This is the half-truth in existentialism and constructivism. Publicly – the qualifier is important – existential meanings are not out there in the world; case by case, individuals must read them into the situations they find themselves in. It is important to realize that, appearances to the contrary notwithstanding, this in itself does not count against life's meaning. Bewildered by life's complexity, often not knowing which way to turn, one naturally wishes that the world came decked with signposts. But Kierkegaard is good on this point. What he says in effect is that though we might think we would like an answer book to life, if we had it we would not be pleased. For though it would simplify life, it would undercut our dignity by turning us into automatons. All we would have to do is look up the answers to our problems and apply them.

So if life cannot be publicly shown to be meaningful, can anything be said for the claim? In the absence of proofs, are there at least considerations that carry some objective weight?

To explore that possibility I shall lift two leaves from Kant's notebook. Taken as a whole his epistemology has had its day,[6] but his distinction between noumena and phenomena, things as they are in themselves and as they appear to us, and his recognition that the mind contributes actively to the knowing process, remain useful. Putting them to use, it seems appropriate to draw back a bit from my confident, opening, *jnanic* reading of life's meaning and admit that noumenally life's meaning, certainly in its fullness, is beyond us. (Was it Woody Allen who, asked about the meaning of life, replied, "Do you think we are wise enough to read the mind of God?") As for its phenomenal meaning – the way life comes through to us – life delivers four features so regularly that it is not outlandish to think (Kant-wise) that those features are generated by categories that are built into the human makeup. Paralleling Kant's epistemic categories that structure human knowing, we may have built into us existential categories that configurate the way we have to experience life. They begin with problems, for if we found nothing awry in life, nothing that needed to be changed, our experience would not be human. As if in rebound, these problems instinctively give rise to hope in the expectation that they can be solved, or at least ameliorated. Solving them calls for effort on our part, and we would not expend it if we did not expect our actions to be met by support. For we are not solipsistic monads. There is a world out there, and (to cite the simplest example I can think of) if I did not expect the ground on which I walk to support me, I would never step out.

Now, if it is the case that these four categories structure the way life comes to us, religions must conform to their combined mold. Suffering, the Buddha's *dukkha* – which in the context of this chapter includes the sense of life's meaninglessness when it moves in – is the paradigmatic problem religion takes off from. Hope and effort do not need to be changed, but support translates religiously into grace. I find it useful to pattern these four categories in the shape of a Maltese cross. Suffering is its lower tip; hope its apex. Effort is at the left end of its horizontal arm, and at the arm's right end stands grace.

That religions can be stretched like goatskins on the frame of this Maltese cross seems obvious, but for the sake of concreteness I will do the stretching once, dipping into the common pool of religions for my examples because their analogs seem so clear that there is no point here in separating them. Judaism's "valley of the shadow of death" parallels Buddhism's *dukkha.* Hope runs all the way from crude images of pearly gates and streets of gold to the rare instance in the Pali canon where the Buddha broke from his preferred *via negativa* and spoke positively of nirvana: "There is, O monks, an Unborn, neither become nor created nor formed ... Were there not, there would be no deliverance from the formed, the made, the compounded."[7] Buddhism likewise comes to mind in connection with effort, most obviously for its being the sixth step in the Eightfold Path, but also because of the Buddha's memorable gloss on that step:

> Those who follow the Way might well follow the example of an ox that marches through the deep mire carrying a heavy load. He is tired, but his steady gaze, looking forward, will never relax until he comes out of the mire, and it is only then he takes a respite. O monks, remember that passion and sin are more than the filthy mire, and that you can escape misery only by earnestly and steadily thinking of the Way.[8]

As for grace, its nuances differ among the religions, but the sentiment that the hymn "Amazing Grace" has immortalized, invests them all.

I hope that the point of this Kantian excursion and the Maltese cross I have extracted from it is clear, but let me make sure by restating it. The religious ambiguity of life and the world make it impossible to prove that the religious "take" on life (in the cinematic sense of that word) is true. But I think it can be reasonably argued that its vision of life stretches *tighter* on a *larger* Maltese cross than do other philosophies.

First, the cross's size – both of its arms extend farther in their respective directions than one finds elsewhere. Religion is often charged with wishful thinking, and the charge is understandable, if one thinks only of the height to which the ascending arm of the cross extends, for religious hope is of no small proportions. Salvation, heaven, the beatific vision, enlightenment, and *moksha* are not ordinary notions. What the charge overlooks is that the vertical axis of the cross plummets downward as far as it rises. "Vanity, vanity, all is vanity"; "out of the depths have I cried unto thee"; "*Eli, Eli, lama sabachthani*"; "wretched man that I am; who can deliver me from this living hell?" – groans such as these could only have issued from souls who knew clearly how the world can carve the heart down to a bitter nub. It is not going too far to think of religions as responses to the unblinking realization that unredeemed life is little short of agony. To touch on only the short list, there is fear of losing or hurting what or who we love; fear of death, bereavement, and becoming dependent; fear of loneliness and of being unloved and unlovable. Through the systematic use of imagination and hope, into which a certain amount of denial and rationalization inevitably creep, religion seeks to transform this underlying agony and anxiety into the joy and gratitude we can feel for the gift of life, our own included. Many charges can be leveled at religion, but when we think of the sheer length of the vertical axis of the Maltese cross, it is hard to see how superficiality or the pollyanna response can be one of them, for the distance between eternal salvation and eternal damnation is the greatest that the human mind can conceive. Experientially, it is infinite. The proportions of that distance are on the one hand an inducement to effort to effect the right outcome, while on the other they bring into clear relief the need for grace to augment efforts that are unequal to the task. Paradoxes yawn in the foundations of religion just as they do in science, and Joseph Sitler produced a striking instance when, in a course on the New Testament at the University of Chicago, he compressed Paul's theology into the conclusion "You have to work like hell because it's all been done for you."

To summarize the last page or two: without reneging in the least on my admission that the religious posit cannot be objectively demonstrated, I am suggesting that it can be objectively argued that it raises life's stakes and, through the tight stretch of the skin on the enlarged Maltese cross, brings a tonus in life that is otherwise lacking. Working with the existential categories that human experience has no choice but to conform to, it pushes the content of all four of those categories – their percepts, as Kant would say – into new waters.

Of course, the decisive arm of the Maltese cross for religion is the one that soars upward in hope. Whether its extravagant hope is well founded has been the question for this second half of my chapter, and I am surprised to discover that in the course of it I haven't even mentioned faith. That is surprising, because one way to think of religions is as gigantic faith claims. At the center of the religious life is a particular kind of joy, the prospect of a happy ending that blossoms from necessarily painful beginnings, the promise of human difficulties embraced and overcome. (Note, in passing, the presence of all four arms of the Maltese cross in that sentence.) At some strange level, in some strange way, the religious life *is* joyful, but its joy derives in part from appropriating into the present, through anticipation, the happiness of its ending in the "other world." In worldly terms, faith in the reality of that world is simply one posit among others, though Pascal advanced it as the smarter bet and others commend it as the choice of the most creative hypothesis. But within the religious purview, faith assumes a different cast. It has ontological stature. Neither an emotion nor an opinion, it is our clogged but unsevered umbilical cord to the perfection from which we derived. As such, it is a force which, working against the world's friction, draws us toward truth. In Thomas Merton's words, it is "the opening of an inward eye, the eyes of the heart, to be filled with Divine light."[9]

Appropriately for the conclusion of this chapter, we are drawn back to life's objective religious ambiguity.

NOTES

1. "This is that eternal Asvattha Tree with its root above and branches below ... In that all worlds are contained," *Katha Upanishad,* III.1.1.
2. Wallace Stevens, *Collected Poems* (New York: Alfred A. Knopf, 1995), p. 786.
3. Both quotations appear, unreferenced, in *The Eastern Buddhist,* n.s., 16, 2, Autumn 1983, p. 10.

4. Thomas Merton, *Love and Living,* ed. Naomi Burton Stone and Brother Patrick Hart (New York: Farrar, Straus & Giroux, 1985), p. 1.
5. John Betjeman's wording, abridged from his poem, "Christman," reads: "And is it true? And is it true,/This most tremendous tale of all . . . /That God was Man in Palestine/And lives today in Bread and Wine."
6. Nicholas Wolterstorff's "The Limits of Kant" (*Harvard Divinity Bulletin,* 26, 4, 1997) shows one important way to move beyond him.
7. *Iti-vuttaka,* 43; *Udana* VIII, 3.
8. Quoted in J.B. Pratt, *The Pilgrimage of Buddhism and a Buddhist Pilgrimage* (New York: AMS Press, 1928), p. 40.
9. Thomas Merton, *New Seeds of Contemplation* (Toronto: New Directions, 1961), p. 126.

Plate 12 The Lokesvararadja Buddha in Fengxian Temple in the Longmen caves, carved in 672 CE during the Tang Dynasty and partially destroyed by Red Guards during the Cultural Revolution, Henan Provence, China. Photo: *Nancy M. Martin*

15

THE RELIGIOUS MEANING *of* LIFE

John Hick

The notion of the meaning of life is initially extremely vague. In order to be useful, it has to be specified further, and different people will quite reasonably do this in different ways. I must therefore begin by saying in what sense I shall be using the expression here.

PRACTICAL MEANING

First, then, not semantic meaning, the meaning of words and sentences, but what for want of a better term I shall call practical meaning, that is to say, meaning that makes a difference to the way in which, actually or potentially, we act and react in the world. And by the practical meaning for us of a thing, event, or situation – including our situation as part of the universe – I mean the dispositional state it evokes in us as a result of our identifying, or misidentifying, it as being that particular kind of thing or event or situation.

So an object's meaning to us consists in the actual or potential difference that it makes for us – that is to say, it consists in what in relevant circumstances we find it appropriate to do or avoid doing in relation to that object. To take a trivial example, I believe that what I am holding is a tennis ball if it is true of me that I will treat it, in circumstances in which the issue arises, as a tennis ball rather than, say, as a cricket ball or a hand grenade or anything else. Its meaning for me is such that I will treat it in this way.

This practical meaning is always both species and culture relative: a kitten might see the tennis ball as something to play with, and a stone-age person, translated here in a time-machine, would not have the concepts of tennis or tennis ball and would accordingly see the same object as something quite different. So already a basic epistemological truth, classically propounded by Immanuel Kant, comes into view, namely that perceivers contribute significantly to the meaning that their environment has for them.

Let us now move on from the meaning of objects, such as a tennis ball, to the meaning of situations. A situation is a complex of objects which has its own meaning over and above the sum of the meanings of its constituent objects. A situation is formed by selective human attention operating on a higher level than in object-awareness – higher in the logical sense that it presupposes object-awareness – and human life is ordinarily lived on this higher level of situational meaning. To take an example, the meaning for us of being at a session of an academic conference is such that we behave in ways that are appropriate. Its accepted meaning within our culture is such that I read aloud my paper, and you politely listen whilst thinking up difficult questions to raise in the discussion period. But the stone-age persons whom I mentioned earlier, if suddenly materialized among us, would not find the same meaning in this physical configuration. For them it would constitute a very different situation, because they would not have such concepts as conference, university, academic paper, philosophy, and so on that are familiar elements of our own cultural world.

I want in due course to move from limited situations such as this to the unlimited situation of our existence in the universe. But first I want to stress again a basic point that has already emerged, namely the contribution of the perceiver to all our awareness of meaning. During the two centuries since Kant this has become an increasingly widely accepted idea, and has in our own time been further reinforced by the development of cognitive psychology and the sociology of knowledge. Its significance for the epistemology of religion was first suggested to me by Wittgenstein's disciple, John Wisdom, in his lectures in Cambridge in the early 1950s, after Wittgenstein's death in 1951 – although neither he nor Wittgenstein would necessarily have approved of the use that I want to make of it. But in the *Philosophical Investigations* (part II, section xi), Wittgenstein discusses what he called, "seeing as" – as when you see an ambiguous picture first in one way and then in another. It seems natural to expand this into the concept of experiencing-as, which we need if we are to apply the basic idea to situations. But John Wisdom took this further. Attending his lectures was a strange experience. One would listen to his apparently formless and unprepared meanderings, bored stiff, for weeks on end, and then suddenly he would say something so excitingly illuminating that one had to keep coming back for more. For example, he once spoke of doing metaphysics as being like seeing the pattern in a puzzle picture. As was typical with Wisdom's lectures, this was a tantalizingly suggestive throw-out remark which he never, so far as I know, developed further. But to me it was a clue to the nature of religious awareness and hence of the religious understanding of the meaning of life.

The general point, then, thus far is that consciousness of our environment is an interpreted awareness of it as having practical meaning for us. Here "interpretation" is not of course theoretical interpretation, as when we interpret a text or a detective interprets the clues, but the perceptual interpretation that is taking place all the time in our continuous awareness of a meaningful environment within which we are able to act and react in ways that we take to be appropriate.

PHYSICAL, MORAL, AND AESTHETIC LEVELS OF MEANING

I now want to take note of the different levels of meaning that we discern in human situations. These are the physical, the social or ethical, the aesthetic, and the religious; and I refer to them as *levels* of meaning because the ethical and the aesthetic presuppose and are mediated through the physical, whilst the religious can presuppose and be mediated through each or all of the others; whereas the reverse does not hold. We are primarily interested here in the religious meaning both of limited situations and of the unlimited situation of our presence in the universe; but the same epistemological structure runs through the whole hierarchy of forms of awareness.

However there is no time here to discuss the physical, ethical, and aesthetic levels of meaning. I will only note that ethical presupposes physical meaning, and religious presupposes both ethical and physical meaning. Aesthetic meaning has a more fluctuating position within the logical hierarchy, which I shall not pursue here. But the pattern throughout, I suggest, is that of levels or layers of meaning such that the higher meaning includes and is mediated through the lower; and also that the more value laden the meaning the greater our cognitive freedom in relation to it. This freedom (and attendant responsibility) is minimal in the case of physical or natural meaning, but much greater in the case of aesthetic and moral meaning, and at its maximum in the case of religious meaning – to which we now turn.

RELIGIOUS MEANING

Here I must move quickly through the meaning of particular sacred objects and places and of the situations that consist in the enactment of religious rituals. Sacred objects include totems, and the clay, wood, or stone figures of Hindu deities, of the Buddha and Bodhisattvas, of Christ, the Virgin Mary and Christian saints, etc.; and such sacred writings as the Torah scroll, the Bible, the Qur'an, the Adi Granth, etc.; and such symbolic images as the cross, the crucifix, the Islamic crescent moon, Hindu and Buddhist mandalas, and so on; and again, sacred buildings include stone circles, synagogues, churches, chapels, cathedrals, mosques, gurdwaras, etc.; and sacred places include Benares, Jerusalem, Mecca, and so on; whilst religious events include the ancient Vedic rituals, the Christian Eucharist, the Muslim *salat*, and solemn processions and sacred dances, etc. All of these are designed, or more often have evolved, to evoke a dispositional response which is, generically, a move toward the centering of the life of the individual and the community in the sacred, the divine, the transcendent in the particular form selected by this symbolic object or event – thus reinforcing communal dedication to a local deity or producing a greater degree of devotion to Vishnu or to Shiva, or to the Adonai of rabbinic Judaism, or to Christ, or to the Holy Trinity, or to Allah, or a greater degree of inner transformation in response to the Dharma or the Tao.

But our concern now is with a larger and more general form of practical meaning, the meaning of life, the religious meaning of our existence in the universe. We are concerned with religious ways of experiencing our total environment, and with our correlative dispositional responses.

The way in which we inhabit the universe – not necessarily from day to day but in the overall tenor of our lives – is a reflection of the character that we conceive and hence experience it to have. And so the meaning-of-life question is: What is the nature of this universe in which, and as part of which, we find ourselves? Above all, is its ultimate nature, so far as we humans are concerned, benign or hostile or indifferent? I say "so far as we humans are concerned" because we are minute fragments of the universe, and it seems very unlikely that we have the conceptual equipment to comprehend the nature of reality as a whole. We may however be able to comprehend in our own human terms what its nature is in so far as it affects us. As John Stuart Mill said, "If to know authentically in what order of things, under what government of the universe it is our destiny to live, were not useful, it is difficult to imagine what could be considered so. Whether a person is in a pleasant or in an unpleasant place, a palace or a prison, it cannot be otherwise than useful to him to know where he is."[1]

Each of the great world religions offers a comprehensive conception of the nature of the universe; and insofar as such pictures are believed, and are thus built into our dispositional structure, they automatically affect the way in which the believer experiences the universe and lives within it. In other words they determine what the overall meaning of life is for us. We are of course talking here about genuine beliefs, belief on which we are prepared to act – what Cardinal Newman called real as distinguished from notional assents.[2]

As a relatively trivial example of the fact that the way in which we experience our environment affects our dispositional state, consider the following imagined situation. I am in a strange building, and walking by mistake into a large room I find that a militant secret society is meeting there. Many of the members are armed, and as they take me for a fellow member I think it expedient to acquiesce in this role. Plans are being discussed for the violent overthrow of the constitution. The whole situation is alarming in the extreme. Its meaning for me is such that I am alarmed and apprehensive. Then I suddenly become aware in the dim light above us of a gallery in which there are silently whirring cameras, and I realize that I have walked by accident onto the set of a film. This realization consists in a change of interpretation of my immediate situation. Until now I had automatically interpreted it as "real life" and as demanding considerable circumspection on my part. Now I experience it as having a quite different significance. But at ground level there is no change in the course of events; the meeting of the secret society proceeds just as before. And yet my new awareness of the more comprehensive situation alters my experience of the more immediate one. It now has a new meaning for me, such that I am in a different dispositional state in relation to it. For example, if one of the "conspirators" noticed my arrival and threateningly pointed his gun at me, I might pretend to be terrified but would not be so in fact.

This is not an adequate analogy for our religious situation, because the cameras and their operators in the balcony are only more of the same kind of reality as the set and the actors at ground level. But it does nevertheless perhaps help to make intelligible the suggestion that the religious understanding of our lives as taking place in the presence of, and as grounded in, the Divine, the Transcendent, the ultimately Real, can make a profound difference to our understanding of the meaning of our life now.

RELIGION AS COSMIC OPTIMISM

Let me now put to you the hypothesis that the great world religions are different forms of what I shall call cosmic optimism. "Cosmic optimism" is not a term that figures in the distinctive vocabulary of any of them. But my suggestion is that it is a generalization of their distinctive affirmations about the ultimate character of reality as this affects we human beings. Concerning that reality the great monotheisms affirm, in the case of Judaism, that "as the heavens are high above the earth, so great is [the God of Israel's] steadfast love towards those who fear him" (Psalm 103:11); or that the heavenly Father of the New Testament is a limitlessly loving God; or that the Allah self-revealed in the Qur'an is ever gracious and merciful. Most Hindus are also theistic, but turning to the great non-theistic faiths, advaitic Hinduism affirms that in our deepest nature we already are the *saccidananda*, being–consciousness–bliss of Brahman, but have yet, so to speak, to become what we are; or again, that our true nature is the universal Buddha- or dharma-nature of the universe which is reflected within human experience as the limitless compassion of the Buddhas – and again we have to become what in a sense we already are. In each case they teach that we can, whether suddenly or gradually, whether on earth or in heaven, whether in this life or through many lives, receive or achieve the salvific transformation to a new relationship or a newly discovered identity with that ultimate reality.

Each tradition draws a radical distinction between, on the one hand, the state from which we desire to be saved or released or from which we need to awaken, and on the other hand the limitlessly better state to which it shows the way. There is a deeply pessimistic view of our present predicament, combined with a highly optimistic view of what is ultimately open to us. The pessimism is an understanding of ordinary human life as fallen into sin and guilt, or lived in disobedience and alienation from God, or as caught in the unreality of spiritual blindness (*avidya*) and the consequent round of suffering existence (*samsara*). But there is also the affirmation of a limitlessly better possibility which is available to us because the Ultimate is benign from our human point of view. By divine grace, or divine mercy, or by a gradual transcending of the ego point of view and a realization of our own deepest nature, we can attain or receive the highest good, variously conceived as heaven, paradise, unity with God, harmony with the Tao, absorption into Brahman, nirvana. Insofar as this limitlessly better state is said to be available to everyone, the message of each of the great religions constitutes good news.

I mean, then, by the cosmic optimism of the world religions that in each case, if their conception of the nature of the universe is basically correct, we can be glad to be part of the universe and can rejoice and be thankful for our present human existence. That is to say, the meaning of life is such that we can have an ultimate trust and confidence, even in life's darkest moments of suffering and sorrow.

However, I think that we have at this point to draw a distinction like that which Cantwell Smith draws between what he calls faith and what he calls the cumulative traditions.[3] I do not personally think that his term "faith" is the best word for what he is referring to, namely the actual response to God, or to the Transcendent, that informs an individual's life. And so, although this may not be the best term either, I shall speak of life responses to the Transcendent, distinguishing these from religion in the sense in which this is studied by anthropologists, sociologists, and historians. For it makes no difference to work in these disciplines whether or not God exists or whether or not there is, more broadly, a higher and ultimate spiritual reality. It is sufficient, for the scientific study of religion, that individuals and communities have believed that there is. In other words, the scientific or objective study of religion is the non-religious study of it. This is entirely legitimate, and indeed extremely valuable; but I want to insist that the religious study of religion is no less legitimate. The two, although importantly different, are only rivals if the methodological naturalism of the scientific approach is treated as a dogmatic naturalism.

Otherwise not. And from the point of view of a religious interpretation of religion, responses to the Transcendent are to be distinguished from the institutions and practices of the cumulative traditions. At the same time, although they are to be distinguished, in practice they are mingled together; for religious responses to the Divine are normally expressed in and through the religious practices, organizations, and belief-systems constituting the historical traditions. But the distinction enables us to recognize that these traditions do not always or everywhere or fully embody a response to the Transcendent. They have their own autonomous existence, in virtue of which they can be the subject of scientific study. And sometimes they can proceed on through history even when largely devoid of any response to the Transcendent – like an aeroplane that continues its flight after the pilot has bailed out!

And so there is generally a wide gap between the meaning of life as taught by our religion and the immediate concrete meanings in terms of which we live our daily lives. It does not follow from the fact that our religion teaches a form of cosmic optimism that we, as believers, are always in a cheerful and optimistic frame of mind! Nor does the belief that human existence is ultimately good mean that our present self-centered, unredeemed, illusion-bound existence is good, even though there is a great deal that is good within it. Pain and suffering, starvation and disease, war and genocide, repression and exploitation are real, and they effectively blot out the ultimate goodness of human existence for very many people for much or even most of their lives. That human existence is good means that it is a process or project, leading to a totally good conclusion. But although the religions explicitly teach this, the majority of men and women of each faith live much of their daily lives without any such thought. Belief in the goodness of the Ultimate from our human point of view is probably for most people most of the time a notional rather than a real belief – although it is one that may come vividly to life in some moment of crisis.

Further, even the teachings of the great traditions contain elements that conflict with belief in a wholly good outcome of the human project, so that the cosmic optimism hypothesis has to be carefully qualified. We have to consider to what degree the great ethnic religions, Hinduism and Judaism, are optimistic only concerning their own community but pessimistic concerning the rest of humankind; and in the end the answer of most Hindus and most Jews is that salvation is *not* confined to their own community. Again, it has been believed within the monotheistic faiths, and strongly so in the medieval period, that the large majority of the human race are destined to an everlasting hell – either because they are outside the Church or because they are infidels, not of the "people of the book." And within each religion there is today a large fundamentalist wing that retains that medieval view; and we have to say that insofar as any tradition teaches the exclusion of a proportion of men and women from the fulfillment of the human project, to that extent it is a form of cosmic pessimism rather than of cosmic optimism. However, there is the complication that within each tradition wicked individuals who die unrepentant have been believed to be consigned to an eternal damnation, so that for them no redemption is then ever possible; and we have to distinguish – though how much we should make of the distinction is a difficult question – between being excluded from the ultimate good fulfillment by the structure of the universe and being self-excluded by one's own free actions. And so the situation is complex, and we shall find in the history of religions the picture offered by each tradition has been a mixture of good news and bad news concerning the ultimate destiny of humankind as a whole.

It must also be made clear that when we speak of the ultimate goodness of the universe from our human point of view, we are talking about the total character of a reality which far exceeds anything that we can presently see or that the physical sciences can discover. For it is clear from the evils that afflict humanity, and from the equally evident fact that the realization of the human potential is seldom fulfilled in this present life, that if the process is ever to reach its completion, it must be continued beyond this life. The faith that, in the words of the Christian mystic Julian of Norwich, "all shall be well, and all shall be well, and all manner of thing shall be well" presupposes a conception of the ultimate structure of reality that makes this possible.

The great traditions and their sub-traditions have developed different pictures of this structure and of the final fulfillment as heaven, paradise, union with God, the beatific vision of God, an absorption into Brahman in which separate ego existence has been transcended, nirvana, the universal realization of the Buddha-nature of all things, and so on. But it is important to note that the idea of a good outcome of the life process does not require that any one of these specific conceptions of it will turn out to be accurate. Indeed, thoughtful people within each tradition have always been aware that the scriptural accounts of heaven/paradise are presented in a poetic imagery which points beyond the range of our present imagination; or in the Eastern faiths that the final unity that is sought is, once again, not thinkable in any earthly terms.

There are, then, two closely related conditions that qualify a religion to be a form of what I am calling cosmic optimism. One is that it conceives of that which is ultimately real as benign from our human point of view; and the other is that it conceives the structure of the universe to be consonant with this.

The next step, if there were space, would be to look at each of the great world religions to see whether or to what extent they fulfill these two conditions. I only have space, however, to do this for one sample case, for which I have chosen Buddhism.

BUDDHIST COSMIC OPTIMISM

Buddhism is not of course a single uniform entity, as our modern Western reifying name might suggest, but a history of experience and thought launched in northern India some twenty-five centuries ago, and developing since within different cultures to form a distinctive family of traditions. In its early centuries the Buddhist movement was strongly influenced by the pervasive "Hindu" outlook of India, although also reacting against some central aspects of it; for the Buddha's *anatta* teaching rejected the idea of an eternal unchanging Atman, and the Buddhist *sangha* rejected the hierarchical caste system of India. When Buddhism moved north, early in the Common Era, the Mahayana Buddhism of China, Tibet, Korea, Japan, and Vietnam took forms that are in some ways different from the southern Theravada (or Hinayana) Buddhism of Sri Lanka and Southeast Asia. Very roughly, the more world-denying ethos of religious life in India gave way in China to a more earthly and world-affirming outlook – the two eventually coalescing, it can be argued, in Zen Buddhism with its discovery that nirvana and *samsara* are identical: that is to say, earthly life in its full concrete particularity becomes nirvana in the experience of those who have entirely transcended the ego point of view.

The terms enlightenment, liberation, awakening, nirvana, *shunyata* ("emptiness"), Dharmakaya, and so on range in connotation between the psychological and the metaphysical. Some Westerners, usually in reaction against what they see as the anthropomorphism of Christian conception of

God as a greatly magnified person, have responded eagerly to Buddhism, seeing it as a psychological technique for attaining inner peace and serenity without involving any notion of a transcendent reality. This particular Western appropriation of Buddhism parallels the contemporary non- or anti-realist versions of Christianity, according to which God is not a transcendent (as well as immanent) reality but an imaginary personification of our human ideals. But, whilst there are Buddhists who adopt a non-realist epistemology, it seems to me impossible to sustain such a picture from the Pali scriptures.

The Buddha taught the insubstantiality of the world, as a single universal interdependent process of ceaseless change (*pratitya samutpada*) in which each movement in some degree conditions and is conditioned by every other in a vast network of dynamic mutuality. Everything is compounded of elements (*dharmas*) with only a fleeting momentary existence; and the appearance of solid enduring entities, including the human self, is illusory. Indeed it is the deep realization of this that can free us from the self-centered outlook that makes our experience of life so often one of anxious craving, sorrow, and joylessness – in Buddhist terms *dukkha*.

The Pali *nibbana* (or in Sanskrit, nirvana) means, literally, "blowing out," as in the blowing out of a flame. However, this is not a ceasing to exist, but the blowing out, or destruction, of illusion and its fruits: "The destruction of lust, the destruction of hatred, the destruction of illusion, friend, is called Nibbana."[4] And this is not only an individual psychological state, but a reflection in a particular momentary occasion of the ultimate universal reality that is variously referred to as nirvana, the Dharmakaya, *shunyata*, the Buddha-nature of the universe. Thus nirvana is described in the Pali scriptures as an eternal reality, "the unborn ... unageing ... undecaying ... undying ... stainless."[5] In a famous passage the Buddha teaches, "Monks, there is a not-born, a not-become, a not-made, a not-compounded. Monks, if that unborn, not-become, not-made, not-compounded were not, there would be apparent no escape from this here that is born, become, made, compounded."[6] The contemporary Theravadin scholar Narada Mahathera accordingly speaks of nirvana as "the permanent, immortal, supramundane state which cannot be expressed by mundane terms."[7] And Takeuchi Yoshinori, of the Kyoto school of philosophy, quotes with approval Friedrich Heiler's words, "Nirvana is the equivalent of what Western mysticism understands as the

'Being of beings,' the supreme and one reality, the absolute, the divine ... Nirvana is the infinite, the eternal, the uncreated, the quality-free, the ineffable, the one and only, the highest, the supreme good, the best, the good pure and simple."[8] Again, Edward Conze, a leading Western authority, says that

> It is assumed first of all [in Buddhism] that there is an ultimate reality, and secondly that there is a point in ourselves at which we touch that ultimate reality. The ultimate reality, also called Dharma, or Nirvana, is defined as that which stands completely outside the sensory world of illusion and ignorance, a world inextricably interwoven with craving and greed. To get somehow to that ultimate reality is the supremely worthwhile goal of the Buddhist life. The Buddhist idea of ultimate reality is very much akin to the philosophical notion of the "Absolute," and not easily distinguished from the notion of God among the more mystical theologians, like Dionysius Areopagita and Eckhart.[9]

However, the focus of Buddhist attention is always upon the present life and indeed upon the present moment. The dharma is wholly practical, a way to liberation. Gautama said, "As the great ocean is saturated by only one taste, the taste of salt, so this teaching and system is saturated by only one taste, the taste of salvation [i.e. liberation]."[10] Metaphysical speculations about the ultimate structure of the universe are accordingly discouraged as a distraction from the demanding and all-absorbing search for enlightenment. Thus when asked whether the world is eternal or not eternal, infinite or not infinite in space, whether (putting it in modern terms) mind and brain are or are not identical, and whether a fully enlightened one, a Buddha, exists after bodily death, Gautama refused to answer, saying that it is not necessary for liberation to know these things. Such knowledge, he said, "is not connected with the goal, is not fundamental to Brahma-faring, and does not conduce to turning away from, nor to dispassion, stopping, calming, super-knowledge, awakening nor to nibbana."[11]

But it is important to realize that this emphatic exclusion of a philosophizing that can so easily become a substitute for the spiritual quest occurs within the context of the belief, continuously either affirmed or assumed, that the karmic project of which we are each the present incarnation progresses through many lives until enlightenment/liberation/awakening is at least attained. Thus it is taken for granted that the structure of the universe is such that human existence is moving, on a vast time-scale, towards a limitlessly good fulfillment. This is not thought of (as generally in Western religion) as the perfecting of the individual self or community of selves, but as a state lying beyond the range of our present conceptualities. And so when a monk, Vaccha, asked the Buddha where, in what kind of existence, a Buddha arises after completing the long process of rebirths, the Buddha says "'Arises,' Vaccha, does not apply," and the dialogue continues:

> "Well then, good Gotama, does he not arise?"
> "'Does not arise,' Vaccha, does not apply."
> "Well then, good Gotama, does he both arise and not arise?"
> "'Both arises and does not arise,' Vaccha, does not apply."
> "Well then, good Gotama, does he neither arise nor not arise?"
> "'Neither arises nor does not arise,' Vaccha, does not apply."

Vaccha now expresses his bewilderment, and Gautama replies, "You ought to be at a loss, Vaccha, you ought to be bewildered. For Vaccha, this *dhamma* [that is to say, the nature of *parinirvana*, or final nirvana beyond the series of earthly lives] is deep, difficult to see, difficult to understand, peaceful, excellent, beyond dialectics, subtle, intelligible to the wise."[12] It is a state to which our present intellectual categories do not apply. But it is not therefore nothing. Indeed the Buddha explicitly repudiated the idea of annihilation: "There are some recluses and brahmans who misrepresent me untruly, vainly, falsely, not in accordance with fact, saying: 'The recluse Gotama is a nihilist, he lays down the cutting off, the destruction, the disappearance of the existent entity.' But as this, monks, is just what I am not, as this is just what I do not say, therefore these worthy recluses and brahmans misrepresent me untruly, vainly, falsely."[13] And it is equally clear that whilst the Buddha did not teach a final cessation of existence, neither did he teach the immortality of the present self. The nirvanic fulfillment of the human project lies beyond our earthbound conceptualities: "Freed from denotation by consciousness is the Tathagata [Buddha], Vaccha, he is deep, immeasurable, unfathomable as is the great ocean."[14]

Normative Buddhism, then, offers a picture of the universe as structured towards the "nirvanization" of all life. Different schools of thought hold either that enlightenment (*satori*) is possible in this life for all who seek it with all their heart and mind, or in this life only for those who have already approached it through many previous lives; that it occurs suddenly, that it occurs in stages; that when it occurs it liberates us *from* the material world and that when it occurs it liberates us *for* the material world. There is thus immense variety within Buddhism. But in all its forms it holds that none are excluded from the ultimate fulfillment of the human project. Buddhism is thus unambiguously a form of cosmic optimism.

Given this Buddhist worldview, what is its correlative dispositional response? How are Buddhists taught to pursue enlightenment/liberation/awakening/nirvana? The Buddha teaches a practical way to release from *dukkha*, the pervasive anxiety and insecurity of ordinary human life as we encounter pain, sorrow, grief, despair, frustration, sickness, aging, and death. Life has for us this *dukkha* quality, he taught, because we experience the world as centering upon ourselves. I experience everything in its relation to *me*, as welcome or unwelcome, propitious or threatening, as likely to satisfy or frustrate my desires; and this way of experiencing life creates a basic *angst* which is sometimes conscious and sometimes unconscious. Liberation from this is achieved by transcending the ego point of view in order to participate in a more universal perspective.

There is, incidentally, an interesting analogy between the role of the universal point of view in Buddhism and in the Kantian ethic. According to Kant, morally right action is action that is best, not in the private interests of the agent, but from a universal and impartial point of view in which every individual is valued equally as an end in him- or herself. This point of view is achieved, according to Kant, by applying a "universalization" criterion. Can we not say that Buddhism teaches the inner spiritual attitude of which the Kantian ethic teaches the practical application?

The way to this inner spiritual attitude is the "Noble Eightfold Path," which is both ethical and spiritual. Ethically it consists in developing a universal compassion (*karuna*) and loving-kindness (*metta*). There are concrete steps to this. We are enjoined to practice right speech – not lying or slandering or maliciously gossiping; right action – not stealing or acting dishonestly, not taking life, not indulging in illegitimate sex; and right livelihood – not earning one's living in ways that harm others such as by dealing in armaments or in harmful drugs. Thus within Buddhism – as within the other world faiths – the religious meaning of our situation in the universe presupposes its ethical meaning, which in turn presupposes its physical meaning. Spiritually the way to enlightenment is that of prolonged meditation producing a realization of the insubstantial and fleeting nature of the self, leading to an eventual detachment from the ego point of view. This is a transcendence both from egoity and to – and here there is a variety of terms – enlightenment, liberation, awakening, nirvana, *shunyata* ("emptiness"), conscious participation in the Dharmakaya or in the universal Buddha-nature. What the ultimate reality is with which we become one in enlightenment cannot be stated in human concepts. For it is for us *shunyata* – empty of everything that the human mind projects in its activity of awareness.

All who have an inkling of this state will seek it in this present life. For "Above, beyond Nibbana's bliss, is naught;"[15] and again "He that doth crush the great 'I am' conceit – this, even this, is happiness supreme."[16] In the *Dhammapada*, a collection of the Buddha's sayings which constitutes for many a Buddhist Bible, there is a continual stress upon the blessedness of approaching the nirvanic state now: "happily do we live without hate among the hateful ... happily do we live without yearning among those who yearn ... happily the peaceful live, giving up victory and defeat ... there is no bliss higher than Nibbana ... Nibbana, bliss supreme ... Nibbana is the highest bliss ... the taste of the joy of the Dhamma."[17]

And so, because the nirvanic state is limitlessly good, and is open without restriction to everyone, the message of Buddhism is clearly a form of cosmic optimism.

OTHER COSMIC OPTIMISMS

I believe that an analogous case can be made for the cosmic optimism of Christianity, Judaism, Islam, and Hinduism. There has only been space here to spell the case out in one instance, and I chose Buddhism because it is in many ways so different from the Christianity within which I myself live. But I can now in closing indicate the broad outline of the argument in relation to the other great traditions.

Christianity presents itself as a gospel, good news. In Jesus' teaching there is a very clear affirmation, expressed in parable after parable, of the goodness and love of God. Although his mission was primarily to his fellow Jews, there are several indications that he did not see God's saving love as confined to them. On the contrary, "many will come from east and west and sit at table with Abraham, Isaac and Jacob in the kingdom of heaven, while the sons of the kingdom [i.e. the children of Israel] will be thrown into the outer darkness" (Matthew 8:11–12). This saying does however also remind us of the doctrine of hell, which I have recognized above as undermining religious cosmic optimism. This has played a prominent part in Christian belief, particularly in the pre-modern period; and Jesus certainly spoke vividly of dire consequences beyond death for evil-doers, the criterion of judgment being always moral rather than theological. However, I do not think that it can be shown that he taught an *eternal*, and therefore necessarily unredemptive, punishment. The relevant passages are sparsest in the earliest gospel, that of Mark, and most prominent in the latest, that of John. But in the majority of the parables of judgment the punishment to come is clearly limited; for example, "till you have paid the last penny" (Matthew 5:26), "till he should pay all his debt" (Matthew 18:34). And when the word eternal (*aeonion*) is used, it does not necessarily mean "for ever and ever" but can mean until the end of the aeon, or age.[18] Thus a Christianity that emphasizes Jesus' teaching of divine love and God's gracious forgiveness of the truly penitent – as in the Lord's prayer and in the parable of the prodigal son – is indeed good news for all, a form of cosmic optimism.

Judaism's cosmic optimism consists in a special covenantal relationship between the people and their God, who is both gracious and just, and in a faith in the people's future welfare and ultimate fulfillment within the divine kingdom. Toward the end of the biblical period the idea of the world to come (*'olam ha-ba'*) became part of Jewish thinking, developed within rabbinic Judaism – particularly in the medieval period – first in terms of bodily resurrection and later of the life of the soul. Further, the rabbis concluded that redemption is not confined to Israel, and that non-Jews do not have to obey the many laws of the Torah to be accepted by God but only the basic moral principles believed to have been revealed to Adam and Noah. Thus whilst Jewish thinking has been compelled by history to be focused on the survival and welfare of the Jewish people, it is in principle universal in scope. In affirming both the loving-kindness of God and the reality of the world to come, Judaism constitutes a form of cosmic optimism.

As a form of cosmic optimism Islam exhibits essentially the same structure as the other great "religions of the book." That is to say, there is an affirmation that the Ultimate is gracious and kindly toward humanity, and that God's good purpose for all who seek him will finally be fulfilled in the life of paradise. Every *sura* of the Qur'an speaks of "*Allah rahman rahim*," God gracious and merciful. And the divine mercy is not restricted to the Muslim community: "Surely the believers [i.e. Muslims] and the Jews, Nazareans [= Christians], and the Sabians, whoever believes in God and the Last Day, and whosoever does right, shall have his reward with his Lord, and will neither have fear nor regret" (2:61). Islam teaches the unqualified unity and the absolute sovereignty of God, the sole ultimate reality, so that our appropriate human response to God is one of total submission and of trust in the divine goodness and mercy. The final judgment is strongly emphasized, and in the mainstream of the tradition it has been assumed – as in traditional Christianity – that many will forfeit paradise. But Islam contains great internal diversity: some of the Sufis thought that hell might be empty![19] It would seem, then, that Islam is a form of cosmic optimism in the same sense – admittedly qualified in much of their histories – as Christianity and Judaism.

Hinduism – that is to say Indian religiousness in its wide variety of forms – sees human existence, both in this life and beyond it, as a journey. On the large scale it is a journey through many lives in which souls (*jivas*) are gradually moving towards their final liberation (*moksha*): "After a number of births, perfected, he reaches the highest goal" (*Bhagavadgita* 5:45). This goal is differently conceived within the theistic and non-theistic strands of Hindu religion. According to the Advaita Vedanta of Shankara and others, our surface personality, or conscious ego, is only a fleeting material individuation of the universal Atman, which is ultimately identical with the universal Brahman, beyond the limitations of personality. On the other hand, according to the great theistic philosopher Ramanuja the material universe, including human selves, constitutes the "body" of God, and the final state is life within the eternal divine life. It is also the case that within the Hindu pictures of the structure of the universe there are many hells and many heavens. But these are not in the same category as the standard heaven and hell of Western monotheism. They are levels of existence in which *jivas* spend limited periods of time. But the ultimate state is eternal and is ultimately for all, whether as union with Brahman in which individual egoity has been entirely transcended, or as life within the life of God. Such a worldview clearly constitutes another form of cosmic optimism.

To summarize, then, the meaning for us of our human life depends upon what we believe to be the nature of the universe in which we find ourselves. The great world religions teach that the process of the universe is good from our human point of view because its ultimate principle (as some would say) or its governor (as others would say) is benign – again, from our human point of view. This is basically a very simple and indeed, I would think, obvious suggestion – though not necessarily any the worse for that.

Notes

1. John Stuart Mill, *Nature and the Utility of Religion and Theism* (London: Longmans, Green, 1875), p. 69.
2. John Henry Newman, *A Grammar of Assent* (1870; New York and London: Longmans, Green, 1947), chap. 4.
3. Wildred Cantwell Smith, *The Meaning and End of Religion* (1962; New York: Harper & Row, 1978).
4. *Samyutta Nikaya*, IV. 250, trans. Frank L. Woodward, in *The Book of the Kindred Sayings*, (London: Luzac, 1956), part 4, p. 170.
5. *Majjhima Nikaya*, I, 163, trans. I.B. Horner, in *The Collection of the Middle Length Sayings*, (London: Luzac, 1954), vol. 1, pp. 206–207.
6. *Udana* 80 (iii), trans. Frank L. Woodward, in *The Minor Anthologies of the Pali Canon* (London: Oxford University Press, 1948), pp. 97–98.
7. Narada Mahathera, introduction to *The Dhammapada*, 2nd ed. (Colombo: Vajiranama, 1972), pp. 24–25.
8. Takeuchi Yoshinori, *The Heart of Buddhism*, trans. James Heisig (New York: Crossroad, 1983), pp. 8–9.
9. Edward Conze, *Buddhism, its Essence and Development* (New York and London: Harper & Row, 1975), pp. 110–111.
10. *Vinaya Pitaka, Cullavagga* 9, 238, trans. I.B. Horner, in *The Book of the Discipline* (London: Luzac, 1963), vol. 5, p. 335.
11. *Majjhima Nikaya*, II, 431, in Horner, *Middle Length Sayings*, vol. 2 (1957), p. 101.
12. *Majjhima Nikaya*, I, 486, in Horner, *Middle Length Sayings*, vol. 2, p. 165.
13. *Majjhima Nikaya*, I, 140, in Horner, *Middle Length Sayings*, vol. 1, p. 180.
14. *Majjhima Nikaya*, I, 488, in Horner, *Middle Length Sayings*, vol. 2, p. 166.
15. *Therigatha*, 476, trans. C.A.F. Rhys Davids, in *Psalms of the Early Buddhists* (London: Luzac, 1964), p. 169.
16. *Udana*, II, 1, in Woodward, *Minor Anthologies of the Pali Canon*, p. 13.
17. *The Dhammapada*, trans. Narada Mahathera (Colombo: Vajiranama, 1972), chap. 15.
18. For a fuller discussion of both the biblical evidence and the philosophical issues, see my *Death and Eternal Life* (London: Macmillan, 1985 and Louisville, Ky. Westminster/John Knox, 1993), chap. 13.
19. For example, Rumi, *Masnavi*, Bk. 5, 432.

Plate 13 The modern high altar of Salisbury Cathedral, England, is framed above by the striking arches of the Holy Trinity Chapel, completed in 1225 CE with ribs of dark marble adding drama to the light Chilmark limestone, and behind by the contemporary *Prisoners of Conscience* windows at the east end. Photo: *Nancy M. Martin and Joseph Runzo*

16

THE WORLD *as* GOD'S BODY[†]

Sallie McFague

"And the Word became flesh and lived among us" (John 1:14a). The scandal of uniqueness is absolutized by Christianity into one of its central doctrines, which claims that God is embodied in one place and one place only: in the man Jesus of Nazareth. He and he alone is "the image of the invisible God" (Colossians 1:15). The source, power, and goal of the universe is known through and only through a first-century Mediterranean carpenter. The creator and redeemer of the fifteen-billion-year history of the universe with its hundred billion galaxies (and their billions of stars and planets) is available only in a thirty-year span of one human being's life on planet earth. The claim, when put in the context of contemporary science, seems skewed, to say the least. When the world consisted of the Roman Empire (with "barbarians" at its frontiers), the limitation of divine presence to Jesus of Nazareth had some plausibility while still being ethnocentric; but for many hundreds of years, well before contemporary cosmology, the claims of other major religious traditions have seriously challenged it. In its traditional form the claim is not only offensive to the integrity and value of other religions, but incredible, indeed absurd, in light of postmodern cosmology. It is not remotely compatible with our current picture of the universe.

But the scandal of uniqueness is perhaps not the central claim of Christian faith. In the model of the universe as God's body, the important

[†] This chapter is reprinted with permission from *The Body of God* by Sallie McFague (pp. 159–160, 163–174 and 182–191), copyright © 1993 Augsburg Fortress.

motifs are "became flesh" and "lived among us." It is the statement of faith that God is embodied and embodied paradigmatically as one of us, a human being, that is critical. It is not the exclusive claim that matters, for one would assume that the source, power, and goal of the universe, its life and breath, its enlivening energy, would be embodied in many forms through its vast reaches. Rather, it is both the concrete, physical availability of God's presence ("became flesh") and the likeness to ourselves, a human being ("lived among us") that matter.

CHRISTIANITY'S DISTINCTIVE EMBODIMENT: INCLUSION OF THE NEGLECTED OPPRESSED

The point at issue is *distinctive embodiment*; that is, what does, could, Christian faith have to say that is special, important, different, illuminating about embodiment – in relation to God, to ourselves, and to the natural world? Religious traditions will say many and different things about embodiment, and, as scholars have reminded us, Eastern, Goddess, and Native traditions, to mention a few, may say more and better things than does the Christian tradition. The question, however, for those of us who choose to remain Christian is: What does, can, the Christian faith contribute to an embodied theology, to an ecological sensibility? Our tradition and its theologians are not called upon to say the whole thing or the one thing; that presumption is a holdover from universalism and essentialism, which refuse to acknowledge the limitations of physical, cultural, historical – as well as religious – embodiment. Christianity is but one attempt, from a particular, concrete location, to speak of the unspeakable: reality. Its constructions are limited and partial, as are all constructions; nevertheless, they can and should be offered to the planetary agenda of our day as a voice in the conversation, a piece in the quilt. Like all other contributions, they will be judged by a variety of criteria, including their compatibility with the current view of reality from postmodern science, their fit with one's embodied (physical, cultural, historical) experience, and the value of the insights for planetary well-being.

What does Christian faith, and especially the story of Jesus, have to offer in terms of a distinctive perspective on embodiment? What is the shape that it suggests for God's body, the universe, enlivened by the breath of God's spirit? Christianity is *par excellence* the religion of the incarnation and, in one sense, is about nothing but embodiment, as is evident in its major doctrines. In another sense, . . . Christianity had denied, subjugated, and at times despised the body, especially female human bodies and bodies in the natural world. This is not the place for a treatise on the sorry history of Christianity's treatment of bodies or even on the rich complexities of various incarnational theologies such as those of Paul, John, Irenaeus, certain medieval mystics, and so on. I want to make a more simple, direct proposal: *The story of Jesus suggests that the shape of God's body includes all, especially the needy and outcast.*[1] While there are many distinctive features of the Christian notion of embodiment, in an ecological age when the development of our sensibility concerning the vulnerability and destruction of nonhuman creatures and the natural environment is critical, we ought to focus on one: the inclusion of the neglected oppressed – the planet itself and its many different creatures, including outcast human ones. The distinctive characteristic of Christian embodiment is its focus on oppressed, vulnerable, suffering *bodies*, those who are in pain due to the indifference or greed of the more powerful. In an ecological age, this ought to include oppressed nonhuman animals and the earth itself.

We need to pause and consider this suggestion, for it is shocking by conventional human standards. Until recently, most people found the notion that the earth is vulnerable, that its many species as well as the ecosystems supporting life are victims, are oppressed, absurd. And many still do. Many will even deny that the destabilizing love that we see in Jesus' parables, which overturns the conventional dualisms of rich and poor, righteous and sinner, Jew and Gentile, should include the dualism of humans over nature. And yet a cosmological or ecological perspective demands this radicalization of divine love: God's love is unlimited and oriented especially toward the oppressed – whoever the oppressed turn out to be at a particular time. The definition of who falls into this group has changed over the centuries, most recently focusing not on the spiritually poor, but the physically poor, those oppressed through the deprivation of bodily needs or through discrimination because of skin color or gender. Thus, the liberation theologies based on oppression due to poverty, race, or gender (and their interconnections) have arisen to claim that the gospel of Jesus of Nazareth has a preferential option for the poor, the poor in body, those whose bodies and bodily needs are not included in the conventional hierarchy of value. These are bodies that are devalued, discarded, and destroyed; these are bodies that can claim no intrinsic value in themselves but are of worth only because they are useful to others. In the organic model, bodies are basic, have suggested, and how they are treated – how they are fed and housed, valued in their differences, honored in their integrity – is the primary issue. One of the most fundamental aspects of the story of Jesus, the love that overturns conventional dualistic hierarchies to reach out to the outcast and the victim, ought, I suggest, be extended to another dualistic hierarchy, that of humanity over nature. Nature is the "new poor," and in an embodiment, organic perspective, this means bodily poverty.

It is important to be clear about this suggestion of nature as the new poor. It does not mean that the "old poor" – poor human beings – are being replaced, or that every microorganism is included in God's love in the same way as human beings are.[2] It does, however, suggest that nature is the "also" poor, and that even microorganisms have their place in creation, a place this is not merely their usefulness (or threat) to human beings. There are two interrelated issues in the notion of nature as the new poor. The first is nature's value as such and to God; the second is its relation to human beings as well as what human beings are presently doing to nature. A statement from the World Council of Churches on the meaning of the phrase "the integrity of creation" is helpful here: "The value of all creatures in and for themselves, for one another, and for God, and their interconnectedness in a diverse whole that has unique value for God, together constitute the integrity of creation."[3] This definition underscores the *intrinsic* value that each living being has in and for itself as a creature loved by God as well as the *instrumental* value that living beings have for one another and for God as parts of an evolutionary, weblike creation.[4]

Intrinsic versus instrumental value is the critical issue. It means, quite simply, that other creatures as well as our planet as a whole were not created for our benefit, as we have already learned from the common creation story. Therefore, when we consider some part of it solely in terms of usefulness to ourselves as, for instance, in the metaphors of "silo" (food), "laboratory" (experimental material), "gymnasium" (recreation), or "cathedral" (spiritual uplift), we transgress "the integrity of creation."[5] Nature as the new poor does not mean that we should sentimentalize nature or slip into such absurdities as speaking of "oppressed" mosquitoes or rocks. Rather, nature as the new poor means that *we have made nature poor.* It is a comment not about the workings of natural selection but of human sin. It is a hard, cold look at what one part of nature, we human beings, have done to the rest of it: we have broken the integrity of creation by the excesses of our population and lifestyle, by our utilitarian attitude toward other creatures as well as toward our own vulnerable sisters and brothers, by our refusal to acknowledge the value of each and every aspect of creation to itself and to God. Nature is not necessarily and as such poor; it is so only because of *one* species, our own, which threatens the vitality and viability of the rest of nature. To say that the inclusive love of Jesus' destabilizing parables ought to be extended to nature does not, then, imply a sentimental divine love for each and every cell or bacterium. Rather, it brings to mind the righteous judgment of the Creator whose body, composed of many valuable, diverse forms, is being diminished on our planet by one greedy, thoughtless, albeit self-conscious and hence responsible, part of the that body – ourselves. It means that nature needs to be liberated and healed because *we* have enslaved it and made it sick. This perspective claims that in the twentieth century on our planet, human beings have caused nature to be the new poor in the same way that a small elite of the human population has created and continues to create the old poor – through a gross imbalance of the haves and have-nots. Those "other" people (the old poor) and nature (the new poor) are, in both cases, there "for our use."

Of course, all aspects of creation – including human beings – have instrumental as well as intrinsic value (we all live on top of, in between, and inside each other), but this cannot mean within the Hebrew and Christian traditions that *any* aspect of creation is nothing but fuel or fodder for others. The recognition of intrinsic value means, at the very least, that when we use other creatures for our benefit, we do so with humility, respect, and thanksgiving for these other lives. Moreover, to add nature as the new poor to God's inclusive love does not mean that each and every cell, elephant, or Douglas fir will thrive and prosper any more than it means that each and every poor human being does. In our complex world of natural selection, fortune and misfortune, human freedom as well as sin, nothing could be further from reality. It might mean, however, that *we* would look at nature with new eyes, not as something to be misused or even just used, but as our kin, that of which we are a part, with each creature seen as valuable in itself and to God. Indeed, we might see nature in our time as the new poor of Jesus' parables.

A cosmological and theocentric perspective – valuing the natural bodies around us because they are intrinsically worthwhile in themselves and to God, rather than for our purposes – is conventionally alien to us, but so is the overturning of the other hierarchies in the message of Jesus.[6] The central claim of the gospel is, then, not only that the Word became flesh, but the particular shape that flesh took – one that presented a shock to our natural way of considering things in terms of value to ourselves. And for us to admit that nature is the "new poor" is also a direct affront to our anthropocentric sensibility. Our first response, in fact, might well be that such a radical perspective, a theocentric–cosmological one, is useless in light of the ecological crisis we face, where increasing numbers of poor, needy people *must* use the natural environment to provide for their own basic needs. We do not need to add yet another category of the oppressed, especially that of nature. But the shape of the body of God from a Christian perspective suggests otherwise. That shape, we have suggested, is given its basic outlines from one of the central features of Jesus' ministry – his destabilizing parables that side with the outcast. Extended to the natural world, to our planet and its many nonhuman creatures, the parabolic ministry of Jesus names a new poor, which is by definition poor in body, for those creatures and dimensions of our planet are primarily body. An incarnational religion, a bodily tradition, such as Christianity, should not have to strain to include the natural world and its creatures, for they epitomize the physical. They are, as it were, the *representative* bodies.[7]

If we press this issue still further in light of other motifs in the ministry of Jesus – his healings and eating practices – we can develop our theme more deeply. Jesus' healing ministry has often been an embarrassment to the Church, especially in light of the Church's spiritualization of salvation; moreover, the healings appear to fall into the category of miracles and thus suggest a breaking of natural laws. But they are unmistakably central in all versions of Jesus' ministry, as central as the parables. As a symbol of focused concern, of what counts, the healing stories are crucial. We have suggested that in the organic model the body is the main attraction, and the healing stories seem to agree. Whatever else one wants to say about them, they focus attention on bodily pain and bodily relief. Since Christians understand Jesus of Nazareth as at least paradigmatic of God, that his ministry is a place to gain hints and clues about divine concern, then the centrality of the healing stories stands full square against any minimizing of the body. Bodies *count*, claims the healing ministry of Jesus, in the eyes of God. This perspective, of course, fits very well indeed with an ecological sensibility. It suggests that redemption should be enlarged to salvation: redemption means to "buy back" or "repay" through, for instance, a sacrifice, whereas salvation means healing or preserving from destruction. The first applies only to human beings who have offended (sinned) and hence need to be rescued through a substitutionary act of reconciliation, while the second can include the natural order, which, along with human beings, needs to be healed and preserved.

The healing metaphor for salvation is a modest claim. It does not suggest ecstatic fulfillment of all desires but rather preservation from destruction or, at most, the restoration to adequate bodily functioning. If the parables are the deconstructive phase of Jesus' ministry, overturning the oppressive, dualistic hierarchies, then the healing stories are the middle or reconstructive phase, not promising the kingdom but only what in ecological terms is called "sustainability," the ability to function in terms of bodily needs. The healings are a modest statement in light of the radical character of the parables. And yet, in another sense, at least in a cosmological or ecological context, they deepen the radicality of the parables, for they imply that bodily health and well-being is a priority of the gospel – and given the inclusiveness of the parabolic message and its bias toward the needy, this must mean not just human bodies but other vulnerable ones as well.

A third characteristic aspect of Jesus' ministry, his practice of eating with sinners, might be called the *prospective* phase, in contrast to the *deconstructive* (parables) and *reconstructive* (healing) dimensions. This practice was as much a scandal to Jesus' contemporaries as were the destabilizing parables and miraculous healings.[8] It is also, although for different reasons, scandalous to an ecological era. It suggests that *all* are invited to the banquet of life. In the stories of Jesus feeding the multitudes as well as in his unconventional invitations to the outcasts to share his table, two motifs emerge. First, whatever food there is, be it only a few loaves, should be shared, and second is the hope of abundance, of a feast that satisfies the deepest hungers of all creatures, of all creation. One could say there is a minimal and a maximal vision: the exhortation that the basic needs of all creatures, including the most needy, be met from available resources, and the faith that the deepest needs will also be met in the future. By focusing on food, which, along with breath, is the most immediate and necessary component of bodily health, the motif of God's love for all, especially the outcast and the vulnerable, is deepened and radicalized. Moreover, the food imagery includes, without any additional explanation or rationalization, the non-human creatures and the plants of our planet. Food is basic to all life and is, increasingly, a symbol of the planet's crisis: the exponential growth of the human population and the lifestyle of some in that population at the expense of all other living things. So, this one metaphor of food includes not only what is most basic but also what is deepest. The eating practices and feeding stories of Jesus not only suggest a survival strategy for the diversity of life-forms, but also project a vision when all shall gather at one table – the lion, the lamb, and human beings – and eat their fill. It is a vision of salvation as wholeness, characterized not by the overcoming of differences, but by their acceptance and inclusion. Such visions have a prophetic edge, for they serve both as a critique of current practices and as a goal toward which to strive. They are not, then, so much about the future as about the present; they propose an alternative to the present, not necessarily realizable but at least as giving a direction toward which to aim.

Jesus' eating stories and practices suggest that physical needs are basic and must be met – food is not a metaphor here but should be taken literally. All creatures deserve what is basic to bodily health. But food also serves as a metaphor of fulfillment at the deepest level of our longings and desires. The Church picked up and developed the second, metaphorical emphasis, making eating imagery the ground of its vision of spiritual fulfillment, especially in the eucharist. But just as the tradition focused on the second birth (redemption), often neglecting the first birth (creation), so also it spiritualized hunger as the longing of the soul for God, conveniently forgetting the source of the metaphor in basic bodily needs. But the aspects of Jesus' ministry on which we have focused – the parables, healings, and eating stories – do not forget this dimension; in fact, Jesus' activities and message, according to this interpretation, are embarrassingly bodily. The parables focus on oppression that people feel due to their concrete, cultural setting, as servants rather than masters, poor rather than rich, Gentile rather than Jew; the healing stories are concerned with the bodily pain that some endure; the eating stories have to do with physical hunger and the humiliation of exclusion. None of these is primarily spiritual, though each assumes the psychosomatic unity of human nature and can serve as a symbol of eschatological fulfillment – the overcoming of all hierarchies, the health and harmony of the cosmos and all its creatures, the satiety of the deepest groanings and longings of creation.

Our focus, however, has been on the bodily basics, because the major established traditions within Christianity (except for sectarian, monastic, and now liberation theologies) have neglected them, and because it allows us to include human as well as planetary well-being. The shape, then, of God's body from some central motifs in the ministry of Jesus is one that includes the rich diversity of created forms, especially in regard to their basic needs for physical well-being. *The body of God must be fed.*

But even this exhortation, let alone the fulfillment of creation's deepest longings, is difficult, perhaps impossible, to bring about. We have suggested that the distinctive feature of a Christian view of embodiment is inclusion of the outcast and the oppressed. This is a scandal by conventional human standards and (here the issue deepens and darkens) in light of the process of natural selection in evolutionary biology. In neither framework do the vulnerable get the basics, let alone any glory.

EVOLUTION AND SOLIDARITY WITH THE OPPRESSED

We have looked at this scandal in terms of conventional human standards, but what of natural selection? What consonance can there possibly be between Christianity's inclusion of the outcasts of society, as well as our extension to include our vulnerable planet and its many creatures, and biological evolution, in which millions are wasted, individuals are sacrificed for the species, and even whole species are wiped out in the blinking of an eye? Does not the Christian overturning of hierarchies, the healing of bodies, and the concern with basics of life for all seem like an absurdity – or, at least, hopelessly naive? Is there any fit between the distinctive embodiment perspective of Jesus' ministry and the common creation story? The answer is both yes and no; there is both consonance and dissonance.

Jesus voiced the yes in the stories we have of his life and death: human beings can choose to side with the vulnerable and the outcast. Evolution is not only or solely biological; it is also historical and cultural. Once evolutionary history reaches the human, self-conscious stage, natural selection is not the only operative principle, for natural selection can be countered with the principle of solidarity.[9] The notion of siding with the vulnerable is not the sole insight of Christianity by any means. All human beings, despite the historically dismal record of slavery, oppression of women and homosexuals, and genocide, just to name a few of our more heinous crimes against the vulnerable, have, nonetheless, the option of deciding differently – and sometimes do. That is, once evolutionary history reaches the self-conscious level, other principles can function as to which individuals and species live and thrive. Cultural evolution can expand ethical regard to include more and more others besides the dominant males of a culture: women, people of all races and classes, the physically challenged, gays and lesbians – and even animals and the earth. This is a democratizing tendency that counters the fang and claw of genetic evolution as well as its two basis movers, chance and law. Human choice, the expansion of who survives and prospers, can and has enlarged the pool, so that, for instance, the physically challenged are not necessarily cast aside as they would be if only genetic selection were operative. Enlarging the pool, however, is often a minimal step, for we all know that equality for all does not follow. Ethical regard is practiced differently for African-Americans than for whites and for gays and lesbians than for heterosexuals.

Nonetheless, once the scales have fallen from our eyes and we recognize that human beings have reached a plateau where both choice and power are involved in who lives and how well they live, we see that cultural evolution is as (if not more) important than natural selection – at least on this planet at this time. We now know that natural selection is not the only principle: something else is possible. We know that the recognition of the intrinsic value of other life-forms is an alternative. Some form of this insight is evident in the practice of most cultures and religions, though which life-forms count varies enormously. The point is that some do; that is, *all* life-forms are not simply grist for the biological mill, as natural selection holds. The issue becomes, then, where one draws the line in terms of intrinsic value. The model of the universe as God's body, composed of billions of different bodies, implies that all are valuable. The theocentric–cosmocentric view implicit in the organic model is radically inclusive: God loves the entire creation and finds it valuable. The Christic paradigm suggests a further shaping of the body, with particular attention to those parts of the body that hitherto have been excluded by human sin. In this reading, Christianity intensifies a cultural process we find in many different forms and places in human history: a radicalization of intrinsic value that is counter to the principle of natural selection (and this occurred, of course, centuries before those principles were known).

Solidarity with the oppressed, then, becomes the Christian form of both consonance with and defiance of the evolutionary principle. It is consonant with it because it claims that there is a next stage of evolution on our planet, one that is not primarily genetic but cultural: the necessity, for survival and well-being, for all life-forms to share the basic goods of the planet. It is defiant of it because it suggests that the principle needed for this to occur is not natural selection or the survival of the fittest, but the solidarity of each with all. We have reached the point where war, ecological destruction, sexual and racial discrimination, poverty and homelessness, are counterproductive to planetary well-being. We have also reached the point where we realize that the interrelationships and interconnections among all forms of life are so deep, permanent, and mysterious that the various species of plants and animals need one another. But solidarity of each with all should perhaps remain at this utilitarian level: we *need* each other to survive. The scandal of Christianity goes further: it insists on solidarity with the outsider, the outcast, the vulnerable. Does not this make Christian faith a surd, if not absurd, in view of postmodern science, rather than merely counter to it? Would not the planet be better off without these "outcast" types?

At this point, I believe we have no choice but to admit that the radical inclusiveness that is at the heart of Christian faith, especially inclusion of the oppressed, is not compatible with evolution, even cultural evolution. For as we have seen, its view of sinful human nature deepens the notion of the ecological sinner: the bloated self refusing to share. Hence, even the best of cultural evolution, from a Christian perspective, is lacking, for we "naturally" construct our worlds to benefit ourselves, including only those who are useful to us. Christian solidarity with the oppressed, therefore, will have some special, peculiar characteristics that are both counter-revolutionary and countercultural. One form will entail resistance to evil or the liberation of the oppressed, and another will involve suffering with those who, nonetheless, suffer. The first form is the primary one, what we have discussed under the rubric of the embodiment ministry of Jesus – his parables, healings, and eating practices that attempt in deconstructive, reconstructive, and prospective ways to free suffering bodies and fulfill their needs. The second form, the suffering of God – and ourselves – with those who, nonetheless, suffer, recognizes that irremediable, unconscionable, unremitting, horrific suffering *does* occur both to individuals and to whole species, suffering that is beyond our best efforts to address and seemingly beyond God's as well.

In both forms of Christian solidarity with the oppressed, the active and the passive, liberation and suffering, the cross and resurrection of the

Christic paradigm are central to an embodiment theology. The death of our natural, sinful preference for hierarchical dualisms that favor the wealthy, healthy, well-fed bodies is a necessary prerequisite in the embodiment ministry of Jesus. His parables, healing stories, and eating practices demand our deaths – just as the practice of his embodiment ministry also brought about his own death. Neither biological nor cultural evolution includes this radical next step of identification with the vulnerable and needy through the death of the self. What is clear in the New Testament stories of the Christic paradigm is that for those who respond to its call, the way of solidarity with the oppressed will demand the cross (in some form or another). What is less clear, but hinted at, is that *bodies*, all suffering bodies, will live again to see a new day. Regardless of the difficulty of imagining what resurrection might mean, then or now, what is clear is the focus on the body, the physical basis of life. Faith in the resurrection of the body is the belief that the spirit that empowers the universe and all its living forms is working with us, in life and in death, to bring about the well-being and fulfillment of all the bodies in creation. Resurrection of the body puts the emphasis where it should be in an ecological theology: on the physical basis of life. As often as Christianity has forgotten and repudiated that basis, its most ancient and treasured belief in the resurrection of the body reminds it of its denial of the physical.

THE DIRECTION OF CREATION AND THE PLACE OF SALVATION

The immediate and concrete sense of the cosmic Christ – God with us in liberation and in defeat – is the first level of the scope or range of God's body. But there are two additional dimensions implied in the metaphor that need focused and detailed attention. One is the relationship between creation and salvation in which salvation is the *direction* of creation and creation is the *place* of salvation. The metaphor of the cosmic Christ suggests that the cosmos is moving *toward* salvation and that this salvation is taking place *in* creation. The other dimension is that God's presence in the form or shape of Jesus' paradigmatic ministry is available not just in the years 1–30 CE and not just in the Church as his mystical body, but everywhere, in the cosmic body of the Christ. Both of these dimensions of the metaphor of the cosmic Christ are concerned with *place* and *space*, with where God's body is present in its Christic shape.[10] Christian theology has not traditionally been concerned with or interested in spatial matters, as we have already noted, priding itself on being a historical religion, often deriding such traditions as Goddess, Native, and "primitive" for focusing on place, on sacred spaces, on the natural world. But it is precisely place and space, as the common creation story reminds us, that must now enter our consciousness. An ecological sensibility demands that we broaden the circle of salvation to include the natural world, and the practical issues that face us will, increasingly, be ones of space, not time. On a finite, limited planet, arable land with water will become not only the symbol of privilege but, increasingly, the basis of survival. Geography, not history, is the ecological issue. Those in the Christian tradition who have become accustomed to thinking of reality in a temporal model – the beginning of creation; the middle in the incarnation, ministry, and death of Jesus Christ; and the end at the eschaton when God shall bring about the fulfillment of all things – need to modify their thinking in a spatial direction. We need to ask where is this salvation occurring here and now, and what is the scope of this salvation?

In regard to the first dimension of the cosmic Christ, what does it mean to say that salvation is the *direction* of creation and creation is the *place* of salvation? To say that salvation is the direction of creation is a deceptively simple statement on a complex, weighty matter. It is a statement of faith in the face of massive evidence to the contrary, evidence that we have suggested when we spoke of the absurdity of such a claim in light of both conventional standards and natural selection. Some natural theologies, theologies that begin with creation, try to make the claim that evolutionary history contains a teleological direction, an optimistic arrow, but our claim is quite different. It is a retrospective, not a prospective claim; it begins with salvation, with experiences of liberation and healing that one wagers are from God, and reads back into creation the hope that the whole creation is included within the divine liberating, healing powers. It is a statement of faith, not of fact; it takes as its standpoint a concrete place where salvation has been experienced – in the case of Christians, the paradigmatic ministry of Jesus and similar ministries of his disciples in different, particular places – and projects the shape of these ministries onto the whole. What is critical, then, in this point of view about the common creation story is not that this story tells us anything about God or salvation but, rather, that it gives us a new, contemporary picture with which to remythologize Christian faith. The entire fifteen-billion-year history of the universe and the billions of galaxies are, from a Christian perspective, from this concrete, partial, particular setting, seen to be the cosmic Christ, the body of God in the Christic paradigm. Thus, the direction or hope of creation, all of it, is nothing less than what I understand that paradigm to be for myself and for other human beings: the liberating, healing, inclusive love of God.

To say that creation is the place of salvation puts the emphasis on the here-and-now aspect of spatiality. While the direction motif takes the long view, speaking of the difficult issue of an evolutionary history that appears to have no purpose, the place motif underscores the concrete, nitty-gritty, daily, here-and-now aspect of salvation. In contrast to all theologies that claim or even imply that salvation is an otherworldly affair, the place motif insists that salvation occurs *in* creation, in the body of God. The cosmic Christ is the physical, available, and needy outcast in creation, in the space where we live. In Christian thought creation is often seen as merely the backdrop of salvation, of lesser importance than redemption, the latter being God's main activity. We see this perspective in such comments as "creation is the prologue to history" or "creation provides the background and setting for the vocation of God's people,"[11] and in Calvin's claim that nature is the stage for salvation history. In this way of viewing the relation between creation and redemption, creation plays no critical role: it is only the stage on which the action takes place, the background for the real action. But in our model of the body of God as shaped by the Christic paradigm, creation is of central importance, for creation – meaning our everyday world of people and cities, farms and mountains, birds and oceans, sun and sky – is the place where it all happens and to whom it happens. Creation as the place of salvation means that the health and well-being of all creatures and parts of creation is what salvation is all about – it is God's place and our place, the one and only place. Creation is not one thing and salvation something else; rather, they are related as scope and shape, as space and form, as place and pattern. Salvation is for all of creation. The liberating, healing, inclusive ministry of Christ takes place *in* and *for* creation.

These two related motifs of the direction of creation and the place of salvation both underscore expanding God's liberating, healing, inclusive love to all of the natural world. This expansion does not eclipse the importance of needy, vulnerable human beings, but it suggests that the cosmic Christ, the body of Christ, is not limited to the Church or even to human beings but, as coextensive with God's body, is *also* the direction of the natural world and the place where salvation occurs.

NATURE AND THE COSMIC CHRIST

These comments lead us into the second dimension of the metaphor of the cosmic Christ, which also concerns spatiality. The world in our model is the sacrament of God, the visible, physical, bodily presence of God. The cosmic Christ metaphor suggests that Jesus' paradigmatic ministry is not limited to the years 1–30 CE nor to the Church, as in the model of the Church as the mystical body of Christ, but is available to us throughout nature. It is available everywhere, it is unlimited – with one qualification: it is mediated *through bodies.* Our model is unlimited at one end and restrictive at the other: the entire cosmos is the habitat of God, but we know this only through the mediation of the physical world. The world as sacrament is an old and deep one in the Christian tradition, both Eastern and Western. The sacramental tradition assumes that God is present not only in the hearing of the word, in the preaching and reading of scripture, and not only in the two (or seven) sacraments of the Church, but also in each and every being in creation. While Christian sacramentalism derives from the incarnation ("the Word became flesh"), the sense of the extraordinary character of the ordinary or the sacredness of the mundane is scarcely a Christian insight. In fact, it is more prevalent and perhaps more deeply felt and preserved in some other religious traditions, including, for instance, Goddess, Native, and Buddhist ones.[12] Moreover, Christian sacramentalism has usually been utilitarian in intent, that is, using the things of the world as symbols of religious states. They are often not appreciated in their own integrity as having intrinsic value but rather as stepping stones on one's pilgrimage to God. This perspective is evident in a famous passage from Augustine's *Confessions*, in which all the delights of the senses are transmuted into symbols of divine ecstasy: "But what is it I love when I love You? Not the beauty of any bodily thing ... Yet in a sense I do love light and melody and fragrance and food and embrace when I love my God – the light and the voice and the fragrance and the food and embrace in the soul...."[13] This tradition is rich and powerful, epitomized in a sensibility that sees God in everything and everything full of the glory of God: the things of this earth are valuable principally as vehicles for communication with the divine. A different sensibility is evident in this Navajo chant:

> May it be delightful my house;
> From my head may it be delightful;
> To my feet may it be delightful;
> Where I lie may it be delightful;
> All above me may it be delightful;
> All around me may it be delightful.[14]

The delight here is in and not through the ordinary; the ordinary is not chiefly a symbol of the divine delight. The difference between these sensibilities is epitomized in two lines, one from Hildegard of Bingen, a medieval German mystic ("Holy persons draw to themselves all that is earthly") and one from Abraham Heschel, a contemporary Jewish theologian ("Just to be is a blessing, Just to live is holy").[15] The first perspective transmutes all things earthly into their holy potential, while the second finds ordinary existence itself to be holy.

Nevertheless, in spite of its limitations, traditional sacramentalism is an important perspective, for it is the major way Christianity has preserved and developed an appreciation for nature. It has encouraged Christians to look upon the world as valuable – indeed, as holy – and has served as a counterforce to two other perspectives on nature within Christian history, one that divorces it totally from God through secularizing it and one that dominates and exploits it. Traditional sacramentalism has, in its own way, supported the principal thesis of this essay: the model of the world (universe) as God's body means that the presence of God is not limited to particular times or places but is coextensive with reality, with all that is. It has been one of the few traditions within Christianity that has encouraged both a spatial and a historical perspective; that is, Christian sacramentalism has included nature as a concern of God and a way to God rather than limiting divine activity to human history. For these and other reasons Christian sacramentalism should be encouraged. It is a distinctive contribution of Christianity. From its incarnational base, it claims that in analogy with the body of Jesus the Christ all bodies can serve as ways to God, all can be open to and give news of the divine presence. But it does not claim, at least primarily, that bodies have intrinsic value. The great theologians and poets of the Christian sacramental tradition, including Paul, John, Irenaeus, Augustine, the medieval mystics (such as Julian of

Norwich, Meister Eckhart, Hildegard of Bingen), Gerard Manley Hopkins, and Pierre Teilhard de Chardin, love the things of this world principally *as expressions of* divine beauty, sustenance, truth, and glory.[16] It is not a sensibility that in a homey phrase wants "to hold on hard to the huckleberries."[17] The value of huckleberries as huckleberries is not a major concern of Christian sacramentalism.

Again, we need to remind ourselves that for the purposes of the planetary agenda, no one tradition needs to claim universality or the whole truth. What is more helpful is to specify the *kind* of insights that are distinctive of different traditions. The Christian tradition does not underscore the intrinsic value of all things earthly but does express richly and deeply the symbolic importance of each and every body on the earth: each in its own way expresses divine reality and is valuable for this reason. Unfortunately, traditional sacramentalism is not a central concern for many Christians; in fact, some Protestant churches scarcely attend to it. Yet it can be a way that Christians, at least, might begin to change their exploitative, utilitarian attitudes toward nature – as well as toward other humans whose bodies are also expressions of God. As Hopkins puts it, "Christ plays in ten thousand places, lovely in limbs, lovely in eyes not his."[18] If use is to be made of our earth and its people and other creatures, it can only be a use, says Christian sacramentalism, for God's glory, not for our profit.

Nevertheless, we suggest two qualifications of traditional sacramentalism. The first is implicit in the direction of this entire essay: the need to replace the utilitarian attitude toward other beings that accompanies anthropocentricism with a perspective that values them intrinsically. If we are not the center of things, then other beings do not exist for our benefit – even for our spiritual growth as ways to God. They exist within the vast, intricate web of life in the cosmos, of which they and we are all interdependent parts, and each and every part has both utilitarian and intrinsic value. Within our model of the world as God's body, all of us, human beings included, exist as parts of the whole. Some parts are not merely means for the purposes of other parts, for all parts are valued by God and hence should be valued by us. We do have a distinctive role in this body, but it is not as the ones who use the rest as a ladder to God; rather it is as the ones who have emerged as the caretakers of the rest.

The second qualification of traditional sacramentalism picks up on this note of care and might be called "negative sacramentalism." It focuses on bodies not as expressions of divinity, but as signs of human sin and destruction. It is a perspective on the earth and its many bodies that sees them not as telling of the glories of God but of human destruction. The bodies of the earth, human and nonhuman, that are vulnerable and needy cry out for compassion and care. These bodies appear to us, at the end of the twentieth century, not primarily as expressions of divine loveliness, but as evidence of human neglect and oppression. The focus is not on their use to help us in our religious pilgrimage but on our misuse of them, our refusal to acknowledge these bodies as valuable in and for themselves and to God. One of the motifs of our analysis of the model of the world as God's body from the perspective of the common creation story is that all bodies are united in webs of interrelatedness and interconnectedness. This motif has been radicalized by the Christic paradigm that reaches out to include especially the vulnerable, outcast, needy bodies. Hence, I would suggest that a form of Christian sacramentalism for an ecological era should focus not on the use of all earthly bodies but on our care of them, in the ways that the Christic paradigm suggests. We are suggesting that the Christic shape to God's body be applied to the full scope of that body, especially to the new poor, the natural world. Nature, its flora and fauna, therefore would not simply be addenda to human salvation, avenues providing deeper communion between God and human beings; rather, the Christic salvific paradigm would also be applied to the earth and its many creatures. This is what a cosmological or ecological context for theological reflection demands: the whole cosmos is God's concern, not just its human inhabitants and not merely as our habitat.

In what ways, then, should the Christic paradigm be applied to the natural world? In the same ways as applied to other outcasts: the deconstructive phase (liberation from oppressive hierarchies as seen in the parables), the reconstructive (physical sustainability as suggested by the healing stories), and the prospective (inclusion of all as manifest in the eating practices). These primary, active dimensions of the Christic paradigm – the shape of the cosmic Christ given to God's body – are balanced by a secondary, passive phase, the suffering of God with the despairing and defeated. What does each of these themes suggest to us as we reflect on the deteriorating, needy body of our planet earth?

Just as, in the overturning of oppressive, dualistic hierarchies, poor people are liberated from their enslavement by the rich, people of color are liberated from discrimination by whites, so also the earth and its many nonhuman creatures are liberated from oppression and destruction by human beings. The dualistic hierarchy of people over nature is an old and profound one, certainly as ancient as the patriarchal era that stretches back some five thousand years.[19] Until the sixteenth-century scientific revolution, however, and the subsequent marriage of science with technology, human beings were not sufficiently powerful to wreak massive destruction on nature. But we now are. The first phase, then, of extending the Christic paradigm beyond human beings is the recognition, which involves a confession of sin, of our oppressive misuse of the major part of God's creation in regard to our planet, that is, everything and every creature that is *not* human. The destructive phase is a breaking down of our "natural" biases against nature; our prejudices that it is, at best, only useful for our needs; our rationalizations in regard to activities that profit us but destroy it. The hierarchy of humans over nature has been, at least in the West, so total and so destructive for the last several hundred years that many people would deny that nature merits a status similar to other oppressed "minorities." Nature is, of course, the *majority* in terms of both numbers and importance (it can do very well without us, but not vice versa). Bracketing that issue for the moment, however, many would still claim that it does not, like poor or oppressed people, deserve attention as intrinsically valuable. Nature is valuable insofar as and only insofar as it serves human purposes. Thus, in a telling phrase, many speak of wilderness as "undeveloped" land, that is, of course, undeveloped for human profit, though it is excellently developed for the animals, trees, and plants that presently inhabit it.

The liberation of nature from our oppressive practices, the recognition that the land and its creatures have rights and are intrinsically valuable, is by no means easy to practice, since immediately and inevitably, especially on a finite planet with limited resources and increasing numbers of needy human beings, conflicts of interest will occur. These conflicts are real, painful, and important, but the point that our model underscores is that the resolution of them from a Christian perspective cannot ignore the value and rights of 99 percent of creation on our planet. The model of the world as God's body denies this attitude, and the model of the cosmic Christ intensifies that denial. Whether we like it or not, these models say that all parts of the planet are parts of God's body and are included in the Christic liberation from dualistic hierarchies. It is for us to figure out what this must, can, mean in particular situations where conflicts arise. The preferential option for the poor is uncomfortable wherever it is applied; it will be no less so when applied to the new poor, nature.

The second phase of the Christic paradigm, the healing phase, is especially appropriate to the nonhuman dimensions of creation. It is increasingly evident that the metaphors of sickness, degeneration, and dysfunction are significant when discussing the state of our planet. The pollution of air and water, the greenhouse effect, the depletion of the ozone layer, the desertification of arable land, the destruction of rainforests are all signs of the poor health of the earth. One of the great values of the organic model is that it not only focuses on bodies and includes the natural world (unlike many models in the Christian tradition), but it also implies that salvation includes, as the bottom line, the health of bodies. While the model helps us to focus on basic justice issues for human beings – the need for food, clean air and water, adequate housing, education and medical benefits – it also insists that we focus on the basics for other creatures and dimensions of our planet. The organic model focuses on the basics of existence: the healthy functioning of all inhabitants and systems of the planet. Jesus' healing stories are extremely valuable in a time of ecological deterioration and destruction such as we are experiencing. They refuse any early and easy spiritualizing of salvation; they force us, as Christians, to face the deep sickness of the many bodies that make up the body of God. These embarrassing stories are part of the mud of our tradition, the blood-and-guts part of the gospel that insists that whatever more or else Christian faith might be and mean, it includes as a primary focus physical well-being. And nature, in our time, is woefully ill.

Most of us, most the time, refuse to acknowledge the degree of that sickness. It is inconvenient to do so, since curing the planet's illnesses will force human inhabitants to make sacrifices. Hence, denial sets in, a denial not unlike the denial many people practice in relation to serious, perhaps terminal, illness when it strikes their own bodies. But denial of the planet's profoundly deteriorating condition is neither wise nor Christian: it is not wise because, as we increasingly know, we cannot survive on a sick planet, and it is not Christian because, if we extend the Christic healing ministry to all of creation, then we must work for the health of its many creatures and the planet itself.

This brings us to the third and final phase of the Christic paradigm as extended to the whole body of God: the inclusive fulfillment epitomized in Jesus' eating practices. As with the healing stories, the stories of Jesus feeding the multitudes and inviting the excluded to his table are embarrassments, perhaps scandals, in their mundanity and inclusivity. Neither conventional standards nor natural selection operates on the themes of sharing and inclusion; these stories are countercultural and counterbiological, but they are hints and clues of a new stage of evolution, the stage of our solidarity with other life-forms, especially with the needy and outcast forms. The time has come, it appears, when our competition with various other species for survival will not result in a richer, more complex and diverse community of life-forms. The human population is already so dominant that it is likely to wipe out many other forms and probably seriously harm its own, if predictions of our exponential growth prove true and the profligate lifestyle of many of us continues. The good life rests in part, then, on human decisions concerning sharing and inclusion, with food as an appropriate and powerful symbol of both bare existence as well as the abundant life. In the Christian tradition food has always served these dual functions, though the emphasis has often been on the latter meaning, especially in the eucharist as a foretaste of the eschatological banquet. But in our time, the value of food is precisely its literal meaning: sustainability for bodies, especially the many bodies on our planet that Christians as well as others in our society think of as superfluous. In a telling reversal of the need of all bodies for food, many people assume that other creatures not only do not *deserve* food but are themselves *only* food – food for us.[20]

The paradigmatic Christic shape of the body of the world, then, suggests some hints and clues for Christians as we, in an ecological age, extend that shape to be coextensive with the world, superimposing, as it were, the cosmic Christ on the body of God. We look at the world, our planet and all its creatures, through the shape of Christ. As we do so, we acknowledge the distinctive features of that form, especially liberation from our destructive oppression, the healing of its deteriorating bodies, and the sharing of basic needs with all the planet's inhabitants, that the Christian tradition can contribute to the planetary agenda.

But we are not left alone to face this momentous, indeed, horrendous task. Ecological despair would quickly overwhelm us if we believed that to be the case. The cosmic Christ as the shape of God's body also tells us that God suffers with us in our suffering, that divine love is not only with us in our active work against the destruction of our planet but also in our passive suffering when we and the health of our planet are defeated. An attitude of sober realism, in view of the massiveness of ecological and human oppression that faces us in our time, is the appropriate – perhaps the only possible – attitude. We and our planet may, in fact, be defeated, or, at least life in community, life worth living, may no longer be possible. The situation we face is similar in many respects to that portrayed in Albert Camus' powerful allegorical novel *The Plague*, in which a mysterious and devastating plague overwhelmed and destroyed most of the inhabitants of a contemporary Algerian town. It was a symbol of the modern malaise, but for our purposes "the plague" can serve as a literal description of deepening planetary sickness. The response of one of the book's chief activists fighting the plague is a soberly realistic one: "All I maintain is that on this earth there are pestilences and there are victims, and it's up to us, so far as possible, not to join forces with the pestilences."[21] When the work of healing fails in spite of all efforts to make it work, one must, Christians must, not "join forces with the pestilences." The cross in the Christic paradigm does not, in our model, promise victory over the pestilence, but it does assure us that God is with the victims in their suffering. That is the last word, however, not the first.

Actually, the cross is not the last word. The enigmatic appearance stories of the risen Christ, the Christ who appeared in bodily form to his disciples, is the witness to an ancient, indelible strain within the Christian community. It is the belief and the hope that diminishment and death are not the last word, but in some inexplicable manner, the way to new life that, moreover, is physical. This is an important point for an embodiment theology. The death and resurrection of Jesus Christ are paradigmatic of a mode of change and growth that only occurs on the other side of the narrow door of the tomb. Often that pattern has been absolutized as occurring completely and only in Jesus of Nazareth: his death and resurrection are the answer to all the world's woes. In his death all creation dies; in his resurrection all arise to new life. The absolutism, optimism, and universalism of this way of interpreting the ancient and recurring relationship between death and new life – a relationship honored in most religious traditions as well as in evolutionary biology – are problematic in a postmodern, ecological, and highly diverse cultural and religious era. What is possible and appropriate, however, is to embrace these strains in Christian thought as a deep pattern within existence to which we cling and in which we hope – often as the hope against hope. We must believe in the basic trustworthiness at the heart of existence; that life, not death, is the last word; that against all evidence to the contrary (and most evidence is to the contrary), all our efforts on behalf of the well-being of our planet and especially of its most vulnerable creatures, including human ones, will not be defeated. It is the belief that the source and power of the universe is on the side of life and its fulfillment. The "risen Christ" is the Christian way of speaking of this faith and hope: Christ is the firstborn of the new creation, to be followed by all the rest of creation, including the last and the least.

NOTES

1. See Sallie McFague, *Models of God: Theology for an Ecological Nuclear Age* (Philadelphia: Fortress Press, 1987), pp. 45ff. for another analysis of this point.
2. My position is close to that of liberation theologian Ingemar Hedstrom:

   > In light of [the] ravaging of people and land in Central America, we realize that the preferential option for the poor, characteristic of Latin American liberation theologies, must be articulated as a preferential *option for life.* To exercise this option is to defend and promote the fundamental right to life of *all* creatures on earth. The right to life in all its fullness involves partaking of the material base of creation, that is, of the material goods that permit life.

   "Latin America and the Need for a Life-Liberating Theology," in *Liberating Life: Contemporary Approaches to Ecological Theology,* ed. Charles Birch et al. (Maryknoll, N.Y.: Orbis Books, 1990), p. 120.

   The position is substantially different from that of deep ecology, which also defends the right of all life forms (see also ibid. "Us Versus It: Living a Lie in Relation to Nature").
3. Ibid., p. 277.
4. As Jay B. McDaniel writes, "the phrase 'integrity of creation' refers to both kinds of value simultaneously. It is 'the intrinsic and instrumental value of every living organism in its relation to its environment and to God'" ("Revisioning God and the Self: Lessons from Buddhism," in ibid., p. 231). See also the discussion of instrumental and intrinsic value in Charles Birch and John Cobb, Jr., *The Liberation of Life: From the Cell to the Community* (Cambridge: Cambridge University Press, 1981), chap. 5.
5. Charles Birch, "Christian Obligation for the Liberation of Nature," in Birch et al. (eds.), *Liberating Life,* p. 64.
6. This perspective is thoroughly and eloquently argued by James M. Gustafson in *Ethics from a Theocentric Perspective,* vol. 1: *Theology and Ethics* (Chicago: University of Chicago Press, 1981).

7. To speak of natural bodies as the *representative* bodies is analogous to speaking of the representative human being of our time as a third-world woman of color. In both cases, we are pointing to the numbers and vulnerability that epitomize the category. In our time, because of the severe deterioration and destruction facing natural bodies (animals, trees, oceans, and so forth), their bodies rather than ours should stand as the symbol of bodily life. Such bodies are *primarily* body and they are at severe risk.
8. See McFague, *Models of God*, pp. 51ff.
9. One of the first to recognize what is now broadly accepted, namely, the importance of cultural evolution as a further stage beyond biological evolution, as well as a counterforce to it, was Pierre Teilhard de Chardin. See esp. *The Future of Man*, trans. Norman Denny (New York: Harper & Row, 1964), and *Science and Christ*, trans. René Hague (New York: Harper & Row, 1965). Also, for an analysis of Teilhard's position, see Philip Hefner, *The Promise of Teilhard* (Philadelphia and New York: J.B. Lippincott & Co., 1970). Another and very interesting version of cultural evolution, and one to which my analysis is indebted, is by Gerd Theissen in *Biblical Faith: An Evolutionary Approach* (Philadelphia: Fortress Press, 1985). See also Philip Hefner, "The Evolution of the Created Co-Creator," in *Cosmos as Creation: Science and Theology in Consonance*, ed. Ted Peters (Nashville: Abingdon Press, 1989), pp. 211–233.
10. One of the few instances of serious attention to the notion of space by a Christian theologian is the interesting treatment of Jürgen Moltmann in *God in Creation: A New Theology and the Spirit of God* (San Francisco: Harper & Row, 1985), chap. 6.
11. Bernhard W. Anderson, "Creation in the Bible," in *Cry of the Environment: Rebuilding the Christian Creation Story*, ed. Philip J. Joranson and Ken Butigan (Santa Fe, N.M.: Bear & Co., 1984), p. 25.
12. Two collections of poems and prayers illustrate this point: *Cries of the Spirit: A Celebration of Women's Spirituality*, ed. Marilyn Sewell (Boston: Beacon Press, 1991); *Earth Prayers from Around the World*, ed. Elizabeth Roberts and Elias Amidon (San Francisco: Harper, 1991).
13. *The Confessions of St. Augustine*, Bks. I–X, trans. F.J. Sheed (New York: Sheed & Ward, 1942), 10.6.
14. Roberts and Amidon (eds.), *Earth Prayers*, p. 366.
15. Ibid., pp. 360, 365.
16. This is a complex issue to which we cannot here do justice. There are at least two directions within this tradition, one from Augustine's neo-Platonism, which tends to absorb the things of the world into God, and the other from Thomas's Aristotelianism, which supports greater substance for empirical reality. One sees the former epitomized in the extreme realism of the doctrine of transubstantiation in which the eucharistic elements are

wholly converted into the body and blood of Christ, and the latter in a poet such as Gerard Manley Hopkins with his notion of "inscape," the particular, irreducible, concrete individuality of each and every aspect of creation which is preserved and heightened in its sacramental role as a sign of God's glory. But between these poles are many other positions, with the unifying factor being that in some way or other the things of this world are valuable because of their connection to God.

17. The phrase is from an essay by the literary critic R.W.B. Lewis, and refers to the "suchness" and "thereness" of ordinary things in the world that stand against all attempts to translate them into or use them for spiritual purposes.
18. Gerard Manley Hopkins, *Poems and Prose*, intro. W.H. Gardner (London: Penguin Books, 1953), p. 51.
19. See the analysis by Gerda Lerner in *The Creation of Patriarchy* (New York: Oxford University Press, 1986).
20. On animal rights and vegetarianism, see the following: Carol J. Adams, *The Sexual Politics of Meat: A Feminist–Vegetarian Critical Theory* (New York: Continuum, 1991); Tom Regan, *The Case for Animal Rights* (Berkeley: University of California Press, 1983).
21. Albert Camus, *The Plague*, trans. Stuart Gilbert (New York: Alfred A. Knopf, 1954), p. 229.

Plate 14 The interconnectedness of nature and religion is elegantly presented in a combination of Shinto and Buddhist elements at a Hiyoshi (Shingon) temple in Tateyama at the base of the Japanese Alps in Toyama Prefecture, Japan. Photo: *Joseph Runzo*

SELECT BIBLIOGRAPHY

THE RELIGIOUS PERSPECTIVE

Forward, M. (ed.) *Ultimate Visions: Reflections on the Religion We Choose.* Oxford, Oneworld, 1998
Otto, R. *The Idea of the Holy,* trans. J.H. Harvey. London and New York, Association Press, 1936
Smart, N. *Concept and Empathy,* ed. D. Wiebe. London, Macmillan; New York, New York University Press, 1986
— *The World's Religions.* Cambridge, Cambridge University Press, 1989/1998
— *Dimensions of the Sacred.* Berkeley, University of California Press, 1996
Smith, H. *The World's Religions.* San Francisco, Harper San Francisco, 1991
Smith, W.C. *The Meaning and End of Religion.* San Francisco and New York, Harper & Row, 1978; Minneapolis, Augsburg Fortress, 1990
— *Faith and Belief: The Difference Between Them.* Oxford, Oneworld, 1998
Tillich, P. *Dynamics of Faith.* New York, Harper & Row, 1957
Ward, K. *Religion and Human Nature.* Oxford, Oxford University Press, 1998
— *Religion and Revelation.* Gifford Lectures. Oxford, Oxford University Press, 1994
— *Religion and Creation.* Oxford, Oxford University Press, 1996
Zaehner, R.C. *Mysticism Sacred and Profane.* Oxford, Oxford University Press, 1961

RELIGIONS OF THE WEST

Eisen, A.M. *Galut: Modern Jewish Reflection on Homelessness and Homecoming.* Bloomington/Indianapolis, Indiana University Press, 1986

Forward, M. *Jesus: A Short Biography.* Oxford, Oneworld, 1998

— *Muhammad: A Short Biography.* Oxford, Oneworld, 1998

Hebblethwaite, B. *The Ocean of Truth.* Cambridge, Cambridge University Press, 1988

Hick, J. *Evil and the God of Love,* 2nd ed. San Francisco, Harper & Row, 1985

Jaffee, M.S. *Early Judaism.* Englewood Cliffs, Prentice Hall, 1997

Kugel, J. "Two Introductions to Midrash," in *Midrash in Literature,* ed. G.H. Hartman and S. Budick. New Haven, Yale University Press, 1986

Kvanvig, J.L. *The Problem of Hell.* New York and Oxford, Oxford University Press, 1993

McFague, S. *Models of God: Theology for an Ecological Nuclear Age.* Philadelphia, Fortress Press, 1987

Ochs, V. *Words on Fire: One Woman's Journey into the Sacred.* New York, Harcourt, 1990

Peters, F.E. *Children of Abraham: Judaism, Christianity, Islam.* Princeton, Princeton University Press, 1982

— *Jerusalem.* Princeton, Princeton University Press, 1985

— *Judaism, Christianity, and Islam: The Classical Texts and their Interpretations,* 3 vols. Princeton, Princeton University Press, 1990

Quinn, P.L. "Kierkegaard's Christian Ethics," in *The Cambridge Companion to Kierkegaard,* ed. A. Hannay and G.D. Marino. Cambridge, Cambridge University Press, 1997

Schimmel, A. *Deciphering the Signs of God: A Phenomenological Approach to Islam.* Albany, State University of New York Press, 1984

Swinburne, R. *The Christian God.* Oxford, Clarendon Press, 1994

Umansky, E. and Ashton, D. (eds). *Four Centuries of Jewish Women's Spirituality: A Sourcebook.* Boston, Beacon Press, 1992

Watt, W.M. *A Short History of Islam.* Oxford, Oneworld, 1998

Zebiri, K. *Muslims and Christians Face to Face.* Oxford, Oneworld, 1998

ASIAN RELIGIONS

Abe, M. *A Study of Dogen: His Philosophy and his Religion,* ed. Steven Heine. Albany, State University of New York Press, 1992

Berling, J.A. *A Pilgrim in Chinese Culture: Negotiating Religious Diversity.* Maryknoll, Orbis Books, 1997

Brockington, J.L. *The Sacred Thread: Hinduism in its Continuity and Diversity.* Edinburgh, Edinburgh University Press, 1981

Chapple, C.K. *Nonviolence to Animals, Earth, and Self in Asian Traditions.* Albany, State University of New York Press, 1993

Conze, E. *A Short History of Buddhism.* Oxford, Oneworld, 1998

Dalai Lama. *The Joy of Living and Dying in Peace.* London, Thorsons/HarperCollins, Library of Tibet, 1997

Dumoulin, H. *Zen Enlightenment: Origins and Meaning*, trans. J.C. Maraldo. New York, Weatherhill, 1979
Dundas, P. *The Jains.* London, Routledge, 1992
Eck, D.L. *Darson: Seeing the Divine Image in India*, 2nd ed., rev. and enl. New York, Columbia University Press, 1996
Eliade, M. *Yoga: Immortality and Freedom*, trans. W.R. Task. Princeton, Princeton University Press, 1969
Erndl, K.M. *Victory to the Mother: The Hindu Goddess of Northwest India in Myth, Ritual, and Symbol.* Oxford, Oxford University Press, 1993
Fuller, C.J. *The Camphor Flame: Popular Hinduism and Society in India.* Princeton, Princeton University Press, 1992
Gandhi, Mahatma. *The Selected Works of Mahatma Gandhi.* Ahmedebad, Navajivan Publishing House, 1968
Graham, A.C. *Disputers of the Tao: Philosophical Argument in Ancient China.* La Salle, Open Court Publishing Company, 1989
Hanh, T.N. *Cultivating the Mind of Love: The Practice of Looking Deeply in the Mahayana Buddhist Tradition.* Berkeley, Parallax Press, 1996
— *The Miracle of Mindfulness.* Boston, Beacon Press, 1975
Harvey, P. *Introduction to Buddhism.* Cambridge, Cambridge University Press, 1995
Ivanhoe, P.J. *Confucian Moral Self-Cultivation.* New York, Peter Lang Publishing, Inc., 1993
Jochim, C. *Chinese Religions: A Cultural Approach.* Englewood Cliffs, Prentice Hall, Inc., 1986
Keown, Damien. *Buddhism: A Very Short Introduction.* Oxford, Oxford University Press, 1996
Klostermaier, K.K. *A Short Introduction to Hinduism.* Oxford, Oneworld, 1998
Lipner, J. *Hindus: Their Religious Beliefs and Practices.* London, Routledge, 1994
McLeod, W.H. *The Sikhs: History, Religion, and Society.* New York, Columbia University Press, 1989
Momen, M. *A Short Introduction to the Baha'i Faith.* Oxford, Oneworld, 1997
Padmanabh, S.J. *The Jaina Path of Purification.* Berkeley, University of California Press, 1979
Rahula, W.S. *What the Buddha Taught.* Oxford, Oneworld, 1998
Taylor, R. *The Religious Dimensions of Confucianism.* Albany, State University of New York Press, 1990

LOVE, RELATIONSHIPS, AND RELIGION

Biale, D. *Eros and the Jews: From Biblical Israel to Contemporary America.* New York, Basic Books, 1992
Boyarin, D. *Carnal Israel: Reading Sex in Talmudic Culture.* Berkeley, University of California Press, 1993

Brown, K.M. *Mama Lola: A Vodou Priestess in Brooklyn.* Berkeley, University of California Press, 1991

Buber, M. *I and Thou,* trans. D. Cairns. Edinburgh, T. & T. Clark, 1937

Hawley, J.S. and Juergensmeyer, M. *Songs of the Saints of India.* Oxford, Oxford University Press, 1988

Hess, L. and Singh, S. (trans.). *The Bījak of Kabīr.* 1983; Delhi, Motilal Banarsidass, 1986

Kellenberger, J. *Relationship Morality.* University Park, Pennsylvania University Press, 1995

— *God-Relationships With and Without God.* London, Macmillan; New York, St. Martin's Press, 1989

Klein, A.C. *Knowledge and Liberation.* Ithaca, Snow Lion Publications, 1986

— *Meeting the Great Bliss Queen: Buddhists, Feminists, and the Art of the Self.* Boston, Beacon Press, 1995

Mathews, G. *What Makes Life Worth Living? How Japanese and Americans Make Sense of their Worlds.* Berkeley, University of California Press, 1996

Mbiti, J.S. *African Religions and Philosophy.* New York, Doubleday, 1970

Nozick, R. *The Examined Life.* New York, Simon & Schuster, 1990

Ramanujan, A.K. *Speaking of Śiva.* New York, Penguin Books, 1973

— *Hymns for the Drowning: Poems for Viṣṇu by Nammāḻvār.* Princeton, Princeton University Press, 1981

Singer, P. *How Are We to Live? Ethics in an Age of Self-Interest.* Amherst, Prometheus Books, 1995

GLOBAL VIEWS

Abe, M. *Buddhism and Interfaith Dialogue,* ed. S. Heine. Honolulu, University of Hawaii Press, 1995

— *Zen and Western Thought,* ed. W.R. LaFleur. Honolulu, University of Hawaii Press, 1985

Byrne, P. *Prolegomena to Religious Pluralism: Reference and Realism in Religion.* London, Macmillan; New York, St. Martin's Press, 1995

Esack, F. *Qur'an, Liberation and Pluralism.* Oxford, Oneworld, 1998

Griffiths, B. *The Marriage of East and West.* Springfield, Templegate, 1982

Hall, D.L. and Ames, R.T. *Anticipating China: Thinking Through the Narratives of Chinese and Western Culture.* Albany, State University of New York Press, 1995

Hick, J. *Death and Eternal Life.* 1976; reissue London, Macmillan, 1985

— *An Interpretation of Religion.* New Haven, Yale University Press, 1989

— *God and the Universe of Faiths.* Oxford, Oneworld, 1998

— *The Fifth Dimension.* Oxford, Oneworld, 1999

Kung, H. *Christianity and the World Religions.* Maryknoll, Orbis Books, 1993

McFague, S. *The Body of God.* Minneapolis, Augsburg Fortress, 1993

Nishitani, K. *Religion and Nothingness*, trans. J. van Bragt. Berkeley, University of California Press, 1982

O'Flaherty, W.D. *Other People's Myths.* Chicago, University of Chicago Press, 1995

Parrinder, G. *Avatar and Incarnation: The Divine in Human Form in the World's Religions.* Oxford, Oneworld, 1998

— *Mysticism in the World's Religions.* Oxford, Oneworld, 1998

Quinn, P.L. "Religious Pluralism and Religious Relativism," in *Relativism and Religion*, ed. C.M. Lewis. New York, St. Martin's Press, 1995

— "Toward Thinner Theologies: Hick and Alston on Religious Diversity," in *God, Reason and Religions*, ed. E.T. Long. Dordrecht, Boston and London, Kluwer, 1995

Runzo, J. *Reason, Relativism and God.* London, Macmillan, Library of Philosophy and Religion; New York, St. Martin's Press, 1986

— *World Views and Perceiving God.* London, Macmillan, Library of Philosophy and Religion; New York, St. Martin's Press, 1993

Smart, N. *Beyond Ideology: Religion and the Future of Western Civilization.* San Francisco, Harper & Row, 1981

Smith, H. *Beyond the Post-Modern Mind.* Wheaton, Theosophical Publishing House, 1989

— *Forgotten Truth.* San Francisco, Harper San Francisco, 1992

— *Essays on World Religion.* New York, Paragon Press, 1995

Smith, W.C. *Towards a World Theology.* London, Macmillan; Philadelphia, Westminster Press, 1981

Ward, K. *Concepts of God: Images of the Divine in Five Religious Traditions.* Oxford, Oneworld, 1998

INDEX

Page numbers in *italic* refer to figures.